A Critical Dictionary of

Educational Concepts

Other books by Robin Barrow:

HAPPINESS (Martin Robertson)
RADICAL EDUCATION (Martin Robertson)
COMMON SENSE AND THE CURRICULUM (Allen & Unwin)
MORAL PHILOSOPHY FOR EDUCATION (Allen & Unwin)
INTRODUCTION AND COMMENTARY ON PLATO'S APOLOGY (JACT)
PLATO UTILITARIANISM AND EDUCATION (Routledge & Kegan Paul)
PLATO AND EDUCATION (Routledge & Kegan Paul)
LANGUAGE AND THOUGHT (Althouse Press)
THE CANADIAN CURRICULUM (Althouse Press)
SPARTA (Allen & Unwin)
GREEK AND ROMAN EDUCATION (Macmillan)
ATHENIAN DEMOCRACY (Macmillan)
THE PHILOSOPHY OF SCHOOLING (Harvester Wheatsheaf)
INJUSTICE, INEQUALITY AND ETHICS (Harvester Wheatsheaf)
GIVING TEACHING BACK TO TEACHERS (Harvester Wheatsheaf)
UNDERSTANDING SKILLS: THINKING, FEELING, AND CARING (Althouse Press)
INTRODUCTION TO PHILOSOPHY OF EDUCATION (Methuen) (with R. G. Woods)

Other books by Geoffrey Milburn:

TEACHING HISTORY IN CANADA (McGraw-Hill Ryerson)
CAUCUS: CANADIAN POLITICS IN ACTION: A SIMULATION (Nelson) (with W. A. Houston)
NATIONAL CONSCIOUSNESS AND THE CURRICULUM: THE CANADIAN CASE (OISE Press) (contributing editor, with J. Herbert)
CURRICULUM CANADA VI: ALTERNATIVE RESEARCH PERSPECTIVES: THE SECONDARY SCHOOL CURRICULUM (The University of British Columbia) (editor, with Robin Enns)
ISSUES IN SECONDARY SCHOOLING (Althouse Press) (editor, with R. J. Clark and R. D. Gidney)
RE-INTERPRETING CURRICULUM RESEARCH: IMAGES AND ARGUMENTS (Falmer Press) (contributing editor, with I. F. Goodson and R. J. Clark)

A Critical Dictionary of

Educational Concepts

An Appraisal of Selected Ideas
and Issues in Educational Theory
and Practice

Second Edition

ROBIN BARROW
Professor of Education, Simon Fraser University

GEOFFREY MILBURN
Professor of Education, University of Western Ontario

Teachers College, Columbia University
New York and London

First published 1986 by
Harvester Wheatsheaf
66 Wood Lane End, Hemel Hempstead
Hertfordshire HP2 4RG
A division of
Simon & Schuster International Group

Second edition, 1990

Second edition published in the United
States of America in 1990 by Teachers
College Press,
1234 Amsterdam Ave., New York, NY 10027

First edition published in the United
States of America in 1986 by St. Martin's
Press.

Library of Congress Cataloging-in-Publication Data

Barrow, Robin.
    A critical dictionary of educational concepts : an appraisal of
selected ideas and issues in educational theory and practice / Robin
Barrow, Geoffrey Milburn. — 2nd ed.
      p.   cm.
    Includes bibliographical references.
    ISBN 0-8077-3058-0
    1. Education—Dictionaries.   I. Milburn, G. (Geoffrey), 1932–
II. Title.
LB15.B29   1990
370′.3—dc20
                                  90–36532
                                    CIP

For Joan

Contents

Acknowledgements

We are grateful to many colleagues for their advice and counsel, especially Richard Aldrich, Derek Allison, Maryann Ayim, Bob Clark, Carol Crealock, Kieran Egan, John Gingell, Don Gutteridge, Paul Hirst, Grant McMurray, Garth Lambert, Ron Marx, Paul O'Leary, Jim Sanders, Don Santor, Merrill Sitko, Al Slemon, Roger Straughan, Jaap Tuinman, Max van Manen, John Walsh, John Wilson, Phil Winne, and Jack Wrigley.

Two research assistants, Gwen Davis and Kathy Grebenc, and two members of the Althouse College Library, Jean Colhoun and Anna Holman, were indefatigable in their pursuit of references, while Frances McSephney, Melanie Hamilton, Katherine Butson, Wanda Borré and Mary Misangyi prepared copy with their usual efficiency. Surjeet Siddoo of Simon Fraser University, did a superb job of co-ordinating our separate efforts. A research grant was generously provided by the Faculty of Education, The University of Western Ontario.

Preface

In our introduction we explain more fully the nature of this dictionary and the criteria whereby we selected entries. However, since the use of the word 'dictionary' may otherwise mislead some readers, it seems prudent to stress here, briefly, certain distinctive features of the book.

We have called this a dictionary because it contains entries arranged alphabetically for a number of key educational concepts, and because it is designed as a reference book. This seems to us a legitimate use of the term, and it is hard to find a more appropriate one.* However, we have carefully qualified the term in our title, in order to guard against various reasonable, but in this case misplaced, connotations that the word 'dictionary' may have for particular individuals. In particular, it should be noted that this dictionary does not purport to be exhaustive, definitive, or free from any view of the nature of education and educational theory. On the contrary, it is based upon a particular view that is, we hope, clearly articulated, consistently adhered to, and coherently argued for in the course of the various entries.

Given that educational theory does not at present amount to a fully explicated and uncontentious body of principles commanding widespread assent, it seems to us inevitable that a dictionary that is going to advance beyond the uncritical level of reporting the various meanings that different groups attach to different words, and that seeks to explore and make sense of conflicting and sometimes confused or obscure ideas, should involve a particular view or perspective. That being so, we have thought it best to reveal and argue for our position overtly.

There will be those, we imagine, who will take exception to the fact that in some measure we have selected entries by reference to what we think important, rather than, for example, by reference to the most often cited terms in educational textbooks. But this is not designed as a compendium of frequently used terms. It is designed as a dictionary of ideas that, for various reasons explained in the introduction, we believe to be worth contemplating and examining.

---

* OED Dictionary. 2. 'A book of information or reference on any subject or branch of knowledge, the items of which are arranged in alphabetical order.'

Foreword to Second Edition

The publication of a second edition of this dictionary is a matter of considerable importance because it has given us the opportunity to add material, make changes and improvements, and extend the bibliography.

In order to understand the limits of our intentions and how to use the book, what its benefits may be and what it does not seek to do, the reader is advised to read the original introduction. Here we would like to emphasize the point that this dictionary is not, and does not profess to be, 'neutral' in the sense of 'uncommitted'. We were very fortunate in our reviewers (for which we are duly grateful), but it was noticeable that the only hostility we encountered was not due to the fact that we had done what we did badly, but to the fact that we had done what we did. Exception was taken to the fact that a thesis steadily emerges from the separate entries – a thesis to the effect that education is a certain kind of thing, and human beings are constituted in a certain sort of way, such that it makes sense to educate or to inquire into this or that aspect of education in this way rather than that way. We can only remark, once again, that that was our express intention, and that we believe such an approach may be useful. We have attempted to provide a set of relatively brief and good-humoured comments and arguments, designed to suggest the error of certain ways, the wisdom of others, and the truth, falsity, clarity, obscurity, uncertainty, etc., of various ideas. In other words, this is not the kind of dictionary that facelessly describes the state of play in a field; it is one that engages in the debate that constitutes and surrounds the activity.

In writing the introduction to the first edition, we decided against summarizing the gist of our overall argument, for fear of losing one of the groups of readers with whom we would like and need to debate. For, generally, it seems fair to suppose that if people can classify a book as taking a position they themselves do not take, they ignore it! But on this occasion we will take the risk of coming out of the closet, in order to dispel any idea that we are doing something clandestine or illicit. In general terms, we take the view that human beings, being a unique kind of animal, need to be studied in ways that take this into account. Education we regard as a distinctively human concept, and key mental concepts, such as intelligence, imagination and thinking, we believe also need to be understood as being peculiarly human. This leads us to the conclusion that the study of humans in general, and education in particular, must not be exclusively scientific in manner, and the specific criticism that in many respects it too often is. Superficially this could be mistaken for hostility to science. It is not: it is an attempt to show that one can take science too far, and that perhaps this has happened in educational research.

It will be noted that we do not refer to the above as a 'bias' or even a 'perspective', since strictly speaking it is no such thing. It is a conclusion that emerges from the argument contained in various key entries. The only proper way to deal with it is to consider the various arguments and conceptual claims put forward, and either recognize their strength or show by further reasoning where the argument presented is deficient.

In preparing the second edition, we should like to acknowledge the particular help that we received from Kieran Egan and John Walsh. The former made some positive suggestions relating to the entries on recapitulation and memory. The latter provided copious, detailed and very convincing arguments dealing with a number of points in entries relating to psychological topics. We have as a consequence made a number of minor but important changes.

Robin Barrow
Geoffrey Milburn

Introduction

NATURE OF THE DICTIONARY

There are several dictionaries of education already in existence. To our knowledge, this is quite unlike any of them, for they are all, in their different ways, concerned only to define and describe, whereas the prime purpose of this book is to probe and critically assess some of the key concepts in education. It is designed for those concerned with a broad perspective on education, on the grounds that even the specialist researcher or teacher should base his activity on a complete and coherent understanding of the educational enterprise as a whole. This introduction is largely concerned with explaining how we came to select our entries and why they take the form they do.

To put it simply, this is a dictionary of words, ideas, and issues in education that we think people ought to be familiar with and to think about. To some extent it is a dictionary of contemporary educational discourse: it sets out to provide comment and discussion on expressions that crop up a lot and that seem to have some significance for, or emotive impact upon, people, whether for good or bad reasons. People talk about **creativity, developmental theory, ideology, subjectivity, curriculum design, feminism**, and the relativity of **knowledge**, with a gusto and frequency that they do not show in respect of mind, clear argument, authority, and the pragmatic theory of truth. Accordingly (although this will be more fully explained as we proceed) there are entries here relating to the former set of concepts but not to the latter. ·

The reference to what 'people talk about' should be understood to cover professional educators of all types, and what is written as well as said. The language and concepts of classroom teachers, faculties of education, and educational journals are our prime concern, rather than the substantive issues that currently preoccupy newspaper editors or parents, in so far as they differ. We should also stress that we are interested both in concepts that loom large in the context of school practice and those that belong primarily to educational theory. We have entries, for example, under **mainstreaming, programmed learning, behavioural objectives, multiculturalism,** and **stereotyping**, all of which have clear relevance to practitioners, and under **correlation, systematic observation** and **metaphor**, which might seem mainly of interest to the researcher or theoretician. Most entries are of potential interest to both groups (e.g.

1

needs, core curriculum, readiness, skills, and **intelligence**). However, because this is a dictionary set out in terms of the exploration of ideas, its treatment tends to the theoretical rather than the practical: it is concerned with questions such as what might the arguments for and against a core curriculum be, rather than with outlining a specific core curriculum; it is concerned with what **critical thinking** may be and whether so-called exercises in critical thinking truly develop it, rather than with delineating a critical thinking programme.

We have avoided matter that we regard as being of essentially specialist interest. We do not have an entry under the teaching of mathematics, for example, nor do we have entries for specialist theoretical interests such as adolescence. We have tried to concentrate on matters that we think all educationalists ought to be apprised of in order to set their own work in a truly educational perspective. Therefore, we do not offer a breakdown of every psychological concept such as perception and dysfunction, and we do not provide resumés of research into anxiety, motivation, and so forth. On the other hand, there are entries relating to key methodological issues in **research**, and on concepts that we think have a wider educational significance. There are, for example, entries under **operant conditioning** and **behaviourism**, as well as on **indoctrination, interests**, and **understanding**. There are also a number of entries relating to various types and areas of research (e.g. **ethnography, teacher effectiveness**). We do make reference to substantive issues such as anxiety, self-esteem, and motivation under some of these other headings. But another reason for excluding separate entries for them is revealed in the entries relating to research: we are concerned that research has not reliably established much of educational importance in relation to such concepts. Perhaps we may summarize this paragraph by saying that our interest is less in cataloguing unquestioned the claims of researchers about motivation, anxiety, etc., than in critically examining the nature of the research behind such claims.

Given that the pattern adopted is to provide a critical entry examining the sense of, say, **learning** theory, rather than to have entries describing particular theories in detail, or to discuss the value of **models** of curriculum theory rather than to describe the various models that have been proposed, one might say this is a philosophical dictionary. We might even have so entitled the book, had we not feared that many people with but a hazy idea of what 'philosophical' means would have been frightened off by the word. What is meant by describing it as philosophical is little more than that it has the emphasis that has been explained: it is interested in clarifying ideas that are often referred to but are none the less somewhat obscure, questioning assumptions that may be widely taken for granted but are not necessarily reasonable, and considering arguments for and against various practices (actual and proposed) in relation to the school or research and theory.

We are not interested in providing merely verbal synonyms which ignore any question of what we really have in mind, or what we really think we are talking about, when we use a term. Thus we do not say, as a dictionary of the English language would do, that 'education' is 'the bringing up of children'. We examine what kinds of condition have to be met for something to count as **education**, for, whatever an English language dictionary may say, education is fairly obviously a rather special kind of bringing up. One is not educating one's child if one 'brings her up' in a locked room on bread and water and terrifies her into stealing. Similarly, we do not just list or describe views and claims, whether about practice or theory. We question them. Our object is to provoke a degree of reflective, critical examination of educational practice and theory in our readers, by probing the clarity, sense and coherence of prominent ideas and claims ourselves. (On this important matter, see further the entries under **analysis** and **concept**.)

METHOD OF SELECTING ENTRIES

Having said something about the nature of the book, we turn now to the question of how entries were in fact selected. The main point to note is that the entries are of various different kinds.

A few entries may be classified as jargon. These terms may provide genuine but straightforward puzzlement to one not familiar with them, as the French word for 'dog' puzzles someone who does not speak French, without being inherently complex. But they may also, of course, turn out to refer to complex or even incoherent ideas. An example of the first type is **'lateral thinking'***: it may be an unfamiliar term to some, but, whatever we might choose to say about claims made about it, it is not difficult to explain what it means. An example of the latter type, some would argue, is **'brainstorming'**, for, critics might suggest, this term has been coined to describe an idea that veers between being complex, empty, and nonsensical, depending on who is using it.

The distinction between jargon and technical terms may be a fine one in practice, the latter being a less pejorative phrase but likewise implying a special meaning in a special context. For example, some might regard 'lateral thinking' as a technical term rather than as jargon. None the less, there are some clearly technical terms, such as **'validity'** and **'reliability'**, which have quite specific meanings in empirical research that differ from

---

* Throughout this book we follow the convention of using quotation marks to indicate reference to a word (e.g. 'education' has nine letters) as opposed to a concept (e.g. education is desirable).

their meaning in everyday discourse. Or again, **'summative'** and **'formative' evaluation** may be judged technical terms, since, typically, people do not consciously engage in such activities or think about them: they belong to the world of the professional evaluator (and by extension, educator).

The initial question about both jargon and technical terms is a verbal one: 'What does this term mean?', asked in the same way as one might ask what the Latin word *nauta* means. Sometimes the answer to the verbal questions will lead to a conceptual question, that is to say, to a request for further elucidation of the idea in question. ('I see. You tell me that "brainstorming" means "the generation of ideas involving free-flowing creative thought and spontaneous non-critical expression of ideas". Now tell me what *that* means? What does it amount to? What are you actually trying to convey by that description?') The majority of our entries have been selected on the grounds that they are conceptually interesting or complex. And a great many of them have been chosen on the grounds that they are central to the enterprise in which we are engaged – namely schooling and education. Thus, **schooling** and **education** themselves, **knowledge, intelligence, moral education, socialization, culture,** and **language** are examples of concepts central to the practice we are concerned with. While other concepts (such as **objectivity, reconceptualists, research,** and **necessary condition**) are central to the theoretical study of education.   The remaining entries will be seen to be concerned with specific issues of educational theory or practice that invite discussion and argument, if not outright disagreement: Should we **deschool**? What are the problems associated with teacher **accountability**? What forms of **assessment** are desirable? What are the respective merits of **quantitative** and **qualitative** research?

All our entries will be found to belong to one or more of the above categories. But we still had to select. What, apart from our preferences, limitations of knowledge and competence, and partial judgements – restraints too familiar to be worth dwelling on – determined our final choice of entries? What criteria did we use to select amongst the jargon, the technical terms, the concepts central to theory or practice, and the substantive issues?

The overriding criterion has been our judgement as to the importance of a proper understanding or consideration of the idea, issue, or argument in question, for rational practice or theorizing. Such judgement is admittedly both partly subjective and complex, in that criteria for importance may themselves vary. But we have tried to bring together those concepts that we regard as constituting the essence of schooling and the essence of educational theory and research, and those that we recognize other teachers and theoreticians would make similar claims for. Thus, it seems to us clear that **education, knowledge, culture** and **autonomy** are central concepts, and we recognize that, regardless of our views, many others would make the same claim for **creativity, emotions,** and **communication**. So there are entries under each of those headings.

A second criterion is provided by the dominance of an idea, issue, or argument, in contemporary debate. In some cases such dominance will of course be a matter of the importance of a concept. But in others it may rather be a matter of passing fashion (e.g. **child-centred education, sex education**) or the continued openness or debatability of a topic as, perhaps, with questions to do with **aesthetic value** and **class**. The basic point is that for one reason or another some potential entries have more immediate topicality or currency than others, and we have tried to pay due attention to this point.

Some terms and concepts invite confusion more than others, and this provides us with a third, probably more significant, criterion for including one at the expense of another. Such confusion may arise from a variety of sources: some words are confusing because they are used in different ways by different people (e.g. **'creativity', 'objectivity'**), some words refer to confused ideas or concepts (e.g. **'critical thinking'**), while some ideas are confusing because they are inherently complex and difficult to comprehend (e.g. **knowledge**). We have attempted to include entries for concepts that have a tendency to cause confusion, whatever the reason, even if they do not seem to meet our other criteria. Conversely, concepts that, though perhaps important and dominant, seem to us to be relatively unproblematic and clear, have often been ignored. For example, we do not have a main entry for play.

To summarize, we have tried to provide entries for those concepts and issues that we regard as being fundamental to the enterprise of schooling and education or to educational theory and research, and for those that are currently in vogue, especially where they are inclined to cause confusion. We would not pretend that the above criteria always make it easy to decide whether an entry merits inclusion, nor that others would have made the same selection in the light of these criteria. None the less they indicate the manner in which we have proceeded.

REFERENCES

The dictionary is arranged alphabetically, containing some 150 main entries, and a number of others that merely refer the reader to one or more of the main entries. For example, there is a main entry under **ethics**, but the reader looking up extrinsic value will be referred to the main entries under **worthwhile** and **value judgements**. Cross referencing within main entries has been kept as simple as possible: a word that has its own separate entry is distinguished by bold print once (usually but not always on its first appearance) in any other entry in which it appears. In addition, cross references are sometimes added in brackets and marked with an asterisk at the end of an entry, paragraph, or sentence. Sometimes we have had to distinguish cognate forms of a word rather than the word as it actually appears at the head of an entry. For example, **educational** or **educated** should be understood as referring to the entry under **education, creative** to **creativity**, and **emotional** maturity to **emotions**.

Many entries are followed by one or more references, consisting simply of author's name and date of publication. Full references will be found in the bibliography at the end of the volume. The bibliography in no way purports to be comprehensive or fully representative of published work in education. We have confined ourselves to noticing some works that are relevant to the argument of most of the more substantial entries, and for the most part we have limited ourselves to citing books rather than articles.

PURPOSE OF THE DICTIONARY

In our experience one of the most glaring and paradoxical weaknesses in students of education at all levels is their lack of education, in the sense of a broad and critical understanding of various disciplines, different kinds of question, and distinct theories and claims. Too much educational philosophy proceeds in a vacuum, without reference to practical constraints, to sociological challenges to some philosophers' perception of their activity, or to psychological claims relating to the phenomena under scrutiny. Too much sociological research is conducted without reference to psychological research in the same field, and vice versa. Too much empirical work generally is conducted without an adequate feel for conceptual and logical points. Above all, too much work in educational theory, research, and practice, is undertaken without any attempt to set the particular project in some wider coherent educational context.

Our main intention has been, by scrutinizing some of the key concepts in educational theory and practice, with an emphasis on probing their coherence, clarity and implications, to provide an antidote to the over-narrow specialist interest of so many educationalists. It is hoped that by referring to this book, the philosopher can conveniently apprise himself of much that is going on in the field of empirical research and the arguments surrounding various practices; that the psychologist and the sociologist can broaden their repertoire to engage with other than merely technical questions about the coherence and educational value of aspects of their research; that classroom researchers likewise can come to focus on wider issues concerning their work than its validity and reliability, such as, most notably, its appropriateness to a specifically educational setting. We hope to have made a small contribution to the attempt to enable all educationalists to think rather more carefully about the meaning, implications, and sense of such notions as the educationally **worthwhile, relevance, natural, accountability, evaluation, logical order, giftedness**, and **skills**. Above all, we hope that this dictionary will help students to formulate a clearer conception of the nature of education and educational theory and research, that does justice to the complexity of the enterprise as a whole.

A

Academic

Once the proudest word in the vocabulary of the student and scholar; now something of an embarrassment. The word derives from Plato's Academy, founded in Athens in the fourth century BC as something like the first university, and so called after the grove sacred to the demigod Akademos where it was situated. The cynicism evident in the following quotation, however, is not unique: 'Academy, n. 1. Historically, a place of Higher Learning. In that sense the word is obsolete; so is that kind of learning. 2. Currently known as Academia, it suffers from intellectual anaemia, being inhabited by Schools of Education and Business Administration . . .' (Volkart, 1986).

No doubt the use of the word 'academic' to contrast with 'practical' has something to do with its current connotations of 'irrelevant', 'pedantic', 'fussy', etc. It is not clear to what extent that usage was itself determined by a low estimation of theoretical pursuits, or to what extent the pejorative implications have developed as people's attitude to the non-practical have changed. Is it that increasingly we have come to think academic work impractical, or is it that we increasingly think the worse of the non-practical? (*theory)

Professors are sometimes asked to provide an 'academic' response to, say, a new educational policy. What is an academic response? Ideally, it is a well-articulated, well-informed response, that refuses to be browbeaten or restricted by current political restraints, while none the less being solicitous of **logical** and other inevitable limitations. There is no **necessary** reason why 'academic' should be contrasted with practical, **relevant** or **professional**, as it often is.

REFERENCE

Volkart (1986).

Accountability

The demand that **educational** institutions (particularly publicly funded elementary and secondary schools) should become more accountable for

9

what they do (that is, provide evidence that they are providing acceptable service in return for tax support) has become a prominent feature of political debates in recent years. The reasons for this demand are varied, but not necessarily consistent. Some critics were anxious to ensure that schools were efficiently managed in a technical sense, and that educators' 'secret gardens' were opened to public scrutiny. Others seemed convinced that **academic** and personal standards within state-supported school systems had plummeted to such depths that severe remedies were needed (for example, that teachers should be held responsible for what Johnny learned). Members of the public were puzzled by the fact that educational costs did not behave in the way they had expected in a period of declining enrolment. In some countries, the counsel of educational experts was subjected to the same type of cynical scrutiny as the arguments of commercial hucksters for any big business. In a general malaise of declining economic performance, the school systems were obvious targets, even if the causal link between **schooling** and an economic down-turn was never clearly established. While questions of coherence persist in respect of all of these arguments, their general effect cannot be mistaken: schools in many countries are being asked to provide evidence to justify the sums being spent upon them. This request is often backed by the threat of withdrawal of financial support.

It is easier to list reasons for regarding accountability as desirable than to establish what the nature of such accountability should be. First, it is sometimes difficult to identify what schools are supposed to be accountable for. Given the neglect of national goals, it is not easy to make a plausible case that schools should be held accountable for reaching specific goals. Even in those jurisdictions in which specific goals are stated, they are often phrased in such vague terms that discussion of attainment is rendered impossible. Secondly, it is not clear who should be judged accountable. Are local authorities to be accountable? Principals? Teachers? Students? Parents? Although, in principle it would not be difficult to argue that each one of these important constituents of the schooling industry ought to take responsibility for its success or failure, few political systems have tackled the political difficulties that would arise from any attempt to lock any one of these parties into a system of strict accountability. Thirdly, even if it were decided who should be accountable, it is far from clear to whom these persons should be accountable. To the national government? Local authorities? Principals and headmasters? Professional associations? Parents? Students? Finally, there seems to be little agreement on how accountability is to be measured. Some politicians argue that the achievements of students ought to be measured on standardized tests, while others recommend the assessment of a variety of features of the programme under study.

Many of those demanding greater accountability seem to overlook the formal and informal means of accountability that already exist within educational systems. In many jurisdictions, the quality of schooling is assessed by visiting experts or supervisors. Teachers are expected to report to their heads of department or principals. Some schools in some countries use the results of **competitive examinations** to assess school performance. While these informal methods are far from being as all-inclusive or certain as some critics require, they provide a rough-and-ready means of gauging the quality and effectiveness of educational programmes (***assessment, measurement, research, teacher effectiveness**).

Two countries that have gone furthest in introducing accountability procedures are the United States and England. In the former, the principal method used is the checking of student performance against prespecified objectives by means of standardized tests. This process, however, has been widely criticized. Some scholars have argued that use of this type of measurable objective is extraordinarily limiting if not actually anti-educational (***aims, behavioural objectives**). In England the Assessment of Performance Unit (APU) was established in the late 1970s to monitor student performance across the curriculum by examining six 'lines of development' that transcend particular school subjects: mathematical, language, scientific, physical, and personal and social. Although seemingly much broader than the American practice, APU has been subjected to significant criticism concerning such matters as the **validity** of the 'lines of development' on which it is founded, and the relationship between **curriculum** content on the one hand and general qualities of thinking on the other (***critical thinking**). Others have pointed to the limiting effect that national testing programmes have upon the curriculum. In addition, some important statistical problems have been identified in the types of tests used in the APU monitoring programmes. Given the complexity of the educational process, any attempt to introduce a simplistic model of accountability is almost certain to be fraught with difficulties.

That is not to say, however, that all accountability measures should be abandoned. Some researchers, for example, have been attracted by the process criteria characteristic of such self-governing professions as medicine and law. From such examples, they have extracted notions of principles and of practice that depend upon the logic of reflective self-government and the provision of expert services rather than upon prespecified success measures. Such alternative models of accountability stress the delivery of more varied types of information to a wide range of authorities or constituencies. The task of developing the special **skills** required to identify these measures, however, appears to be in its infancy (***practical principles, teaching**).

REFERENCES

Barbee and Bouck (1974), Becher and Maclure (1987b), Becher, Eraut, and Knight (1981), Eraut (1981), Lawton (1980), Lello (1979), MacDonald (1978, 1979), Pring (1981), Sockett (1980).

Achievement/task words

A distinction is made by the philosopher Gilbert Ryle between words that logically imply success in an undertaking, e.g. 'finding', 'arriving', 'killing' (achievement words), and those that logically leave the question of success or failure open, e.g. 'searching', 'travelling', or 'fighting' (task words). (NB The success implied by achievement words relates to completion of a task rather than quality, moral worth, wisdom, etc., of an activity. For example, 'marrying' is an achievement word.) The interest of some words may lie in the fact that they are hard to classify in these terms, e.g. 'torturing', 'loving' or 'forgiving'.

Peters (1967) argued that 'just as "finding" is the achievement relative to "looking", so "being educated" is the achievement relative to a family of tasks which we call processes of education'. He acknowledged that ' "education" is of course different in certain respects from the examples of achievements that Ryle gives. To start with "education" like "teaching" can be used as both a task and an achievement verb.' But none the less, he maintained, 'if I talk of [people] as educated there is an implication of success'. That is surely correct. The question of importance now becomes 'What are the criteria of educational success?' (*aims, analysis, education, teaching).

REFERENCES

Peters (1967), Ryle (1949).

Action research

As several commentators have pointed out, it is easier to state what those who practise action research are *against* than what they are *for*. Advocates of action research argue that the prevailing pattern of educational research based on controlled, **empirical** investigation of **phenomena** is impoverished for a variety of reasons: it focuses only on observable **behaviour**, separates means from ends, detaches **facts** from **values**, and produces generalizations and **theories** that often have little applicability in particular classrooms. The search for such theories tends to reduce teachers to 'subjects' of research over which they have no control (and elevate researchers – many of whom have little experience in the classroom – to an **élitist** status). Because **educational theory**, it is argued, is imposed from above, teachers tend to be subjected to changing imperatives that have the effect of continually reducing their effectiveness in the classroom. In consequence, teachers receive little encouragement to reflect critically upon their professional practices or on conditions in the classroom, and, as a result, hopes for change, amelioration, or reform are dimmed, if not extinguished. This litany of protest may be familiar, but it is keenly felt none the less.

The notion of action research has been seen as an answer to some of these difficulties. The term was first used widely in the United States in the 1930s and 1940s (some scholars trace action research to much earlier sources) in the work of social scientists concerned with improving the capacity of disadvantaged groups to learn about their own problems and devise democratic practices for discussing and assessing their own actions. These broad principles were first used in educational settings in the 1950s (Corey, 1953), and after a period of neglect emerged again in the 1970s in somewhat broader discussions that included arguments from **curriculum** studies, qualitative and naturalistic research, and **critical theory**. Stenhouse (1975b) drew attention to the notion of 'the teacher as researcher' which became a prominent feature in several important curriculum publications. Other scholars, particularly Stenhouse's colleagues (Elliott, 1978; Kemmis, 1984), extended the range of methods in action research and included new arguments, especially from critical-emancipatory and liberationist sources, to justify their use. Interest in action research on several continents is now so great that observers have labelled it a 'full blown' movement (Carr, 1989, p. 85) and a 'broad church' (Kelly, 1985, p. 129) – characterizations that do not engender a great deal of confidence (****quantitative/qualitative research**).

It is possible to find unanimity among various groups of action researchers only by listing some general notions to which the greater number (but by no means all) adhere: they place the teacher at the centre of the research process in terms of identifying a problem, and selecting methodologies; they recognize the significance of involvement, participation, and democratic procedures; they stress the importance of critical reflection on practice; and they wish to ameliorate current conditions in schools. But that unanimity breaks down when these statements are examined in detail.

For example, the appropriate role of the teacher and the outside researcher in initiating and conducting action research is subject to debate (some allocate exclusive responsibility to the teacher, others perceive an important role for the outsider). Little agreement seems to exist on the types of **research** procedure appropriate to action research – some advocate the use of a limited set of naturalistic approaches, others recommend a much wider range of techniques (including traditional empirical methods). There are disputes about what counts as research in action research, with some scholars arguing that every curricular act undertaken by a teacher may be considered a form of research, others that more exclusive tests (including publication) should be adopted. Some theorists have offered schemata for conducting action research (which usually include 'cycles' or 'spiral sequences'), while others suggest that such formal methods not only are **prescriptive** in the same sense as the much despised empirical models, but also mystify the very teachers that they were supposed to assist.

The most heated arguments have resulted from the attempts of some scholars to link action research principles to critical-emancipatory or liberationist theories. Such theorists (e.g. Carr and Kemmis, 1986) reject **positivist** notions of **objectivity**, rationality and truth, and focus on ways in which practitioners may discover distortions in the social fabric and learn to overcome aspects of the social order that inhibit democratic change. To others (e.g. Gibson, 1985; McKernan, 1988) such an interpretation of action research appears **ideologically** committed, inherently uncritical (particularly of itself), naïve, and unrealistic. The climate of this debate, as one observer has pointed out, has been 'hostile' and 'harsh' (McKernan, 1988, p. 196).

Few will dismiss as unimportant the central argument in this discussion: that teachers should be reflective and critical. Whether such a desirable objective requires the ideological commitment and methodological apparatus illustrated in the work of many action researchers is much more debatable.

REFERENCES

Carr (1989), Carr and Kemmis (1986), Corey (1953), Ebbutt (1985), Elliott (1978), Gibson (1985), Hustler, Cassidy and Cuff (1986), Kelly (1985), Kemmis (1984), McKernan (1988), McNiff (1988), Nixon (1981, 1987), Rapoport (1970), Stenhouse (1975b), Winter (1987).

Administrative leadership

Administration is an important aspect of **education**. Large numbers of teachers hold positions of special responsibility. Professional associations of principals and superintendents are among the strongest of their type. In-service courses on leadership and administration are numerous and well subscribed. Graduate schools of educational administration produce a large proportion of all graduate degrees in education. Many professional and scholarly journals are devoted to the subject, and publishers report that books on school management frequently outsell those on other educational topics. Depth of interest, however, is not necessarily accompanied by clarity of thought about the nature of the activity being undertaken. This is particularly evident in discussions about the nature of leadership in educational situations. Views of what such leadership means, how leaders should be identified, and what qualities leaders should have, have been subject to various interpretations and changing **ideologies**.

A dominant view defines leadership in instrumental terms. Given the interest of school authorities in controlling complex systems and implementing centrally devised policies, administrators are expected to put into effect policies devised by others, rather than to originate, or question, those policies. Thus, when talking of the characteristics of such implementers, scholars frequently refer to the ability to influence a group to achieve certain goals, to solve organization problems, or to prescribe the behaviour of subordinates. Thus, leadership is often defined in terms of the possession of certain general **skills**.

Some of these instrumental techniques have been derived from business practices. At the turn of the century, American schools became enamoured of the 'cult of efficiency' spawned by what observers regarded as a highly successful period of national industrialization. Recently, the call has been for the application to schools of 'lessons from America's best run companies' or for the use of techniques of 'middle management' in educational situations. Other techniques have been devised by those social scientists interested in placing the notion of leadership within a broader conception of a rational science of administration, in which **behaviour** in educational organizations may be described and explained by reference to **empirically** derived generalizations and **theories**. Some scholars, for example, have sought to identify the traits that successful leaders possess, or the situational variables that affect success. Several schemata have been invented to categorize leaders in respect of their **interest** in achieving goals and their capacity to work effectively with others.

Given this reliance upon business methods on the one hand, and social scientific theory on the other, it is not surprising that the daily tasks of principals are often expressed in performance-based or skill-based language. The American Association of School Administrators (1982), for example, identifies seven competencies of administrative leadership: school climate improvement, political skills, systematic programme planning, instructional management, school evaluation, resource allocation, and use of resources. Similarly, many school systems have obliged their leaders to operate within the framework of such general models as 'management by objectives' (MBO) and 'programme planning and budget systems' (PPBS).

These simplistic notions, however, have been subjected to criticism from a variety of sources. Social critics have pointed out that prevailing views of leadership reinforce pathologies evident in many educational systems, many of which are ideologically based. (Perhaps it is in the work of such novelists as George Orwell that the dangers of commitment to organizational **cultures** are most strikingly revealed.) **Feminist** scholars, in particular, have argued that many of the so-called principles of administration are inherently male dominated (and thus exclude female experience and **knowledge**). Other scholars have argued that notions of leadership should be redefined in cultural terms: what is important are not general skills but the ability to work in particular social or micropolitical situations (to which theoretical explanations have limited applicability).

Others go much further: they argue that while technical competence may be a necessary condition of leadership, it is insufficient; what is needed is an acknowledgement of questions of **value**. This may be expressed simply as the need for an educational leader to establish a defensible 'mission' for his school. Others perceive the task as much more complex: a leader is one concerned with the analysis of **language**, audit of values, **ethical** options, and the control of affect, rather than with management.

What seems to be emerging, therefore, is a restatement of the argument that leadership in education should not be defined exclusively in terms derived from business models or social scientific theory, nor based on general skills or notions of performance. **Schools** exist for certain educational purposes that are quite distinct from those of industry, and therefore the qualities needed in a leader are those that encourage the achievement of such purposes. Given the nature of those purposes, and the variety that exists among educational institutions, the application of either general skills of leadership or theories derived from social scientific research is inappropriate. What is needed in an educational leader, it is argued, is a well-endowed mind, and a capacity to make principled and **intelligent** decisions in specific school situations.

REFERENCES

American Association of School Administrators (1982), Ball (1987), Block (1987), Callaghan (1964), Fullan (1988), Greenfield (1979), Hodgkinson (1983), Hoy and Miskel (1987), Hoyle (1986), Lewis (1974), Peters (1976), Peters and

Waterman (1984), Shakeshaft (1987), Simon (1965), Smyth (1989a, 1989b), Waldo (1968).

Aesthetic value

How does one determine aesthetic value or quality within the arts? Various responses have been given to this question, ranging from the view that emphasizes the instructional or didactic value of art to that which stresses the essentially aesthetic and locates artistic quality in pure form.

As in the case of other types of **value judgement**, it seems mistaken to deduce from the undoubted fact of **cultural** and temporal variations in taste that judgements of aesthetic value are simply a matter of preference. Although it has proved difficult to explicate a clear and uncontentious conception of art, and to delineate unambiguous and generally acknowledged aesthetic criteria, it can hardly be denied that aesthetic considerations are to be distinguished from moral, economic, prudential, **utilitarian**, or unqualified pleasure considerations. There is something *sui generis* about aesthetic value. It is also, surely, certain that the question of what constitutes a good painting, a good symphony, or a good novel, is not to be decided simply by surveying popular opinion. Despite the difficulty of gaining agreement on answers to questions of aesthetic value, it is possible to be explicit about the appropriate way in which to approach them: it is necessary to combine a careful consideration of the **concept** of art and theories of art in general with a full understanding of the grammar of any particular art form. That is to say, for example, that judgements about the artistic value of a novel, if they are to be truly that, must take some account of what art is and of what novel-writing is.

It is true that different people may have different views. But, as has been indicated, there are limits to possible views on these matters: one cannot choose to define art in terms of economic value, for that is to treat it as something different from what it is. One may prefer novels to have happy endings, but to seek to define the novel in terms of such a criterion is to show ignorance of the domain of novel-writing.

This means, in effect, that informed value judgements in aesthetics can be distinguished from ill-informed, ignorant, and irrelevant judgements, and that to make informed value judgements presupposes understanding of aesthetic theory and of the nature of particular types of art (*art education).

REFERENCES

Adams (1971), Aldrich (1963), Alexander (1968), Beardsley (1981), Bell (1914), Jones (1975), Langer (1958), Sparshott (1982), Tolstoy (1898).

Affirmative action *see* Positive discrimination

Aims

Any practical activity must have an aim or set of aims to give it purpose and the kind of definition that allows us to talk about success or failure, quality, improvement, etc. If sailing has no specific aims, then one might reasonably sink the boat and call that sailing. Similarly, soccer, pharmacy, and horse-breeding are all partially defined in terms of their aims. Arriving at a clear conception of the aims of **education** is essential, therefore, both for understanding the enterprise and for assessing or designing **research** concerned with it. If we do not know what the aims of education are, how can we tell whether a person has been successfully educated, whether this is an effective way to educate, or whether that is appropriate research?

Certain philosophers have exercised great ingenuity in distinguishing aims from such related things as objectives, goals, purposes, and ends, not to mention differentiating between, for example, the aim conceived of as the target of the enterprise and the aim conceived of as the endeavour. It is not entirely clear that much is gained by such fine **discrimination** in this particular case, nor on what grounds some of the distinctions are made. On what grounds, for example, does one legitimately stipulate that 'aim' should be used of long-term goals and 'objective' reserved for short-term goals (as tends to be the practice in educational discourse, following philosophical advocacy)? Certainly not on the grounds that this accords with ordinary usage of the words, nor by reference to the dictionary. (Webster has 'the object to be attained; intention or purpose' for 'aim', and 'something aimed at or striven for' for 'objective'.)

It is important to recognize the variety of aims there may be: long-term, short-term, unrealizable, attainable, aims that are consequences of an activity (e.g. working with the aim of getting rich), aims that are the end product of an activity (e.g. building with the aim of completing the building), aims that though extrinsic to the activity are linked to a specific activity (e.g. building with the aim of owning the house), aims that are inherent in the activity (e.g. the aim of tightening the muscles or keeping fit while participating in a fitness class), general aims, specific aims, etc.

It has been argued that the aims of education are intrinsic to it. One does not educate for the sake of some further reward or goal, but for its own sake, and determining the aims of education is therefore essentially the same thing as clarifying the concept of education (Peters, 1966). But we must also recognize that people do sometimes have extrinsic goals when they pursue education. For example, certain parents may regard socio-economic advancement as the primary aim of education for their children (*behavioural objectives).

REFERENCES

Hollins (1964), Peters (1966), White (1982), Whitehead (1929).

Analogy

Educationalists frequently resort to analogy, comparison, **metaphor**, and simile in the course of argument about the nature of **education**. **Teaching** is likened to conducting an orchestra, filling buckets, or watering a garden; administration is compared with running a business or captaining a ship, education is metaphorically depicted as a process of birth, and the air is replete with settings allegedly analogous to the classroom: parent/child interaction, the work place, the prison, the church, the community at large, etc. Occasionally we resort to analogy in these pages. None the less it is a practice to be wary of. The hoped for advantage is that the vividness, familiarity, or shock of the analogy will spur one to seeing the real object of interest in a fresh light, while stimulating understanding by the comparison. The considerable disadvantage of arguing in this way is that the questions of whether things truly are analogous, and if so in what respects, are never directly addressed and, paradoxically, could only be satisfactorily answered by one who already had full understanding of both analogues. (For example, I wish to explain to you what is involved in being a parent. I say, it is analogous to being a **creative** artist. That may stimulate you – even give you some ideas, some of which are accurate. But there is no way of checking that. There is no way of knowing whether you have seized on the appropriate point of comparison. There is no way of knowing whether it is a good analogy, unless one already has full understanding of both being a parent and being a creative artist, in which case the analogy is unnecessary.) Arguing by analogy is particularly hazardous in respect of matters such as education where there is considerable confusion and disagreement among the experts on its nature and workings. For, if it is bad enough that I, who am an expert in physics and understand atomic fusion, should run the various risks involved in presenting it to you in analogous terms, it is considerably more dangerous that I, who have only a partial and contentious view of the nature of education, should none the less present it to you as analogous to watering a garden (about which I also know little). The solution is to hand: we should be examining and talking about education itself, instead of hiding behind imperfect comparisons between two imperfectly understood ideas.

One should perhaps distinguish between the practice of saying, for example, 'schools are like prisons', and the practice of saying 'schools are prisons'. The former is certainly to be preferred, particularly if one adds specific reference to the points of comparison (*metaphor).

Analysis

An important aspect of philosophy is its concern with analysis. Various philosophers and schools of philosophy, however, have had different views of its nature. Here, we will briefly review a few of these views, emphasizing their differences. In addition, since a great many of the other entries in this dictionary involve our attempts at analysis, we shall try to make it clear exactly what we conceive the task to involve. (The labels that we give to the views considered are not necessarily in universal currency.)

Platonic or absolutist analysis. Plato argued that the physical world presents to our senses a number of particular instances of things (whether concrete or abstract) that in various ways fall short of perfection. Appearances deceive: I do not see a particular table exactly as it is, for I see it only from a particular angle or perspective. In addition, particular tables, rocks, or trees change as time goes by, and various conditions, such as the immersion of a stick in water, may change the appearance of the object. When it comes to abstract concepts, such as love, courage, or education, the difficulty of seeing them as they are becomes even more acute. Such points led Plato to the view that particular instances lack reality in a way that ideal conceptions do not: no particular triangular shape in the world perfectly embodies triangularity. No particular table is a sufficient representation of tableness. He therefore posited a world of what he called ideas or forms – for example, the forms of tableness and triangularity. The important task for mankind, he believed, was to understand the forms of things, rather than to rely on the senses applied to particulars.

The main problem in interpreting Plato's theory of forms is to determine what sense to make of the claims that the forms exist and are imperishable, and that there is a world of forms that is more real than the physical world of experience. However, we need not concern ourselves with those problems here (see Barrow, 1976b).

From our point of view the important point is that Plato's views have given rise to the notion that what education essentially is, or what tableness or courage actually are, is fixed and determined for all time. Opinions about such things may change, but that merely indicates mankind's inability to find and hold on to the truth. On this view, therefore, the task of analysing concepts is seen as one of getting hold of the correct and eternally true account of it. Education, for example, is what it is, and the concept waits to be captured and pinned down, rather lke a butterfly being pursued by a lepidopterist. Since concepts are seen as ideas that are what they are, we may talk of some accounts of concepts being mistaken, and others being correct, or partially correct.

When expressed clearly in this way, it may be doubted whether many philosophers would admit to being absolutists, but none the less many proceed to analyse concepts as if this is what they believed: they search for the **necessary** and sufficient conditions of tableness, education, or courage, as if there could only be one correct account, regardless of time or place.

Sociological analysis. In stark contrast to any such view is what may be termed sociological analysis. Some people, impressed by the fact that different **cultures** and different historical periods have different conceptions of, for example, courage and education, proceed to analyse particular concepts in culturally specific terms, with particular reference to the institutionalization and practical manifestations of concepts. Thus marriage and education are defined in terms of the way a particular culture (usually one's own) embodies them. Education is what the school system provides; marriage is whatever our laws and customs make it. There is, with this approach, no answer to the question 'But what is the true conception of marriage?'; there are only various cultural definitions.

Consensual analysis. Some have been tempted to look for underlying similarities in the different conceptions of different cultures, and to see the essential or true concept in terms of what is common to all. Thus, granted that different cultures have some very different moral rules, for example, we may none the less detect some underlying principles that are common to all, and these, it may be suggested, guide us towards a universal and in some sense true or correct conception of morality. For example, some cultures regard adultery as wrong, while others actually favour it. But these differences can be accounted for by seeing the different particular practices as being the product of the same general principles (of things such as benevolence and trust) being worked out in very different circumstances (*ethics).

Linguistic analysis. Linguistic analysis has enjoyed considerable favour amongst philosophers of education in recent years. This view suggests that the way to analyse the concept of education is to consider how the word is used. By studying what one can sensibly say in respect of education and what one cannot, one comes to a better understanding of it. It would seem nonsensical to say 'He is physically very weak, so his education has been imperfect', from which we deduce that education is not to be defined in terms of physical health; on the other hand 'He knows absolutely nothing, but I must admit he is very well educated' seems contradictory, and suggests that education necessarily has something to do with knowledge.

The view to which we have committed ourselves in preparing this dictionary starts from the observation that there are problems and limitations in each of these positions, and that exclusive preoccupation with any one approach is to be avoided.

It is difficult to make sense of the notion that all concepts are eternally unchanging (unless it is interpreted to mean that all things that are logically conceivable are in principle conceivable at all times). On the other hand, although different cultural groups do sometimes entertain markedly different conceptions, as the Soviet Union and the United States have different conceptions of democracy, to remain on the level of sociological analysis is a most conservative procedure. If education is just whatever our schools provide, how are we ever going to be able to change or improve it? The consensual approach has something to contribute, for it often leads to recognition of much greater similarities between people than superficial appearances would suggest. But here again we must ask why we should be committed to the view that whatever is common to all views of morality is the true essence of morality? And what do we do when, as in the case of education, some conceptions appear to have nothing in common?

Linguistic analysis we regard as a most useful technique, provided that it is seen as being only that, and only one of many. This technique will uncover a number of presumptions about education, but they will only be presumptions of a particular culture. Studying how the word 'education' functions will give us many ideas about the enterprise, but it will at best give us the ideas embedded in the minds of the English-speaking world.

We therefore suggest that the very idea of a true or correct conception be set aside, and the business of analysis be seen as an essentially personal business.

The attempt to analyse the concept of education thus becomes the attempt to articulate precisely what one ideally takes it to involve, and to tease out the various implications of one's view. This task will be assisted considerably by consideration of what one's own and other societies do or have done in the name of education, and of what they regard as meaningful and coherent uses of the word. But such techniques will only give one a number of possible thoughts about the concept. The individual must then forge a coherent concept for himself. In point of fact, given a shared linguistic and cultural background, this will lead to much uniformity of conception. But where it does not, where one conception of education manifestly differs from another, important progress has none the less been made: the participants in the debate have a clear idea of what they are respectively talking about in the name of education, they know that they differ, and they can move on to intelligible arguments about the rival value of their different types of education. To try to establish that one of them has a mistaken conception seems to us fruitless, if not meaningless.

It follows from the above that what we have to say about concepts such as **autonomy, education**, and **indoctrination** in this dictionary, though presented as if it were simply the correct account of these concepts, in fact purports to be no more than our conception of them. Their value lies in the fact that they are, we hope, clearly and fully articulated conceptions which cohere with one another, as well as internally, and which probably do represent articulations of concepts that readers share (though in some cases they will not have articulated them), because they share a broadly similar background.

The criteria for assessing whether a concept is well analysed, on this view, are clarity, internal coherence and consistency, making implications explicit, and coherence between those implications and other beliefs. For example, one's account of what constitutes an educated person should arise out of reflection on various cultural practices and views, combined with close consideration of what it makes sense to say in respect of 'the educated person'; but what is ultimately required is an account sufficiently full and unequivocal to enable others to see all the implications of one's conception, and the implications of which are neither themselves incompatible nor incompatible with other conceptual positions one holds (for example, a conception of an educated person that was not clearly distinguishable from one's conception of a trained person, could be criticized on that ground, if one was known also to hold the view that the two are to be distinguished).

Strategies for engaging in conceptual analysis include comparing apparent opposites (e.g. education and indoctrination), comparing distinct concepts that none the less belong in the same domain (e.g. education and **training**), considering border-line cases (e.g. the brilliant but narrow

academic), and searching for necessary and sufficient conditions, besides the more general procedures referred to above (***behavioural objectives, concept, degree words, etymology, facts, research**).

REFERENCES

Alston (1964), Austin (1962), Barrow (1976b, 1981b, 1983, 1985b), Graham (1977), Plato (1974), Wittgenstein (1958).

Analytic truth *see* Contingent

Aptitude treatment interactions

The study of aptitude treatment interactions (ATIs) is a particular branch of **teacher effectiveness** research. An 'aptitude' is defined as any relatively stable student characteristic that may be related to achievement (e.g. a psychological process, personality trait, or age), and a 'treatment' is any manipulable variable (e.g. teaching style, or time-on-task). Those interested in ATIs are motivated by a desire to fit teaching behaviours to individual student characteristics rather than to rely on general laws of learning designed for all students.

Questions related to ATIs have required researchers to supplement or combine traditional psychological research methodologies as new studies are conducted or previous reports re-examined for evidence of interactions. To date, such investigations have extended over a wide range of instructional settings, including programmed instruction, reading, mathematics and science instruction, and many types of **teaching** methodology.

Despite twenty years of effort, the findings of ATI research have not been encouraging. Some experiments are methodologically weak, or inconclusive in their results. Critics in the field have noted that the range of factors involved in matching learner aptitudes and methods is so awesome in breadth that any attempts to establish causal links are likely to founder. A strong case may be made that current research efforts have failed to establish any ATIs that are useful for instructional purposes.

Several critics have pointed to **conceptual** weaknesses in ATI research. Some dispute the central conviction that teaching behaviours are causally linked to student learning. Others have suggested that the attempt to identify and confirm particular interactions will result in the destruction of an essential component of dynamism in the teaching act.

In addition, some critics have noted that ATI research appears to have taken little cognizance of the effects of different types of subject matter upon particular interactions.

The nature and current status of ATI research highlights several general questions concerning the relationship of social scientific theory to educational **research**. ATI investigators assume a **behavioural** view of teaching and learning that is not held by all scholars. The search for effective and predictable interactions seems to rest on the premiss that there is a limited number of ways in which learning may take place in particular situations. **Education** in general (and **learning** in particular) is too complex an undertaking to be restricted to the study of single dimensions of particular teaching styles or particular student aptitudes.

REFERENCES
Cronbach and Snow (1977), Jackson (1970), Koran and Koran (1984), Tobias (1981, 1982), Tom (1980, 1984).

APU *see* Accountability

Art education

Art education has often occupied a hinterland of its own in schools, as if it were an 'optional extra', as indeed it used to be in certain private schools. This state of affairs may be partly due to the fact that art education has sometimes been narrowly defined to mean only painting, or perhaps craft work in general. It has had at least one unfortunate consequence in that the bulk of general curriculum theorizing has rather ignored art and any particularities it may have. (Particular authors, e.g. Eisner, 1979, and Ross, 1984, have of course stepped in to fill the gap.)

In order to talk coherently about art education a number of possible distinctions need to be appreciated. We may be concerned with performing arts (e.g. drama, music-making), creative arts (e.g. pottery, painting), or consumer arts (e.g. appreciating music). There are the familiar distinctions between, for example, music, painting, sculpture, mime, poetry, and literature. More generally we have to be clear whether talk of the arts includes, for example, **history**, the study of languages (particularly such dead languages as Latin and Greek), and philosophy. It is not that art education must be defined once and for all, still less that there is a correct answer to the question of how it should be defined (*analysis), but it is impossible to follow particular arguments about the arts without a clear idea of what the proponent of the argument takes art education to involve. It is probably fair to say that 'the arts' are usually taken to refer to the **liberal** arts (philosophy, history, English, etc.) and are contrasted with the sciences, while 'art education' is confined to creative art.

If art **education** is to be truly that and to be distinguished from, for example, **training** in art, then it should mean initiation into the **theory** of painting, music, **literature**, etc. Many would argue that art education in this sense is under constant threat from the vocational and **utilitarian** demands of government and industry, and that it should play a more prominent role in the **curriculum**. However that may be, there are a number of questions that have not received the attention they deserve: Is there a good case for schools seeking to encourage performance in the arts? If so, on whose part? If so, what arts? Why? For the sake of art, for the sake of the child's **nature**, therapy, or what? Should we likewise seek to produce true **creative** individuals? Is knowledge of the arts part of being a fully developed person? What claims can plausibly be made about the relationship of music, painting, sculpture, etc., to **knowledge** or **emotional** development? (***aesthetic value, communication, culture, schooling, value judgements**)

REFERENCES

Eisner (1979), Gribble (1983), Osborne (1984), Ross (1984).

Assessment

Students may be assessed for a number of different reasons and in a number of different ways. We may, for example, wish to test the level of student attainment, to gather data to aid inquiry into our teaching or for purposes of **accountability**, to make predictions concerning the student's future, to set standards, or to motivate students. The range of types of assessment runs from the conventional written essay, through oral tests and practical projects, to various types of objective test. Sometimes tests will be classified as norm-referenced, sometimes as criterion-referenced. This distinction will not necessarily be marked in the nature of the test, but rather in the use to which it is put. Tests designed and used primarily to rank order students are norm-referenced, those designed and used to indicate mastery of subject matter are criterion-referenced. (A particular test may be used for both purposes.) Some tests are in addition standardized, which is to say that prior research will have been carried out to establish a norm for performance on the test either in general or in respect of particular groups, especially age groups. Thus a standardized vocabulary test will indicate the scores to be expected of a class of a given age.

Many further variations may be noted within this broad range of tests. The traditional written exam may be modified to allow particular books to be taken along and used by the student, or the questions may be given in advance. The questions themselves may invite anything from simple recall (e.g. 'Describe the content of the 1944 Education Act'), to argument or creative expression. Objective tests are also, and perhaps better, termed selective-response tests, for they differ from the essay type **examination** in that they limit the options open to the student, and look for a particular response. Whether that truly makes them objective depends partly on what is meant by 'objective' and partly on recognizing the limits of what they are testing. (A selective-response test may test such things as correct recall of a date, or knowledge of the meaning of a particular word, objectively, but not things such as the student's breadth of knowledge or verbal fluency.) These tests too may be primarily concerned with recall (e.g. 'Who said/wrote X?'; 'Complete the following quotation'; 'Complete/label the accompanying diagram'), or recognition (e.g. 'Which of the following statements are true/false?'; multiple-choice questions and matching items). There are a number of traps for the unwary that need to be guarded against in constructing such tests (for example, avoid giving clues to the correct answer in the grammar/ wording of the question; in multiple-choice questions avoid any overlapping answers; avoid confusing questions, and questions where the answer belongs to the realm of opinion rather than **fact**). And researchers have made some claims about desirable practices in constructing them. (For example, four is said to be an optimum number of alternatives in a multiple-choice question; increased length of test can help to ensure reasonable coverage of material.) But the most crucial consideration is that a selective-response test, and the particular form chosen, should be suited to that which we wish to assess (*objectivity).

Many advantages and disadvantages both to formal assessment procedures in general and to specific forms have been noted. It is said that any form of assessment that is public promotes a **competitive** spirit. It is pointed out that no type of assessment can get round the fact that individuals may not do themselves justice, for reasons that have little to do with their ability or achievement (or the teaching they have received). No test, for example, can satisfactorily allow for the individual who feels sick or has just experienced some emotional trauma. Some fear that any system of examination may lead to domination of the **curriculum** by the requirements of the examination system, and others deplore the fact that such systems tend to emphasize the value of the written word at the expense of the oral.

There is some truth in the descriptive part of all these claims. What is not so clear is that they are necessarily objectionable. Whether people should be encouraged to be competitive, and if so to what extent, is a contentious question to which there is as yet no obvious route to an easy answer. We need to establish not only what counts as being competitive (i.e. where it begins and ends: is an individual's concern that his children shall be prosperous part of his competitive edge? is his desire to do as well as anyone else at any job to which he sets his hand?), but also what effects it does in fact have (is it true that it brings a measure of satisfaction to mankind? is it true that it makes people more inventive, more hard-working?) and whether these effects are to be valued or not (*value judgements).

It is true that no examination system can guarantee that no extraneous factors will ever affect the results. But one might argue that it is not the purpose of examinations to test a person's performance under artificial clinical circumstances, but rather under the typical pressures of daily life. As to the question of domination of curriculum, that is surely not an objection in itself. Provided that the examination system assesses what we can argue ought to be assessed, then it is desirable that it should affect the curriculum. Similarly, many would argue that the written word should dominate, partly because of the educational importance of reading, and partly because it is easier to monitor and improve precise and accurate language use in the written form (*language).

Points made against the use of the essay as a form of examination include: the difficulty of marking essays objectively (many studies suggest that not only do different markers often give widely disparate assessments of the same essay, but also that the same marker may vary in assessment according to such factors as his mood and circumstances); the time that it takes to administer; the relatively low content validity that such a form of examination tends to have (for example, one does not test a student's knowledge of Tudor history as a whole by setting two or three essays on topics covered in the programme); and the fact that it handicaps children who, while able, clever, and making good progress in learning, are not verbally very fluent or are weak in areas such as grammar and punctuation. At the other end of the spectrum it has been pointed out that though selective-response types of examination are relatively easy to administer, they are correspondingly difficult to set in the first place; and that they do not allow points to be pursued in depth or at length.

There is, however, something rather curious about pursuing the question of the merits and demerits of particular forms of examination in the abstract. The crucial consideration should surely be what kinds of thing one wishes to encourage and monitor. Selective-response tests are ideal when one is only concerned to test for discrete items of knowledge and wishes to ensure coverage of a wide area. But if one is concerned that students should be able to use the language well, to sustain arguments, to pursue points in depth, to show evidence of rational thinking/**critical thinking/intelligence/creativity**, then such tests are incomparably inferior to the more open-ended essay examination. Since the major worry about essays (apart from length of time required to administer them) appears to be that they are not objectively assessable, it should be pointed out that this is not just another fact about them, so much as a necessary consequence of the kind of thing they are and what they are trying to do. There is no way of ensuring marker-uniformity on an essay, because an essay is a complex response involving too many potential elements to allow them all to be pre-categorized, and too many elements that do not lend themselves to **measurement**. In short, the reason that selective-response tests can be said to be more objective is simply that they ask less complex and equivocal questions and concern themselves with features of student response that are easier to recognize (for example, recall of correct date rather than interpretation of evidence). Quite obviously, essay tests do handicap those who have difficulties with grammar, punctuation, and, more generally, the written word. But for many educators that is one of the reasons they are to be preferred as a means of assessment. **Education**, it may be argued, should be particularly concerned about this kind of competence, and any form of assessment that avoids testing it is grossly inappropriate.

The above paragraph is directly relevant to the more general issue of the **validity, reliability** and **objectivity** of testing procedures. We do not want tests to be unreliable (i.e. giving rise to inconsistent results for no apparent reason), invalid (i.e. testing something other than what they purport to test), or subjective in the sense of being based on irrelevant or unstated criteria (*subjectivity). On the other hand, we should be cautious about relying on claims about high reliability, validity, and objectivity, and it is important to remember that they are not sufficient conditions of a good test. When a test is allegedly shown to have high reliability, it is seldom the case that the test designers can legitimately claim to have rigorously established that no extraneous factors have had or could have anything to do with the results. A test that does indeed test what it sets out to test under any conditions may none the less be a poor test for a number of reasons (for example, that it tests something trivial). For such reasons, due caution and allowance for margins of error are formally counselled on all sides, although it may be suggested that such tests are none the less treated too reverentially in practice.

A more important question is whether such technically good tests are likely to focus on the sorts of thing that educationalists really need to know. It follows from the nature of validity, reliability, and objectivity that only certain kinds of thing lend themselves to testing with high ratings in these respects. For example, it is relatively easy to construct a technically good test of vocabulary, numeracy, and certain other specific **skills**, but relatively difficult to do so in respect of appreciation, sophisticated understanding of complex arguments, and critical or creative thinking. Yet the latter would be thought by some to be rather more important **aims** of education. It should at least be recognized that most classroom research, in relying heavily on technically sound tests of achievement as an index of student progress, contributes to a conception of successful education in terms of a limited number of fairly specific and unsophisticated skills. (The situation would be potentially less misleading if such tests were thought of as tests of specific competency rather than tests of achievement. By all means let us say that a particular student has demonstrated a certain knowledge of vocabulary or computing skill, but not that we have demonstrated that he has been successfully taught, still less, well educated.) (*behavioural objectives, literacy, research, teacher effectiveness, teaching)

REFERENCES
Bloom, Hastings and Madaus (1971), Burt (1923), Ebel (1972), Gronlund (1974, 1977), Popham (1978), Thorndike (1971).

Authority *see* Neutrality

Autonomy

Autonomy means self-government. An autonomous person is one who thinks and acts independently, rather than one whose decisions are controlled by other persons or agencies. It has been widely promoted as a goal of **education** (*aims).

Autonomy is to be contrasted with heteronomy, which implies subordination to some outside agency, be it another person or persons, custom, ideology, religion, etc. The word is derived from the two Greek words *autos* (self) and *nomos* (law). Heteronomy is derived from *heteros* (other) and *nomos*. Autonomy is to be distinguished from freedom. A man may be free to do as he pleases in various respects, but none the less fail to act autonomously, if, for example, he simply does what other people tell him to do. (A person may autonomously choose to obey someone else; but as soon as he begins acting in response to orders he ceases to be autonomous. In cases where people do not choose to obey others or to follow the dictates of some ideology, but do so unreflectively, they are not proceeding autonomously.) Conversely a person may be unfree, but still act autonomously: a prisoner may have very little freedom, but in so far as he conducts himself as he sees fit to do, within the limits of possibility, and thinks for himself, he is being autonomous.

It might be argued that, if autonomy means self-direction as opposed to being subservient to any external agency, it is an unrealizable goal. For, although it is quite often possible to be free of other people's orders, it is not possible to get away entirely from systems of belief or **ideology**. Thus, although I may think my decision to leave my wife is autonomous, it will in fact be the product of various assumptions, values, etc., that I am sometimes not consciously aware that I am committed to. However, although it is no doubt true that we are all to some extent influenced by a range of assumptions and beliefs that we take for granted when we make particular decisions, it is extremely doubtful whether we are all necessarily unthinkingly committed to, and hence governed by, some ideology. There is in principle a clear distinction between one who accepts an ideology without question and decides particular questions in the light of that ideology, and one who is willing to question and decide for himself the merits of his beliefs. And, though few of us will ever be completely autonomous, we may clearly approach more or less fully to the goal of autonomy. An unquestioning commitment to, say, Catholicism, combined with a refusal to think about a particular issue such as abortion except in terms of current Catholic orthodoxy, clearly involves less autonomy than a willingness to think about the grounds for one's faith independently and/or to examine the issue of abortion without prior commitment to the Catholic view. Being autonomous is essentially a matter of seeing oneself as responsible for one's beliefs and assumptions (even if they were initially thrust upon one by other people or one's environment), and being willing to examine them for oneself. It is not a matter of holding idiosyncratic views. One might be exceedingly conventional and highly autonomous. It is a question of how one approaches decision making rather than what one's decisions are (*degree words).

Implicit in the previous paragraph is the point that autonomous behaviour is not necessarily wise or sensible behaviour. An autonomous person thinks for himself; he does not necessarily think well. This raises two problems: how does one distinguish between a lack of autonomy and such things as stupidity or ignorance? And what does this imply for the value of autonomy?

Many people may appear to lack autonomy because they seem to accept and to be governed by a variety of beliefs or people rather than by their own thinking. But it may be that some people are merely unable to see any problems in received opinions or that they believe in the superior wisdom of certain other people. Am I unautonomous, if I trust my medical advisers rather than get engaged in examining medical theory for myself? Am I lacking in autonomy, if I lack any marked capacity to see problems and weaknesses in the philosophy of the political party which I have always supported? Here it is necessary to distinguish between a practical problem and a theoretical one (*theory and practice). It is certainly the case that it will often be difficult to determine whether an individual is behaving autonomously, in practice. But the distinction that we are looking for can still be explained in principle: if I decide to trust my medical advisers, because I recognize their superior knowledge, then I make an autonomous decision. In following their advice, I cease to act autonomously, but none the less to act thus was itself an autonomous decision (and might well be accounted a wise one). Likewise, if I decide for myself that there are good reasons to support and follow the party as a matter of principle, I may claim to be an autonomous person to some degree, even though, having made the decision, I allow the party to direct me. If, on the other hand, the reason that I follow the instructions of medical experts or party is that it never occurred to me to question them, then to that extent I lack autonomy. It may indeed be difficult to say whether a person who is committed to a certain interpretation of the world is so because he has thought about it and decided for himself that it is the only reasonable one, or because he was brought up in the tradition and never thought to question it; or perhaps it is because his ability to question it seriously was so slight as to make it impossible for him to begin to recognize the problems at issue. But it remains clear that only the first position involves autonomy. The second response is straightforwardly unautonomous, while the third provides an instance of autonomy being hampered by intellectual shortcomings. Autonomous thought, as we have said, is not necessarily sensible or wise thought, but autonomous thought does require a certain minimum intellectual competence. In order to proceed autonomously, it is necessary to understand something of the nature of what one is concerned with. Making up one's own mind about particular medical matters does not logically require making the correct decisions, but it does require some understanding of the nature of medicine and medical research. This is because without such understanding one could hardly refer to it as genuine thinking about medical problems, let alone autonomous thinking (*critical thinking).

But, if it is the case that an autonomous individual may none the less make a number of poor decisions, to what extent should we value autonomous thinking? Is it not more important that people should hold true beliefs than that they should make them their own, and that they should do the correct, right, or wise thing than that they should do what they autonomously decide? Some might go further than this and suggest that it is more important to ensure a happy society, a just society, or an ideologically sound society, than to cultivate autonomous individuals.

The weakness of such views is that they presuppose that somebody can determine beyond reasonable doubt what is correct, wise, and right. Whereas the truth is that in many cases even views about what means are appropriate to given ends is legitimately hotly disputed (*research, teacher effectiveness), while in the case of ends, whether they involve moral, educational, aesthetic or political values, there is not even universal agreement on how one should proceed to determine them, let alone what they actually are. Autonomy must be valued by anyone who values truth and who recognizes the openness of many fundamental questions (*value judgements, aesthetic value, ethics).

In addition, autonomy seems necessarily to be one of the values that schools should be concerned with, because **education** is logically tied up with it: to be educated implies having **understanding**, rather than mere information or a set of rules and beliefs learned by rote, and to understand is to make something one's own. It would be a mistake, therefore, to assume that, since autonomy means self-direction, a school system that wishes to develop it should necessarily leave children to direct themselves in all particulars all the time. If we wish to end up with autonomous adults we need to ensure appropriate understanding, and this might be best developed in situations where much of the time students are not granted much autonomy. On the other hand a school system that at no point encourages the exercise of autonomy is not likely to lead to the emergence of autonomous adults (*normative).

REFERENCES

Barrow (1975), Cohen (1982), Dearden (1972a), Doyle (1973), Godfrey (1984), Quinn (1984).

B

Basics

The terms 'basics' and 'basic education' refer to those essentials in **learning** that every student should possess, or upon which many other subjects or areas of study depend. In particular, 'basics' frequently appears in the phrase 'back to the basics', which usually implies that an educational system has abandoned the **teaching** of certain desired skills or subject matter in favour of unnecessary frills or fringe activities. A movement to basic education is often at least mildly conservative.

Over the centuries, what has been considered essential for every young person to learn has varied from one society to another. Classical Sparta emphasized gymnastics and obedience to the state (and gave short shrift to subject matter approved as important in such states as Athens). Certain eighteenth- and nineteenth-century reformers argued that every student should either study science or be trained in desired industrial skills. Some jurisdictions have always demanded the inclusion of religious studies of one sort or another in every student's programme. In common parlance over the last hundred years, however, the term 'the basics' has been associated with 'the three Rs', reading, writing, and arithmetic (the supposed foundation for every other subject, and the source of skills desired in the working place), and those subjects have dominated the elementary school curriculum.

The reasons for recent heightened interest in the basics are not difficult to locate. Schools have produced graduates whose writing habits have dismayed university professors and personnel officers. Scores on standardized tests of language and mathematics appear to have declined over the last decade (although the **empirical** evidence on this question is far from clear). Some parents, angered by alleged lack of **discipline** in schools, argue that schools are not ensuring adequate **academic** achievement. In addition, lack of money has forced **administrators** to eliminate certain subjects from the curriculum. Given these perceived ills in the school system, a return to basics has been seen by a growing number of citizens and educators as a panacea.

What it is that schools are supposed to return to is not always very clear. Many recommend an emphasis on a revised version of 'the three Rs' in the old sense, with computer competency or **computer literacy** being added. Some advocate a return to more clearly defined rules of behaviour: witness, on the one hand, the introduction in some places of stricter discipline within school buildings, and dress regulations for both sexes, and, on the other hand, the downgrading of teaching techniques that encourage social interaction or inquiry. Others recommend a curricular emphasis on national literature and **history**, or on selected civic competencies. Another group (in itself greatly varied) requires all students to include one or more of the following as part of their basic education: **religious education, sex education**, environmental studies, and life and leisure **skills** (and others of varied importance). Some writers interpret the notion of basic education quite broadly to include a wide range of subject matter reflecting a variety of forms of **knowledge**. Because this may result in little room being left for optional studies, basic education has become confused with **core curriculum (*topic-centred education**).

Despite the ill-defined nature of the 'back to the basics' movement, it has affected schooling throughout the English-speaking world in the last decade. In particular, the balance between optional subjects and required subjects has shifted in favour of the latter. Curriculum guides and handbooks have listed skills and competencies that all students ought to possess. Some school systems have adopted courses of study that give greater attention to skills desired in the workplace. New schools have been established (so many in some jurisdictions that the existence of a public system has been threatened) that emphasize not only basic subject matter and tight discipline but also adherence to particular religious denominations.

Current interest in 'back to the basics' by parents' groups may be considered part of a generally conservative movement to regain social control of the school. At its best, the call to re-examine what is basic in an educational process requires careful reflection on such important issues as the relationship of subjects and disciplines to one another, the content of the curriculum at each grade, and the goals of education. At worst, however, advocates of 'back to the basics' appear to be openly anti-intellectual and anti-educational. The issues involved in any serious discussion of basic education are too complex to respond to one-sided solutions (***education, curriculum, literacy, schooling**).

REFERENCES

Barrow (1979), Cox and Dyson (1969), Eisner (1982), Federation of Women Teachers' Associations of Ontario (1978), Hodgetts (1968), Hodgetts and Gallagher (1978), Jackson (1979), Kohl (1982), Morgan and Robinson (1976), Ohmann (1976), Sublette (1982), Vickery and Smith (1979), Wallace (1982), White (1982).

Behavioural objectives

'Behavioural objectives' are defined as **aims** or goals of instruction intended to change the observable behaviour of learners. Such objectives are pre-specified; they determine in advance the performances of students, strategies of teachers, and methods of student assessment in a particular course, a section of a course, or a lesson. Behavioural objectives often indicate the conditions under which the desired change of behaviour takes place, and state the minimum standard of performance by which the required behaviour may be judged. In writing such objectives, stress is placed on words thought to be unambiguous in their reference to behaviour (e.g. 'write' or 'jump'), rather than words considered to have no obvious behavioural connotations (e.g. 'know' or 'appreciate'). Behavioural objectives, therefore, are to be distinguished from those aims or goals that refer to the mental states of learners (e.g. what they 'think' about an issue or subject).

One of the principal complaints of those advocating use of such behavioural objectives is that there has often been a difference between teachers' stated goals and the actual student achievement in the classroom. To improve instructional techniques, and encourage teachers to be more effective in the classroom, the argument goes, general educational goals should be broken down into specific instructional objectives designed to elicit behavioural change that may be carefully monitored. For example, in place of a general statement of aim such as 'be able to solve problems in algebra', we write: 'Given a linear algebraic equation with one unknown, be able to solve (write the solution) for the unknown without the aid of references, tables, or calculating devices.' (Mager, 1975, p. 50).

It is probably true that many teachers do, in fact, deceive themselves about the degree to which lofty aims are put into effect in terms of student learning. In many skill-based topics in such areas as mathematics, grammar, health sciences, technical subjects, managerial studies, and physical education, careful attention to performance components and standards may be productive. A reliance upon performance-based goal statements is thought to have been successful in a number of training tasks in the Second World War, and in the 1950s and 1960s many school systems, encouraged by the writings of certain educational psychologists, experienced a varying degree of success in incorporating behavioural objectives into most subjects in the **curriculum**. (So great was the demand in the United States that several entrepreneurs made the assembly of banks of behavioural objectives a successful commercial undertaking.)

What is at issue in these discussions about behavioural objectives is not the question of whether there ought to be any objectives or aims in specific school subjects or courses. It would be absurd to argue that no purposes at all should exist in an educational enterprise of any order, or that the achievement of learners in an instructional setting should not be assessed. What is disputed is that these purposes should necessarily be framed in behavioural terms.

Several important questions have been raised about behavioural objectives. First, it is not clear that certain desired aims in education can be written satisfactorily in behavioural terms. What are the behaviours, we may ask, that characterize '**autonomous** thinking' or 'the ability to make independent judgements'? While it is true that behavioural examples of such desired educational goals may be generated quite easily, it is by no means certain that the simple performance of the behaviours in the examples is evidence of the desired end state. A person who sorts through the arguments within a political tract, for example, may simply be following instructions by rote rather than exercising independence of judgement – the behaviour in itself does not tell us which. The aims of **education** are far too complex to be satisfactorily characterized in terms of lists of behaviours. Indeed, strict adherence to behavioural objectives suggests commitment to the questionable position that knowing and **learning** are the same as behaving.

Second, from the point of view of forms of **knowledge** or **disciplines** additional difficulties arise. Some disciplines do not lend themselves to the types of pre-specified performance required by behavioural objectives. Certain subjects within the humanities, such as **literature** and philosophy, call for expressions of taste and judgement that are particular and unique – and certainly resistant to both behavioural pre-specification and expression. How can a teacher pre-specify a student's reaction to a painting or a poem, or insist that that reaction be exclusively demonstrated in terms of performance? Even in those subjects which at first glance may lend themselves more readily to behavioural objectives, such as certain sciences, pre-specification in experimental investigations may be hostile to important understandings within the disciplines.

Third, it has been argued that the task of writing behavioural objectives presents more difficulties than their exponents have recognized. For example, the notion that ambiguity in a given purpose is removed by using such action verbs as 'assess' or 'evaluate' is questionable. Few rules or guides seem to exist for deciding the level of specificity of behavioural objectives in particular instances – if the list is kept short, the objectives often seem vague; and if the list is not vague, it is often impossibly long. In particular subjects or disciplines, the relationship between objectives in certain topics may be far more complex than a written list may suggest. The suggestion that there are unitary **skills** in breaking down general statements into specific objectives flies in the face of the contextual nature of knowledge – the fact that a teacher is capable of breaking down a general statement related to government, for example, is no guide whatever to his competence in doing the same task for statements in chemistry. Even if behavioural objectives could be written with any degree of clarity or certainty, the fact remains that such objectives remain symptoms – a student does not write out three causes of the American Civil War, he recalls them first in his head, and then writes them out (*critical thinking, generic fallacy, transference).

Behavioural objectives, therefore, may have value in specific areas of the curriculum designed to improve selected skills and processes. Attention to such objectives may encourage educators to consider the effectiveness of their practices in the classroom. Nevertheless, an over reliance on behavioural objectives may be dangerous. Their use limits the range of alternatives available to teachers, and encourages them to concentrate on trivial ends in the educational process. If the task of the teacher is seen to be directed principally to the pre-specification of behaviours, then his attention is turned from a far more important question: what ends should he be pursuing in the curriculum? (*assessment, behaviourism, curriculum design, research, teacher effectiveness, teaching)

REFERENCES

Barrow (1984), Bloom (1956), Furst (1981), Hirst (1975), Hurst (1984), Kelly (1977), Krathwohl, Bloom and Masia (1964), Macdonald-Ross (1975), Mager (1975), Popham (1969), Pratt (1980), Pring (1971a).

Behaviourism

The term 'behaviourism' appears in a variety of educational contexts. Some use it in a general sense to denote the philosophy of science concerned with the subject matter and methods of psychology. Others use it in a strictly methodological sense to identify the practices of studying behaviour scientifically. Different approaches to behaviourism are located in the work of particular scholars, for example in the pioneering work of J. B. Watson two generations ago and in the more recent publications of B. F. Skinner. Educational psychologists differ in the extent to which they believe that **phenomena** should be, or can be, explained in terms of behaviour: some take doctrinaire positions, while others are more eclectic.

Nevertheless there is agreement on a number of general principles. Scholars in the behaviourist tradition rely upon observation of what human beings do, that is, their actions or behaviour, just as other scientists rely on observation in investigations of other members of the animal world – human beings may be more complex to study, but the process remains the same. Both natural scientists and behavioural scientists follow the same scientific practices in their search for laws of behaviour. Explanations for behaviour are sought in the observable interaction of human beings and their environments, rather than in such unobservable features as human predispositions, **emotions**, feelings, and free will. In the study of that interaction, special attention is paid to the systems of rewards and punishments that affect human behaviour in particular situations. Behaviourists, in consequence, are environmental determinists rather than biological determinists.

Two aspects of behaviourist theory are of particular interest to educators: social engineering and conditioned learning. Because environmental features play a determining role in human actions, it is possible, behaviourists argue, to improve human society by the deliberate manipulation of environmental features. Improvements in society, therefore, may be engineered by behavioural modification. Rather than rely upon such factors as spiritual inspiration or individual will, what we ought to do to improve our condition in life is change the environment, and the system of rewards and punishments, to ensure that the desired state is achieved. Applied to **schooling**, this notion of change through social engineering has proved irresistible to many jurisdictions.

Inherent in behaviourist theory is the notion that how we behave, and therefore what we learn, depends on conditioning – the extent to which our responses are reinforced, either positively or negatively. From this point it is a short step to arguing that decent people can be produced by a scientific application of reinforcement procedures. As one behaviourist put it, by following the dictates of conditioning and applying techniques of reinforcement, a saint can be turned into a sinner, and a sinner converted to a saint.

Such behaviourist notions (and others related to them) have had a powerful effect upon schooling. Given the premise that societal improvement can be deliberately designed and engineered, great attention has been paid to the specific tasks that schools are asked to undertake, and to the observable changes that they are intended to produce. Such general **aims** become the basis of the objectives of particular schools, stated in behavioural terms, for which they will periodically be held accountable. Competencies expected from students are planned in advance, monitored in progress, and tested for achievement. **Curricula** are based on notions of performance and desired knowledge translated into behavioural objectives. **Teaching** techniques stress management of student behaviour, and implementation of appropriate strategies to reinforce that behaviour.

It is not always easy to separate substance from rhetoric in the debates that have occurred on the contribution of behaviourism to educational thought and practice. The categories in which behaviourists converse (reinforcement, conditioning, and the like) often seem to obscure the phenomena under discussion. On many educational issues, the general aims of behaviourists and their opponents seem remarkably consistent. Particular suggestions of behaviourists concerning the treatment of children in schools, for example in the use of praise to reward effort and achievement, make good sense in any terms.

But at the heart of the matter, the rifts between behaviourists and their opponents are as important as they are wide. Arguments persist on the question of the acceptability of the claims upon which behaviourism is constructed. Some critics maintain that behaviourists' belief in environmental determinism is metaphysical rather than scientific. Others suggest that the forms of social engineering advocated by behaviourists are visionary or Utopian rather than verifiable in the scientific sense. In short, such critics attack both the foundation and consistency of the principal tenets in behaviourist beliefs.

Opponents have questioned the kind of social engineering associated with behaviourism. Who is charged, some critics ask, with the responsibility for that design? The prospect of well-intentioned engineers tampering with human society is not one that is welcomed with enthusiasm by all observers. Others have questioned particular **concepts** in behaviourism. Whereas behaviourists regard behaviour as a key to all aspects of human nature, their opponents claim that in some circumstances such a claim is absurd. It may be simple to recognize a person as 'running' by noting the movement of his legs, but what behaviour denotes 'musical appreciation' or 'thinking' or any number of other important human conditions? Similarly, it may be difficult to agree that learning can be expressed behaviourally in all circumstances. Obviously, if a person has learned a scale on the piano, he may demonstrate that learning by playing it (although even here there are important questions about the nature of the performance), but what behavioural demonstrations unambiguously reveal a capacity for insight?

In educational contexts, the attack on behaviourist notions has been particularly forceful. Critics have suggested that the search for behavioural objectives, performance-based teaching, **accountability**, and curriculum management – all of which are evidence of the application of behaviourist notions – has led educators to an impoverished conception of the nature of **education**. An exclusive reliance upon such behavioural notions is based on the mistaken notion that knowing and **learning** are reducible to ways of behaving. Although behaviour in schools is important, the argument runs, it is not central to many principal educational aims; an over-emphasis on behaviour will inevitably lead to the abandonment of intellect for the pursuit of the trivial (***microteaching, natural, nature/nurture, operant conditioning**).

REFERENCES

Barrow (1984), Egan (1983), Newsome (1974), Power (1982), Rachlin (1970), Schwartz and Lacey (1982), Skinner (1971), Steinberg (1980), Turner (1965).

Bilingualism

'Bilingualism' means the ability to speak two languages fluently. In the world of **educanto**, however, some writers confine bilingualism to individuals and use 'diglossia' to characterize societies. Distinctions are also made between those who are fluent in both languages ('balanced') and those whose knowledge of the second language is merely passable ('unbalanced'). In some countries there are arguments about what counts as a language; it is not always clear, for example, whether Creole counts as a language in certain West Indian countries, or whether Black English is a distinct language in the United States.

If the aim of bilingual policies were international **communication**, then governments would have the option of introducing into their schools an artificial international language such as Esperanto (which still has its devotees), or agreeing to teach one of the more commonly used languages already in existence. (The most common mother-tongue is Mandarin, trailed by English, Russian, Spanish, and Hindi.) Neither alternative has attracted much support.

The traditional or classical justification for second-language instruction is that fluency in another tongue has many benefits (for example, improved intellectual and communicative abilities). Given the relationship between a society and its **language**, a full appreciation of the **culture** of that society is only possible through its language. Some critics, however, attack such an argument on the grounds that it is likely to appeal only to those sections of society that can afford the luxury of a language-enriched **curriculum** (for example, élite groups or the middle classes).

Some authorities use bilingual education as a means to political survival. Where many languages are spoken within a national boundary, a second or standard language may be required to meet the basic needs of social communication and commerce. (Papua–New Guinea, to take an extreme example, boasts about 700 languages among its two million souls.) It is not always easy to distinguish between the **teaching** of a common language for purposes of social communication and the outright assimilation of minority groups, some of whom complain that second-language programmes have resulted in erosion of their culture and identities. Other countries use bilingualism in schools as a means of maintaining agreed political balances or compromises. In Canada, for example, new bilingual policies (however imperfectly designed or implemented) played an important role in maintaining national unity among Anglophones and Francophones in the 1970s.

In other jurisdictions, the opposite policy has been followed: second-language instruction has been designed to encourage the survival of languages other than the standard language. Provision of Welsh language instruction in Wales is an outstanding example, although that experience is mirrored in several ex-colonial territories around the world. Some countries have experimented with various types of heritage language programmes that attempt to satisfy the cultural aspirations of such minority groups as native Indians or recent immigrants.

In some jurisdictions, second-language programmes have served a so-called remedial function – to encourage immigrant groups to stay in schools or improve their test scores. Because some Spanish-speaking immigrants in the United States experience severe **learning** difficulties in English-speaking schools, several states have introduced programmes in which the language of instruction is Spanish. Similar difficulties have been experienced in member countries of the European Community, and various compensatory programmes have been attempted, not always with the intended results.

A great deal of time and money has been spent examining the results of second-language programmes. A generation ago some data derived from verbal tests of **intelligence** seemed to suggest that students enrolled in second-language programmes were lagging behind their colleagues, but those claims have since been challenged. More recent research seems to indicate the contrary, especially among balanced as opposed to unbalanced bilinguals. Concern has also been expressed by some observers that second-language instruction might impede facility in the mother-tongue. However, the weight of evidence is perhaps sufficient to allay that anxiety (***assessment**).

A great deal of discussion has arisen on the question of whether students ought to begin their **schooling** in their mother-tongue and learn a second language later, or be immersed in the second language on entering school. No hard and fast rules can be drawn from contemporary experience: in some situations (for example, with some Indian children in Mexico) the first path was successful; in others (especially in Canada) the second worked very well. In assessing second-language learning, social context and political realities seem much more important than methodological principles.

Bilingual education programmes tend to be controversial. Politicians are not slow to make hay out of such culturally sensitive issues. Introduction of new programmes almost inevitably alarms teachers' unions; jobs may be in peril, or teachers asked to undertake assignments outside their areas of expertise. In addition, second-language programmes may serve as inadequate band-aids: members of minority-language groups may continue to experience **discrimination** in the job market even after they have gained fluency in the second or standard language of a community.

REFERENCES

Cummins (1983a, 1983b), Genesee (1983), Hornby (1977), Lewis (1981), Shapson, D'Oyley and Lloyd (1982), Spolsky and Cooper (1977), Swain (1976), Swain and Lapkin (n.d.), Tosi (1984), Valverde (1978).

Body language *see* Communication, Language

Brainstorming

'Brainstorming' is defined by Webster's dictionary as 'the unrestrained offering of ideas or suggestions by all members of a conference to seek solutions to problems'. Such a definition makes it clear that what is referred to is a strategy that may or may not be productive, and that might take any number of specific forms. A brainstorming session might consist in a completely undirected cataloguing of distinct and even incompatible suggestions, or it might in various ways be more directed, perhaps requiring some cohesion between, and development of, suggestions. Whatever form it takes, it is evident that it may result in more or less sensible, appropriate, or searching ideas. The value of brainstorming in this sense, therefore, the wisdom of engaging in it, and the question of what it involves in terms of specific procedures, are as open as they are in the case of engaging in dialogue, attending a seminar, or thinking itself. Sometimes these are good things to do and well done, sometimes one or the other, and sometimes neither.

However, the connotations of the term in educational discourse are sometimes rather different. There may be a suggestion that more specific procedures are involved, and there may be strong evaluative overtones, so that 'brainstorming' comes to be thought of as an identifiable and inherently desirable **skill** or set of skills. A definition from a recent curriculum textbook illustrates this shift in meaning: 'The generation of ideas or solutions to problems involving free-flowing creative thought and spontaneous non-critical expression of ideas; often conducted in a group' (Pratt, 1980). Here the reference to 'solutions' and use of **emotively** powerful words such as '**creative**' serve to suggest that brainstorming is an inherently desirable activity. In addition, the choice of the phrase 'the generation of ideas' (as opposed to 'the unrestrained offering of ideas'), particularly when the notion of it being a group activity is made a **contingent** rather than a **necessary** feature, suggests that some specific skill is being referred to. There is a strong implication that one might learn to brainstorm as one might learn to write, and that it is an equally useful skill to acquire.

Any such implications would seem to be without foundation. It is not clear what is meant by creative thought; it is not clear why the non-critical expression of ideas should be valued; it is not clear why this activity should be presumed to lead to **worthwhile** or good solutions, nor why we should value solutions that are not good ones. It is clear that what is referred to is merely an activity we may choose to engage in, rather than an identifiable skill that can be developed or **trained** to a level of perfection. Brainstorming resembles joking rather than acquiring the skill of timing in telling jokes. Brainstorming, like joking, is certainly an activity we may wish to engage in, but it may be well or badly done, it may be appropriate or inappropriate to engage in it, and it describes only the general class of activity one is engaged in; it does not refer to any clearly definable skill or set of skills.

REFERENCE

Pratt (1980).

C

Caring

'Today, caring and responsibility are vogue-words applied vaguely to any endeavour except the language' (Hughes, 1988). 'Caring' has certainly become a popular word in educational circles, and its use is for the most part vague and largely **emotive**. However, a recent book by Noddings (1984) analyses the **concept** and develops an approach to **ethics** based upon what is alleged to be an innate sentiment of caring, in contrast to the traditional notion that an ethical system must be based upon a set of principles.

It may be argued that some of Noddings' polarizations are rather extreme and artificial: she does not maintain that women necessarily care or that men necessarily do not, yet insists that caring is feminine and rationality masculine. She suggests that the presumption that a moral system must be based upon absolute principles might be misplaced, and that one's intuitive sense of concern for a person(s) might be a better guide to truly moral behaviour; but that falls a long way short of establishing that ethics does not require any general principles, or that reasoning should follow on emotional response. Her conception of caring unexpectedly involves both 'engrossment' (by which she means the capacity to feel as the person about whom one cares is feeling) and recognition from the cared-for person.

But whatever difficulties Noddings' account gives rise to, it is a serious attempt to pin the concept down and to explore the implications for ethics and **education**. That is unusual. While many other educationalists talk about caring, most neither make it clear what they mean, nor explain or justify the educational significance of the concept. It is simply another buzz word in **educanto** as it is in political and social commentary generally. Not surprisingly, as such, it inspires the wrath of many commentators. 'A tedious and much-used word . . . one is not required to care for anyone or anything in particular. One just cares, a state of mind which not infrequently involves an impertinent degree of intrusion in other people's lives . . . often means absolutely nothing at all [as in] "this caring, exquisitely wrought book" [*New Yorker*, 20 September 1981]' (Hudson, 1983). 'A political buzz word of the moment . . . an ideological signpost and slogan rather than a description' (Howard, 1988). While the conservative philosopher Roger Scruton (1982) makes no bones about describing, e.g. 'the caring society', as 'a cant phrase . . . introduced by liberal-socialist journalism'.

The noun 'care' has a number of meanings ranging from 'worry', by way of 'an object of concern', to 'serious attention'. The verb, likewise, may mean 'I worry' ('I don't care about that'), 'provide support' ('I will care for her'), or 'have concern for' ('I care about her'), amongst other things. The questions of interest are what is involved in 'caring' in the sense of 'having concern for', and in what ways and to what extent should teachers 'care' in this sense and/or seek to develop such caring in their students?

A less demanding analysis than Noddings' might suggest that for a teacher to be properly described as caring about his students, he should recognize them as individuals in their own right, wish them success on their own terms, and respect them as persons. Such a view allows us to acknowledge that sometimes one simply cannot 'care for' X, because X is so vicious, mean, or depraved that one cannot wish him success on his own terms. This conception is to be distinguished from any view that identifies caring with the experience of sentimental attachment. One might care about X and also experience various **emotions,** but the strength of one's sentiment or feeling has no necessary connection with the question of whether one truly cares (***logical order**).

A problem with Noddings' more idiosyncratic conception is that it is not clear, despite her arguments, that it really has much to do with education. Clearly, if one believed that 'caring' involved the features that she suggests, and if one valued it highly, one would want schools to exhibit and foster such caring rather than its opposite. But it does not follow and it is not the case, even if such caring were indeed the basis of morality, that schools should be dominated by concern for care. In **schooling**, educational considerations come before moral considerations, provided only that educational considerations do not lead to a clash with morality. Caring in the more orthodox sense, however, does have an obvious if modest role in the business of schooling. As defined above, it is both a good in itself and a virtue closely related to educational purposes. Education seeks to develop the **autonomy** of individuals. The idea of autonomy presupposes the idea of **respect for persons**, which is an element in caring.

REFERENCES

Howard (1988), Hudson (1983), Hughes (1988), Hult (1979), Mayeroff (1971), Noddings (1984), Scruton (1982).

Censorship

Following such recent events as the attempt by Islamic fundamentalists to have Salman Rushdie's *The Satanic Verses* banned, the British government's determination to suppress Peter Wright's *Spycatcher*, the Chinese government's crackdown in Tiananmen Square, and the latest legal challenge to teaching evolution from creationists in the United States, we have no excuse for imagining censorship to be a non-issue.

The issue has always been alive, as witness Aristophanes, who was (unsuccessfully) charged with defamation of character in the fifth century BC; Ovid, who had to write somewhat pathetic recantations to regain the favour of the Emperor Augustus in the first century AD; or Leonardo da Vinci's struggles with the church in the fifteenth century. More recently, there have been innumerable small-scale incidents of censorship specifically in the context of schools, usually relating to text or library books, whether emanating from school board policy directives, the individual whim of principals, teachers, librarians, or parental complaint.

Empirical research undertaken in Canada suggests that the seven most common grounds of complaint by parents relate to (in order): obscene language, sexual references, religious ideas, vulgarity, violence, inappropriate materials, and moral values (Davis, 1979). It seems clear that many instances of censorship are not the result of calculated policy, but rather are the response that schools (particularly in the form of head teachers) make to aggressive complaints, in order to avert further trouble. A number of commentators have argued that the situation would be markedly improved, if schools were to adopt and publicize a clear set of criteria for the selection of books and other similar materials, in the light of which particular cases could be judged. There is some evidence that such guidelines both diminish the number of censorship problems that arise (Olsen, 1974), and lead to a less restrictive selection on the part of librarians (Pope, 1979).

But should there be any censorship of school reading material? An important distinction must be drawn here, for, of course, schools must select (given limited resources). Not only will they (frequently) be obliged to take one book rather than another on no particular grounds beyond personal taste, availability, price, or flip of a coin, but they will properly be expected to make some selection on educational grounds. Thus, a certain book will be rejected from the elementary school library on the grounds that its style is too sophisticated for the age-level of the students in question; another, on, e.g. the collecting of antique furniture, will be turned down as being insufficiently central to the educational aspirations of a school library. Undoubtedly, therefore, there will be some arbitrariness, idiosyncracy, and questionable **value judgements** behind the selection of school books. But this is to be distinguished from censorship, if only in that it is inevitable while the latter is not.

Censorship may take various forms – compare, for example, the preventative (or prior) censorship practised in the Soviet Union and the punitive (or *post eventum*) censorship more commonly practised in the West. Compare also direct legal control, the influence of institutions which may be powerful without having any legal status and individual prosecutions for libel, etc. But censorship is essentially the deliberate, formal, suppression of material on the ground that it is offensive or dangerous. It is, thus, usually on **moral** or political grounds that a work is censored.

The argument put forward in favour of individual acts of censorship is almost always a species of 'freedom of speech is good. But there are limits to it'. The limits, by definition, are set by 'offensiveness', and, in practice, of course judgements of 'offensiveness' are made in terms of what upsets, harms, or ignores the **interests** of the complainant. Thus, the mechanics of censorship are essentially the suppression of expression of a view by an individual or group powerful enough to get its way. But, as John Stuart Mill (1962), whose classic chapter on this topic in *On Liberty* still demands the closest attention, points out, it is 'strange . . . that men should admit the validity of the arguments for free discussion, but object to their being "pushed to an extreme"; not seeing that unless the reasons are good for an extreme case, they are not good for any case.'

Mill's case is clear, concise, and still unrefuted: freedom of thought and expression should be absolute because: (a) no one, individually or collectively, is entitled to claim infallibility (hence any judgement that something is false, blasphemous, objectionable, etc., could be wrong); (b) rarely, if ever, is any position entirely coherent and correct (thus, however well founded, the censor's position will contain something of error, the censored something true, and only by the interplay of imperfect ideas can we refine more perfect ideas); (c) even if the censor's opinion were indeed the whole truth, if it is perpetuated by coercive measures that prevent it being challenged, it will become empty dogma, rather than vital, understood, truth; (d) and finally opinions that are not constantly put to the test become not only inert but altered. As Mill points out: the triumph of Christianity as a religion has made it something quite distinct from what it was for the early Christians, who had to mould and sustain their opinions, their faith, in the crucible of opposition (**autonomy, ethics, moral education, religious education*).

A point not often remarked, but to be stressed here, is that this argument is essentially an educational one. Indeed at one point Mill observes not only that the advantages of free thought are exclusively to do with the advancement of truth (one of the prime concerns of **education**), but also that the benefit he looks to is not 'solely or chiefly to form great thinkers' but 'to enable average human beings to attain the mental stature which they are capable of'.

Thus censorship, in the sense of the deliberate exclusion, suppression, or removal of a book (film, etc.), simply on the grounds that it advocates, enshrines, or presents opinons that are deemed by some to be offensive or incorrect should never be tolerated, least of all in an institution such as a school which is dedicated to the idea of promoting **understanding** and truth. Attempts (all too often successful) to filter material through the sieves of racism, **feminism**, fundamentalism, etc., are all necessarily repugnant to the ideals of education (*****indoctrination, multiculturalism, nationalism**).

(Note: David B. Guralnik, Editor in Chief of *Webster's New World Dictionary*, Second College Edition of 1970, excluded slang racial terms such as 'dago', 'kike', 'wog', and 'wop', despite the fact that Webster has always been primarily a record of oral usage, as contrasted with the Oxford English Dictionary, which is primarily a record of written usage – as Hughes, 1984, puts it, 'The British model focuses on the highest common factor: the American on the lowest common denominator.' Guralnik claimed that the move was justified because such words are 'true obscenities' and are 'in any case, encountered with diminishing frequency'. The claim that a term such as 'wop' is a 'true obscenity' is a fair indication of language-inflation, and how our sensibility is becoming such that while we are sensitive to the slightest wound we can no longer **discriminate** between a slight wound and butchery. If 'wop' is a 'true obscenity', what, pray, were recent events in Beijing, let alone the atrocities of the Nazi concentration camps. Be that as it may, it is evident that Webster is practising censorship of a deliberate **ideological** kind. R. W. Burchfield, supervisor of the OED Supplement (1972–86), coined the term 'Guralnikism', which, he pointed out, is 'the racial equivalent of Bowdlerism' – Dr Bowdler led the field in nineteenth-century Britain in expurgating classic texts, such as those of Shakespeare, largely to remove sexually offensive material.)

REFERENCES

Davis (1979), Hughes (1988), Mill (1962), Olsen (1974), Pope (1979).

Child-centred education

The essence of child-centred education is, self-evidently, that the child should be at the centre of our concerns. This emphasis is commonly contrasted with subject-centred education. It is also characteristic of child-centred educational theory to lay stress on the individuality of each child, and the importance of individual growth in contrast to social demands. It will be readily seen that child-centred education is a somewhat general and imprecise **concept**. Thus defined it has a long history, Jean-Jacques Rousseau commonly being seen as one of its earliest exponents. During this century it has frequently been associated with a number of more specific axioms such as that education should be based on children's **needs** or **interests**, and that **teaching** should proceed by reference to children's **readiness** rather than by reference to some a priori assumption about the suitability of introducing subject matter at prespecified times. Explicitly or implicitly, child-centred educationalists tend towards a view of **education** being a process of leading out rather than of imparting knowledge, and favour **metaphors** such as that of the gardener cultivating the soil in which flowers can grow, rather than that of the craftsman making a product (or, more unkindly, filling a bucket with water). Methodologically, child-centred education is associated with concepts such as learning by discovery and learning how to learn (**analogy, etymology, learning*).

The phrase 'child-centred' has strong favourable **emotive** overtones. How could one deny that the child should be at the centre of our concerns as educationalists? On the other hand, this must be a question of degree. It may be foolish or wrong to plan an educational system purely in terms of subjects that ought to be studied, without reference to individual differences. But it is equally foolish to imagine that what children do or study is neither here nor there, and that becoming educated is just a matter of a natural **process** of flowering. Indeed the concept of **nature** is one of the more problematic of concepts for educationalists of all sorts: what is human nature, how does one determine what is **natural** to an individual, and what is meant by natural behaviour?

If it is granted that there seems no reason to commit ourselves to an extreme form of child-centred education, implying that we do no more than protect the child from outside interference so that he may develop naturally, it becomes clear that arguing about the merits of child-centred education is rather meaningless. The **aims** of **schooling** are not necessarily served in the course of the individual's natural development, even supposing that natural development can in fact occur. Becoming educated, socialized, morally mature, etc., are not inevitable processes (**socialization, moral education*).

The question therefore becomes what sense can be made of, and what guidance obtained from, the more specific claims about needs, interests, readiness, etc., that are commonly associated with child-centred education.

It has been said that 'only child-centred education is education' (Wilson, 1971). But that is plainly either an unhelpful truism or false. If it means that an approach that had no concern for the individual child would scarcely count as education, the point may be conceded, but it gives us no guidance as to how we should proceed. If it means something more specific, such as that the nature of education should be dictated by the child's interests, then it is false (*open education).

REFERENCES

Barrow and Woods (1982), Entwistle (1970), Rousseau (1972), Wilson (1971).

Child development see Developmental theory

Choice see Knowledge, Understanding, Worthwhile

Class

Investigations of the role that class plays in **education** have ranged from very broad speculations to specific **empirical** investigations of relatively minute **phenomena**. Prominent among the many topics that have been examined are class interests in the provision of education, class factors affecting student achievement in schools, and the types of **curriculum** appropriate for different classes of students. There are few **concepts** in education that are not touched, directly or indirectly, by discussion of class.

Such a level of attention and concern, however, is no guarantee of clarity in purpose, method, or result. Many writings on social class are so marked by political bias (or blinkered by political **ideology**) that their arguments can almost be foretold simply by mentioning the authors' names. Since notions of class depend on geographic or **cultural** contexts, transfer of findings or conclusions from one country to another is by no means easy. Empirical investigations into the relationship of class to educational phenomena are subject to the usual difficulties of isolating particular features in human societies. In consequence, any so-called findings on such matters have to be treated with more than the usual caution.

The criteria for the stratification of society into social classes are neither uniform across societies nor clearly defined. In some regions of the world, parentage is virtually the sole criterion of membership of a class. In contrast, in industrialized countries social classes are usually categorized according to income or occupational level. A person's class may also be affected by his status or political power – neither of which are necessarily linked to income or occupational level. Some investigators have included in the notion such factors as speech patterns, artistic preferences, clothing habits, and location of residence. Others, on the contrary, have argued that class exists only in people's minds as a cultural phenomenon (that is, it should be viewed solely as a form of popular myth). A few writers, despairing of the usefulness of the term, recommend that it not be used in any circumstances. In short, definitions of social class have taken such a variety of forms that its use in the examination of any social issue, educational or not, ought to be greeted with some scepticism.

Although the question of the relationship of the class system (however broadly defined) to education has exercised thinkers since Greek times, the issue assumed particular importance in the latter part of the nineteenth century when industrialized countries began to demand certain levels of schooling from great numbers of their citizens. While **schooling** came to be considered as a social service, it was at the same time a focus for political power-plays among various interests – some of them class-based – within society. Some historians have made much capital out of the fact that schools appear to have been introduced in a period when entrepreneurs in the industrial world were anxious to reap the benefits of a time-conscious and disciplined work-force. Political theorists have argued that the primary beneficiaries of compulsory schooling have been those members of the large middle class created by the new industries who have been able to take advantage of the credentialling policies of state schools. Sociologists have maintained that schools have become complex sorting systems that serve to slot citizens into approved jobs that best serve the needs of privileged or ruling classes. The nature of the political power of the middle class in reaching its goals – its so-called hegemony – has also been hotly disputed.

The educational policy of governments, as it relates to questions of social class, may take many forms. In some nations, as a deliberate act of government, the educational system simply confirms the existing distribution of privilege and power; in others, the educational system is designed to ameliorate class distinctions by providing social and economic mobility; and in still others, the purpose of the educational system is to break down all distinctions based on social class. Whether any of these measures succeed depends partly on how success is **measured**, and partly on how the price for success is **assessed**. Some commentators maintain that the introduction of popularly based comprehensive schools (particularly at the secondary level) has contributed to a softening of class barriers in some societies. Others argue that many such efforts to ameliorate class divisions merely disguise continuing middle-class domination of the schools and of society. In this interpretation, middle-class values are so deeply rooted in the curriculum that schools simply function as reinforcers of the hegemony of the middle (or any other ruling) class. This type of argument (despite the cold water thrown on it by analytic philosophers in particular) has provoked some governments to take action to ensure that only approved 'liberating' **knowledge** should be taught in schools, and incited some political theorists to argue that the framework of educational institutions should be dismantled – that society, in effect, should be **deschooled**.

The relationship of social class to educational attainment has long been of interest to those concerned with **equality** of opportunity. As a result, this topic is one of the most closely examined in the empirical literature related to education. On one conclusion drawn from those empirical investigations there is virtual unanimity: social class is related to educational attainment; children of families in the higher occupational categories do better, in general terms, by any number of measures, in elementary and secondary school, than children of families in the lower occupational categories, and occupy disproportionately more seats in universities. There is much less agreement on why this is so. Some scholars argue that the notion of parental occupation as a **correlate** of school success needs to be supplemented by consideration of other factors, such as number of children within the family, reading habits within the home, or presence of such inhibiting environmental features as socially disorganized neighbourhoods. Others maintain that what counts is parental attitude towards schooling, or presence of particular achievement ethics within the family – both of which cross class boundaries. If such attitudes are positively related to educational success – and it appears that they are – government programmes based exclusively on minimizing class influences are not likely to be successful.

One debate has focused on the question of whether different social classes ought to be provided with different types of curriculum. Some have maintained that important differentiations may be noted in the **language** patterns and cultural interests of particular classes. It has been argued, for example, that the linguistic differences that have been found in the middle class and lower working class reflect entirely different modes of speech – an elaborated code on the one hand, and a restricted code on the other. Other writers have suggested that two traditions exist within society: one that is the expression of a literate minority culture, while the other, that of the majority, is essentially oral and behavioural. These views have been used to support such educational policies as: (a) streaming students; and (b) a differentiated curriculum based on class characteristics.

The weight of opinion seems to suggest both of these notions should be handled with care. In the first place, the original formulations of the ideas are far from clear. Secondly, even if language differences between classes can be noted, the conclusion that any one type is functionally unsuited to **learning** does not necessarily follow. Thirdly, given the wide variety of differences that are likely to appear in any one group of students, the task of differentiating them solely on the basis of two categories of language is likely to be very misleading. In any case, the question of what type of curriculum ought to be considered **worthwhile** is not to be determined exclusively by sociological surveys or empirical analyses, however valid those investigations may be (*reconceptualists).

REFERENCES

Anyon (1981), Bernstein (1971–3), Calvert (1982), Entwistle (1978, 1982), Furbank (1985), Hurn (1978), Illich (1971), Jencks (1972), Labov (1969), Lawton (1968, 1975), Marland (1977), Morrison and McIntyre (1971), Reynolds and Skilbeck (1976).

Classical conditioning *see* Operant conditioning

Classroom observation *see* Ethnography, Interaction analysis, Systematic observation, Teacher effectiveness

Cognitive development *see* Developmental theory, Emotions, Nature/nurture

Common curriculum *see* Core curriculum

Communication

The object of improving communication is generally approved. But 'communication' is a very general term. There is a variety of situations in which people may hope to see improved communication. Curriculum guidelines often specify improved communication as an objective, particularly in English, but also for example in the sciences. Educationalists may also be concerned about communication between teacher and students, between head teacher and staff, between school and parents, between school and government, or between parents and children. It is not self-evident that an individual's ability to communicate in one set of circumstances implies an ability to do so in others. There are also various distinct types of communication. For communicating with people in the broadest sense is partly a matter of intellectual or cognitive exchange, and partly a matter of psychological rapport or having a sympathetic relationship. If you and I communicate well with one another without qualification, then we both exchange ideas and get on with one another.

It is advisable to examine the distinguishable elements separately, since one may be more developed in one aspect of communicative ability than another, and it is likely that different parts of the school **curriculum** have different contributions to make to the two main elements.

First, there is the intellectual aspect of communication. Here we are referring to the ability to communicate ideas and arguments, in the sense of articulating them in clear and comprehensible terms. A straightforward example of communication in this sense would be provided by two scholars who have never met each other, but who are able to exchange, understand, and give critical attention to one another's ideas by correspondence. Sometimes communication, even in this sense, will not be between equals. The scholar, if he is to communicate effectively as teacher, will need not only the ability to operate articulately within his **discipline**, but also the ability to couch what he wants to say in terms that are suitable to his audience. This ability is also important in respect of communication between schools and parents, and the other examples given above that involve differing degrees of expertise and **knowledge**.

This aspect of communication, whether in reference to people equally or unequally familiar with the subject matter, is centrally a matter of general command of language combined with command of any specialist sphere in question. If this is a part of what we mean by improving communication, then it follows that we have to develop precision in language use, with special reference to nuances of style, **conceptual finesse**, and logical coherence. It may be debated whether courses in, for example, **critical thinking** or informal logic are effective ways to enhance such general clarity of expression. But English lessons provide one area where the task may be directly tackled, and **history** lessons another. Other subjects, such as mathematics, geography, and physics, have the responsibility of explaining the central **concepts** and logic of their specialism. Although it is certainly not the case that facility in writing is necessary to facility in communication, it may be argued that there is good reason to emphasize writing as a means of developing **language** competence.

A second element in communication is rapport. Some may see this as central, and be more concerned with communication as a matter of people getting along, feeling sympathetic, or sensing some bond, than as the ability to exchange ideas rationally. Questions that arise here are as follows:

1. Can this element be divorced from the intellectual element or is it necessary to effective communication in the first sense?
2. If it is not necessary, does it have its own educational value?
3. Are there ways in which it may be developed?

The two elements can be divorced in practice as well as **theory**. The example of communication between two scholars involved no reference to rapport, except in the trivial sense that both share an interest in what they are doing: but there is no need of any personal tie between them to enable them to communicate intellectually. Conversely, two extremely inarticulate people who are incapable of any serious exchange of ideas, may none the less have intuitive sympathy for one another, or communication in the sense of rapport. However, although the two elements may be separated, very often either element reinforces the other. Our communication at the intellectual level on the state of politics is likely to be forwarded to some extent by a feeling of sympathy, and hindered by any sense of impatience with one another.

Some might argue that communication in the second sense has educational value in its own right. But whilst it is always pleasant to see that people are in rapport, and whilst the world might be a better place if people were more often sympathetic to one another, this seems to have little to do with **education** as such. (More plausible might be the suggestion that it is a proper part of **socialization**.) (*caring)

The real problem here is whether it is reasonable to suppose that we know very much about ways in which to develop people's ability to feel sympathetic towards others, to feel at ease, or to feel rapport. In extreme cases of maladjustment an individual who finds communication in this sense difficult may gain a great deal from psychiatric help or milder forms of encounter group experience. Likewise, it borders on a necessary truth that developing self-esteem and other positive aspects of a self-concept should enhance people's ability to communicate. But whether particular strategies such as refraining from criticism, inviting individuals to participate in sessions that involve physical contact of a mild and superficial sort, or encouraging people to talk about their inner and private experiences and feelings, have any positive contribution to make in the majority of cases is very far from clear. The value of more specific alleged **skills** of communication is open to doubt, whether they properly belong to communication in the sense of rapport (e.g. eye contact) or in the sense of intellectual exchange (e.g. taking up and rephrasing a point just made by one's interlocutor). It is a necessary truth that rapport should involve some kind of engagement, but it is an empirical issue, and one that has not been satisfactorily resolved, as to whether and when it should take particular forms such as engaging in eye contact. It is a necessary truth that intellectual communication should involve mutual understanding, but an unresolved empirical question as to whether and when this should take any particular form (*contingent, research).

Communication between people may take many forms or occur in many modes. It may be egocentric (i.e. centred on the self, despite involving other people). It can consist of questions, the provision of orders, or any other type of combination of speech acts. It may also take place by means of body language anywhere on a continuum between facial expression and engaging in ritualistic behaviours. In addition, there are other non-verbal media of communication such as music and painting. When we are referring to communication in the sense of rapport these may well be powerful media. But conceived of as media of communication in the first sense they are very imperfect. Even when an artist has a clear conception of what he wishes to communicate, which is by no means always the case, what individual members of his audience actually take from it may often be very different. And generally speaking we are not very well informed about what art works do in fact communicate to various people. Attempts at intellectual communication through non-verbal media may well offer something special (for example, they may heighten a perception or jolt one into recognition of something), but they are relatively poor media for communicating intellectually in a clear and organized fashion. Some might suggest that the arts are particularly suited to the communication of emotions. Given the nature of **emotions**, it might be preferable to say that they are well suited to evoking or assuaging images and feelings (*mass media).

Competency-based teaching *see* Microteaching

Competition

Competition, once esteemed as an integral part of **education**, is now widely looked down upon in educational discourse, which is slightly surprising when one bears in mind that this amounts to dissent from a key value in the **ideology** of the countries we are concerned with. (The

game of soccer was recently promoted as a non-competitive sport in a
North American university, so bad have the connotations of the word
become. The mind boggles at the idea of two teams playing soccer non-
competitively. Indeed, it is arguable that, as a matter of **conceptual**
truth, such a game would not be soccer.) Common objections to competition include the claims that it is divisive, that it implies inequality, that
it is discouraging (to those who come off badly), and that it encourages
lack of concern for others.

The claim that competition is divisive seems confused. By definition,
competition involves striving between two or more individuals or
groups, but that is not to say that it need be divisive in the sense of
contributory toward setting one person (or group) against another.
Clearly, some competitors in some cases become rivals in a more
general, hostile, sense. Equally clearly, many do not, and a competitive
structure, such as an interhouse games competition, may foster co-
operation. Competition does indeed imply inequality, inasmuch as it is
designed to establish current differences in ability. It is difficult to take
seriously any objection to the idea of one person (group) being shown to
be more able than another at some particular activity on a particular
occasion. (Rather different is the drawing of general conclusions from
particular competitions. It is not desirable that as a result of coming in
tenth in one race one should be classified as tenth-rate even as a runner,
let alone as a person. But this is an objection to the way in which some
people interpret and draw conclusions from particular competitions, not
to competition itself, and it is certainly possible to have competition
without making such erroneous judgements.) (*equality)

It is not of course possible to have competition without making judgements about the relative achievement or competency of particular individuals in particular respects. Whether that leads to discouragement or
lack of concern for others is an **empirical** question to which we have no
clearly established answer. It is hard to believe that nobody was ever
discouraged by doing badly in competition, but, equally, it is hard to
deny that some remain fairly insouciant, and others, those who do well,
correspondingly gain encouragement from success. There is, besides, the
serious question of whether people who are relatively poor at running,
painting, or Latin grammar, ought not to recognize as much, without
being downhearted at the realization.

The main arguments in favour of competition have been that it serves
as good motivation, and that, in the case of goods which are not available to all, it serves as a rational mode of allocation. To these we may
add the points raised above: competition may prove enjoyable, may lead
to co-operative endeavour, and may provide reassurance and
encouragement.

There may not be a knock-down case for or against competition, and indeed it seems a priori likely that, as with many things, there is no answer to the question of whether it is good or bad in the abstract. For, its employment should depend on who is competing, what they are competing for, why they are doing so, etc. To object to a competitive weekly French test might make sense; to object to a competitive chess game does not make sense.

An interesting question remains: how is it that in a world that is highly competitive, with schools that are in fact competitive, and in the absence of any overriding reason why they should not be, educationalists none the less creep around as if there were nothing to discuss, since this obviously unpleasant practice is foreign to us? The answer must surely lie in something to do with the confused but paralysing **relativism** that is embedded in contemporary thinking generally (***assessment, deschooling**).

REFERENCE

Dearden (1976).

Compulsory curriculum *see* Core curriculum, Religious education

Computer literacy

'**Literacy**' has been compounded with so many words (e.g. 'mathematical literacy', '**visual literacy**', 'technical literacy', and even 'tennis literacy') that it occasions no surprise to find it tied to 'computer' – witness the spate of monographs, texts, and articles that include 'computer literacy' in their titles. If frequency of mention in the popular press is a criterion of importance, computer literacy ranks very high.

Nevertheless there seems to be little agreement on what it actually means. One reason for this confusion may be located in the metaphoric use of literacy. Given the selective transfer of images in a **metaphor** from one **concept** to another, it is by no means clear what qualities of literacy are intended when the word is attached to computer. Is it intended to indicate a somewhat narrow or limited range of abilities with the computer, somewhat analogous to the capacity to read and write at a basic level? Or does literacy in this case indicate complex competencies analogous to being well versed in the nature and use of literary concepts (perhaps including the prized ability to decide what kinds of issue or problem lend themselves to investigation by computers and what kinds do not)? Or does it indicate some desirable but never-to-be-fully-achieved end state such as that suggested when the 'literate' person is identified with the **'educated'** person? Or is it simply a grab-bag term without specific content or connotations, designed to indicate in a very general way some types of general competency in whatever processes are required by the current state of the art in computer technology?

Some writers have argued that the term ought to include certain **emotional** attitudes towards the use of computers. In other words, one of the qualities of a person who possesses computer literacy is a willingness to consider the use of a computer in undertaking a specific project, if not an actual preference for such use. Others maintain that the term also connotes a political or social sensitivity to the effects of improving computer technology on individuals or groups within society as a whole. The nature of those sensitivities or attitudes has not yet been described in any detail.

The evidence to be derived from school examples on the competencies, skills, or attitudes required in the use of computers is far from certain. Some cast the computer in the role of instructor, with the user being subjected to various types of instruction (the many types of computer-assisted instruction seem to fit this mode). Others use the computer essentially as a tool to provide specific services, for example, word-processing. Another group, however, casts the student in the role of a computer programmer, responsible for designing original programmes for solving a wide range of personal or intellectual problems. Since the roles of the student vary with each of these types of computer use, it may be assumed that the competencies implied by the phrase 'computer literacy' may vary also.

One notion that has attracted attention is that computer literacy consists in an ability to pursue all human **knowledge** on a model provided by computational thinking. Rather than rely exclusively upon existing structures of thought or methods of procedure (whether in the arts or sciences) scholars and learners will use an alternative method of investigation based on a computer analogue. So powerful will the computer become that all **cultural** achievement will be written in terms of computer programmes. In short, a claim is made that to think or to **learn** is to acquire a programme. Needless to say, this argument has been subjected to intense criticism. Some thinkers have argued that the notion that the mind processes information in the same way as a computer lacks both logical and **empirical** verification. Others have suggested that the rule-governed nature of computers (which may be very useful in learning tasks at the beginner's level) may, in fact, inhibit a passage to proficiency and expertise. Certainly, it appears doubtful that knowledge of various subject matters (with rules that depend on contexts) can be cut up into discrete units on the information-processing model.

The arguments on computer literacy are rich in colour and enthusiasm, but short on logical analysis and empirical verification. The term appears at best to offer a dubious prospect for further study and at worst to provide fodder for those who argue that most educational innovations are crippled by the slogans they beget(*visual literacy).

REFERENCES

Apple (1987), Beattie (1984), Becker (1984), Dreyfus and Dreyfus (1984), Eisele (1980), Kelman (1984), Lazerson, McLaughlin, McPherson and Bailey (1985), Noble (1984), Olson (1988b), Olson and Sullivan (1987), Papert (1980), Ragsdale (1983a, 1983b), Scriven (1986), Seidel, Anderson and Hunter (1982).

Computers *see* Basics, Computer literacy, Language, Literacy, Relevance

Concept

A concept is an idea or thought, more precisely the abstraction that represents or signifies the unifying principle of various distinct particulars. You grasp or have the concept of redness when you appreciate the idea of the red colour common to all red things. A concept is not an image, athough one may have a mental image of a concept. One cannot have a concept (although one can have an image) of a concrete particular. For example, one cannot have a concept of this pen, but only of penness. (The common use of phrases such as 'that's an interesting concept' in reference to a complex proposal, plan, or set of ideas, is a confusing vulgarism.) It will be seen that concepts and words are distinct, although they are closely related since we label our concepts by words. Thus, I have a concept of love, which is to say an idea of what it is that makes an emotional attitude an instance of love, and I call this idea 'love' – primarily because I believe my concept to be more or less the same thing that others refer to as 'love'. There are things I can say about the word that I cannot meaningfully say about the concept (e.g. 'love' has four letters), and vice versa (e.g. the French are always falling in love). One can sensibly talk of incorrect use of words (e.g. 'love' is incorrectly translated by the French 'joi'; it is a mistake to call a horse pulling a plough a 'tractor'); it is not clear that one can sensibly talk of an incorrect concept (Barrow, 1984, 1985b), though one can certainly talk of incoherent, silly, contradictory, unattractive, unusual or idiosyncratic ones. Defining a word may be a very useful prior stage to **analysing** a concept, but it cannot be identified with it. Educational **research** has often been flawed as a result of failing to appreciate this point and offering a verbal definition of something that is not adequately conceptualized (*degree words, **discrimination, education, ethics, etymology**).

REFERENCES

Barrow (1981c, 1983, 1984, 1985b).

Conceptual analysis *see* Analysis

Conceptual finesse

A phrase coined by Barrow (1981c), drawing on the sense of 'finesse' that implies adroitness, delicacy, and skill, rather than on the sense involved in finessing at bridge. To be possessed of conceptual finesse is to have a large armoury of clearly articulated and finely **discriminated** concepts at one's disposal; to think in relatively specific, clear, and distinct concepts. Barrow argued that conceptual finesse in respect of the 'stuff of daily life' was an important aspect of being **educated**, to be added to conceptual familiarity with various developed **disciplines** of thought (*knowledge).

REFERENCE

Barrow (1981c).

Contingent

A contingent truth, **fact**, event, happening, etc., is one that might have been otherwise, or one that depends upon some particular situation or circumstance, rather than on any necessity. A contingent truth is none the less true for being contingent, and it may remain true for millions of years; but it remains a contingent truth, if some change in the way the world is could render it false. It is a contingent truth that you are reading this entry, that there is fighting in the Middle East, and that the earth is spherical. Contingent truths are to be contrasted with necessary truths, that is, truths that remain constant regardless of time, place, and circumstance. For example, it is a necessary truth that all bachelors are unmarried, that the angles of a triangle add up to 180 degrees, and that, given that all men are mortals and that Socrates is a man, Socrates is a mortal. (Some necessary truths, therefore, are analytic truths, that is, true by definition, but some are truths of logical reasoning. Both are species of logical necessity.) Some wishing to distinguish between contingent truths that seem particularly open to change (e.g. the contingent truths that men wear trousers, that Germany is divided, that America has a Republican President) and those that seem likely to remain true so long as the world remains the way it is (e.g. heavy objects fall straight to the ground when dropped, flowers need water to grow, men will always quarrel with one another), regard the latter as necessary, since they regard them as inevitable and unavoidable. But strictly speaking the latter group of examples are not necessary truths: the world could so change physically that gravity ceases to operate, and people could conceivably change and stop quarrelling. Necessary truths are those that could not conceivably be otherwise – as a circle could not be squared. If the distinction between relatively ephemeral and highly dependable contingent truths is to be marked, it should be done by using some such phrase as 'unchanging' 'unavoidable' or 'certain' truths for the latter.

Most educational **research** is theoretically concerned with seeking out contingent truth (all **empirical** truths are necessarily contingent); for example, 'What do students in the world as we know it find easy, difficult, useful, etc., in an educational context?', 'What happens, as things are, when we adopt this style/technique/approach?', 'Do students with a high IQ prosper at school?' However, many of the conclusions drawn by researchers from their empirical studies turn out to be at least partially necessary truths. For example, 'Brighter people can learn things less bright ones cannot' (Hilgard, 1956) – a truth which could not have been otherwise, since people who could not learn things that less bright people could, would hardly be classified as bright.

Perhaps what might be gained from a rigorous search for and study of necessary truths in the sphere of **education** has not been sufficiently appreciated. It is easy to dismiss necessary truths as tautologous, but: (a) only analytic truths are in fact (the truths of logical reasoning are not); and (b) even analytic truths serve an important purpose, if they draw our attention to, or remind us of, implications that would otherwise pass unnoticed (*logical order).

REFERENCE

Hilgard (1956).

Convergent thinking *see* Lateral thinking

Core curriculum/common curriculum

The terms 'core curriculum' and 'common curriculum' are often confused with each other and with such related terms as 'compulsory curriculum', 'required subjects', and 'basic subjects'. On occasion, these terms are linked together in such phrases as 'common core curriculum', 'compulsory core curriculum', 'basic core subjects', or 'required core subjects'. To some extent, use of one term rather than another is a national characteristic ('common core' is more frequently heard in Britain, 'basic subjects' in North America); nevertheless, the frequency with which the terms are interchanged in the literature is a good indication of underlying problems in fixing their meanings. What this set of terms shares is a relationship to several important questions. Are there reasons for demanding that all students should participate in certain sections of the school **curriculum**? If so, what are those sections?

Interest in giving emphasis to certain types of **knowledge**, and certain **skills**, rather than others, has exercised philosophers and schoolmen since Greek times, but the issue became particularly acute with the introduction of state-required schooling in the last century or so. Given the difficulties of designing a curriculum for many different kinds of students, and the need to satisfy diverse political, social, and educational objectives (and limited resources with which to do it), educators faced the question of identifying those subjects or those competencies that were judged either to be at the core of the educational enterprise, or to be so important that they ought to be shared by all students in common. Needless to say, many alternative views of what is essential have been proposed over the years, some fairly limited in range, and others relatively broad (**curriculum design*).

Limited interpretations focus on literacy and numeracy, those capacities considered essential for progress in all other subjects. Some jurisdictions add a requirement in **moral education** or **religious education**, or any other type of subject matter regarded as essential for preparation for the world outside the school, such as civic competencies or life skills. This notion of core is therefore easily confused with basic education, or the **basics**, on the one hand, and a compulsory curriculum on the other.

Even this very limited definition is not without its difficulties. Stipulating that **literacy** shall be part of a core is a much easier task than explaining what literacy actually means. Some of those who require literacy as part of a core have often been accused of using the term in an instrumental sense, as though **language** were learned separately from other subject matter. Others seem to view literacy simply as the capacity to apply grammatical rules. Similar arguments may be made with numeracy. What does the term mean? Is a person numerate when he possesses a limited range of mathematical skills (and if so what skills?), or only if he is able to design computer-programmed solutions to complex mathematical problems? In addition, the question of the ability of all students to encompass the requirements of even a limited core has not been satisfactorily addressed. What is the point, it may be asked, of issuing instructions requiring students to master a given core, if it is unknown whether a significant percentage are intellectually able to comply? Alternatively, if the level of mastery required in the core is set so low that almost every student can succeed, does it follow that the core is educationally trivial?

Rather than focus upon a limited range of required skills and knowledge to serve as a core, some scholars have suggested that a much larger proportion of the curriculum ought to be devoted to required study by all students – and here the phrase a 'common' curriculum is often preferred to 'core'. Although the reasons for this stand vary from author to author, most argue from one of three positions: that a student's education ought to include some experience in each of the major forms of knowledge, that society has a right to expect students to be aware of the major characteristics of its **culture**, and that students should possess particular skills and abilities to function as intelligent and critical citizens. In the light of these reasons, educators have designed a number of examples of such a common curriculum. Lawton (1973), for example, suggests that a 'common culture individualised curriculum' will include the following core areas: mathematics, physical and biological sciences, humanities and social studies, expressive arts, and moral education. The justification for, as well as the particular nature of, a proposed common curriculum is thus one of the more important questions with which scholars and educators interested in the contemporary curriculum have to contend.

Given the complexity of the issue, it is not surprising that the notion of a common curriculum, and the various proposals for its form within particular curricula, have been subjected to careful scrutiny. Some have argued that our understandings of the distinctions among the various forms of knowledge are not sufficiently clear to support their use as a justification for designing a common curriculum. Others have suggested that the range of abilities and aspirations within the student population is so wide that any attempt to identify a common curriculum is doomed. The arguments for a common curriculum may be interpreted as a hegemonic device to ensure the political and economic survival of either a ruling élite, or a ruling cultural group (to the disadvantage of other groups within the same society), or as a means of enshrining in the schools a particular philosophy of education (that excludes individualistic or experiential conceptions of how the curriculum ought to be organized and implemented). Concern has been expressed that advocates of a common curriculum have underestimated the practical difficulties of co-ordinating or balancing the various parts of such a common curriculum, and ensuring that students of mixed abilities are able to comprehend the curriculum that they share. Some scholars have pointed out that the content in some proposals for a common curriculum leaves little scope for any specialized studies designed for particular students (*giftedness).

Those supporting a common curriculum admit the complexity of the notion, especially when it is applied to a large (and diverse) population, and they acknowledge difficulties in its philosophical justification. They counter by stressing the **educational** significance of certain subject matter, and pointing to the political importance of shared educational experience. On the question of the sensitivity of some ethnic, linguistic, or political groups to some aspects of a common curriculum, they emphasize the importance of developing the capacity for critical and rational thought (*basics, class, integrated studies, multiculturalism).

REFERENCES

Adler (1982), Alberty (1953), Barrow (1976a), Crittenden (1982), Friedenberg (1982), Harris (1977), Holt (1978), Kirk (1986), Lawton (1973), O'Keefe (1986), Reid, M. I. (1979), Reid, W. A. (1981), Reynolds and Skilbeck (1976), Skilbeck (1983, 1989), Toomey (1980), Tripp and Watt (1984), White (1973), Williams (1961).

Correlation

The correlation between events, factors, or variables, refers to the extent that they are found together. Correlations are recorded by means of a numerical score (the correlation coefficient) ranging from −1.00, indicating a strong negative or inverse relationship (i.e. where one variable is much in evidence, the other will be little in evidence, as e.g. low anxiety might be expected to accompany high achievement), through zero, indicating no apparent association, to +1.00, indicating a tight positive relationship (i.e. those variables are found together). A score of 0.70 or above is generally regarded as significant. (To be more precise, such a correlation is generally regarded as statistically significant with sample sizes of five or more. With much larger sample sizes, e.g. thirty, even reasonably small correlations will be statistically significant. With a smaller sample size even a correlation of 0.70 would not be statistically different from zero. It will be appreciated that statistical significance is not the same thing as practical significance. A correlation may be more or less significant, in the everyday sense of 'noteworthy', as a result of factors other than statistical significance, such as, e.g. novelty of associations.)

There is still a disquieting tendency for textbooks (and sometimes even researchers) to treat or interpret high correlations as evidence of cause and effect. For example, there is a high correlation between lung cancer and cigarette smoking, and it is widely inferred that the one is caused by the other. There is a high correlation between a certain style of **teaching** and student achievement, and a causal relationship is suggested. High IQ correlates with large vocabulary, and many people conclude that enlarging the child's vocabulary will improve his IQ.

But, however reasonable it may seem on any particular occasion, one cannot deduce from the fact that A and B are always found together that one causes the other. There may be any number of other factors that are the cause of either or of both A and B. For example, tension might be the main factor that induces people to smoke and to get lung cancer; something about urban life might be the cause of both (since we know that the majority of smokers live in cities); or two or more further quite distinct but unnoticed factors might be at work in those cases where people both smoke and contract cancer, the one the cause of the former, the other the cause of the latter. The correlation between IQ and vocabulary could be the result of the fact that IQ tests, when they are not specifically verbal, are none the less essentially **conceptual**, while most people's vocabulary is more or less coterminous with their conceptual range; or it could be that high IQ leads to greater vocabulary acquisition but not vice versa, or it could be that one or more of a number of other variables (e.g. genetic endowment, environment, individual motivation) are primarily responsible for both. Similarly, it would be rash to conclude from the fact that most competent mathematics students were taught by teachers who continually fired questions at them that the latter was the cause of the former. (It should be added that cause/effect deductions from correlations obtained in a sphere such as **education** are particularly dangerous, in view of the poor conceptualization and inadequate control of variables in most such **research**.) (***intelligence, analysis**)

The value of establishing correlations lies in the fact that they constitute information without which we can plan and decide nothing; for example, never mind the why and wherefore, it is better to know that there is a negative correlation between girls and the study of mathematics, that is, girls by and large do not study maths, than to be ignorant of the fact. In addition, even if it is conceded that the correlations in themselves reveal nothing of cause and effect, they may none the less lead to practical conclusions. I may not know why A and B are found together, but if they are, and I wish to avoid A, it might be sensible to avoid B. (For example, if a certain disease is closely associated with the countryside in summer, then it would be wise to avoid the countryside in summer, even though, for all I know, the cause of the disease is an insect that could well appear in town.)

To finish on a gloomy note, it will be recognized that the value of research that consists only in determining correlational relationships is severely limited in the context of an activity such as teaching where our interest is essentially in cause and effect. (The absence of a positive correlation between two variables – e.g. teacher questioning and student achievement – does of course give one reason to doubt a cause and effect relationship.) (*teacher effectiveness)

Creative arts see Aesthetic value, Art education, Assessment, Creativity

Creativity

Creativity is a **normative** term. We think of creativity as being a good thing. It is not always so clear what we think it means. In fact there are clearly different senses of the word, or different **concepts** of creativity.

1. Those who are unfamiliar with the use of the word in educational contexts generally associate creativity with the production of original work of high quality in any sphere, but particularly in the arts. Thus Beethoven, Van Gogh, and James Joyce are typically regarded as creative artists, Einstein and Fleming creative scientists. A person of many talents such as Leonardo da Vinci might be thought of as creative without qualification, though, strictly speaking, we should say creative in many spheres. Creativity in this sense is sometimes hard to judge, and there may be arguments about whether particular individuals are or are not truly creative. None the less, it is tolerably clear what is meant; and this kind of creativity, being linked to notions of excellence and originality, is likely to be relatively rare.

2. A second conception of creativity minimizes reference to originality and regards the production or creation of any kind of product as creative, provided that it is well done. In this sense all competent craftsmen,

architects, and artists are creative, even if they merely execute their tasks well within a received tradition.

3. A third conception of creativity ignores reference to quality and sees creativity as no more than production. The professor who publishes more papers than another, or the person who produces more matchbox models than another, is thereby more creative, regardless of the quality of what he produces.

4. A fourth conception emphasizes the state of mind of the agent rather than the product. On this view to be creative is to be going through some particular kind of psychological **process**. At the lowest level the process might be identified with self-expression of one kind or another, regardless of the quantity, quality, or originality of what one produces. A more elaborate view associates the creative process with the experience of effective surprise (the generation of effective surprise in the agent himself being identified as **subjective** creativity, the promotion of effective surprise in others being identified as **objective** creativity). Countless other accounts of creativity as a process may be or have been advanced.

5. A fifth conception associates creativity with problem-solving ability, seeing ingenuity in the face of problems as the hallmark of the creative mind.

One could generate further conceptions of creativity, either by adding new criteria, or by combining the various criteria already referred to in new ways (originality, quality, quantity, process, problem-solving ability). But these are the most common conceptions, and they are sufficient for us to raise the following important questions:

1. In which of these senses, if any, does creativity have educational value?
2. How does one measure or otherwise assess creativity in these various senses?

The third conception (creativity as production in quantity) does not appear to have any inherent value, whether educational or any other. There may be occasions where high productivity is valuable for some further purpose, but even then it is hard to see why it should be valued if it is divorced from questions of quality. The second conception, by bringing in the notion of competence, has self-evident value, but the word creativity itself is redundant. Creative craftsmen, students, or shopkeepers, in this sense, are simply good craftsmen, students, or shopkeepers. These we certainly desire, but there is no mystery in principle about how to get them (we need to bring people to understand their craft, their studies, or the nature of shopkeeping), and no point in designating them creative.

The first conception does mark out something valuable and distinctive, and therefore something worth labelling distinctively. Creative people, in this sense, by definition, are the people who contribute to advances in knowledge and achievement. One might perhaps question whether a system of mass schooling should be particularly concerned to develop creativity in this sense (rather than, say, concentrating on competence, and leaving creative genius to emerge); none the less, this is one kind of creativity that has inherent value and could reasonably be argued to have educational worth.

The fourth conception gives rise to a rather different kind of problem. What can we sensibly say about creativity, when it is conceived of as a certain kind of mental or psychological process? If Shakespeare's creativity is a matter of what went on in his mind when he wrote his plays, then we are in no position to say whether he was creative or not, since we know nothing about what went on in his mind. There is something odd about adopting a conception of creativity that does not allow us to form an opinion on the question of whether any of the historical figures normally regarded as creative are in fact so. Nor is it clear that we can say much directly about the creativity, in this sense, of contemporaries. We shall consider the nature of creativity tests in a moment, but it is fair to say here that no test purports to be a direct test of the inner workings of the individual's mind in the process of being creative. (Research into characteristics of so called 'high creatives' in this sense invariably exhibits a degree of circularity. Thus, creative architects have been said to display such qualities as non-conformity and originality, when studied. But the selection of particular architects as creative in the first place appears to have been made in the light of the same sort of criteria as are subsequently cited as the qualities they possess.)

If this type of conception is more specific, as when it identifies the creative process with self-expression, a new conceptual problem arises: what constitutes self-expression? If whatever the individual produces or does when left to his own devices counts as expressing oneself, then the value of creativity in this sense must be questioned. What is the inherent value of my feeble attempts at painting, just because they are the product of my attempt to express myself? It may be suggested that there is some link between self-expression and subsequent creativity in some other sense. But, although self-expression is a necessary part of the first conception of creativity, there is no adequate evidence to support the thesis that encouraging self-expression in the young is beneficial in terms of ultimately producing creative persons in that sense. It may also be suggested that self-expression has therapeutic value or value in boosting self-esteem. But, while that may be true, such reference to extrinsic values would hardly warrant the appropriation of a normative term such as 'creative' to describe the process. In any case, on grounds of clarity alone, one might prefer what is agreed to be no more than self-expression to be called that.

If, on the other hand, something more specific is meant by self-expression in this context, or if the process of creativity is to be identified with anything else, whatever is meant needs to be clearly articulated, and, if we are able to recognize, encourage, and develop it, it needs to be articulated in a way that renders it accessible to us and assessable. One other line of argument should be noted here: it has been suggested that young children in expressing themselves, or going through the creative process in some similar sense, are producing matter that is original to them. Though this may be true, the question remains open as to whether, in what way, and to what degree, this is educationally important (*education, worthwhile).

The fifth conception begs an important question. Is there such a thing as a general problem-solving ability? One can distinguish between good and bad crossword puzzle solvers, good and bad performers on tests in logic or critical thinking, good and bad **lateral thinkers**, good and bad chess players, and so forth, but there is no reason to suppose that the good performer on one test or in one field will be a good performer in another. More importantly, there is no reason to suppose that a good performer on any or all of these tests, will be a good problem solver in the context of his personal life, his business administration, or his physics laboratory. (The reasons why this should be so are examined under **critical thinking**.) But if, this being so, creativity is defined in terms of specific problem-solving abilities, then one must again question its educational importance. Certain problems (for example, in mathematics) obviously have educational worth. But do the sorts of problem predominantly associated with creativity testing? (*generic fallacy)

Creativity tests face the problem of all standardized tests: they seek to quantify competence, and they do so by reference to readily monitorable indices. Creativity in the full sense (the first conception) obviously cannot be **measured** in this way. Rather one has to rely on impressionistic judgements. These judgements should be related to definable criteria, and they are not entirely arbitrary (*aesthetic value, value judgements); but defining the criteria is a contentious matter, and an overall estimate still has to be made, rather than a measurement taken. Whether, or to what extent, the composer John Cage is truly creative depends upon agreement on criteria of quality in music and criteria of originality, and even if agreement is reached on definition, judgement will be required in discerning them. Such estimates are not a mere matter of opinion, but they are necessarily extremely difficult. Judging creativity in this sense is a matter for those with an intimate understanding of the sphere in question and an appreciation of the logic of value judgements. It cannot be monitored by standardized tests (*assessment).

Examples of creativity tests include the following: think of as many uses for a brick as possible; fill in as many circles as possible to form pictures; complete a picture by joining the following shapes: O >; provide suitable titles for a number of short story summaries. Some tests may be more complex, either in the tasks they set or in that they conjoin a number of different such tasks. Some veer more towards problem-solving tests, perhaps presenting a series of problems with closed solutions, perhaps open (as in the case of lateral-thinking tests). They may tend towards the use of spatial, verbal, musical, or other items.

Regardless of the precise form, the logic of such tests remains the same and invites some awkward questions:

1. If the test is marked in purely quantitative terms, its value is plainly open to doubt. Is generating a large number of responses, without reference to quality, worth worrying about?

2. If quality is scored, how is it to be estimated? Who is to say whether a title is appropriate for a story, or a completed circle a good response? Sometimes this question itself is answered quantitatively: the most unusual response amongst those tested is treated as the most original. So it is, in the very precise and limited sense of 'original' employed (i.e. uncommon among this sample). But that is not to say that it is original in any qualitative or wider sense. It is difficult to see why this kind of originality displayed in such trivial and test-specific contexts should be valued. Sometimes more ambitious judgements of originality may be made by the testers, but: (a) their criteria for judgement are often not revealed; (b) where they are, they are often of questionable appropriateness; and (c) they remain at best judgements relating to trivial exercises. We are not aware of any such research that avoids these problems.

3. Given that these are specific tests, why should we value them, even if we could accurately assess good responses? Why should we value the ability to generate good plot titles? There has been some debate as to whether good performance on such tests **correlates** with subsequent creativity. But research into that question cannot be carried out in any meaningful way, until it is conducted in respect of a clear conception of creativity. Whether the student's performance on such a test correlates with subsequent performance on similar tests as an adult is of no educational interest, so long as the tests are confined to such items. The need

is for research that examines the relationship between such test performance and subsequent creativity in the full sense outlined above (cf., in this respect the type of research into critical thinking that is required). One necessary condition of subsequent creativity in a given field, namely understanding of the field, is not tested at all by such tests.

4. Tests of problem-solving ability are similarly lacking in direct **validity** for either creativity in the full sense or problem solving in general. It has recently been fashionable to stress open problems and to develop **skills** in lateral or divergent thinking. Here the problem of estimating the worth of a response is manifest: if there is no gauge of correct or good responses, then how does one determine poor ones? If there are criteria for evaluating responses, then the problems are not entirely open. Here also there is a lack of any adequate evidence to support the supposition that fluency in responding to test items indicates or leads to fluency in coping with real-life problems. Similarly, competence at dealing with closed problems in test conditions would appear to tell one little about people's likely subsequent competence to deal with real-life closed problems. This is natural enough, since real-life closed problems by definition require a range of **knowledge** and **understanding** that is context specific for their solution.

Creativity testing, like many of the tests used in classroom **research** is predicated on the highly questionable assumptions that there are a number of definable skills that invariably come into play in the creative act, that these can be practised and developed to good effect without concern for context, and that performance on such tests is a reliable pointer to subsequent creative performance (*art education, emotive meaning).

REFERENCES

Bailin (1988), Barrow and Woods (1982), Elliot (1971), Lloyd (1976), Lowenfeld and Brittain (1982), Lytton (1971), White (1972).

Criterion-referenced tests see Assessment

Critical theory

The origin of so-called critical theory is located in the intellectual resistance to political and social difficulties that arose in Europe in the 1920s and 1930s. Theorists such as Max Horkheimer, Theodor Adorno and

Herbert Marcuse (the 'Frankfurt School'), drew together ideas from Marx, Freud and other sources to develop a body of arguments to resist political and economic oppression and the rise of authoritarianism. Some of these scholars, such as Erich Fromm and Herbert Marcuse, were forced to move to the United States in the pre-war years. After 1945 their work was extended by such intellectuals as Jurgen Habermas in West Germany, and Pierre Bourdieu and Michel Foucault in France. Ideas derived from critical theory have now become widely disseminated, especially among sociologists and political theorists, and have been extended and applied in a wide variety of social settings. Given this historical development, the singular form of 'critical theory' suggests a coherence and unanimity among its adherents that manifestly does not exist. Nor is the substitution of the plural 'critical theories' – with its evocation of a group of parallel philosophies – entirely satisfactory, although it is suggestive of the diversity and complexity of arguments among critical theorists.

Critical theory, in very general terms, is a form of analysis of social, political and economic life, designed to enable people to gain insight into the oppressive forces that control their lives. In the everyday world, the argument goes, many institutions, practices, and beliefs are so familiar to us that they are accepted unthinkingly. Yet many of these routinely accepted – 'taken for granted' – features of everyday life are inherently unfair, unjust, or undemocratic. For example, in political life, some groups may have inherited special privileges that are accepted unthinkingly by others within the community; in family life, some participants may be ascribed particular authority simply because they are male, older, or a wage-earner; and in economic life, some institutions may benefit because they control sources of information being fed to the public. Such individuals or institutions with special status within society have an inherent self-interest in maintaining the prevailing social structures, and within it their own positions, by promoting **ideologies** that justify their privileges.

Critical theory casts a very wide net. All aspects of social life are historically created ('constructed') for human purposes. Thus in social life there are no permanencies and no 'truths' – every aspect needs to be examined, or reflected upon, to discover the social interests maintaining it, and identify its effects on others. Note that critical theorists maintain that **'knowledge'** itself is 'socially created', and that the academic **'disciplines'** in which knowledge is lodged are themselves human constructions. Given that argument, critical theorists challenge the value-neutral status of traditional notions of a 'science' of human behaviour. They view mainline social science as humanly constructed and inclusive of particular **interests** and distortions: its commitment to **facts** rather than **values**, means rather than ends, predictive generalizations rather than interpretative studies of individuals is evidence not of **objectivity** or the search for truth, but of an underlying interest in control, management and efficiency – an 'instrumental rationality'. What is needed, critical theorists argue, is a form of social science that is reflective, participatory, democratic, emancipatory and reformist.

Few features of social life escape review by critical theorists: personal relationships, social customs, languages, fine arts, popular **culture** and institutions of all kinds. In several areas of social life – for example, human **emotions** and sexuality, the role of literary texts as social documents, and the relationship of **language** to political development – these studies have been bold and original, as well as controversial and unsettling. The topic of **education** serves as an example of the arguments of critical theorists, and illustrates both their strengths and weaknesses.

Their critique is wide ranging. In general terms, critical theorists regard the educational system as a powerful force in the control mechanism of the state (thus schools become agents of 'social regulation'). The focus of interest in the management of **schools** is perpetuation of existing social and economic forms (thus schools are also agents of 'reproduction'). Such reproduction serves to ensure that the prevailing 'ideology' of the state be conveyed through the school system – a frequently used simile is that of the school as a black box in which **equalities** in **class** and gender relationships, and the 'hegemony' of one class over another, are replicated. In that process the **curriculum** in school plays a significant part: academic disciplines within the curriculum, far from serving the emancipatory function envisioned in theories of **liberal education**, in fact serve the interests of particular groups and classes within society, because such knowledge, held by some but not others, becomes a form of 'cultural capital'. As a consequence, the cultural forms of working-class students or minority groups within schools are systematically devalued.

In the classroom, it is argued, teachers and students are victims of the social system. The **educational theory** in which teachers are trained is divorced from the realities of the classroom. Practices in the classroom are derived from an educational science that values abstraction and excessive intellectualism rather than the capacity for reflective thought and action about what happens in particular cases. Relationships between teachers and students (in both personal and academic terms) are authoritarian rather than democratic in any emancipatory sense. Thus the fabric of the interchanges between teachers and students is inherently undemocratic and 'distortive'. Consequently, students are frequently alienated. Given these intellectual broadsides, an observer may be forgiven for concluding that the only remedy for the present condition of schools is to close them at once (a solution advocated by several commentators).

There are undeniable signs in the educational literature of the effects of such criticism. In recent years, articles in **professional** journals have raised questions about the relationship of schools and society more frequently than in the past. Teachers are more aware of the social constraints upon minority groups and women, for example, and less likely to assume that disadvantages are the result of personal failings. There is evidence that materials for schools are being examined more critically than heretofore, and from different perspectives. Alternative types of discussion are being introduced in classrooms to encourage students to resist some of the social and political pressures upon them. Moreover, new forms of curriculum design and of teacher participation in research (so-called **'action research'**) have been spurred by particular interpretations of critical theory. In short, the arguments of critical theorists have enlarged the consciousness of a great number of persons in education, and changed many of their practices.

On the other hand, there can be no denying official resistance to the arguments of critical theorists. Some scholars in the pre-war years were persecuted in totalitarian states – a practice that continues to the present time. Even in democracies the careers of some critical theorists have been adversely affected by reactions to their ideas. The response of those in authority over education – governmental and non-governmental – has often been firm, and occasionally harsh. Teachers, for example, who have attempted to reform schools on the basis of their perception of ideas drawn from critical theory have found themselves the focus of bitter criticism (Clanfield, 1989).

Many of the central notions, arguments, and publications in critical theory are not difficult to attack. Critical theorists have been accused of stating their ideas at such a high level of generality and abstraction that educational **phenomena** have been distorted, and conditions exaggerated or over-simplified. School practices and conditions, their critics claim, are not as uniform as critical theorists state. Some have argued that critical theory is long on statements of **theory**, but short on recommendations for specific change. Others claim that critical theory tends to reduce pedagogy to politics, and in so doing loses sight of the importance of the child in understanding educational phenomena. Several critics have pointed to what they regard as a strong ideological stance in critical theory, in which explanations are inevitably reduced to the failings of capitalism. Others point to a tendency by critical theorists either to regard certain arguable tenets as fundamental truths, or to fail to address moral issues within their arguments. The split between **positivist** scientists and analytic philosophers on the one hand, and critical theorists on the other, on epistemological and methodological grounds is very wide indeed. To some reviewers, some critical theorists in education appear overly conformist and uncritical in their own work – the very features they protest against in others.

REFERENCES

Apple (1979), Bottomore (1984), Bowles and Gintis (1976), Carr and Kemmis (1986), Clanfield (1989), Entwistle (1979), Freire (1973a, 1973b), Gibson (1986), Giroux (1981, 1983b, 1988), Grundy (1987), Habermas (1974), McLaren (1986), Young (1971).

Critical thinking

Critical thinking is widely agreed to be an important **aim** of **education**. It is closely associated with goals such as rationality, **autonomy** and, perhaps, **creativity** and **intelligence**. It is sometimes referred to as a **skill** which may be misleading in that it is plainly not a single activity that one engages in, or a specific technique that one adopts, without variation in any context. Thinking critically about a new tax proposal is different from thinking critically about how to design one's garden, and thinking critically about either one might take many different forms and involve different procedures. Referring to the skills of critical thinking would therefore seem more appropriate.

But while any instance of critical thinking will involve some discernible skills (e.g. following an argument, visualizing a proposal, imagining alternatives), it is not clear that one can identify a set of skills that is common to all instances of critical thinking, except at a very general level (e.g. speaking a language). If we try to be more specific and suggest that all critical thinking involves, for example, the ability to be logical, to generate alternatives, to conceive of the unusual, we run into trouble: critical thinking does not always involve proceeding logically (spontaneous and intuitive responses to situations may sometimes count as examples of critical thinking); what is involved in proceeding logically may vary in kind from one context to another (logical thinking about a moral issue is distinct from logical thinking about a problem in chemistry); the ability to generate alternatives is sometimes an appropriate and useful technique to adopt, but sometimes not; nor is such an ability something that one either has or lacks: I may be rather good at generating alternatives when planning my garden, and rather bad at it when considering tax proposals. Similarly with conceiving of the unusual.

The description of somebody as a critical thinker involves reference to a dispositional element (one tends, or one has an inclination, to assess critically), a basic intellectual element (one has some grasp of fundamental logical principles: one observes the principle of avoiding contradiction; one can see that if all As are B, and this is an A, then it must be a B), a strategic element (one is capable of adopting some suitable strategies to forward one's critical thought), and a contextual element (one knows something about the subject matter concerning which one is trying to think critically). Of these, the last is clearly the crucial element, for without it, without some knowledge of the subject matter in question, one could not conceivably think critically about it, and in addition the contextual element determines what strategies may be appropriate and what steps are logical.

It follows that, if we wish to develop powers of critical thought, we have to do it largely in the context of various subject matters, **disciplines** or forms of **knowledge**. If we do not give people a thorough understanding of the distinct nature of mathematics and **aesthetics**, then they cannot be expected to think critically in those areas; if people do not know anything about economics, government and tax, or about gardens, then their responses to suggestions about them can hardly count as critical thinking. Since we have to include development of contextual understanding, and since appropriate strategies and forms of logical reasoning depend upon context, it would seem sensible to develop the latter elements too in the context of whatever subject matters we deem to be educationally **worthwhile**. Although one might practise various strategies to enhance critical thinking in any context, they none the less have to be practised in some context. Similarly, one cannot cultivate the dispositional element in a vacuum, but only in the context of some subject matter or other. That being so, it would be curious to resist doing it in the context of logically important and educationally worthwhile subject matters.

None the less, perhaps as a direct result of thinking of critical thinking as a skill or a set of skills, the idea has grown up that one can best develop it by exercise in the skills, without reference to particular contexts. Thus some counsel courses in logic (formal or informal) as aids to critical thinking, and others advocate specially designed critical thinking programmes, which generally incorporate a number of points of logic, a number of strategies, and a number of procedures. In addition, some specific programmes (which, being relatively specific, imply a relatively specific and hence narrow conception of critical thinking) such as De Bono's CORT (Cognitive Research Trust) programme have been marketed.

Nobody interested in critical thought could sensibly object to people studying logic. One may, however, question whether learning the principles and forms of logical reasoning in the abstract is the most sensible way to proceed. One can learn to reason logically in a wide variety of contexts, without studying logic in the abstract; equally, some people who are competent students of logic are not very good at being logical in particular contexts. There is no clear evidence to support or reject the hypothesis that the study of logic is beneficial in respect of promoting the goal of critical thinking.

Specific programmes, such as De Bono's, naturally reflect their designer's view of critical thinking. In De Bono's case, the open or ill-structured problem that does not have a correct answer has always been regarded as the characteristic kind of problem that requires critical thought. What he terms '**lateral thinking**', or thinking sideways, has long remained the basic strategy he recommends. Consequently, he proposes a variety of games that one might play, and provides a number of open-ended problems to chew over. It may be presumed that practice on such a programme will make one more adept at such exercises (although it necessarily remains unclear how one judges how adept one's response to problems without correct answers may be); there is no reason to expect it to make one a person of developed critical thinking powers in the full sense described above.

The serious question for schools and universities is whether they should adopt critical thinking programmes *per se*. Should they devote curriculum time to programmes containing such content as: the study of various features of language, grammar and style (e.g. conditional clauses, the meaning of indicator words such as 'therefore', the use of irony); the study of forms of argument (e.g. two premises leading to a conclusion; multiple premises leading to two conclusions); the study of various procedures (e.g. checking inferences, clarifying terms, generalizing); the study of various strategies (e.g. trying to find a counter example; clarifying a term by considering it in relation to its opposite, or to distinct but similar terms). These programmes largely proceed by way of fictitious examples, or examples taken in isolation and out of context, and in any event forming no coherent whole: they do not seek to solve any actual problems, perfect any substantive argument, or develop any body of understanding.

The minimal argument for the adoption of such programmes is that they are likely to develop a keen awareness of the points they introduce and a greater concern for, for example, checking inferences or studying the meaning of words generally. What is not clear is whether they lead to any greater competence at thinking critically outside the context of such programmes. What would be required to throw light on that issue is research into whether there is, on the one hand, a high **correlation** between those who do critical thinking courses and those who display strong powers of critical thought in the context of, for example, **history**, science, politics, and, on the other, a low correlation between those who do not do such courses and those who become good critical thinkers. If these correlations were established, the inference that such courses, while not in themselves producing critical thinkers, none the less contribute usefully to their development, would be a reasonable one. But in point of fact there is no such research to suggest any such thing. (Most research into the effectiveness of critical thinking programmes tests only in relation to a similarly limited conception of critical thinking as that employed by the programmes. It tests only whether people become better at doing the sort of exercises involved in the programme. That is obviously immaterial, so long as we recognize that what we want is critical thinking displayed in various specific contexts, and that that can be achieved through study of the subject matters alone.) (*assessment*)

In the absence of any clear evidence to support the contention that they serve a useful purpose, it might seem reasonable to devote the limited time at our disposal to developing powers of critical thought in the various contexts where we are particularly anxious to see it displayed, whether they be formal subjects such as science and history, or areas of life such as marital relations and work problems (*generic fallacy, reification, transference*).

REFERENCES

De Bono (1970), Hitchcock (1983), McPeck (1981).

Cultural literacy

A phrase recently given prominence by E. D. Hirsch in his book of that title. His argument is that the ability to read with **understanding** is severely impaired for many students today, because their **education** has failed to initiate them into their cultural heritage, and hence reference points, allusions, implications, etc., are largely meaningless to them. The fact is undeniable that most complex and sophisticated writing can be fully understood only if its cultural context is understood. The claim that students today are not sufficiently culturally literate may be correct. Less convincing was Hirsch's positive proposal to deal with the problem: a dictionary of culturally significant names, events, and other reference points. Apart from the predictable argument amongst scholars about which items should be in or out of such a dictionary, many felt that a solution could be found only in sustained immersion in **literature, history** and various important bodies of **knowledge** (*culture, literacy*).

REFERENCES

Hirsch (1987), Proctor (1988), Ravitch and Finn (1987).

Cultural relativity *see* Culture, Objectivity, Relativity, Relevance, Subjectivity

Culture

The word 'culture' has many meanings, ranging from the biological use of the term to refer to the growth of bacteria to its use in physical development to refer to the cultivation of the body. The two senses of particular interest to educationalists are: (a) 'culture' meaning the way of life, manners and customs of a group, as when we refer to Islamic or Welsh culture; and (b) 'culture' meaning a body of works of high quality, particularly but not exclusively in the **liberal arts**. T. S. Eliot offered an account of (English) culture in the first sense as including 'all the characteristic activities and interests of a people: Derby Day, Henley Regatta, Cowes, the twelfth of August, a cup final, the dog races, the pin table, the dart board, Wensleydale cheese, boiled cabbage cut into sections, beetroot in vinegar, nineteenth-century Gothic churches, and the music of Elgar.' The phrase 'a cultured person' must imply the second sense (since everybody is cultured in the first sense, if they belong to some group), and suggests an acquaintanceship with great works of literature, art, and music, or, in Matthew Arnold's phrase, 'the best that has been thought and said'.

Schools are concerned with culture in both senses. Culture in the first sense, sometimes called the sociological or anthropological sense, is essentially what we **socialize** people into, while culture in the second sense, sometimes termed 'high culture', enshrines some part of the excellence of human thought and **understanding** that being educated suggests having come to grips with. (Although **education** is not defined in terms of acquaintance with or appreciation of great works of art, **literature**, and science, one might naturally expect them to play a role in educating, and their appreciation to be one of the rewards of being educated.)

The main problem with the idea of initiating people into culture in the sociological sense is largely revealed in the question 'whose culture?'. Some might object to deliberate initiation into any culture, but it is hard to sustain that objection, since it is a characteristic of cultures to impress themselves on members of the group, and influences towards cultural assimilation are unavoidable. Provided such socialization does not become **indoctrination**, there is little to complain of. (This is to presume that the culture in question is not immoral or repugnant in some way; if it is, that constitutes the ground for objection, rather than the fact of initiating people into a culture.) But in many contemporary societies there are many distinct cultures along lines of race, **class**, and **interest**. Consequently we face the questions of whether to opt for **multiculturalism**, in one form or another, and how to select between cultures.

While cultural differences between sub-groups in a society (for example, between social classes or ethnic communities) may mean a great deal to individuals within the various groups, it is arguable that the role of a national system of **schooling** should be to preserve and continually reforge the dominant culture, precisely because it is a national system and not, for example, a working-class, Inuit, or Asian system. (Such an approach is compatible both with respect for other cultures and with gradual modification of the dominant culture in response to the influence of other cultures.) As against this, it may be argued that typically the dominant culture in Western societies is identifiable as specifically middle-class culture, and that, since the middle class may be numerically a minority, this amounts to the imposition of one out of many sub-cultures, which fact is obscured by reference to 'national' culture and use of the ambiguous word 'dominant'.

There is not much doubt that schools do tend to promote the cultural values, manners, and customs that are commonly thought of as middle class. One might respond by suggesting that the label 'middle class' simply means those who have been successfully initiated into such a culture. That is to say, it may not be that an otherwise identifiable group is imposing its way of life, so much as that the group becomes identifiable once the aim of the schooling system has proved more effective in some cases than others. Either way it cannot be denied that whether we aim to forge a national culture or to preserve many cultures, a process of selection has to take place and judgements about the quality, efficacy, and desirability of particular cultures have to be made (*value judgements, core curriculum).

The two main questions about high culture are: (a) how does one determine what constitutes culture in this sense?; and (b) though it is a **concept** that involves quality and value by definition, does initiation into it have the educational worth that is claimed for it?

Arguments against the schools' preoccupation with this kind of culture have sometimes taken the form of denying any innate superiority in particular examples of alleged cultural excellence. In an extreme version the claim is made that there is no such thing as innate superiority; no works can be cited as being inherently qualitatively distinct. This seems plainly incoherent. If an activity has any identity at all, whether it be soccer, musical composition, painting, science or literature, then some criteria for determining relative quality in the field must emerge from the nature of the activity alone: some soccer players can be shown to be better than others by reference to the nature of the game (*value judgements, worthwhile). However, in some fields, such as art, there is room for a great deal of argument about what constitutes quality, and hence which works possess it to what degree. This is largely because the questions of what art is is a great deal more problematic than the questions of what science or soccer are. Consequently, those who suggest that the sort of works typically associated with culture in the schools (e.g. Shakespeare, Beethoven, Renoir) are not necessarily the best, may have a case. (Here again, there are some who argue that typically it is middle-class taste that in fact determines what judgements of quality are made.) But, in order to tackle this issue, it is necessary to clarify one's conceptions of literature, music, art, etc., and then examine particular works carefully in the light of those conceptions. It is hard to believe that many, if they did this job thoroughly, would deny that, as literature, Shakespeare and other commonly heralded works are superior to, for example, Agatha Christie mysteries. Similarly, in the case of other arts, one would expect some broad uniformity of judgement (*aesthetic value, analysis).

Another objection is that many works of culture are relatively inaccessible to schoolchildren, and that on methodological grounds more serious attention should be paid to works of lesser quality. As a generalization that seems fair, and there is no reason why commitment to the ultimate goal of introducing students to culture should lead to schools being exclusively or even predominantly concerned with cultural works.

But should initiation into high culture be one of the goals of schooling at all? Surely it should. Works of high culture are also a part of our culture in the other sense, and, by definition, they constitute some of the best of its products. In addition, such works are to a large extent models of the very forms of thought and awareness that are aspects of being educated. One could be educated in the full sense without being aware of any particular cultural works. (Education has not been defined in terms of cultural examples.) But it is a necessary truth that the educated mind should recognize the quality of a Tolstoy, a Henry James, a Cervantes or a Flaubert, should it become acquainted with their respective works. (Recognizing the quality does not necessarily imply enjoying.) Likewise, it is part of what it is to be educated to have some understanding of what art is, and hence to be able to recognize at least some instances of good and bad products in that domain. It therefore seems educationally appropriate that students should be led to some direct acquaintanceship with some such cultural products, with some of the best that has been thought, spoken, written, and created (*emotive meaning, ethics, knowledge, mass media, nationalism, normative).

REFERENCES

Arnold (1932), Bantock (1968), Barrow and Woods (1982), Eliot (1948), Holly (1974), Lawton (1975), Reynolds and Skilbeck (1976).

Curriculum

Educators define 'curriculum' in many ways: some use the term in very limited and specific contexts, others attach very broad and general meanings; some define it in descriptive terms (what curriculum is), others in **prescriptive** terms (what curriculum ought to be). Resolving (or even penetrating) such confusion is no easy task.

Its root is located in the Latin verb *currere* 'to run', from which an extension is easily made to the noun meaning 'a course to be run', and (as a **metaphor**) 'an educational course to be covered'. From medieval times the term has denoted the arrangement of subject matter in a school timetable. Many people, particularly those not in education, associate curriculum with the outline of a course programme (e.g. 'O' level mathematics, or Grade 10 history) written on a piece of paper. In this sense, it is virtually synonymous with the term 'syllabus' as it is commonly used in the English educational system. Thus, curriculum has become associated with the official written programmes of study published by ministries or departments of education, local authorities or boards of education, and commercial firms or teams of educational specialists working on specially funded projects.

Some written courses of study are more prescriptive than others. A government official or a **curriculum designer**, for example, may be so anxious to control what happens in the classroom, or fearful of the competencies of teachers, that he may attempt to prescribe every activity in the classroom (action pejoratively labelled 'teacher-proofing'). On other occasions, the same person may issue rather general instructions for a programme (often called 'guidelines'), and expect local authorities or teachers to supplement them as local conditions warrant.

But what is written on a piece of paper may have very little connection with what actually happens in the classroom. A written programme of study in a **history** course, for example, may call for a certain form of inquiry learning that a teacher may not be able (for any number of reasons) to put into effect in a classroom. In consequence, some educators confine use of 'curriculum' to what actually happens in particular classrooms (with special emphasis being placed on the content and nature of the interchange between teacher and students).

These differences between what may be labelled 'the written' and 'the actual' curriculum highlight another distinction. In those cases in which a teacher overtly preaches one message, but by his manner or attitudes conveys a second message (for example, when a teacher advocates democratic values, but personally behaves in an authoritarian style), observers have distinguished between the official curriculum and the hidden curriculum (in which the latter may have more lasting effects than the former on students' learning and attitudes). The hidden curriculum is of particular interest to those sociologists seeking explanations for the persistence of social, political, and institutional structures within society.

A commonly held view of curriculum – one that became popular after the publication of Tyler's (1949) text – defines it essentially by reference to objectives of student **learning** (i.e., the **knowledge, skills** and attitudes actually learned by students). Tyler derived these objectives from studies of the nature of learners themselves, studies of the nature of contemporary life, the work of subject specialists, and the writings of psychologists and philosophers. The curriculum planner's task, Tyler maintained, is to provide **teaching** strategies, learning activities, and evaluative devices, so that these selected objectives may be realized in the classroom (***aims, behavioural objectives**).

One of the long-term (and perhaps unintentional) results of Tyler's interpretation of curriculum is the view that a teacher's role in curriculum is confined to implementing the written goals of ministries, local authorities, or principals. Thus curriculum may be understood in terms of specific skills that teachers need in order to put a particular course of study into operation, including assessing **needs**, designing objectives, selecting strategies, and constructing tests. Curriculum-making is reduced to a process or system. One difficulty with this definition is that it assumes that there are general skills in such curriculum-making, an assumption that is far from proven. For example, a teacher may be able to devise objectives and strategies very successfully in auto-mechanics, but be helpless in history. The putative general skills called for by proponents of this view of curriculum may be far more contextually bound than they realize (***generic fallacy**).

Others have devised a more global definition for curriculum. In some school systems, particularly in North America, curriculum is often defined in terms of 'all the experiences that a child has in school'. On this view, many features of schooling (such as the nature of the subject matter under study, actions of teachers in the classroom, attitudes fostered in students, and texts and other materials used by students) may be subjected to scrutiny under the term curriculum. But such a broad conception raises many questions. What limits does the term now possess, if any? Are we to conclude that what happens in the hall-way should be included in the notion of curriculum? To what goals are experiences aimed? By what criteria are some experiences to be considered of greater worth than others? What, if anything, is distinctly **educational** about a curriculum in this sense?

Finally, some scholars have attempted to resolve these definitional difficulties by considering curriculum as a set of principles to guide prospective teachers and other educators. Thus curriculum is confined to a discussion of the principles that govern, on the one hand, the selection of content and strategies, and, on the other, such matters as evaluation of student progress. What is emphasized is critical scrutiny of curricular issues. Such a definition may be helpful to scholars, but whether it is of much practical use to teachers and others responsible for curriculum design and implementation is another question.

Scholarly work in more recent years has swung from attempts to redefine some previously held interpretations, to hand-wringing over the moribund state of curriculum thought in general. For example, Hirst (1974a) has attempted to derive a curriculum for **liberal education** from the nature of knowledge itself. Lawton (1983) has advocated the location of curriculum in what he calls 'cultural analysis' (requiring answers to questions about the extent to which an existing curriculum meets the needs of society, and about the curriculum changes required to achieve desired societal aims). Schwab (1970) has suggested that the entire field should be reconceptualized by devising new **practical** and eclectic arts that will readily affect actual practice in schools. Given continuing confusion over the meaning of 'curriculum', teachers may be wise to confine their attention to those educational ends or purposes that are particularly worthwhile, and to activities designed to realize them in the classroom (***core curriculum, curriculum change, integrated studies, reconceptualists, schooling**).

REFERENCES

Barrow (1984), Beauchamp (1968), Brent (1978), Giroux (1979), Goodson (1987), Hirst (1974a), Jenkins and Shipman (1976), Kelly (1977), Lawton (1983), Miller (1988), Pinar (1988b), Pratt (1980), Resnick and Resnick (1985), Schubert (1986), Schwab (1970), Smith, Stanley and Shores (1957), Stenhouse (1975b), Taba (1962), Tanner (1988), Taylor and Richards (1979), Tyler (1949).

Curriculum change, curriculum development, curriculum implementation

Many terms are used in educational discourse to denote the task of replacing an existing curriculum with another curriculum: for example, 'curriculum change', 'curriculum development', 'curriculum implementation', 'curriculum dissemination', 'curriculum diffusion', 'curriculum innovation', 'curriculum renewal' or 're-treading', 'curriculum inquiry', 'curriculum research', and even (partly tongue-in-cheek) 'curriculum insemination', and 'curriculum buoyancy'. This variety is caused by such factors as confusion over the meaning of '**curriculum**' itself, the multitude of tasks connected with curriculum change, and particular emphases adopted in specific circumstances. Because the first three terms in the list occur frequently, difficulties in defining them may be taken as characteristic of the entire group.

The phrase 'curriculum change' logically implies any type of change, whether progressive (in which the intention is to substitute a new curriculum for an old one) or regressive (in which a teacher may decide to return to an old curriculum). In practice, the latter meaning is rarely intended: curriculum change almost always implies the intentional introduction of a new and better curriculum. Unfortunately, it is not always clear what criteria are to be used in order to **assess** such improvement.

Much of the literature on curriculum change is concerned with technical methods for changing schools by means of curriculum initiatives taken by local authorities or school boards, or as a result of directives from central governments. Such centrally directed curriculum change has attracted the attention of those who are anxious to develop strategies for change in general, or to identify those common features that may be deemed to encourage or discourage change. Formal **models** of change are usually derived from branches of social scientific research. The 'research, development and diffusion' model focuses attention on the plans of the originator of a proposed change, and provides for the careful sequencing of activities designed to put the proposed change into effect, often on a fairly wide scale. The 'problem-solving' approach to change emphasizes solving specific problems in particular locations. The 'social interaction' model for change relies upon the deliberations of the persons for whom a particular change is intended. Each of these models places the originator of a planned curricular change (often a researcher) and the receiver of that change (usually a teacher) in significantly different positions. All three models (and variants of them) have been used in curriculum projects (large-scale and small-scale). In some countries, reliance on the research, development and diffusion model led to the production of packages of materials, which, however well designed, were not always understood or used by teachers or local school systems. Some observers have argued that this approach tends to reduce teachers to passive receivers of curricular ideas, and to ignore the important personal and political relationships that exist in any school setting.

Another set of models for curriculum change has been derived from studies of the diffusion of social change in general, and adapted to educational theory. In the 'centre-periphery' model the 'centre' assumes responsibility for the design of the proposed change, which is then put into effect in the 'periphery' in a carefully managed organizational pattern. The 'proliferation of centres' model provides for some devolution of authority from the centre, in which secondary centres are provided to serve as stimuli for effective change. The 'shifting centres' model relies on change resulting from shifting points of emphasis in any curricular movement.

Curriculum development is usually considered to be less technical or mechanistic than curriculum change, although the two terms are frequently treated as synonyms. Curriculum development often indicates a formal or informal process for reshaping or designing a curriculum, usually with a practical end in view. For example, a group of university researchers may decide to select or write a set of materials for English classes at a specific grade level; a senior curriculum supervisor within a local board may set out the principles for a new course in mathematics for his jurisdiction; or a couple of teachers in a particular school may discuss the introduction of scholarly documents in a senior secondary school history class. At the other end of the scale, well-funded projects may comprise teams of scholars developing new types of curricula for general adoption. In some countries such curriculum development tasks are more closely controlled from a national office than in others that prefer to encourage local **autonomy**.

Curriculum implementation, on the other hand, frequently refers to difficulties experienced in putting curricular proposals into effect. Some perceive this task as virtually the same as change: identify the principal factors, and establish methodological procedures or models to ensure a pre-specified result. Others suggest that particular attention should be paid to the conditions under which teachers and students function, and to those negotiations required for a curriculum to be introduced successfully. Still others maintain that implementation depends upon reflective and critical discussions by concerned teachers. Current **research** seems to confirm that teachers have difficulties recognizing the intent of curricular proposals developed by others, and usually adapt documents to suit their own purposes and teaching styles. In such conditions, implementation becomes a much more difficult undertaking than had previously been acknowledged.

Educators are beginning to understand the extraordinary complexity of effecting change, development, and implementation in the school curriculum. Greater emphasis has been placed on acknowledging the characteristics of particular settings in which changes are to be considered, and progress appears to have been made in identifying the professional arts that encourage curricular flexibility in teachers. Nevertheless, the emphasis in the educational literature still appears to be on the technical (or manipulative) means for promoting change, rather than upon the quality of the change that is being promoted (***action research, critical theory**).

REFERENCES

Anderson and Tomkins (1981), Bacchus (1986), Barrow (1984), Becher and Maclure (1978a), Bolam (1975), Connelly (1972), Fullan (1982), Galton (1980), House (1979), Hoyle (1970), Kelly (1986), Kogan (1978), Leithwood, Holmes and Montgomery (1979), MacDonald and Walker (1976), Oliva (1988), Olson (1985), Plaskow (1985), Sarason (1982, 1983), Schwab (1970), Shipman (1974), Skilbeck (1984), Stenhouse (1975b), Wallin (1985).

Curriculum content *see* Culture, Interest, Knowledge, Topic-centred education, Understanding

Curriculum design

'Curriculum design' is one of a cluster of commonly used terms (including 'curriculum construction', 'curriculum engineering', 'curriculum planning', 'curriculum structure', and 'curriculum organization') that refer to the principles or procedures upon which a curriculum is fashioned before it is put into operation. What is meant by 'curriculum design' depends first on what is meant by '**curriculum**'. If what we have in mind is a written document to guide a teacher, then problems of design are quite different from a situation in which curriculum is seen as a largely extempore interaction of teacher and student in the classroom. Even if agreement were reached on the question of curriculum, a definition of curriculum design depends further upon the scale, scope, and point of interest of particular enterprises. The task of design may encompass the **theoretical and practical** considerations of such varied enterprises as planning a national curriculum (involving a number of distinct subject matters, and hundreds of schools), planning a research-based curriculum (requiring a team of scholars and teachers) based on a particular curriculum issue, or planning a single course, or part of a course, in a single school. The purpose and scope of a proposed curriculum will directly affect the procedures for putting it into operation.

Some writers take a very mechanistic or technical view of the term 'design'. As if producing an engineer's blueprint, planning is reduced to a series of components, functions, and tasks that are interrelated by arrows or other (sometimes very elaborate) two-dimensional flowcharts. Such an approach, usually couched in a technical vocabulary (and often in **educanto**), is suggestive of the agreed procedures and standards characteristic of a mechanistic interpretation of the nature of design. Such reliance on **modelling** often appears to take precedence over reflection on the quality or **worth** of a curricular undertaking.

Some curriculum scholars prefer to concentrate on a framework, or series of frameworks, derived from philosophical speculation or psychological theory. Thus, it is possible to speak of a discovery model of curriculum design derived from scientific notions of inquiry, a learner-centred model derived from the work of such philosophers as Rousseau or Dewey, a cognitive-development model derived from the work of Piaget, and so forth. Others have speculated on different orientations to curriculum based on different **conceptions** of the nature of **knowledge**, the learning patterns of children, and the ultimate purpose of **schooling**. Such alternative frameworks may be valuable as tools in curriculum research. To the extent that they provide alternatives for curriculum designers or teachers, they may be useful, but if they simply serve as substitutes for serious thought and reflection about the nature and purpose of particular curriculum undertakings, then they perform a positive disservice.

The most commonly used approach to curriculum planning, however, is the so-called 'objectives' model (of which several versions exist). The intention of this approach is to pre-specify, in terms of manifest student behaviour, those objectives that will serve as a guide for selecting teaching strategies and **learning** activities. A prescribed level of such student learning is used as a check on the effectiveness of the objectives. Emphasis is usually placed upon patterns of cognitive, affective, and psychomotor learning identified by empirical psychologists, or upon some type of **needs** assessment at a local or national level. This approach to curriculum design, often articulated in elaborate detail in standard curriculum texts adopted in teacher education institutions, has the seal of approval of many ministries and departments of education.

Criticism of this approach – especially in its most simplistic versions – is widespread. Some philosophers have attacked the notion of basing curricular objectives exclusively on theories derived from **behaviourism**, while others have argued that the general theories of cognitive psychologists do not sit well with the task of identifying aims in specific **disciplines** commonly taught in schools. Many observers find the task of writing certain desired **aims** in behavioural terms problematic, and the types of teacher–student interaction prescribed by the approach poverty-stricken. Even those teachers who pretend to design their courses in accord with the objectives approach usually adapt it, sometimes in virtually unrecognizable form, to their own purposes and styles of **teaching**.

Many alternative patterns of curriculum design have been suggested. Bruner (1960), for example, recommended that curricula should be designed to reflect the concepts and methods located in the structure of each discipline, with the range of subject matter extending that structure in a so-called spiral fashion as the student proceeded through the various grades. Lawton (1983) suggested that a form of **cultural** analysis should form the basis for curriculum planning and design in particular schools. Schwab (1970) outlined a series of practical and eclectic arts that may guide specially designed school committees representing the principal interests in the curriculum. Stenhouse (1975b) argued that teachers should tie curriculum planning enterprise to specific research questions. Researchers employed in large-scale projects of various types (especially in the 1960s and 1970s) used a variety of principles and procedures in the production of written curricula and associated packages. Other researchers maintain that the task of planning should be based on reflective and critical discussions by those classroom teachers responsible for curriculum implementation.

In one sense, the curriculum researcher, education student, and teacher are fortunate in the range of choices in curriculum design open to them in the educational literature (even if the objectives model still appears to have official favour), because variety may encourage reflection and intellectual growth. On the other hand, such optimism must be moderated by acknowledgement of the heavy weight of jargon, especially about technical modelling, that is endemic to the literature. A continual stress upon operations and **processes** tends to blunt interest in the quality and worth of particular programmes. The basic issue in curriculum design, as in most areas of educational thought, is conceptual rather than technical or scientific in nature: how to tease out what is important in various types of subject matter and incorporate it in school programmes in ways that are meaningful for students (***behavioural objectives, core curriculum, curriculum change, integrated studies, reconceptualists, skills**).

REFERENCES

Barnes (1982), Barrow (1986), Bruner (1960), Connelly, Dukacz and Quinlan (1980), Lawton (1983), Macdonald-Ross (1975), Nicholls and Nicholls (1972), Pope (1983), Pratt (1980), Robinson, Ross and White (1985), Schwab (1970), Sockett (1976), Stenhouse (1975b), Taba (1962), Taylor (1970), Taylor and Richards (1979), Tyler (1949), Zais (1976).

Curriculum development *see* Curriculum change

Curriculum evaluation *see* Assessment, Curriculum change, Evaluation

Curriculum implementation *see* Curriculum change

Curriculum integration *see* Integrated studies

Curriculum policy

The term 'curriculum policy' denotes the study of the political, economic, and social forces influencing the **curriculum**. Scholars in the past decade have examined such neglected issues as the social interests underlying the selection and organization of **knowledge**, the rise and fall of school subjects as a response to social change, and the relationship of historical and ethnographic methodologies in the study of schools. This focus on sociological questions has enlarged our conception of the nature and historical development of the curriculum. Despite the value of such work, an over-emphasis upon one kind of research (however justified in terms of previous neglect), or a narrow focus on one set of questions, may be misleading. The study of what is important in **education** in general, and curriculum in particular, should not be confined to questions related to those social forces that happen to be operating at any particular period in history.

REFERENCES

Boyd (1978), Goodson (1983a), Goodson and Ball (1984), Kirst and Walker (1971), Sarason and Doris (1979), Tomkins (1986).

D

Definition *see* Analysis, Ethics

Degree word

This phrase was coined to pick out that class of words which, while they clearly refer to an ideal state, are invariably applied in cases that fall short of the ideal (Barrow, 1980). Thus 'happiness', whatever its precise meaning, is a word that implies an ideal state to which nobody fully attains (at any rate in this life). Yet we apply it to certain people – namely, to those we regard as being happy to a considerable degree; hence, 'degree word'. '**Education**', is a degree word, as is '**creativity**'. On the other hand, '**indoctrination**' for example, is not: one either is indoctrinated or one is not. There can be no such thing as a degree **concept**. Concepts are by their nature ideal: the concept or idea of pen-ness, redness, love, etc., must by definition be of perfect or absolute pen-ness, redness, love, etc. One may have a concept of something imperfect, incomplete, flawed, etc., for example, a concept of evil or a concept of wreckage, but here too the concepts necessarily embody the idea of bona fide evil or bona fide wreckage. If one entertained an imperfect conception, as opposed to a conception of something imperfect, it would in fact be a conception of something other than what it purports to be, just as, analogously, a physical instance of a house that lacks certain key features ceases to be a house and becomes something else such as a shop, a ruin, or a heap of bricks (*analysis).

REFERENCE

Barrow (1980).

Deschooling

The term 'deschooling' was coined by Ivan Illich. To deschool society would be to disestablish the state system of **schooling**, or to remove formal **education** from society. The essence of the argument is not specific to schooling, but refers to a certain type of institutionalization.

93

Institutions (whether church, corporations, schools, etc.) are seen as either manipulative or convivial. Convivial institutions are those that are at the service of their users, and that make no demands on users when not in use, such as the postal system or the public parks system. Manipulative institutions are so-called because, by contrast, they manipulate us in various ways, directly and indirectly, even when we are not using them. Organized business, medicine, religion, and schooling reach out to influence and control us, and, instead of simply providing a service, they shape and mould us to suit their institutional interests.

In addition to the charge that schooling serves to foster the interests of particular economic groups, the claim is that the very existence of institutionalized frameworks necessarily leads to certain evils such as **indoctrination**, competitiveness, and respect for appearances and ritual, rather than for substance. Organized religion, for example, leads to concern for going to church rather than living a religious life. Organized medicine leads to definitions of sickness in terms of what doctors say and do with patients, rather than in any absolute sense – whether you are 'mentally disturbed' is less a question of your state of mind than the medical profession's attitude to that state of mind; and the profession's attitude is partially governed by the pressures of drug companies, the interests of the profession itself, etc. Car manufacturers do not simply try to provide us with good cars. They play upon our beliefs and attitudes in such a way as to make us want certain types of car, often for reasons that have nothing to do with the inherent quality of the vehicles. (It is not entirely clear whether the claim is that any institution might become manipulative, or whether, for example, the postal system is necessarily convivial and the church necessarily manipulative.)

In the particular case of schooling it is argued that the formal system is committed to such things as social role selection and a custodial responsibility that have an anti-educational effect. A compulsory system of schooling is seen as exercising a considerable degree of social control, to the detriment of education, while indoctrinating people with such contentious beliefs as that only the kinds of thing taught in school have any real value, that **knowledge** has to take the sequential and hierarchical form adopted in designing curricula, that what matters is to pass exams and be awarded diplomas and degrees, and that **competition** is desirable. The positive proposal of the deschoolers is that the formal system should be replaced with learning webs, or networks of personnel and resources, to which individuals may voluntarily turn as their **needs**, wants, and **interests** dictate. Such networks would consist essentially of directories of people's interests and of available resources, and de-schoolers show a marked enthusiasm for the potential of recent technological developments to store information and regurgitate it at a rapid rate. They envisage a grander and more ambitious version of the steps currently being taken by open universities and distance learning projects.

That schooling systems with which we are familiar do exhibit some of the features noted by deschoolers, and that some of those features are objectionable, seems beyond dispute. However, it is not clear that a system of schooling necessarily has to exhibit all such features, nor that all of them are objectionable. It may be conceded that schools inevitably preach the message that what schools teach is valuable; but one may reasonably counter that what they teach is indeed valuable (or that, if it is not, it could be), and that there is no necessary reason why they should suggest that what they teach is the *only* kind of valuable **learning**. (It is sometimes said that schools specifically teach that only school learning is 'true learning', but whatever this means, and it is not always clear what it means, it too seems a message that schools *could* overtly preach against.) Schools do not have to be organized on a competitive basis, and, in any case, some might want to argue that they should be. Few would want to defend the notion that a degree is the mark of the educated person, but, again, a system of schooling surely does not have to encourage such a delusion. Besides, what encourages us to identify the symbols with the substance is that we often need to make judgements about people without the benefit of getting to know them in any full sense. So long as that is so, there will be a system of labelling, with or without schools. A minor advantage of the labels that arise out of schooling, as compared with many others, is that we have some idea of what lies behind them: a degree in physics does at least suggest that one has studied physics to a level that some who know about physics believe worth noting.

One of the most useful **concepts** emphasized by deschoolers is that of the hidden curriculum, referring to that set of beliefs, assumptions, and attitudes taught by schools without being advertised in the curriculum. It is certainly important for schools to recognize that they do have a hidden curriculum, part at least of which they may be teaching without being aware of it. As against this, one of the weaknesses in the deschooling argument is its vague use of the word 'indoctrination'. In any specific sense of 'indoctrination', it is simply not true that schools necessarily indoctrinate. The only sense in which it would be necessarily true, would be a very general one that equates 'indoctrination' with 'influence'. Schools do indeed inevitably influence, but on the face of it that is one of the things they should do. Children (and adults) will necessarily be influenced by their environment. Consequently criticism will have to concentrate not on the fact that schools influence, but on objections to particular forms of influence or particular influences. This takes us back to the question raised above: is it clear that there are objectionable influences that schools necessarily exert?

Part of the importance of questioning the deschoolers' emphasis on schooling being a necessarily manipulative institution is that it may affect our response to their alternative proposal. If a system of schooling does indeed necessarily embody various evils, one would turn more readily to deschooling as a solution than one might if one believed that the evils of schooling are in principle eradicable.

It may also be argued that the network of learning systems proposed has its own problems. It is not free of some of the faults attributed to a schooling system. (For example, the personnel and resources to which I am directed to pursue my interest in chemistry or fly-fishing may prove no less influential than the formal classroom, and may effectively preach many of the same messages.) It seems likely that it would contribute to, rather than minimize, the divisive social system generally deplored by the deschoolers. It is a **contingent** matter, but it none the less seems likely that the children of supportive and educated parents will make rather more use of the network than others, thus perpetuating and strengthening the division between the well and the badly educated.

The deschoolers have performed a useful service in pinpointing various deficiencies in the schooling system. But, since they have not established their cardinal point that these are necessary evils, specific to a formal system, they are vulnerable to the powerful counter-argument that an organized system of schooling is the most rational way to seek to combat the evils they note. A formal system of schooling at least allows us to mount an organized attack on the unreflective acceptance of the various beliefs and assumptions that they fear (*class).

REFERENCES

Barrow (1978), Illich (1971), Lister (1971), Reimer (1971).

Developmental theory

Although developmental theory is an established part of psychological **research**, we may still wish to consider the precise nature of such research, how trustworthy it is, and how useful it is for the teaching profession. In principle it is concerned with locating and describing the various stages of **natural** or maturational development through which individuals pass. One might, by contrast, seek to produce an **educational** theory of development, which, in taking account of what we might bring about through **teaching** and in making explicit **value judgements** about what we wish to bring about, would be concerned to prescribe stages through which we should seek to develop children. But psychological developmental theories are theoretically concerned to locate stages of cognitive, moral, or emotional growth without reference to educational or other environmental influences; and they seek to be descriptive rather than **prescriptive**. They seek to describe features of development that human beings must necessarily experience *qua* human beings.

The nature of its concerns inevitably makes research into psychological development difficult, since it is impossible to study children who are not to some extent affected by their environment and, as they grow older, education. Hence emphasis is placed upon wide-scale observation of children from various cultural backgrounds, in the hope that what is observed in all manner of conditions may indeed be part of a maturational process rather than the product of environment. In addition, items used to test stages of development are designed to be culture-free (*culture).

Particular developmental theories (such as those associated with, for example, Piaget, Kohlberg, Erikson, and Isaacs) will consist of the following elements: the location of what are thought to be significant stages, in that they can be clearly distinguished from what precedes and what follows; labels for the stages; and an attempt to associate the stages with chronological age. The initial location of stages may arise out of observation or hypothesis, but clearly a view about the reasonableness of noting a particular state has to be based on observation. Whether, for example, it is plausible to maintain that all children go through a stage at which they are essentially capable of logical operations only in relation to concrete things (Piaget's 'concrete operational stage'), or through one at which they are conspicuously concerned with a search for identity (Erikson's 'adolescent stage'), can only be determined by studying large numbers of children, and verifying both that they all do go through such stages and also that the descriptions of the stages pick out features that are in some way dominant. Erikson's stage of adolescence would clearly lose its force, if a search for identity was everpresent in human beings, or if there was no identifiable stage when it became notable as the central concern of individuals.

Different developmental theories do not necessarily compete with one another. There are more ways than one to slice a cake, and there is no reason in principle why, for example, Piaget, Isaacs, and Erikson should not be equally correct. This might be because different theorists have different interests (e.g. Erikson is interested in aspects of personal maturity, Piaget in cognitive ability); but it might also be because, although interested in the same type of thing (e.g. cognitive ability), one theorist looks for larger or longer lasting stages than another. Similarly, if one were concerned with stages of physical growth, one might be interested in mapping out the broad stages of pre-puberty, puberty, and maturity, or in providing a more detailed breakdown of observable distinctions within the stage of puberty. Judgement therefore is involved from the outset in creating a developmental theory: the researcher chooses to emphasize certain moments in individual development as worth focusing on and describing. In the physical development example it is a fact that at some point the individual goes through puberty, and that within that period genital hair appears. Whether it is particularly worthwhile to draw attention to either of these moments, by locating them as stages and labelling them, is a matter of judgement.

The value of locating a stage is dependent on its subsequent description. Simply to refer to puberty is not very helpful; but to give a detailed account of what is involved in puberty may be. In general, the fuller the description the better. More particularly, a description will be illuminating in proportion to the extent that it describes what is not immediately obvious. Piaget's sensorimotor stage, which begins at birth, describes the child's emerging ability to see himself as different from the objects that surround him, and to regard an object as constant despite changes in its location (amongst other things). These being readily apparent features of early childhood, the stage is less interesting than his description of the later stage of formal operations. The most useful kind of description would be one that drew our attention to a number of features that necessarily occur together, some of them being apparent and some not. A developmental theory that contained such descriptions would enable us to infer abilities or features of particular children's states of mind from observation of other readily apparent features.

A major problem in estimating the coherence and value of developmental theories is that they are clearly not straightforwardly empirical. (In many cases this is explicitly acknowledged. For example, Piaget asserts that his work is partly epistemological.) Claims about the invariant order of stages are to a degree a matter of logical necessity (*contingent, logical order). (For example, Piaget's description of the stage of formal operations incorporates elements that would necessarily have to have been acquired or developed before one could function at that stage.) The implications of this become fully apparent when one also appreciates how tentative the strictly **empirical** claims in a developmental theory are: (a) the description of a given stage seldom, if ever, consists in a set of **necessary** and sufficient conditions for that stage; (b) the association of stages with chronological age is admitted to be rough and ready; and (c) even within that flexibility, the stage/age matchings are acknowledged to be mere generalizations.

For example:

(a) Kohlberg's description of the fifth stage of moral development, in terms of a sense of fairness and legality overlaying a simple sense of duty, and an increasingly critical attitude to rules, does not purport to provide us with criteria whereby we could firmly pigeon-hole every individual as being within or without the stage.

(b) The claim that the stage is entered at the age of twelve is only a rough approximation; even if one could pinpoint a moment when an individual has just entered a stage, which of course one cannot, the researchers are not claiming that *anyone* necessarily enters on this stage at the age of twelve. They are saying that somewhere around the age of twelve, give or take a year or two, one would expect an individual to start showing signs of being in stage five.

(c) In the case of, for example, Piagetian theory, it is widely accepted that this type of rough approximation itself only applies in the case of three out of four children.

The research that lies behind developmental theory has in a number of instances been severely criticized. It has been suggested, for example, that children can handle abstract **concepts** well before Piaget's studies suggest, particularly if they are explained pictorially or with considerable deliberateness. Such a debate serves to remind us that investigating this empirical question is crucially a matter of conceptualization and judgement as to the significance of observable behaviours. (That is, the major difficulty does not lie in such problems of empirical research as ensuring a random sample or producing a **valid** and **reliable** instrument, but in articulating an adequate conception of abstract concepts, in handling them, and in determining trustworthy and observable indices of them.) Again, it has been argued that Piaget did not establish that various children lacked the principle of conservation; for it might equally well be that what the children lacked was the ability to understand the question they were being asked, as formulated.

The above remarks may be put into perspective by brief comparison with a more general type of developmental theory. Bruner believes that there are three stages of growth in the way the child comes to represent his world: the enactive stage, in which we learn by doing things, the iconic stage, in which we learn through images, and the symbolic stage, in which we learn through **language**. Since Bruner allows that adults code experiences by all three means, and that in some cases the enactive or iconic processes may dominate, and since he has little to say about chronological age, this theory tells us more about the non-empirical question of what types of learning there may be, than it does about the empirical question of natural development. The only truly developmental point (that children initially operate with enactive response to the world) has only slight interest for educators, since by the time they reach school children can clearly operate to some extent in all three modes.

Developmental theory therefore seems to offer little that should be allowed to guide or constrain our activity as teachers. From the fact, if it is a **fact**, that three out of four children have been judged to exhibit the features of a given stage to some noteworthy degree between the ages of X–1 and X+1, what should I deduce? Certainly nothing about what I ought to aim to achieve, nor about what I might be able to achieve, if I set my mind to it. The only element in such **theories** which is sufficiently specific and securely established to have clear implications for practice is the logically necessary element that demands that some capabilities be developed before others. Knowledge of developmental theory may be of some value to teachers, if treated as a checklist of features that individuals may possibly exhibit at various ages. But it is evident that what a teacher actually needs to do is make specific judgements about the present capabilities of particular children. That cannot be done by knowledge of developmental theory alone, and it could be done without any knowledge of developmental theory (*emotions, ethics, moral education*).

REFERENCES

Baldwin (1967), Barnett (1966), Barrow (1984), Bruner (1966), Egan (1979, 1983), Erikson (1963), Fontana (1981), Isaacs (1966), Kohlberg (1969, 1970), Peters (1974), Piaget (1930, 1947, 1959).

Diagrams *see* Curriculum design

Dilemma

Unlike the word 'problem', which implies nothing as to the tractability, solubility or otherwise of a given problem, 'dilemma' means a problematic situation (or argument) that allows one only a choice between equally unpleasant, awkward, difficult, etc., alternatives. We are accustomed to thinking of **education** as an area in which there are many problems. But perhaps some of those 'problems' are in reality dilemmas. It is worth noting that 'dilemma' is often the favoured term in moral developmental programmes, notwithstanding the fact that students are sometimes encouraged to treat the matters as problems (*values clarification*).

Discipline

The three main senses of discipline are: (a) a branch of learning or knowledge (e.g. the discipline of mathematics); (b) a system of rules; and (c) corrective or regulative treatment, punishment. Precisely what constitutes a discipline, as distinct from a subject, form of knowledge, field of knowledge, etc., is open to debate, but the word is generally reserved for a subject that is well established and has a recognizable methodology associated with it. For example, science, mathematics, and philosophy are disciplines. French, social studies, and drama are not. Whether, for example, **history** and English should be classified as disciplines or not is a moot point (*knowledge).

It has been argued that discipline in the second sense is a **necessary** feature of any institution such as a school (Wilson, 1979). The fact that schools are specific kinds of institution, designed for some particular purposes, logically implies certain things that come to constitute rules. (For example, schools seek to educate, **education** implies learning, **learning** can only take place in certain conditions, rules define and create the conditions.) One way of categorizing behaviour that may threaten to break such rules (and perhaps require discipline in the third sense) is in terms of: (a) physical aggression; (b) peer affinity (e.g. moving around without permission); (c) attention seeking; (d) challenge of authority; and (e) critical dissension (Kooi and Schutz, 1965). (Most behaviours could fit into several of these categories; e.g. wandering around could be an instance of peer affinity, attention seeking, or challenging authority.) Empirical researchers claim that ignoring disruptive behaviour is one of the most successful ways of containing and discouraging it (O'Leary and O'Leary, 1977), provided that withholding teacher attention is maintained consistently on a number of occasions, and is not offset by peer group encouragement. (One might therefore feel inclined to try other measures!) An even more dramatic suggestion is that one should remove the disruption by eliminating the occasion of the interruption; e.g. 'if fighting occurs primarily during certain games, eliminate those games' (Gage and Berliner, 1979).

Research findings relating to the effectiveness of discipline in the sense of punishment have been contradictory. For example, Sears, Maccoby and Levin (1957) claimed that punishment was ineffective in suppressing undesirable behaviours in children. However, Azrin and Holz (1966) claim that, provided it is administered in appropriate conditions and strongly, punishment definitely reduces such behaviour. (**Empirical research** into such an issue is always up against the problem that failure to suppress disruption may be due to the fact that the punishment was too weak, timed wrongly, satisfied the student's need for attention, etc., rather than to the inefficacy of punishment *per se*; and there is no obvious independent gauge of how much punishment is appropriate, etc., in particular situations.) Equally important questions here are whether it is morally acceptable to punish, and, if so, when and in what way (Acton, 1969; Peters, 1966) (*ethics, moral education).

REFERENCES

Acton (1969), Azrin and Holz (1966), Gage and Berliner (1979), Kooi and Schutz (1965), Kounin (1970), Marshall (1984), O'Leary and O'Leary (1977), Peters (1966), Sears, Maccoby and Levin (1957), Wilson (1979).

Discovery learning *see* Learning

Discrimination

Two senses of 'discrimination' are to be distinguished. The first, perhaps most common, use indicates differential treatment; the second, and older, meaning refers to the drawing of theoretical distinctions. I discriminate between John and Henry, in the sense of differentiate, when I give them different amounts of food. I discriminate, in the sense of note logical distinctions, between socialization and indoctrination. (There is also a transitive use of discriminate in the second sense: e.g. white hair discriminates this group from that, or is the discriminatory factor.)

In the former sense, the word usually has pejorative overtones and strongly suggests (although it does not mean) that the differential treatment in question is unjustified and involves partiality. Hence phrases such as 'racial discrimination' and 'sexual discrimination' have come to be identified with unfair differential treatment (*feminism, stereotyping).

However, discrimination in the latter sense is a most necessary and valuable activity. To develop people's powers of discrimination or teach them to discriminate is part of the school's function, and part of what is meant by **educating** people. **Understanding** in any sphere may be partially characterized as coming to acquire a discriminatory sense in that field, such that one can recognize fine distinctions, rather than remain on the level of broad conceptions that lump similar but disparate things together. Teaching people to discriminate is partly a question of encouraging clear and correct use of **language**; it also involves encouraging people to understand and adopt relatively specific **concepts**. For, although there is nothing wrong with referring to both cats and dogs as 'animals', our knowledge of the world is clearly increased when we are aware of their differences as well as their similarities.

Failure to discriminate may lead to sloppiness and crudeness in thought, and to injustice and inefficiency in action. In the context of education the ability to discriminate between, for example, influence, **indoctrination** and **socialization, educating** and **training, systematic** and **objective**, is a necessary feature of sound **theory** (*__positive discrimination__).

REFERENCE

Barrow (1982a).

Disruptive behaviour *see* Discipline

Divergent thinking *see* Lateral thinking

E

Ecological education *see* Topic-centred education

Educanto

If you are a graduate in educanto, 'You will know that dynamically reinforced growth of your ideational and cross-fertilized learnings has occurred, hopefully through intravariable autorivalry, enriched need arousal, purposeful goal-oriented behaviour, and persistent achievement motivations. Your self-actualization, together with your real-life readiness for situational and retractive testing against Yoakam's Readability Formula will be concretioned . . .', etc. The term 'educanto' was coined by James D. Koerner in *The Miseducation of American Teachers*. As he says, besides masking 'a lack of thought [that] in fact makes thought of any kind difficult', educanto can 'reduce any mildly sensitive layman to a state of helpless fury in a matter of minutes'. Why is it that so many educators are so badly educated? Why, in particular, are they incapable of writing plain English?

REFERENCES
Koerner (1963), Newman (1975).

Education

The central question to be addressed here is the **conceptual** one: 'what is it to be educated?' Without an adequate answer to this question we are in no position to assess whether, in this respect, our schools are doing a good job. Equally, without a clear conception of what it is to be educated, empirical research into the educational effectiveness of programmes or **teaching** strategies cannot begin. Furthermore, unless researchers clearly articulate their conceptions publicly, they place their conclusions beyond the judgement of others (*****empirical, research, teacher effectiveness**).

Education does not have to take place in schools and does not necessarily require teachers. There is nothing incoherent or odd about the idea of self-education. In one sense it is a truism that all education is self-education, inasmuch as nothing in the way of education can be achieved unless the person who is being educated makes what is presented to him his own. But, beyond that, it is possible to distinguish between those who are self-educated in the sense of having gained their education through their own efforts, without the guidance and instruction of teachers, and those who receive their education through formal schooling or through voluntary attendance at classes sponsored by various agencies. Most people today are educated through the school system and, despite the criticisms of **deschoolers**, there seems nothing inherently objectionable in this.

Education is not the name of a particular activity or process. It is a name applied generically to a number of different activities and processes. It is in this respect like the general term 'gardening' rather than the more specific 'planting beans'. Therefore, to be fully understood, the concept has to be characterized by reference to its purpose. In the same way, while a purely procedural or methodological account could be given of planting beans (e.g. place them at certain fixed intervals), gardening has to be explained in terms of the objective of cultivating a lot of land and achieving certain kinds of end result.

'Education' is a word that has to be defined in terms of the intentions, rather than the results, of would-be educators. It resembles a word such as 'hunting', in that it describes the task one is engaged in without reference to success or failure, rather than a word such as 'finding' which describes one's **achievement**. Teachers may reasonably claim to be educating, even if some of their pupils do not end up particularly well educated, provided that what they do is in general appropriate to the development of educated people. The failure of students to become well educated suggests, rather than establishes, that their teachers are poor educators, since a number of other factors such as individual problems, home and other social conditions, and a breakdown in **communication** between particular individuals, may account for the failure. In just the same way hunters cannot be dismissed as poor hunters, simply because they fail to find anything. (Although, after a while, one may begin to wonder.) 'Education' is a **normative** term and a **degree** word: it implies that something of value is going on, and it is a word that we use without qualification of people who are in fact merely more or less well educated.

To educate, then, is to be involved in one or more of a number of possible activities designed to contribute to the emergence of the **worthwhile** state of being to a marked degree educated. The crucial question becomes 'What is to count as being educated?' Is it a matter of acquiring a style of dress, a code of manners, a set of beliefs, or some combination of these? Is it to be identified with specialist expertise? Should we widen the concept to include distinction in any field of school endeavour? Do standardized tests of achievement accurately gauge the level of education individuals have attained (*assessment)?

To all of these questions the answer is probably no, although some of the qualities referred to may bear some indirect relationship to being educated. (For example, it might be the case that academic distinction or good performance in IQ tests correlates with being well educated. As to whether either is in fact so, we cannot say, since the question has never been investigated.)

Although other conceptions are certainly possible, a widespread view is that education is essentially a matter of breadth of understanding. It is thus a cognitive matter. This emphasis may initially worry those who feel that schools are over-concerned with the intellect, or those who wish to stress the importance of, for example, emotional and aesthetic development. However, although education is a normative term, it is not the only honorific label to hand, and there is no need for us to insist that all the various functions of schooling that we value should be seen as part of education. There are, besides, two good reasons for accepting this relatively specific conception of education:

1. There is the largely practical consideration that the more specific the concept the more useful it becomes to us in our thinking. If 'education' is treated as a broad term, akin to, for example, 'upbringing', then we are merely reduplicating our vocabulary, and we still need new terms to focus on various different types or aspects of education/ upbringing, about which we may want to say different things.
2. It does seem rather strange to use the word 'education' in connection with such things as physical fitness or moral worth. There seems nothing logically odd about saying 'Although he is a cripple, he is very well educated', and this suggests that education has nothing inherently to do with physical well-being. In the same way moral weakness or turpitude, aesthetic insensitivity and idiosyncracy of character, though they may indicate a failure on the school's part to serve all its functions, clearly do not necessarily indicate a lack of education. One may be a well-educated crook. (It is important not to confuse the claim that one can be educated and immoral with the claim that one cannot be morally educated.)

The major questions now become: what kind of breadth of understanding is required of an educated person, and is education of any great value?

Use of the word 'understanding', as opposed to 'knowledge', implies that what is at issue is something more than mere information and the ability to relay or act in accordance with formulae, prescriptions, and instructions. (The latter is characteristic of **training** rather than education.) An ability to recite dates, answer general knowledge quizzes, or reproduce even quite complex pieces of reasoning, is not necessary to being educated. Rather, one requires of an educated person that he should have internalized information, explanation, and reasoning, and made sense of it. He should understand the principles behind the specifics that he encounters; he sets particulars in a wider frame of **theoretical** understanding. But would one regard an individual with great understanding of physics, but nothing else, as educated? Surely not. Being educated is a question not only of understanding, but also of breadth of understanding. The educated peson has understanding across a range of human knowledge.

Any more specific account of what the breadth of understanding should incorporate must depend partly on the nature of **knowledge** or what different types of thing there are to be known. But it is a feature of the educated mind that it should avoid errors of understanding and conception (rather than that it should necessarily have familiarity with a wide range of human interests and endeavour). Thus, one would expect it to be capable of recognizing whatever logically distinct types of domain there may be, such as the scientific and the religious. The educated person, as was said above, is not necessarily a moral being or aesthetically sensitive, but he is, by definition, capable of distinguishing a moral question or an aesthetic question from a religious, political, or scientific question.

Other characteristics of being educated that have been proposed include realization of self, growth of the whole person, cultivation and development of one's own **interests**, and the development of a sense of individuality and historical perspective. Each of these suggestions, however, clearly requires considerable **analysis** before one could estimate its worth, and none of them seems likely to oust the contention that the essence of the concept is having understanding of the major categories of thought recognized and refined by man. (Some might explicitly label this a liberal concept of education.)

The value of education, thus defined, can hardly be doubted by those who believe in values such as truth, rationality, and **autonomy**; for education in this sense is both predicated on such values and contributes to them as **aims**. It is, for example, because we value truth and rationality that we want people to be educated rather than **indoctrinated** or merely trained; and educated people will be in a position to act autonomously and pursue the goals of truth and rationality better than uneducated people.

Of more practical concern may be to note that, if this is what education is, it will require some kinds of **curriculum** provision rather than others, and will only be appropriately judged by certain specific kinds of performance towards the end of the process. Reflection on this conception must also lead us to wonder whether much of what passes for education in our schools really is so. Certainly the kinds of ability we seek to test with standardized achievement tests, and the kinds of qualification often sought by industry, would seem to have little to do with education. To this a superficial reply might be that the economy cannot afford the luxury of education, when it needs skilled manpower. How shortsighted such a view may be is not something that can be quantified. But it seems fairly safe to say that in the long run it is educated minds that maintain or fail to maintain a civilization (***art education, etymology, culture, liberal education, nationalism**).

REFERENCES

Frankena (1973), McClellan (1976), Peters (1966, 1967), Peters, Woods and Dray (1973), Scheffler (1973).

Educational theory

'A deplorable subject, taught badly at all schools and colleges of education because there is nothing to teach' (Volkart, 1986). A fairly widespread view. Not to be confused with the truth of the matter, which is that, while there is of course something to be taught, the subject is indeed deplorable because so much of it is very bad. Established **disciplines** have a central body of uncontested, well-wrought **theory** to draw on (almost by definition). **Education**, primarily because it is not a unified discipline, but an amalgam of different disciplines, points of view, **aims**, and practical experience, gives rise to a theoretical corpus that is in part contradictory, in part irrelevant, in part poorly articulated, in part not **empirically** validated, and in part absurd. But in principle educational theory could be as sound as medical theory or baseball theory (***philosophy of education, relevance, research, validity**).

REFERENCES

Dearden (1984), Furlong (1989), Hirst (1983), Volkart (1986).

Educational value/worth *see* Education, Value judgements, Worthwhile

Effective learning *see* Learning

Effective teaching *see* Education, Research, Teacher effectiveness

Effective schools *see* Education, Research, Teacher effectiveness

Elites

A distinction should be drawn between the term 'élitist' which has acquired a purely pejorative connation and means 'one who favours giving power or other advantages to a privileged group that is not deserving of it', and the term 'élite'. The latter simply means the chosen, choice, or best part of a group. Thus, the élite of the academic world are the best scholars, the élite of the soccer world are the best players, and the élite of the washing machine world are the best washing-machine makers. Elites, as T. S. Eliot (1948) in particular argued, are crucial to the well-being and development of a society. If we do not aim to develop élites we cease to concern ourselves about the quality of our life in all its aspects.

The trick is to avoid treating a group that is an élite in some specific respect, as if it were superior in other respects and deserving of greater advantages in general. (It should also be noted that endorsement of the idea of developing élites in this sense is to be distinguished from various theories about élites such as those propounded by Mosca, 1939, Michels 1949 and Miliband, 1977).

REFERENCES

Eliot (1948), Michels (1949), Miliband (1977), Mosca (1939).

Emotions

Emotional development is one of the proper concerns of **schooling**. But a number of different things may be meant by the phrase. One might refer to developing the individual's capacity to experience various emotions, or to developing the power to experience them deeply. One might have in mind the goal of **teaching** people to control their emotions, either in the sense of suppressing some of them (e.g. jealousy, envy), or in the sense of curbing the expression of them. One might, by contrast, be concerned to enable people to recognize emotions in themselves or others. Or one might be aiming at some kind of emotional equilibrium. It is by no means obvious that all of these possible objectives are the proper concern of **education** or even schooling, nor that they are indeed matters of **development**, either in the sense of maturation or in the sense of being deliberately developed by an outside agency.

Emotions cannot simply be equated with feelings, for they involve more than mere sensation. A feeling, such as pain, may be experienced without the agent setting it in any kind of cognitive framework: one may just experience the feeling or sensation of pain. But an emotion, although it involves a feeling, is by definition a feeling that is associated with some specific appraisal of the situation in which one finds oneself. It is necessarily connected by the agent with some cause or explanation. Thus, to experience jealousy is to entertain some feeling or sensation that one associates with some such circumstances as losing one's loved one to another; it is to recognize something such as a betrayal or act of faithlessness as the reason for the feeling. One cannot meaningfully claim that one just woke up with a feeling of jealousy in the middle of the night. Indeed, the feeling element itself is the aspect of an emotion least worth dwelling on, since we have no way of knowing whether the nature of our various sensations are similar. What we do know is that to experience some broadly unpleasant feelings in response to some such set of circumstances is what is meant by being jealous.

It follows that a person may correctly be said to be experiencing jealousy, even if he has no actual grounds for being in that state: the question of whether one is experiencing an emotion is answered by how one sees one's situation rather than by what it truly is. Many who have cause to be jealous, are not; many who do not have cause to be, are. But always the experience of jealousy logically depends upon a feeling being associated with a particular kind of appraisal or view of one's situation. It also follows that no easy divorce between intellect and emotion can be made. There is an intellectual or cognitive element at the heart of the experience of an emotion, and, in practice, consideration of whether or what emotional experiences people are undergoing is a matter of trying to establish how they see their circumstances. (Conversely there is an emotional factor in cognitive development. The developed mind is not simply one that has the requisite breadth of **understanding**; it is also one that is committed to such values as truth, coherence, and rationality. And commitment is a species of emotion: a positive feeling concomitant on adherence to some value.)

Emotional adjustment is no doubt one thing that we would like people to have: we hope that people will not become suicidally depressed, or give way to violent outbursts of temper; we hope that they will be able to cope with bereavement and other kinds of setback. In extreme cases psychological or counselling expertise may be needed to help people find adjustment. But it is likely that in most cases people may achieve some degree of emotional equilibrium through **socialization** and education. The socialization process directly and indirectly discourages us from taking some things too seriously and from exhibiting extreme emotional responses in certain situations, while encouraging them in others. At the same time we learn about emotions both directly through our experience and vicariously through drama, **literature** and the arts.

We may experience emotions in any setting, for example, playing football, or doing science, and one may witness the outward expression of emotion by others in any setting. One may also attempt to study the causes and effects of various emotional states in psychology. But the way in which we most obviously enlarge our understanding of emotional states themselves is by thinking about the subtle range of responses that various particular circumstances may bring about; this is a form of thinking most obviously encouraged in various branches of literature, particularly fiction and history. The other arts, for example, music, sculpture, architecture, serve to evoke feelings in us that may, depending upon circumstance, deserve to be categorized as emotional responses, while performing arts such as drama, allow us to practise thinking ourselves into unfamiliar situations.

It is sometimes assumed that **creativity** is closely associated with emotional maturity. However, although poetry, for example, may on occasion be the quintessence of emotional experience, it would be rash to assume either that young children's creative work has necessarily much to do with the experience or expression of emotion, or that one necessarily learns much about emotion from the work of mature poets. Poetry enhances emotional response only in so far as it increases one's capacity for appraising new situations in a way that calls forth some feeling.

It should be clear that one's capacity to experience emotion is not entirely, and possibly not very importantly, a matter of **natural** development, while one's ability to control one's expression of emotion would seem to be of little concern to the school, except as an aspect of socialization. Where the school can play a part is in helping the individual to put some coherent patterns on what would otherwise be a random, and probably somewhat impoverished, set of feelings (**communication, intelligence*).

REFERENCES

Barrow (1981c), Bedford (1964), Dunlop (1984), Hepburn (1972), Peters (1974).

Emotive meaning

The emotive meaning of a word is the effect it may have on the emotions of an audience. (Some would restrict the use of the phrase to cover only those cases in which the speaker himself has, and intends to convey, a particular attitude of approval or disapproval to the matter in question.) There is a school of thought that regards all **ethical** utterances as essentially only emotive – for example 'honesty is good' is seen as conveying no more meaning than the intimation that the speaker favours honesty. Most philosophers, however, would argue that emotive meaning is at best only one aspect of moral utterances. A large number of key educational words are, or may be, rich in emotive meaning, for example, **indoctrination, socialization, brainstorming, creativity, culture, child-centred eduation,** and **stereotyping** (*normative).

Empathy *see* Communication

Empirical

'Empirical' means 'relying or based solely upon experiment and observation', or, more colloquially, 'confirmed by one or more of the five senses'. Those things that we have seen, touched, etc., are empirically established, and are to be contrasted with truths of logic and definition. Educational researchers have been anxious to establish as much as they can about their field empirically. Sometimes, perhaps, in their haste and eagerness, insufficient attention has been paid to the points: (a) that the fact that something is an empirical issue does not necessarily mean that it can be empirically established (e.g. whether or not **teaching** children mathematics is useful to them in later life is an empirical question, but not one that would easily lend itself to empirical research); and (b) that empirical research can only be as good as the **conceptual** and logical base on which it is grounded (e.g. one could not in any case research the above question until one had a clear idea of what counts as 'teaching mathematics', 'useful', etc., and a logically coherent way of reasoning to a cause and effect conclusion from the data one empirically gathered) (*analysis, facts, knowledge, research).

Empirical research *see* Facts, Objectivity, Reliability, Research, Transference, Validity

Empowerment

As with the verb 'to enjoy', there is nothing wrong with the word 'empowerment' but something to be desired about its current usage. 'To empower' meaning 'to invest formally with power' is first recorded in 1654. But in its original usage it meant either 'to authorize' or 'to enable someone to do something'. What is striking about contemporary usage is that, in common with 'enjoy', it is used without any reference to what a person is empowered to do (or what they are to enjoy). (E.g. **critical theorists** argue that the purpose of **education** is 'to empower' students.) Its meaning is thus vague, and the speaker is empowered to take a holiday from thinking. 'I empowered her to sign the deed' (meaning I gave her legal authority to do so), and 'I empowered her to give up smoking' (meaning I gave her the support and hence the strength or power to do so) both make sense. 'I see my job as empowering', 'I empower the kids', 'empowerment should be our objective', could mean anything from 'making someone good at anything' to 'making them feel good'. If empowerment is your bag, it helps to know whom you wish to empower in what respects.

Ends *see* Aims, Needs

Environment *see* Curriculum, Deschooling, Developmental theory, Feminism, Nature/nurture, Operant conditioning

Epistemology *see* Knowledge

Equality

Equality, freedom, and happiness are the most commonly lauded values in the Western tradition. There are three common ways of interpreting the principle of equality: as the view that all people should end up with the same amount of material benefit; as the view that all people should be treated in the same way; and as the view that everyone should have the same opportunity.

The first position, though it is sometimes associated with socialism, is not widely canvassed: it seems too apparent that we cannot successfully devise a mechanism for ensuring it, except by barbarous intrusions on people's freedom and happiness; furthermore, many question the implication that matters such as desert, hard work, talent, and **training** are irrelevant to the issue.

The second view was convincingly rebutted, as stated, by Plato's observation that no sane person would insist on giving a baby and a prize wrestler equal portions of a large steak. The resulting modification to the view, endorsed by Aristotle, that no distinction ought to be made between people who are equal in all respects **relevant** to the kind of treatment in question, is generally accepted. It is, however, only a **formal** principle. Everything hinges on what one judges to be relevant respects: the racist will maintain that a certain racial characteristic is relevant to differential treatment; his opponent will deny it. (However, all is not lost: there are some arguments and some **facts** that establish that certain particular claims to relevance are false, absurd, or misconceived. E.g. Hitler was just mistaken in his empirical claim that all the great works of art have been produced by Aryans, and his **concept** of an Aryan was in various ways inadequate.)

Equality of opportunity is widely valued in Western democracies, because it is compatible with a large degree of freedom. We should provide everyone with a similar opportunity, runs the argument, regardless of weight, size, family, gender, lovableness, race, or anything else – but then it is up to the individual to make what he or she can of it. But this is problematic too, as the widespread acceptance of, e.g. certain aspects of the welfare state indicates. At what point should the 'opportunity' that is being provided begin and end? Opportunity for or to do what? Anything? Presumably not, but, if not, by what criteria do we decide? Should this apply to both limited and unlimited goods? For example, are we to have an equal opportunity to compete for scarce goods, so that one person's gain is another's loss, (e.g. money), or for unlimited goods such as, e.g. happiness, or both? Do we, in any case, really believe that the down and out should get nothing, since they have had their opportunity? And did they in fact? What about the consideration that people may be victims of genetic or socially determined disadvantage?

Education is an unlimited good in one sense: in becoming better educated, I do not diminish a fixed stock of education so that there is less left for others. On the other hand, in the world as it is, we do not have the resources to make equal educational provision for all. The North

American educational system and the politically dictated transition from the tripartite to the comprehensive system in most of England and Wales in the 1960s and 1970s are based on the principle that, broadly speaking, all students should receive the same education. But this premiss has often been challenged, whether soberly (e.g. Bantock, 1965, 1968) or stridently (e.g. Cox and Dyson, 1971), particularly by those who would prefer to adopt a principle of equality of opportunity. The view that all students should receive the same education depends partly upon the questionable view that they are in all educational respects equal – i.e. either that there are no differences (such as intellectual ones) or that, if there are, they are irrelevant.

The real difficulty has been the entwining of social and educational issues: some of the reasoning behind differential schooling was both questionable and (to many) objectionable. For example, behind the British tripartite system there was an implication that some were born to be labourers, could not conceivably become other than labourers, and should therefore be schooled as labourers. Conclusions were also drawn about the relative worth of different types of schooling. But if the social factors are divorced from educational considerations, as some maintain they can be, both in **theory** and practice, it is far from clear that the idea of different curricula for different types of student is morally offensive. Possibly a more telling argument for similarity of educational provision is provided by the view that education necessarily involves certain types of study and activity, and that therefore all students should experience at least a variant of a **core/common curriculum**.

REFERENCES

Bantock (1965, 1968), Cox and Dyson (1971).

Essay *see* Assessment, Measurement, Objectivity, Reliability

Essentially contested concepts

The phrase 'essentially contested concept' was coined by W. B. Gallie. People may argue about the meaning of any **concept**, but in many cases serious disagreement will be limited by constraints of logic or nature. For example, one is not at liberty to argue for square circles or married bachelors, because such conceptions would be contradictions in terms. And, while selective breeding might produce new creatures that are hard to classify, at any given moment what one is at liberty to say about the concept of, say, cow is severely restricted by the features that cows actually possess.

However, concepts such as beauty, justice, and democracy are not clearly restricted either by logical or **empirical** considerations. They are essentially contested, inasmuch as their very nature makes it impossible to rule out any conception as logically or empirically absurd. (The most one might do is point out that some conceptions of, for example, democracy are at odds with most people's use of the word.)

Education itself should probably be classified as an essentially contested concept. If someone were to define education in the way that others define **indoctrination**, the only objection we could make would be that a verbal mistake is being made. We could not establish that it is logically incoherent in the way that square circles are, or that it is empirically at fault in the way that defining cows as udderless would be.

However, the fact that a concept is essentially contested does not mean that one can say anything one likes about it: to be acceptable, the **analysis** of the concept still has to meet criteria of clarity, coherence and fullness.

REFERENCES

Barrow (1983, 1985b), Gallie (1955).

Ethics

Ethics is important for **education** in two main respects. First, **schooling** gives rise to a number of ethical issues (e.g. Is punishment morally acceptable? What rights do students, parents, etc., have? What is the morality of compulsion? Are there immoral ways of **teaching**?). Secondly, schooling seeks to provide **moral education**.

It is not possible to review here all the moral theories to be encountered in the history of ethics, but an attempt will be made to map out features of the moral domain as it is broadly conceived today. Ethics is concerned with the good and the right. There is argument about the precise relationship between the two, but goodness is normally attributed to persons or states of affairs, while rightness is a property of actions. Thus, an act may be described as right because it produces a state of affairs that is regarded as good. One distinction that may be noted is that between teleological theories, that see rightness in terms of goals or consequences being attained, and deontological theories, that see rightness as a property of certain actions regardless of consequences.

(One might seek to accommodate the two by seeing each one as concerned with a different sphere: teleological theories concern themselves with whether behaviour is morally productive; deontological theories concern themselves with whether the individual is a moral agent.)

An initial problem is that the central term 'good' is widely thought to be indefinable. Many **concepts** are defined by being broken down into the constituent parts (e.g. a horse is an animal with strong hoofs, flowing mane and tail, etc.). But certain terms cannot be defined in this way; for example, 'yellow'. One may offer an explanation of the conditions that produce yellowness, but the only way to get somebody to understand what it is, is to show it to them. If it is agreed that goodness is a simple concept (i.e. non-complex) that cannot be explained by being broken down, but can only be seen (intuitively recognized?) by those who have a correctly attuned moral sense, then it is clear that we cannot acquire moral understanding by way of **analysing** that term.

However, some agreement about the nature of the moral sphere may be reached. Moral language is generally thought to be partly **prescriptive**, partly **emotive**, and essentially universalizable. That is to say, when we make moral utterances (e.g. 'you ought to do this', 'this is good', 'that was wrong') as contrasted with, say, prudential, self-seeking, flattering, descriptive, **aesthetic** or religious utterances, we necessarily: (a) indicate our own emotive support for/objection to the act/state of affairs/person in question; (b) indicate that we enjoin others to feel likewise and, when appropriate, act accordingly; and (c) indicate that the judgement in question would retain its force, other things being equal, no matter who the people concerned might be. These are logically indicated by the nature of moral remarks; they are not simply psychological points that people wish to get over when using moral language. The utterance 'kindness is morally good', if made in sincerity, must reveal that the speaker values kindness, enjoins others to do so too, and presumes that it is always good to be kind to anyone, other things being equal. Whereas there is no impropriety in my changing my mind on a matter of taste, or accepting one judgement from you and an incompatible one from someone else concerning enjoyment of something, if I make a truly moral commitment to the effect that A should not do B, then part of what is meant by phrasing it in moral terminology is that I too should refrain from B, other things being equal, and that you and others should share my conviction.

It has also been argued that by definition morality is concerned with certain specific values, most obviously impartiality, freedom, and people's well-being. Even though many people may have done cruel things in the name or morality, if they sincerely believe themselves to have been acting morally, then they must have seen themselves (however mistakenly) as acting for the good of people, without partial favour to any particular individual or group. Thus, while certain religious inquisitors may conceivably have acted morally, however wrongheadedly, in their zeal, by no stretch of the imagination could the concentration camps of Nazi Germany or Soviet Russia be classified as within the realm of morality. It is not a question of having different moral values: those who ignore the well-being of some group(s) for no adequate moral reason, by definition, though they may have values, do not have any recognizable moral values. And a degree of freedom would seem to be a necessary aspect of moral behaviour, since what we mean by a moral action is partly one freely chosen, as opposed to forced upon us, engaged in at random, etc.

We see that in the moral sphere, as in any other, **value judgements** have a certain logic arising from the nature of the domain itself, although an area such as morality is a lot less clear than an area such as football. It should also be observed that the fact that communities in different places and times have had different moral values is of very little significance for argument about the extent to which such values are **objective** or **subjective**. In the first place, different local customs may need to be explained in terms of the same broad principles. (As Herodotus noted, some burn their dead, some bury their dead, but all alike have respect for their dead.) In the second place, there is less differentiation amongst **cultures**, at the level of broad principle, than the differences of practice enumerated by the anthropologist might suggest. Most important of all, the fact, if it was one, that different cultures had distinctly different basic principles would no more establish that all were equally true, than differing opinions about the shape of the earth make that a matter of opinion.

However, the main problem in ethics is probably that of attempting to set out proofs for the retention of particular principles, and a large part of the history of ethics has been concerned with trying to establish ethical theories that might explain both what our moral duty is and why it is so. Examples include **utilitarianism**, that sees morality as ultimately deriving from man's inevitable pursuit of happiness, intuitionism, that sees certain principles of morality as being self-evident, and transcendentalist theories, that seek to establish certain moral principles by appeal to the canons of reason alone.

Few think that these or any other theories have been entirely satisfactorily articulated. However, it is perhaps worth remembering that the fact that something cannot be proven to be true, does not show that it is not true. A **fact** is not to be identified with what has been **empirically** demonstrated. It might be a fact that one ought to be kind, as certainly as it is a fact that the earth is spherical. And indeed the strength of our sentiment might incline one to the view that this is one of the more plausible claims to have been made over the centuries. One might even say, paraphrasing Voltaire's remark about God, that, if there was not an ethical truth, mankind would have to invent one (*knowledge).

REFERENCES

Hospers (1961), Hudson (1970), Warnock, G. J. (1967), Warnock, M. (1966).

Ethnography

There are two main strands in educational research: the **positivist** tradition, derived from mainstream social science, and the naturalist tradition, derived from nineteenth-century conceptions of **subjective** understanding. Most educational researchers, especially those trained in the United States, are positivists: they treat social facts as being identical to natural facts, form generalizations based on those facts, and from those generalizations derive bodies of **theory**, on the pattern of physicists looking for universal laws. Those in the naturalist tradition, as the name implies, seek to understand the educational world in its own terms, without the use of such preformed categories and understandings. The emphasis on one or other approach may vary according to subject matter, and some scholars attempt to bridge both traditions (***action research, life history**).

Educational researchers have adopted the term 'ethnography' (first used by anthropologists to indicate a method of describing **cultural** groups by extended observation) to denote naturalistic approaches to examining schools and **schooling**. Claiming that positivist approaches exclude essential elements within educational settings, ethnographers attempt to evoke the life in institutions as authentically and as sympathetically as possible. They are interested in exploring particular modes of existence in schools as expressed in values, beliefs, motives, rituals and rules, and attempt to come to terms with the life experiences, however mundane, of students and teachers.

Ethnographers typically use a case-study approach for examining and reporting educational affairs. Data within a case study are usually gathered by personal (participant) observation, a technique derived from anthropology. Participant observation demands extended periods of on-site observation by an observer who is respectful of, and sensitive to, the special or unique features of particular schools and classrooms. An observer may participate in the life of the classroom, not as the 'fly on the wall' in the positivist tradition, but as a full member of the group, interested in discussing issues openly with others in the group, students as well as teachers. In addition to participant observation, ethnographers use such related techniques as textual analysis, conversational analysis, and unstructured interviews.

Case-study reports are usually descriptive or narrative. They consider the subject of study in a holistic and expansive manner rather than attempt to identify or manipulate particular sets of variables, or reduce findings to numbers. Sections into which reports are divided may reflect a particular image of the subject of study that the investigator wishes to bring to life, and the style in which the reports are written tends to be personal and vivid. Writers of ethnographic texts are not averse to using striking quotations, allusions, and **metaphors** in making a point, or to giving force to their observations and conclusions by the ironic juxtaposition of instances and ideas.

Given such principles and procedures, ethnographic research is difficult. Field studies of the detailed nature demanded by ethnographic methods often entail large investments of time and money; for example, keeping a person in the classroom for months may be a very expensive business. Gaining access to particular schools for this type of research is not always easy, and winning the confidence and trust of administrators, teachers, and students is a task demanding special skills in negotiation, and agreed rules for confidentiality. During an ethnographic study, some researchers may find themselves in positions in which their various roles are in conflict; for instance, while they are acting as participants, they may discover information that does not sit well with their responsibilities as observers or even as citizens. Because ethnographic studies are often concerned with particular individuals, their treatment during the investigation, and particularly in the text of the report, raises moral and legal questions concerning the rights of others to privacy.

In the context of the prevailing tradition of educational research, ethnographic studies have attracted their share of critical comments. In some circles these approaches remain highly suspect, and young academics are occasionally warned that their futures may be in peril if they become too enamoured of ethnography. Because different observers do not necessarily agree in their accounts of particular situations, the spectre of **reliability** haunts ethnographic approaches; it is joined by its twin, **validity**, because observers using ethnographic techniques admit that their accounts may be subjective or even idiosyncratic. Written reports often appear to others to be so particular in nature that they could have no general significance, or so subjective that they resemble a work of fiction.

On the one hand, ethnographers maintain that their research will reveal views of schools and classrooms that have not previously been available in the educational literature. In their opinion their work has the practical value of evoking the nature of life in institutional settings, and uncovering the distortions of official policies that affect teachers and students alike. On the other hand, critics argue that the work of ethnographers cannot be taken seriously until it is subjected to some public form of warrant or test – the fact that a written report enlarges understanding does not make it true.

These comments on the nature of ethnography, and its relationship to conventional methodology, underscore the problematic nature of eductional **research** in general. Discussions seem long on claims, but short on analysis, and scholars appear to be more willing to spend time guarding the boundaries of what they call their '**paradigm**' than finding and justifying appropriate means of dealing with *educational* issues.

REFERENCES

Burgess (1982, 1984), Fetterman (1984), Hammersley and Atkinson (1983), Jackson (1968), Johnson and Johnson-Lee (1988), LeCompte and Goetz (1982), MacDonald and Walker (1975), Norris (1977), Phillips (1985), Simons (1980), Stake (1985), Walker (1985), Werner and Rothe (n.d.), Woods (1977, 1985, 1986), Zigrami and Zigrami (1980).

Etymology

Studying the etymology of words, fascinating and illuminating as it may be, is not necessarily a particularly useful way of arriving at understanding of the modern meaning of words, still less of the **concepts** behind the words. For example, the word 'happiness' derives from the Middle English word 'hap' meaning 'chance' or 'fortune' (whether good or bad), but it does not follow that contemporary English speakers mean by 'happiness' 'a chance or accidental state of mind' of some kind, or that happiness is in fact a matter of chance or fortune. Similarly, the obvious etymological link between the words 'doctrine' and 'indoctrination' does not provide a compelling argument for confining the notion of **indoctrination** to those cases where doctrines are being imparted. '**Education**' itself provides a particularly interesting example: it is arguable that it derives either from the Latin *educare* (to train) or from the Latin *educere* (to lead out), and some have tried to defend a traditionalist conception of education as a matter of direction and instruction by claiming that the word stems from the former, while others have advocated a more **child-centred** conception on the grounds that it stems from the latter, and therefore implies a process of bringing out what is innate in the child. But (a) it is difficult to be sure which it does derive from; (b) in point of fact, although *educere* has a primary meaning of 'lead out' and *educare* of 'train', both words were used by the Romans with reference to educating children, while the former was also sometimes used to mean 'train' and the latter to mean 'nourish' (of plants); (c) even if the case were different and it could be unequivocally established that the word derives from a particular Roman word which unambiguously means this or that, it does not follow that our conception of education either does or should remain the same.

None the less it is of interest to note that a number of key words in educational theory are more or less direct transliterations of Greek or Roman words. In addition to education, Latin gives us, e.g. cognitive (from *cognosco*: I learn, recognize), **intelligence** (from *intellego*: I understand) and **reification** (from *res*: a thing and *facio*: I make). From the Greek we get, e.g. etymology itself (from *etymos*: true, real, and *logos*: word, account), **paradigm** (from *paradeigma*: a model, impression or blueprint), epistemology (from *episteme*: **knowledge** and *logos*: a rationale, account), **autonomy** (from *autos*: self and *nomos*: law), **aesthetic** (from *aisthenesthai*: to perceive) and **theory** (from *theoria*: contemplation).

A few words have been transplanted without alteration. These include the Latin *datum* and **curriculum** (literally 'the having been given' and 'the course to be run') which have a plural form ending in 'a' (data; curricula), and the Greek *criterion* and **phenomenon** ('means of judging' and 'a having appeared thing'), which also have a plural form that ends in 'a' (criteria; phenomena). Aspiring academics might care to note that their 'c.v.' stands for 'curriculum vitae' and not 'curriculum vita' ('vitae' being in the genitive case), but that, when the word 'curriculum' is dropped, the form should be 'vita' in the nominative.

Evaluation

Educational discourse has many words that relate to the broad tasks of judging the worth of a person, programme, or piece of work, including 'evaluating', 'measuring', 'assessing', 'appraising', 'examining', 'testing', 'marking', 'grading', and 'scoring'. Such words are often confused: one person's 'testing' is another person's 'assessing', and 'marking' in one country may be 'grading' in another. Nevertheless, these words are not all synonymous. 'Scoring' is usually applied to the act of checking responses to **objective** questions (a task that may be completed by a machine). 'Marking' and 'grading' (British and American equivalents?) indicate that a teacher is judging the worth of written scripts submitted

by students, either in **examination** conditions or as part of course requirements. 'Testing' and 'examining' usually suggest the application of
a standardized (as in tests of basic **skills**) or teacher-devised instrument
to gauge the progress of students during or at the end of a course of
study. '**Assessing**' and 'appraising' are general terms that may indicate a
variety of intentions and activities, such as measuring progress in a
strictly experimental sense, estimating certain qualities in a programme,
or judging the worth of an educational activity. On different occasions,
therefore, both these words have been used as synonyms for very different terms: 'measuring' on the one hand, or 'evaluating' on the other.

The differences between measuring and evaluating are important.
Measuring generally has a very precise denotation: assigning numerals
to objects or events according to rules. Consequently, those interested in
measurement typically search for observable indications of properties of
objects or events under study, apply rules to those properties, and then
allocate a number to the result, often using statistical techniques. Thus,
in measuring **creativity**, researchers identify a particular range of behaviours that are thought to indicate creativity, apply a test that requires
students to demonstrate those behaviours, and then derive and rank a
series of scores based on the results of that test. Consequently, a number
indicating relative creative ability may be attached to each student. An
important aim is that each experimenter will obtain the same result.

In the opinion of some scholars, this procedure is often unsatisfactory
in **educational** contexts. They claim that it is not always possible to link
specified behaviours with desired educational **aims** with any degree of
certainty. They reject the notion, for example, that it is possible to score
a person's creativity by means of the types of test that are commonly
applied by educational researchers. They also claim that some activities
which cannot be judged or appraised by numerical systems are none the
less educationally important. As **literature** and paintings defy such
methods of appraisal, so do such things as **teaching**, school programmes
and curricular materials. What is needed, therefore, is a kind of evaluation that ranges far beyond numbers, and that is not necessarily tied to
the notion of inter-observer **reliability**. In order to distance themselves
from traditional **empirical** techniques of measuring, some of those involved in tasks of making educational judgements call themselves
evaluators.

Unfortunately, not all evaluators agree on the nature of evaluating.
Readers should expect to find that in the educational literature some
evaluations of educational **phenomena** are virtually identical to meas-
urements of the same phenomena, others are based on quite different
principles, and still others are mixtures of the two. Disagreement exists
on the purpose of evaluation: some argue that it should assist in decision

making, others that it should simply lay bare the characteristics of what is being examined; some say that it should be concerned with debating the merits of an activity or programme, and others that it should be concerned with working out the effects of an activity. In each of these perspectives, different types of evidence may be needed, and different types of reporting may be offered. Contemporary evaluators, in consequence, travel to a variety of educational destinations carrying many different kinds of methodological baggage.

Nevertheless, several arguments offered by contemporary evaluators have attracted wide agreement. First, many subscribe to the principle that the job of evaluation is to make an overall judgement: to assess the educational **worth** of an activity or programme. They therefore reject such practices as judging an activity solely by reference to the extent to which it achieves declared objectives, or assessing a programme solely by student scores on standardized tests. They prefer criteria that will encourage others to reflect upon the quality of an activity or programme, with no preconceived limits on the range of judgements to be offered.

Secondly, many contemporary evaluators have attempted to use research techniques that lie outside the range of traditional social scientific methodology. They have pioneered new uses for the case-study approach and applied techniques derived from **ethnography**. Some have examined critical techniques in the humanities as a source for principles and practices in the assessment of educational activities. Such techniques have been labelled 'qualitative' as opposed to '**quantitative**' methods of research.

Thirdly, some have experimented with different types of educational reporting. Rather than rely almost exclusively on numbers, they have produced, for example, reports that are written in prose (and require writing skills that are not often found among educational researchers). Such written reports may share many of the **subjective** characteristics of humanistic critiques of novels or plays.

Alternative approaches to evaluation that lie outside the accepted understandings of measurement have attracted a certain amount of critical comment. Some argue that a search for quality, however important it may be, cannot be allowed to divert attention from certain important practical issues facing school administrators. Whether a programme is efficient in its use of limited resources, for example, is a question that ought not to be avoided. Critics have maintained that many of the new forms of written evaluation are narcissistic and pretentious, involving too many personal and subjective statements and too few dispassionate comments about the object of study. Others have suggested that some new forms of educational evaluation are **ideologically** committed. Still others point to the failure of practitioners of newer forms of evaluation to explicate criteria whereby their work may itself be subject to scrutiny and criticism. No resolution to contemporary debates on the nature and techniques of educational evaluation appears likely in the immediate future (*curriculum change, formative/summative evaluation).

REFERENCES

Adelman (1984), Broadfoot (1979), Eisner (1979), Guba and Lincoln (1982), Hamilton (1976), House (1980), Jenkins, Kemmis, MacDonald and Verma (1979), Lacey and Lawton (1981), Stake (1967), Tawney (1976), Tyler, Gagné and Scriven (1967).

Examinations

'The hand that rocks the cradle rules the world' according to a popular song. (The origin of the cliché is to be found in the poem 'What rules the world' by the American William Ross Wallace, 1819–91.) More certain is that the **assessment** system that a school system adopts dictates much of the nature of the teaching. Some respond to this truth by condemning the very idea of assessment, others by arguing that responsible teachers should take account of the fact and teach to the requirements of the system of assessment. Both responses fail to note that the connection is only **contingent**, and that the question of what form assessment should take in particular cases has to be decided by the varying nature of what is being taught and why. There is no necessary need for a teacher to direct his efforts to ensuring student success on popular forms of assessment, and, obviously, he should not do so when he has reason to view them as anti-educational. Thus the ubiquity of **intelligence** tests, standardized achievement tests, and other professed registers of **generic** ability, should not blind us to their inappropriateness; they should be, for the most part, rejected by the teaching profession, and replaced by tests related to the subject matter in question. Similarly, multiple-choice examinations on, say, philosophy would seem to be singularly inappropriate.

A question that arises, whatever form of examination one adopts, is whether the **evaluation** should be in the hands of outsiders or those who do the **teaching**. There are some obvious advantages in internal examinations. Teachers can make allowance for special circumstances; they bring more understanding of individuals to the task. But if the object is to ensure **objectivity**, it is a risky approach. With a system of public examination we can come nearer to the ideal of ensuring similarity of treatment, of minimizing personal favouritism or antagonism, of freeing the teacher from the conflicting roles of supporter and critic of students, and of removing grounds for suspicion of the system (*deschooling).

REFERENCE

Montgomery (1978).

Expanding horizons curriculum *see* Logical order

Experience *see* Literature

Extrinsic value *see* Value judgements, Worthwhile

Eye contact *see* Communication

F

Facts

Everybody in the field of **education** would love to get at the facts. But what is a fact? The widespread assumptions that in the realm of educational values there are no facts, and that claims made about the effectiveness of certain **teaching** methods are facts, suggest that to many people: (a) facts are always **empirical**; and (b) anything empirically researched is a fact. Some slight warrant for this confusion of the terms 'fact' and 'empirical' may be found in the etymology of the former, for it derives from the Latin *factum* meaning, 'what is done'. However, its essential meaning today is 'that which is true'. In this sense the above two assumptions about facts are not themselves facts, but are somewhat factitious and factious (i.e. untrue and a cause of confusion).

Firstly, it is not the case that all facts are empirical (i.e. matters to be attested by observation). For instance, $2 \times 2 = 4$ is a fact, although not an empirical one, as are the observations that all bachelors are unmarried and that the angles of a triangle add up to 180 degrees. It has been maintained by some that all facts are either analytic (truths of definition), as these examples are, or propositions capable of empirical verification. No other utterances, though they may have some point or purpose, are capable of being true or false, or, therefore, of being classified as facts. But that suggestion is oversimple. In the first place it would imply that claims such as 'I love her' or 'God exists', which on the face of it are meaningful and either true or false, are non-factual claims, since they are neither true by definition nor capable of being empirically verified. In the second place this principle of verification falls by its own logic. The claim that it makes, being neither analytic nor capable of empirical verification, cannot be a factual one.

It might more reasonably be suggested that anything that is a fact (i.e. true) is so either by definition or by virtue of the nature of experience. This is to shift emphasis away from the idea that, if a claim is non-analytic, it needs to have been demonstrated empirically (if it is to be regarded as a fact), to the idea that it must in principle be capable of some experiential test, even if we do not have agreement on what forms such a test should take in particular cases. This would allow us to regard 'I love her' and 'God exists' as factual claims, without having to commit ourselves to the view that they are established facts.

127

Either way it is clear that not all facts are empirically demonstrable in principle, and many that may be so in principle are not empirically demonstrable in practice.

Secondly, conversely, the exhaustive empirical examination of an issue does not in itself make the conclusion a fact. Whether a claim is true is a question of the way things are. Empirical investigation will confirm a fact only in so far as such investigation is both relevant and of adequate quality. No amount of empirical research helps to confirm that all bachelors are unmarried, since it is a fact that is not in any way empirical. And no amount of empirical research will establish that X loves Y, unless it can first adequately conceptualize and identify **phenomena** such as love.

There are good grounds for saying that most of the facts that we have in relation to education are either not empirical or not empirically demonstrated, while most of the empirical research has failed to establish facts. But the facts that we do have, remain facts, even though in many instances they are noted as the result of logical reasoning, insight, and intuition.

Facts or the factual are sometimes loosely contrasted with **theory**. ('Give me facts; I've no time for theory.') Such a contrast is absurd: there are theoretical facts and practical facts, and the particular perception or construction of a fact is usually partially dependent on the theoretical framework with which we operate. (For example, the fact that it is a poor expedient for teachers to treat students in certain ways, derives partly from certain particular views about the nature of education, the nature of human beings and the nature of morality.) (*objectivity, research, teacher effectiveness, value judgements)

Faculty psychology *see* Mental faculties

Feelings *see* Emotions

Feminism

'Feminism' is a label for a commitment or movement to achieve equality for women. Given that definition, the term ought to apply to committed men or women, although in common parlance it is confined to committed women only. Although there is evidence of feminist thought in most periods of recorded history, it became a particularly powerful social movement in the 1960s and 1970s, following the publication of such books as Betty Friedan's *The Feminine Mystique* (1963) and Germaine Greer's *The Female Eunuch* (1970). In many countries, feminism now ranks high as an influential social force.

All feminists share the general view (which can scarcely be disputed) that male domination (to be found in every important aspect of contemporary society – legal, economic, occupational, social, religious, and educational) is the source of social inequalities and injustices that affect the life of every woman, and it is worth stressing, every man also. They object to the notion that a woman's worth in society is determined principally by her gender, and to the view that women are by **nature** subservient to and less **intelligent** than men. They oppose the sexual exploitation of women in the media, the market-place, and the workplace. They also, by and large, support the removal of the most obvious barriers to equal social and economic opportunities for women, and of sexist and **stereotyped** content in the media and in **education**.

Given the complexity of the issues, it is not surprising that divisions persist within the feminist movement. There are moderate and extreme positions on such general questions as the role of marriage and the family within the society, and the role of heterosexuality. Feminists differ in their views about the importance of the capitalist system in maintaining historical inequalities. They also disagree on the nature of the practical solutions to perceived inequalities: for example, on the details of affirmative action programmes, or on provision of social services specifically designed for women. Like many other political reformers, feminists have found it easier to adopt common cause against injustices than to agree among themselves on the reasons for the status quo, or the appropriate remedies (**positive discrimination*).

Feminists have often complained about traditions, policies, and practices within the educational system. It is argued, for example, that most elementary school readers depict females in subservient roles. **History** and social studies texts tend to ignore the part played by women in historical events. The language used in schoolbooks of all types seems to many feminists to be riddled with sexism (the generic use of 'man' and 'he' causing particular offence). Teachers frequently encourage so-called feminine qualities in the deportment and manners of girls in elementary and secondary schools (and manly qualities in boys), and guidance counsellors tend to advise females to consider those careers that have historically been filled by women (such as the secretarial trades and the nursing profession). In secondary schools, female students are traditionally underrepresented in those subjects (mathematics and science) that qualify students for entry into the more highly paid professions and occupations. At the university level, the provision of services and facilities (for example, in graduate school placements) has contributed more to the advancement of men than of women. The very structure of the educational system, in which women teachers clearly hold subordinate positions, offers a sexist role-model for all students.

In recent years many jurisdictions have taken steps to correct the more obvious inequalities, principally through enlightened teacher-education courses and programmes, changed practices in schools (for instance, encouraging female students to take such previously male-dominated subjects as technology and mathematics), and the revision of texts and other classroom materials to ensure the removal of sexist language on the one hand, and the inclusion of more references to the part played by women in society on the other. At the tertiary level, limited progress has been made in the introduction of affirmative action programmes for women. Whether this improvement in the treatment of female students (many feminists argue that it remains slight) should be credited to actions by education authorities, or to a heightened awareness of the issue in society as a whole, is an open question.

To critics of the movement, several aspects of the arguments offered by feminists, and the actions they recommend, are disquieting. Those critics suggest that important definitional questions concerning the nature of **equality** between males and females have not been resolved. They argue that the societal issues raised by feminists are too complex to admit of what amounts to a one-dimensional answer. Moral discussions of the family, church, and schools should not necessarily be confined to those issues raised by feminists. Other critics maintain that feminists underestimate the dangers inherent in requiring governments or censor-boards to take legislative or administrative action to change current practices, and some find feminist attempts to 'police' **language** more than faintly ridiculous. Specific views of groups of feminists also often find strong challenges (for example, that feminine exploitation is the result of a male conspiracy, or that women's liberation is impossible without the overthrow of the capitalist system).

Concern has also been expressed about some of the actions being taken in schools. Opinions differ on the nature and extent of sex-role stereotyping (and its alternative) in schools. Whether both female and male students should be required to take such subjects as mathematics in the same order will depend, at least in part, on the findings of **empirical** studies on the nature of their **learning** processes, evidence for which is, at best, inconclusive. Nor is it at all clear that the fight against the inculcation of sexist attitudes would be won by banning literature that portrays such attitudes, let alone that it would be well won. Some critics have suggested that attempts to rewrite school textbooks so that the role of women is acknowledged runs the risk of simple-minded and crude manipulation of the past (particularly by bureaucrats). Other observers, holding educational values derived from particular **cultural** or religious traditions, detect significant threats to those traditions in the growth of the feminist movement (*****censorship**).

The inequality in the status of women is widely acknowledged, and attempts in all aspects of society (including **schooling**) have been made (with mixed success) to resolve it. The road ahead, however, is more cluttered with **conceptual** difficulties than many seem prepared to acknowledge. Whether these difficulties will be cleared away in an atmosphere of rational **analysis** or knee-jerk **ideological** disputation remains to be seen (*****critical theory, giftedness**).

REFERENCES

Barrow (1982a), Batcher, Brackstone, Winter and Wright (1975), Culley and Portuges (1985), De Beauvoir (1953), Fennema (1982), Firestone (1972), Fowlkes and McClure (1984), Fox and Tiger (1971), Frazier and Sadker (1973), Friedan (1963, 1982), Goldberg (1973), Greer (1970, 1984), Grumet (1988), Lewis and Simon (1986), Martin (1985), Millett (1970), Nilsen, Bosmajian, Gershuny and Stanley (1977), Partington (1985b), Roy (n.d.), Spender (1982), Stacey, Bereaud and Daniels (1974), Stanworth (1983), Stockard and Wood (1984), Warren (1980).

Field studies *see* Ethnography, Quantitative/qualitative research, Teacher effectiveness

Fields of knowledge *see* Knowledge

Formal research *see* Interaction analysis, Objectivity, Quantitative/qualitative research, Systematic observation

Formal/substantive

Certain principles, particularly **ethical** ones, are termed formal. They state how one should in principle proceed, but they do not dictate or reveal the particular form the procedure will take in specific cases. A substantive principle, by contrast, provides explicit guidance. Thus, the principle of impartiality is formal. It states that one should not show favour to an individual for irrelevant reasons. I therefore know that, *if* being my daughter is an irrelevant reason for giving this student a good grade, I ought not to give her a good grade. I do not know that I should not in fact do so, however, until I have determined whether the reason *is* irrelevant.

There is a danger of being dismissive about principles that are 'merely formal', because they do not prescribe specific practice. But they are not entirely without teeth. Better to gain agreement that people should be favoured only when there are **relevant** grounds for so doing, than to continue in a world in which people see nothing wrong with partial treatment. Although what is relevant in a particular situation is a distinct question, not directly answered by the formal principle of impartiality, it is none the less the case that many instances of relevance/irrelevance can be instantly agreed upon, and others can be sensibly argued about. It may be unclear whether it is 'impartial' to give a stiffer sentence to a thirty-year-old than to a twenty-five-year-old for the same offence. But there is no doubt that it is not impartial to give a stiffer sentence to a stranger than to your son.

Formative evaluation/summative evaluation

The terms 'formative' and 'summative' evaluation are currently used to indicate the making of judgements at two different stages in the life of a project or course: while it is in progress ('formative'), or when it is concluded ('summative'). They were first used in reference to the role of evaluators and **evaluation** in the specific context of course improvement. Some evaluators, dissatisfied with evaluations based exclusively on summative tests of student behaviour, suggested that courses could be improved by conducting revisions while they were in progress. (Such an argument was stimulated by the practical requirement that funded research projects produce their materials within tight time-limits.) Evaluators were also interested in exploring methods of judging the **worth** of programmes using methods that were qualitative as well as **quantitative**. More than one evaluator suggested that formative evaluation based on a wide range of indicators was more important in the task of course development and improvement than summative evaluation.

In this context, the distinction between the two terms became blurred. If the purpose of formative evaluation is to make judgements of major **aims** on a course, or to effect revisions of the nature of a course, then it is performing much the same function as that ascribed to summative evaluation.

Many social scientists of the behaviourist tradition, wedded to a concern with assessing student **learning**, retain a distinction between the two terms by careful definition: formative observations are designed to assess the degree of student mastery of specific tasks, while summative evaluation is directed to assessment of the degree to which major objectives have been attained by students. Discussion of the meanings of these terms, therefore, at this point merges into broader issues of the nature of **education**, and the purpose of **schooling** (*assessment, behavioural objectives**).

REFERENCES

Bloom, Hastings and Madaus (1971), Cronbach (1963), Guba and Lincoln (1982), Patton (1980), Sanders and Cunningham (1973), Scriven (1967).

Forms of knowledge (Platonic forms) *see* Analysis; (Hirstian forms) *see* Core curriculum, Critical thinking, Ethics, Knowledge, Religious education

Freedom *see* Autonomy, Ethics

G

Games *see* Simulations

Generic fallacy

In *Democracy in America* (1863), the perceptive Alexis de Tocqueville noted two features that he regarded as 'a deplorable consequence of democracy'. The first was a general lack of precision in **language**, which he attributed to the fact that all users of the language were presumed to be equal (and therefore no clear distinction could be made between what some linguists refer to as high-register, common-register, and low-register vocabulary and speech patterns). The second was a particular instance of this general lack of clarity in vocabulary (and hence **conceptual finesse**), namely 'the continual use of generic terms or abstract expressions'. 'A democratic writer will be apt to speak of *capacities* in the abstract for *men of capacity,* and without specifying the objects to which their capacity is applied.'

Ignoring the question of the connection between language habits and democracy, there can be no denying that North America is particularly prone to endorse the equal correctness of all utterances and to sacrifice precision to **weasel words**, pacifiers, jargon, and other forms of avoiding offence and commitment. It is also second nature for North American educationalists to talk of 'capacities in the abstract', **skills**, faculties, etc., rather than to refer to people, in whom alone such capacities can be realized.

At the turn of the century, faculty psychology was in the ascendant, and with it the idea that a human being had various distinct faculties, such as **memory**, imagination, creativity, etc., each of which was a discrete element that might be more or less well-developed. The terminology of faculty psychology has now been largely set aside. But judging from the way in which many educationalists talk and from the things that are done in reference to determining or cultivating, e.g. creativity, thinking has not really advanced beyond the days of faculty psychology and the imprecise and continual use of generic terms noted by de Tocqueville.

This is unfortunate, since it is clear that whatever may be involved in such concepts as **creativity, imagination, critical thinking, values**

clarification, etc., it is not the case that being creative, or being a critical thinker, is a matter of having some general capacity that can be readily exercised in any situation. It is apparent on a moment's reflection that one cannot be imaginative, creative, critical, etc., except in relation to something: there has to be a context, a something to be imaginative, creative or critical about. This does not preclude the possibility of, e.g., some factor that is necessary and common to all instances of creative thought, just as a certain muscular strength is necessary to a variety of physical movements. But, just as dribbling a soccer ball, shooting it at goal from twenty-five yards, controlling a basketball, and rowing all require very different overall talents, despite having a certain minimum muscular competence in common, so, being an imaginative writer, being imaginative in response to political theory, and being an imaginative poet, all require contextual understanding. The form that creativity, logic, etc., take necessarily changes from context to context – a logical argument in mathematics is of a different order from a **logical** argument in **ethics**. It follows that a person may be very creative in one sphere and not in another. And it follows that to develop people's capacity to be creative, etc., one needs to exercise the capacity in specific contexts.

Individual entries relating to, e.g. critical thinking, creativity, will indicate a host of related misconceptions surrounding popular ideas of these central mental concepts, such as a lack of precision in use of the terms 'skill' and '**transference**'. But perhaps one of the most debilitating as well as most dominant of contemporary assumptions is this one that an individual brain houses a number of discrete abilities that can be exercised and developed in and of themselves. That is the generic fallacy – the fallacy of assuming there is a something there to be exercised, rather than that by developing **understanding** of various particular subject matters, we enable a person to respond to more subject matters creatively, critically, and so on.

(It follows that standard **intelligence** tests, creativity tests, critical thinking tests, etc., cannot be true tests of intelligence, creativity, etc., since such notions are not coherent except understood in the manner described. Yet, since the tests are clearly not devoid of content, they must test something. They test one's ability to respond creatively, critically, etc., to isolated, generally trivial, artificial problems.)

REFERENCES

Barrow (1990), de Tocqueville (1863).

Genetic endowment *see* Nature/nurture

Geography *see* Knowledge, Nationalism

Giftedness

At the beginning of this century, the term 'gifted' referred to a person with a high IQ as measured on one of the standardized tests used to select students for secondary school. The limitations of such tests encouraged researchers and educators to identify persons with other kinds of above-average abilities, for example, the highly creative person, the artistically talented, the person with performing or athletic ability, and the person able to demonstrate outstanding leadership ability. However, in identifying such abilities, it was not always clear whether students' current giftedness or a supposed potential was being assessed. (Educators soon noticed that some students seemed to possess abilities that they were disinclined to use, while others were prepared to persevere in exercising their talents.) In short, there are many definitions of giftedness in common use, the term is applied to a wide range of abilities and talents, and (partly for these reasons) there is little agreement among researchers on the proportion of school students who are endowed with those abilities (**creativity, intelligence*).

Some educational jurisdictions have offered a variety of programmes for gifted students. A few have built separate schools for academically gifted students or (much more rarely) artistic students. Others have provided special classes or opportunities within mixed-ability schools, by instituting streamed groupings for the gifted, offering enriched **curricula** for able students, or accelerating high achievers more quickly through the grades than the majority of students. All of these provisions have incited, on occasion, heated, and even acrimonious debate.

A partial explanation for this controversy may lie in claims concerning the social context of giftedness. **Feminists** and others have noted that certain types of gifted class are disproportionately filled with male students. Some researchers have argued that the tests used to identify the gifted favour white, middle-class students, and discriminate against students who are non-white or poor. Others maintain that the provision of separate schools for the gifted, or even of separate classes within mixed-ability schools, has contributed to the growth of political and social **élitism** in society at large. In England, for example, the question of offering educational programmes to gifted students became embroiled in the arguments over the existence of private – the so-called 'public' – schools.

While these debates take place, the lot of the gifted students has not always been happy. They have been subjected to a variety of **metaphoric**

labels (such as 'racehorses' or 'fine china') that have misleading connotations. In some families, parental pressure has been exerted on some
children to 'reveal' gifted characteristics whether or not they possess
them. Among their peers, gifted students (for example, those that publicly affirm academic interests) may find themselves shunned. Gifted
students have been vested by governments with the additional duty of
solving pressing economic and social problems. Given such attitudes and
pressures, it is scarcely surprising that some students respond with a
variety of behaviours intended to disguise their condition. Special difficulties exist for two classes of gifted persons: women and handicapped
students. Pressures of traditional role-models in society often divert the
former from pursuing interests that may be considered non-conforming;
the latter may find that hidden abilities are either ignored or unnoticed
in the stresses of their condition.

Such is the controversial nature of giftedness that many observers
have argued that provision for gifted education is a threat to public
schooling. What is needed, such critics argue, is not special education for
the gifted, but high quality **education** for every student.

REFERENCES

Barbe and Renzulli (1981), Benn (1981a, 1981b), Burt (1975), Croll and Moses
(1985), Dowdall and Colangelo (1982), Getzels and Dillon (1973), Guilford
(1967), Hudson (1966), Ogilvie (1973), Renzulli (1978), Renzulli and Delisle
(1982).

Global education *see* Topic-centred education

Goals *see* Accountability, Aims

Grading

It might be worth pondering why grading or assigning some rank order
to student performance should have increasingly become something of
an embarrassment. Presumably, reluctance to grade an essay, project,
etc., is partly the consequence of the age's increased lack of confidence
in itself and in the idea of truth or **objective value**. That seems unfortunate since, while any system of grading (e.g. A, B, C; 95 per cent, 80 per
cent, 50 per cent; first-rate, competent, acceptable) will involve arbitrary
notation, and will either grade the incontestable or will involve

judgement rather than **measurement** and hence be subject to challenge, it is none the less in the nature of **education** that grading should take place, in some way or another. It might be formal or informal, public or private, communicated to students or reserved in the teacher's mind, but if the teacher is truly seeking to educate, then he is necessarily seeking to develop **understanding**, and the degree of one's understanding is therefore a paramount consideration. A teacher who did not mind whether my understanding of *Macbeth* was great, average, or weak, or who had no way of estimating it would be undesirable. (This is not to say that grading necessarily need be a frequent occurrence, nor that whatever cannot be satisfactorily graded cannot have educational significance.)

Objections to grading seem to be of two broad types: those that centre on its undesirability, and those that focus on its difficulty.

In the first group, some maintain that it is an 'intrusion upon the relationship' between teacher and student (Noddings, 1984), that it distorts the nature of **learning** or that it teaches the wrong message. It is of course true that grading can interfere with the relationship but so may concern for truth, quality, and honesty. **Teaching** is not primarily about forging any kind of relationship, however useful some kinds of relationship may be to the goal of educating someone. Similarly, while it may well be true that individual students come to think it more important to get straight As than to take in, enjoy, or even understand something, or draw any number of other false messages from the system (such as that people who get more As are superior people; that to get Cs is to be an irretrievable dunce, etc.), they may take equally erroneous messages from any other mode of procedure (e.g. that quality of work is immaterial, that everyone is equally able at everything). Objections that apply to any way of behaving, and that are only **contingently** related to a particular practice, are no objections to that practice. It is difficult to discern any evils that are necessarily implicit in grading.

Difficulties in doing the job well and accurately of course there are. But the fact that a job cannot always be done perfectly does not mean that it is not worth doing at all. The besetting sin of much debate on this issue has been the fallacious assumptions that, if grading cannot be 100 per cent precise, it cannot be acceptable, and that it cannot be precise at all except in so far as it is measurable. Both errors fairly obviously arise from the dominance of the scientific **paradigm** in our lives, especially in education. When we are operating in the field of the natural or exact sciences, we very properly expect a degree of precision, a quantifiable and accurate mode of measurement, and a particular form of objectivity. To expect the same in other areas that are logically distinct in kind is, as Aristotle long ago noted to little avail, the mark of the foolish. When, for example, we are determining the quality of a new novel by Peter

Ackroyd, we cannot expect a similar degree of precision, we cannot and should not look for a quantifiable mode of measurement, and our objectivity will be shown in a different way – it will take a distinct form. This does not imply that our judgement of the novel need be **subjective** in any pejorative sense, arbitrary, or mere opinion. It can and should be an objective, well-established, judgement. It differs from the scientific judgement essentially only in being arrived at by different means, less precise (which does not mean less accurate: it is accurate to say that he is over forty, but less precise than saying that he is forty-five), and, as it happens, more debatable. (But more debatable does not mean subjective, arbitrary, etc. Some scientific claims are more debatable than others, so are some literary claims. Some scientific claims are more debatable than some literary claims.) Grading, therefore, may often be far from precise, but none the less accurate and important. And accuracy is a function not of any mode of **assessment** *per se*, but of a proper understanding combined with a mode of assessment that is suitable to the type of endeavour under consideration. That is to say, for example, good teachers of **history**, being people who understand the nature of history and what they hope to achieve in teaching it, are qualified to assess how their students are progressing by means they can judge to be appropriate to the occasion, and to grade accordingly, should they so wish, to exactly the same extent as the good carpenter can measure the angles of the cupboard he is making (*examinations).

REFERENCE

Noddings (1984).

H

Handicapped children *see* Giftedness, Mainstreaming

Happiness *see* Etymology, Subjectivity, Utilitarian

Heredity *see* Nature/nurture

Hidden curriculum *see* Curriculum, Deschooling, Ideology, Reconceptualists

History

To some extent historians disagree about the nature, the purpose, and the value of studying history. Does it unfold in a methodical manner, repeat itself, or follow no recognizable pattern? Is it a science, a **discipline**, a form of **knowledge**, or a subject matter? Does it reveal 'the general in the particular' (Carr, 1961), generalizations, laws, or particulars? Does it broaden the mind, is it intellectually stimulating, does it increase self-knowledge, or provide practical instruction? Those who do not value history wonder how ignorance of past events can impair life in the present. In what way could ignorance of the battle of Thermopylae, the death of Julius Caesar, the first Crusade, the French Revolution or the Second World War possibly make me a worse husband, financier, citizen – indeed anything other than a worse teacher of history?

But such debate should not be allowed to obscure the large measure of agreement that does exist. It is true that no particular body of historical knowledge is necessary to living a good, useful, or happy life, and that many people have lived their lives in total ignorance of history (other than the immediate, contemporary, and local). None the less, few dispute that knowledge of the past illuminates and improves our lives: by giving us greater **understanding** of particulars (e.g. a full understanding of the American Constitution requires some appreciation of how and why it was conceived); by enlarging our **imaginative** scope (e.g. a

person with knowledge of Russian history is likely to take a more imaginative attitude to the possibilities embodied in *glasnost* than one who
presumes that Russians are just Americans in the East); by helping us to
understand why things are as they are (e.g. a proper understanding of
events in South Africa requires an appreciation of the way in which it
was settled, colonized, fought over, and governed during the last hundred years); and, more generally, by developing an awareness of the
diversity, possibilities, and limitations of humanity. Some parts of history might be argued to be more worth studying than others, because
they illustrate more important themes, or because they deal with issues
of greater significance to the human conditions or to our times; but the
main **educational** value in studying history lies in developing a broad
sense of history rather than in deriving particular lessons or conclusions
from it. It is said that during the Second World War a force of British
soldiers escaped capture at Thermopylae because their commander
knew about the famous battle of 480 BC. True or false, history has more
often served people to a deeper and greater extent indirectly and sub-
liminally. One who had never studied any history could not be aware of
the extent to which mankind and its exploits are historical constructs,
could not appreciate the full explanation of various aspects of contemporary circumstance, could not be open to the possibility of change, and,
in a number of other ways, could not have a true perspective on people
and events.

There is scope for choice from a wide variety of periods of study, but
there are criteria to be met in making a choice. One is not looking simply
for **relevance**, but for educational relevance. One is not, therefore, necessarily led to the study of one's own immediate past, or 'our neighbour-
hood in our grandparents' time'. On the contrary, it is likely that the
history of long ago and far away will very often be better suited to the
aim of opening the mind to a historical dimension. None the less, many
would argue that a priority should be given to developing understanding
of our own culture and civilization. For example, a student in Melbourne
would study the history of Australia in the wider context of Western
civilization, rather than the history of Palestine in the context of Islamic
civilization. It may be argued that in these **multicultural** days to adopt
such a view is chauvinistic and that, e.g. white English people in Brad-
ford rather urgently need some sense of the history of the Indian
peoples and their **cultural** inheritance. No doubt nothing but good could
come of that, but the argument put forward here is that the first thing
one needs to understand is the tradition that has generated oneself. In
any case, contemporary **religious** and cultural differences should not
blind us to much that is shared by many different groups. Dido and
Aeneas are part of the cultural history of a Kentucky farmer and a

Libyan camel-driver. Whether you are a Nigerian or a New Zealander, there is much that you need to know in common, from biblical times to the present, if you are fully to understand yourself and your society.

The study of history is not advocated simply because it allows one to understand common reference points and to make sense of **literature** that would otherwise be unintelligible, though it does those things. It is not even advocated simply because it enlarges our understanding of the present, true and obviously important though that is. It is crucially important because, in conjunction with other arts subjects, it may moderate what would otherwise be a one-dimensional view of man generated by the natural and social sciences. The social sciences have increased our understanding of human activity and behaviour and they have helped to modify an uncritically individualistic view of man, brought to its apogee in the Romantic period largely through the study of the humanities. There is a danger that the pendulum is now swinging the other way, giving us an uncritically mechanistic and deterministic viewpoint. The social scientist's job involves sorting particulars into categories, classifying particularities under general headings, and explaining diversity in terms of general principles. The understanding he provides is, and is supposed to be, couched in terms of general laws, (though, increasingly, social scientists settle for generalizations). But human beings are not simply rule-governed animals, and there is much that is true of them which is barely susceptible to, and is certainly not well caught, in generalization (*liberal education).

It is this other kind of truth to which the historian contributes. While indeed we aim to draw conclusions of general significance from our study of particular events, the study is none the less in-depth study of a host of interrelated particulars in their full complexity, as contrasted with the study of broad phenomena in isolation (in so far as that is possible), which is the business of the social scientist. The psychologist, for example, wants to undestand the **phenomenon** of anxiety and to establish that anxiety does, or does not, do this or that, to these people or those. The historian wants to study an event and draw conclusions about all sorts of things including, perhaps, the role that anxiety played. One might compare the difference to that between statistical knowledge relating to cricket and personal knowledge of particular batsmen. You know that X had a bowling average of 10 for 50 in his professional career and took more wickets than anyone else in first-class matches; whereas I was unaware of that, but I did see him bowl about a hundred times. These are equally important, but very different kinds of knowledge (*analogy).

Though the knowledge of the social scientist and the historian may be equally important in themselves, historical understanding is more important from an educational point of view. To understand the science of human beings is less important in respect of developing the mind, and is of less practical significance for most people in living their lives, than to understand the story of our past and something of how we became what we have become (*art education, curriculum, feminism, logical order, nationalism, moral education).

REFERENCES

Carr (1961), Elton (1967), Finley (1975), Gardiner (1988), Handlin (1979), Marwick (1970), Stanford (1986), Strayer (1943), Tosh (1984).

History of education *see* Research, Theory

Humanities *see* Core curriculum, Liberal education, Metaphor, Quantitative/qualitative research

I

Ideology

'Ideology' has been used in a wide variety of senses and contexts over the last two hundred years. First employed in the late eighteenth century in a very specialized sense to denote a particular science of ideas, the term became common two generations later in discussions of the belief systems and ideas that characterize or dominate the thinking of communities or groups within society. Marxist thinkers, in particular, paid attention to the role that belief systems held by certain classes play in mystifying or masking the nature of **class** conflicts. The term is now used by all those interested (e.g. sociologists and educationalists) in uncovering what they regard as the taken-for-granted ideas or **theories** dominating thought and practice, especially in the study of **language, knowledge**, and institutions. (Note that some writers also use the term as the rough equivalent of 'theory', 'idea', or 'view', as in 'the ideology of IQ', or 'the ideology of higher education'.)

When not too loosely conceived, the notion usefully draws attention to the fact that what people believe or even know is often determined by the society in which they live, rather than by their own reflections or thought. For example, particular groups within society may hold strongly a wide range of political beliefs that govern their voting behaviour, even if those political beliefs are not always in their own best **interests**. Within society, certain institutions or classes may have a vested interest in promoting particular sets of beliefs, and on occasion be able to use the weapons of state or other authority to enforce those beliefs. Evidence of a dominating thought or prevailing belief system may be found in, for example, language systems, class structures, sex differentials, or possibly knowledge patterns – all of which play powerful roles in the daily life of schools. The way students and teachers talk to one another, the type of knowledge served up in **curricula**, and the means of **teaching**, it is claimed by some, often carry a particular political message, or serve a special economic purpose. Such interests may be overt (e.g. in promoting **nationalistic** feelings in a **history** class), or covert (e.g. in promoting class interests in mathematics lessons by use of specific examples). Identifying ideologies in education, and showing how they may affect patterns of curricula and human relations in schools, are important tasks for sociologists and educators.

Nevertheless, the search for ideological influences on society in general, and **schooling** in particular, carries with it some hidden dangers. Given the interest of specific political groups in such **research**, the findings appear at times to be fairly simplistic; there is a disconcerting inevitability about research into evidence of class interests in societal **phenomena**. Some discussions of such research seem far from openminded either on the evidence or on the interpretation that is placed upon it. In addition, on the question of the social origin of knowledge, it is a comparatively short step from arguing that knowledge is affected by social context, with which most people would agree, to maintaining that knowledge is determined by social context, with which most would disagree (*action research, critical theory, reconceptualists).

REFERENCES

Apple (1979), Bernbaum (1977), Bowles and Gintis (1976), Brown (1973), Carson (1983), Defaveri (1983), Freire (1973b), Gilbert (1984), Giroux (1983a), Karabel and Halsey (1977), Plamenatz (1970), Schnell (1979), Shapiro (1982), Sharp (1980), Willis (1977), Young (1971).

Imagination

In common with **creativity**, and to a lesser extent **intelligence** and **critical thinking**, imagination is commonly thought of as a species of inspirational visitation. 'Imagination' serves as an **emotively** positive term that suggests a capacity to be inventive, unusual, or productive of ideas. It tends to be associated with the arts more than the sciences, and differs from creativity, if at all, in being associated with ideas rather than visual or musical images. One tends to talk, for instance, of a creative composer but an imaginative writer.

This broad everyday understanding of the term is not entirely wide of the mark. But it is necessary to pinpoint certain features of imagination that are ignored or glossed over in any such common sense account, and, in particular to combat the idea that imagination is essentially a form of inspiration. For the logic of imaginative is very similar to that of creative, and to be imaginative necessarily involves mastery of certain branches of **understanding**.

The **generic fallacy** needs to be avoided. Imagination is not a faculty that one possesses, as one possesses a leg or a liver. 'It' is not anything, for there is no organ of the imagination. It is the name we give to an abstract idea that arises because people may do certain things imaginatively. (It well may be that a certain part of the brain in good working order is a necessary condition of imaginative behaviour, but that no more makes it equivalent to the imagination than the heart that is necessary for the pumping of blood makes the heart the same thing as the flowing of blood.) A person, then, does not literally have imagination, and one's ability to do some things imaginatively tells one nothing about one's ability to do other things imaginatively.

We describe an individual as imaginative in so far as he is capable of conceiving of unusual and effective ideas, solutions, etc. Thus, quality and competence are built in to the concept. While it is conceivable that a person should by **nature**, chance, act of God, etc., have original and useful ideas relating to, for instance, the writing of poetry, atomic fission, or planning a golf course, a reasonable presumption is that deliberate study of these and other areas will be required, if one is to be imaginative in the areas in question.

There may be such things as flair, inspiration, etc., but one requires disciplined understanding in a given sphere to be imaginative in it. The cultivation of the imagination would therefore seem to be best served by a combination of developing understanding of various important and **worthwhile** subject matters, and by providing examples and illustrative models of imaginative work and behaviour.

REFERENCES

Egan and Nadaner (1988), Warnock (1976).

Immersion

The term 'immersion' is applied to a particular type of **schooling** for second-language instruction, associated especially with French-language instruction among Anglophones in Canada. For a variety of reasons (political and social, as well as **educational**) a growing number of English-speaking Canadians have demanded that their school systems produce graduates who are fluent in French – an ability that many students taught by traditional methods conspicuously lack. One remedy, attempted first in English-speaking parts of Quebec, is to restructure the entire early-school programme to provide for French as the exclusive medium of instruction in all subjects (thus students were 'immersed' in the second language). The objective of this change was to reproduce in school the environment in which students had learned their first language. Although other formats were devised (introducing programmes at later points in a student's career, or devoting only part of a timetable to subject matter taught in French), they were not considered as effective as the early-school model, which is now provided on an optional basis by many jurisdictions across the country.

French-immersion programmes have not been without their critics. Some argue that students in French-immersion programmes are held back in the development of their first **language**, others that only students of superior abilities can benefit from immersion. (Recent research results appear to allay these fears.) Many jurisdictions cannot obtain qualified staff in sufficient numbers to mount their immersion programmes, and others experience difficulties in reallocating personnel and resources. Some concern has been expressed about the persistence of traditional pedagogies in immersion classes, to the exclusion of more interactive or dialogic patterns. Despite these problems, however, French-immersion programmes have been welcomed, for the simple reason that their graduates are not only fluent in French and English, but also appear to perform at least as successfully as their non-immersion contemporaries in standard tests of achievement.

A larger educational question remains in dispute. The provision of immersion programmes needs justification, not on political, but on educational grounds, and it is not clear that such justification has been provided. It could be argued, for example, that the emphasis upon one language may deflect attention from other desirable educational goals. Furthermore, although the results from standardized tests are encouraging in themselves, any conclusions from these findings should be modified by reflection on the limited range of such tests (*research). Finally, granted that immersion students become fluent in French, any considerations of its worth should take into account its expense.

It is uncertain to what extent the French-immersion example applies in other contexts. Canadians themselves are not obviously persuaded of the usefulness of immersion in other situations which at first sight seem parallel: for example, second-language instruction of non-anglophone native peoples. The results of immersing native children in English from the very first days of school have not proved entirely beneficent: their facility in the second languge (i.e. English) is often considered unsatisfactory, and their experience in the 'immersion' environment appears to alienate them both from their schools and from their own **culture**. (Some scholars use the term 'submersion' rather than 'immersion in such settings.) Consequently, many critics argue that what is needed is not an immersion approach to the second language, but a much stronger provision for the vernacular. This argument has been echoed in many other jurisdictions – Wales and Ireland are but two examples – in which **bilingualism** is a contentious issue.

REFERENCES

Cummins (1983b), Cummins and Swain (1986), Day and Shapson (1988), Safty (1988), Toohey (1985).

Impartiality *see* Neutrality

Implementation *see* Curriculum change, Reconceptualists

Impressionistic appraisal *see* Intelligence, Objectivity, Research

Indoctrination

Despite the fact that historically the word 'indoctrination' has been used as a mere synonym for 'instruction', it now generally carries pejorative overtones. Indoctrination is something that we wish to avoid, something that we are inclined to accuse those we do not like of doing. How, then, is it to be characterized and to be distinguished from, for example, **education, socialization**, influence, and **training**? It is true that the word is often used very loosely in educational (and political) writings. (For example, the **deschoolers** argue that all **schooling** is necessary indoctrinatory. But that could only be true if the word is interpreted to mean something very general such as influence.) But this is to be resisted, essentially because the connotations of disapproval and condemnation that remain (and are usually supposed to remain from the speaker or author's point of view) are not warranted, unless the concept is taken in some particular and specific way that can be seen to be objectionable. (For example, if schooling does indoctrinate, but only in the sense of influence or form various beliefs and values, then indoctrination can hardly be objected to: in the first place, such influence cannot be avoided; in the second place, there are many strong arguments, to do with social cohesion and personal security, that suggest such influence, which is closely akin to socialization, is highly desirable.)

Research into the **concept** has revolved around four criteria. Some see indoctrination as essentially a matter of **teaching** or imparting information in a certain kind of way (method criterion); some see it as marked by a certain kind of intent (intention criterion). Some argue that the hallmark is the type of information one puts across (content criterion); and some see indoctrination as an **achievement** word such as 'finding', in that one is indoctrinating if, and only if, one succeeds in closing somebody's mind on an issue (consequence criterion). In addition, various combinations of these criteria have been proposed.

Although the view that to be an indoctrinator one has to succeed in closing the mind of someone is not common, it is generally agreed that a necessary feature of the indoctrinated person is that he should have a closed mind. A closed mind is to be distinguished from one that has commitment to or a firm belief in something. A closed mind implies less about the strength of beliefs than the way they are seen, or their status. The hallmark of the closed mind is that it sees its beliefs as ungainsayable – it gives them the status of unquestionable truths. The closed mind is therefore a psychological state, and the person with a closed mind may develop a number of techniques for fending off challenges to his beliefs. It is important to distinguish between the mind that is closed in this sense, and the mind that remains committed to its beliefs as a result of ignorance, laziness, stupidity, etc. The indoctrinated mind insists on the correctness of its views in defiance of any question or challenge.

Although it is the case that to be in an indoctrinated state necessarily involves a closed mind, it does not seem sensible to attempt to define the act of indoctrination in such terms. For we surely object to certain kinds of teaching on the grounds that they are indoctrinatory, whether they succeed in closing the mind or not. This would lead some to argue that it is the intention to close the mind that is the hallmark of the indoctrinator. One might, for example, teach Darwinian theory simply with a view to explaining what was involved in it and suggesting that it had some plausibility. In such a case one would not be an indoctrinator, even if one's students ended up regarding the Darwinian theory as unquestionably correct. On the other hand, on this view, one would be an indoctrinator, whatever effect one had, if one's intention was to persuade students that the theory was beyond question.

One problem with that view is that sometimes it surely is the teacher's intention to close the mind on an issue (because there is no doubt about the issue, we claim) and we do not wish to condemn such teaching as indoctrination. For example, since two times two does equal four, since certain things do happen if you mix certain chemicals, since certain facts about the Second World War are established, etc., teachers are expected to impart such information and make it stick. Such considerations may lead to examination of the other two criteria. For, first, it may be said that there are different kinds of content, some of which it is appropriate to close the mind over, some of which it is not. Secondly, it may be suggested that the idea of closing the mind needs further refinement, with particular reference to the method whereby information is imparted.

Where the information is amenable to clear proof in terms that are publicly accepted, it has been argued, we may indeed wish to make the information stick. There is nothing wrong with imparting an unquestioning commitment to the belief that two and two equal four or that certain things happen when one mixes certain chemicals, and we will not call such teaching indoctrination. But where the information is not amenable to proof in any publicly agreed way, as might be said to be the case with certain historical claims, and would certainly be the case with certain **religious, aesthetic**, and **moral** claims, then one should not close the mind on particular beliefs. Thus to commit the individual to an unquestioning belief in the existence of God would be to indoctrinate. (To put the matter formally, this would be to say that indoctrination involves imparting commitment to unprovable propositions. Others would go further and suggest that the etymological connection of the word 'indoctrination' with 'doctrines' indicates that it is only propositions that are part of a doctrinal system that can be indoctrinated.)

A problem with the view that indoctrination is simply a matter of imparting a certain kind of content is that it is not entirely clear where the type of content in question begins and ends. Some would argue that the natural sciences, usually taken as the **paradigm** of **objective** truth, are not as straightforward and securely known as is popularly supposed; at the other extreme some would argue that, for example, certain claims in morality and art are not beyond rational demonstration. This may lead some commentators to argue that what matters is the method whereby one imparts information. Provided that one provides whatever reasons one can to support the truth of any claims considered, and acknowledges that their truth is assumed on the basis of the reasoning alone, which may turn out to be inadequate, faulty or false, one is teaching acceptably. But so soon as one resorts to non-rational techniques of persuasion (whether they be hypnotism, torture, charisma, appeals to authority, etc.) then one is indoctrinating.

The method criterion alone cannot sensibly be said to define indoctrination. For, if it did, we should be guilty of indoctrinating every time we persuaded young children to refrain from putting their hands on hot stoves or walking across busy roads. But it does seem a **necessary condition** of indoctrination. Our view would therefore be that indoctrination involves the use of non-rational means in an attempt to impart unquestioning commitment to the truth of certain unprovable claims with the intention of making them stick (*emotive meaning, etymology, normative**).

REFERENCES

Flew (1966b), Hare (1964a), Snook (1972a, 1972b), White (1967), Wilson (1964).

Infer *see* Linguistic error

Informal research *see* Ethnography, Objectivity, Research, Quantitative/qualitative research, Subjectivity

Information processing *see* Programmed learning

Inherent value *see* Creativity, Value judgements, Worthwhile

Innate differences *see* Nature/nurture

Inquiry learning *see* Integrated studies, Learning

Instruction *see* Teaching

Integrated studies

In the last twenty years many attempts have been made to unify or integrate various subjects within the school **curriculum. Teaching** by themes that cross disciplinary boundaries, or teaching for critical thinking without limitations on the area of search, have become particularly popular. Several well-funded curriculum projects have published a variety of types of package designed to combine the study of more than one discipline. For example, in Britain, the Humanities Project, in the United States, *MACOS (Man: A Course of Study)*, and in Canada the projects undertaken by the Canada Studies Foundation, included major elements of curriculum integration.

Despite these examples, however, it is not clear how 'integration' ought to be defined, nor are the principles governing the integration of subject matter easy to isolate or justify. The distinctions between 'integration' and such related terms as 'a co-ordinated curriculum', 'a fused curriculum', 'interdisciplinary studies', 'cross-disciplinary studies', and 'multidisciplinary studies' are not always evident. On occasion, subjects have been integrated simply to solve immediate social problems (e.g. raising the school-leaving age, or new requirements for career education) rather than as a result of reflection upon the nature of the epistemological issues involved in the enterprise of integration itself.

It is worth noting that 'integration', rather like **'child-centred'** and **'needs'**, is a loaded term among educators. As Pring (1971b) has demonstrated, 'integration' carries in educational discourse strong connotations of approval that the phrase 'subject-based' lacks. 'Integration' implies unity (which seems generally to be approved), while 'subjects' imply compartmentalization, departmentalization, or divisional structure (all of which are widely regretted). In published integrated studies projects and courses, however, it is not always clear who or what is responsible for the actual integration. In some cases, teachers are expected to make themselves familiar with propositions and methods of inquiry in a number of **disciplines**; in others, teachers and students are expected to draw their own conclusions from collections of material derived from several disciplines. Other versions put students in the position of integrating a variety of ideas on one topic offered by a team of subject-based teachers. These confusions may account for the conceptual and practical problems that integrated studies courses have experienced.

Perhaps the most frequently used means of integration involves bringing ideas, **concepts**, or **facts** from a second discipline to bear on issues or problems raised in a particular subject-based class. A teacher examining the changing political climate of eighteenth-century European **history**, for example, may introduce related notions from the arts and music into his discussion (or invite the fine-arts teacher and music teacher to illustrate parallel developments in their own disciplines). This type of integrative activity is obviously unexceptionable and perhaps desirable, in that it simply recognizes that different forms of knowledge are clearly related to one another, and that developments in one subject may influence or affect developments in others. The situation becomes somewhat more complex when teams of teachers in many disciplines offer different perspectives on a single topic, especially if the task of integration devolves upon students.

Some exponents of an integrated curriculum, however, make much more ambitious claims. They argue that, since all **knowledge** is one, a sort of 'seamless web', all distinctions among subjects and disciplines ought to be removed. Given this vague exhortation, it is scarcely surprising that methods of implementing its intent vary from curriculum to curriculum: some favour examining themes or topics, while others recommend grouping subjects under such umbrellas as environmental studies or current issues. Unfortunately, such curricular integrations, however well meaning in purpose, ride roughshod over a number of epistemological problems. Within the several disciplines or forms of thought, propositions, concepts, and methods of inquiry differ significantly, and little is gained by treating them as if they were identical, as may happen in an integrated studies course. Effective investigation of many themes or subject-groupings may depend upon a prior knowledge of facts, concepts, and methods of procedure appropriate to those disciplines to which the themes are related. (In environmental studies, for example, appropriate investigation of certain issues may depend upon a prior knowledge of chemistry.)

The same argument may be applied to those patterns of integrated study based on such notions as **creative** thinking, **critical thinking**, or inquiry learning. Some curriculum proposals encourage students to follow their own **interests** after selecting a particular concept. A person choosing 'exploration', therefore, might conceivably end up looking at either medieval literary texts or twentieth-century space metallurgy (or perhaps both). Students practising the process of inquiry in an integrated setting may similarly be encouraged to follow those paths that their interests (or whims) dictate. In such undertakings the dangers of aimless or idiosyncratic wanderings in alternative subject matters, without invoking any type of public test, are obvious. This is not to say that personal exploration or speculation is undesirable, merely that it is worth stressing that the results of such investigations need to be examined in relation to public traditions and by means of accepted methods of verification.

A shift within a school to any type of integrated studies (even if well articulated and carefully justified) may cause some stress among administrators and teachers. Headmasters and principals may be unwilling to accommodate the timetabling demands of an integrated studies programme. Teaching staffs may be divided: some teachers who spend all their spare time attempting to keep up with publications or new ideas in one discipline may resent being pushed into unfamiliar areas, while others may welcome the opportunity provided by integrated studies to get out of an academic rut in which they find themselves after many years of service. If both types of teacher are employed in the same staff (not an unlikely event), then a person advocating integrated studies may be required to be flexible and tactful rather than zealous or dogmatic in his aims and approaches.

Integrating subject matter is a difficult task; the range of alternative approaches is wide, and some are easier to justify than others.

Integrated studies have some advantages, not the least of which may be revitalizing a moribund curriculum or shaking up staid teachers. But there are other methods for reforming a curriculum, and if teachers were better educated and more imaginative, many of the pressures for integrated studies (and a good many other educational problems) would vanish overnight (*open education, team teaching).

REFERENCES

Barnes (1982), Bolam (1972, 1973), Bruner (1966), Gibbons (1979), Hirst (1974b), Hodgetts and Gallagher (1978), Kelly (1977), Pring (1971b, 1973, 1976), Schwartz (1970), Shipman (1974), Stenhouse (1970b, 1980), Underhill and Telford (1979), Warwick (1973).

Integration

In educational discourse, integration may typically refer to: (a) **integrated studies**; (b) **mainstreaming** or the integration of various distinct categories of learner, such as learning disabled and dyslexic children; (c) integration of otherwise differentiated grade levels, as in a current British Columbia proposal to break down or integrate the categories from kindergarten to grade 4; or (d) mixed-ability grouping amongst regular students. This entry is concerned only with the final category.

Mixed-ability grouping is usually contrasted with streaming, and **empirical** evidence is generally thought to show it to be preferable. Thus the Royal Commission on Education in British Columbia states that 'research evidence clearly shows that all students benefit when they are grouped heterogeneously', and the Radwanski *Study* (1987) in Ontario similarly summarizes the situation thus: 'the practice of consistent homogeneous ability grouping can no longer be justified in a system of education committed to achieving successful outcomes for all students.' In fact one may question these verdicts. First, they are overstatements of the research findings they are actually citing; for example, Radwanski is summing up this slightly more cautious summary of the research made by Esposito (1973). 'Homogeneous ability grouping as currently practised shows no consistent positive value for helping students generally . . . among the studies showing significant effects, the slight gains favouring high ability students are more than offset by evidence of unfavourable effects on the learning of students of average and below average ability.' Secondly, there is some, though perhaps not very persuasive, counter-testimony. For instance, Joan Lunn (1970) found that students in streamed schools seemed to do slightly better in a set of attainment tests (although in a longer study she found no difference). Thirdly, there is the major question of how far the kind of **research** that lies behind any of these claims is in fact **reliable** or trustworthy.

In this case, however, the issue does not have to be debated in terms of whether research does or does not establish what it claims to have established, for a striking feature of most of the individual studies (on the basis of which final positions are being taken), is that they have involved comparison between streamed and mixed ability groups, 'streamed' meaning 'divided into particular ability groupings for all purposes'. Thus the contrast is between categorizing individuals as of high, average, low, etc., ability across the board and making no distinctions. Now, whether empirical research has confirmed it or not, a priori one would be inclined to believe, and one's own limited experience tends to confirm, that individuals are seldom of the same ability at everything: on the contrary, many individuals are good at mathematics, but poor at languages; moderate historians but excellent chemists; average at English and worse at physical education, etc. That being so, classification according to some notion of a fixed across-the-board ability (an instantiation of the **generic fallacy**) seems unconvincing, and may well be supposed to have shown no particular advantages over mixed-ability grouping.

The issue should obviously be one of whether to adopt setting or not. That is to say, whether particular classes in, say, mathematics, should consist of people of differing mathematical background and competence, or people of similar present proficiency. To this issue, the body of research conventionally cited does not appear to speak at all. Common sense suggests that, while in a mixed-ability class less advanced pupils might be inspired by more advanced ones, and while there will be opportunity for peer tutoring which, it has been claimed, is beneficial to both parties, the business of **teaching** will be considerably harder (and therefore may in the event more often fail), some of the more advanced may more readily become bored, some of the less advanced more despondent, and that it is an impossibility to stretch all ability groupings to their capacity, without in some way distinguishing them.

It will be noted that even if the research cited were in no way questionable and spoke to the issue at hand, it still does not decisively conclude that mixed-ability teaching is preferable: it says rather that it is marginally better in certain very limited respects.

Why, then, the unseemly rush to adopt integration in this sense? The answer, yet again, would seem to be a failure of nerve in the face of contemporary confusion over the concepts of truth, **value**, and **education** – a mistaken confusion between achieving currently fashionable social objectives and achieving timeless educational objectives.

REFERENCES

Esposito (1973), Lunn (1970), Radwanski (1987), Wright (1977).

Intelligence

Gage and Berliner, in a standard textbook on educational psychology (1979), write: 'As everyone knows, it became possible during the twentieth century to measure individual differences in intelligence.' However, this claim is highly misleading, if not actually false. It became possible to administer tests that were called 'intelligence tests'. In what sense such tests truly **measure** intelligence, and whether it is truly intelligence that they **assess** are further questions. There is still some truth in Boring's judgement that intelligence tests only test intelligence, if intelligence is defined as 'what the intelligence tests test'. And there is still room for argument, despite attempts at refinement of tests over the years, as to how accurate an estimate they provide even of what they test.

Intelligence testing is usually taken to have started with the work of the French psychologist Binet and his collaborator Simon in the 1890s. But their concern was specifically to devise tests to reveal the individual's competence in respect of various specific things such as attention span, ability to perform certain logical operations, and to make **moral** judgements. Their intention was to devise tests that would enable distinctions to be made between students' suitability for the work of the regular classroom, more reliably than by means of the teacher's impressionistic judgement. (The latter could clearly be susceptible to distortion as a result of, for example, a child's quietness in class, the likeableness of a child, or his hearing difficulties.) In principle there are no problems about the idea of such tests: they have direct **validity** in respect of clearly defined **skills**, and they are being used only to establish relatively extreme cases where such skills are lacking. But already one may wish to raise the question of whether the ability to display competence, as defined by the tester, in respect of a number of specific skills, as selected by the tester, constitutes intelligence. When I refer to Einstein's intelligence, is it to such a stock of basic competencies that I intend to refer?

Subsequent developments in intelligence testing have produced a more systematic approach and more sophisticated tests, as well as allegedly more data. (It is necessary to write 'allegedly' because of the problem, endemic in such **research**, that new tests are largely validated against other tests. In so far as there are fundamental flaws or weaknesses in the idea or design of such testing, such validation is largely immaterial.) They have also produced more ambitious attempts at a definition of intelligence.

At one time it was popular to conceive of intelligence in terms of some general factor (named the g factor by Spearman) and a range of specific ability factors (s factors). On this view, any given intelligent act would involve both g and the s factors appropriate to the act. However, even if it were true that there is a g factor, it would be impossible to measure it on its own, since by definition it is always found in conjunction with s factors. (That is, if one uses a spatial test of intelligence, whatever happens, it will not be possible to distinguish what is due to various spatial abilities and what to the g factor.) Furthermore, there does not appear to be the high **correlation** between different kinds of intelligence test that one would expect, if they all measure to some extent the common factor g. Consequently many people prefer a multi-factorial model of intelligence, which is to say one that represents intelligence in terms of many particular competencies. Guilford, for example, has posited 120 mental factors which in one combination or another may be involved in an intelligent act. Such detailed and extensive **models** naturally encourage fairly elaborate **conceptions** of intelligence. Thus Stoddard suggested that 'intelligence is the ability to undertake activities that are characterized by (a) difficulty; (b) complexity; (c) abstractness; (d) economy; (e) adaptiveness to a goal; (f) social value; and (g) the emergence of originals, and to maintain such activities under conditions that demand concentration of energy and a resistance to emotional forces.' But can the tests plausibly be thought to measure intelligence so defined?

Tests may take many forms. They may emphasize verbal abilities, numerical, or memory abilities (or some combination of such things). The items too may take a variety of forms. (For example, complete the following: 'A table is made of wood; a window of—.' 'A bird flies; a fish—.' Recite a series of digits backwards. Name a number of small models of things such as bed, chair, and table. When asked what one uses to drive about in, or to drink out of, either point to a model car or cup respectively, or give the word 'car' or 'cup'. Look at a series of pictures and say what is odd about them – a couple sitting out on the porch in the rain, perhaps, or a rabbit chasing a dog.) But, whatever the precise nature of the test item, it is liable to be an item that simply tests vocabulary, numeracy, the ability to recognize shapes, the ability to recapitulate material, or some common observation knowledge about the world with as little reference to specialist knowledge as possible. The material is scaled in difficulty for different age groups (a test of vocabulary suitable for a three-year-old would not be very appropriate for a twenty-three-year-old). But it will be noted that, the more complex the test item, the more uncertain it becomes whether competence in respect of it suggests something about intelligence as opposed to something about what one has been taught. Perhaps there is something that may reasonably be classified as low intelligence involved when a three-year-old appears to have acquired very little of the vocabulary normally found in children of that age. It becomes much less clear that a similarly small vocabulary relative to other eighteen-year-olds should be interpreted as a sign of poor intelligence in an eighteen-year-old. Other items may present other, though logically similar, problems. The ability to memorize or, more specifically, recite numbers backwards does not obviously seem to have much to do with intelligence or to have any intrinsic importance. Likewise, whether it seems odd that a rabbit should be chasing a dog seems more a question of one's experience and knowledge than one's intelligence. The overriding problem would appear to be that though it is possible to conceive of test items that are relatively culture-free and context-free, they will tend to be trivial and not obviously related to anything that matters very much, still less to any normal conception of intelligence. If on the other hand they are constructed to test abilities that seem to us significant and really to involve intelligence, then, whether there is some general factor of intelligence or not, they will necessarily involve testing acquired learning as well (*culture).

So far we have considered tests simply as if they were tests for individuals, and as if intelligence were judged only in terms of success or lack of it on the test. But tests are more often group tests, and scored in a particular way. Because the basic assumption has been that such testing is not simply testing the individual's ability to do certain specific things at a specific time, but rather is testing some permanent element(s) called intelligence, it has been supposed necessary to produce a system whereby we can relate the individual's test score (the raw score) to some notion of what is normal or appropriate for his age. Raw scores are converted to standardized scores, and these are interpreted in the light of the test's norms. The scores are usually expressed in terms of 100 being the average. One other point about scoring is extremely important: the assumption is made that intelligence is normally distributed throughout the population. Just as most people are grouped in the middle so far as height goes, with a small number of very small people and a small number of very big people, so it is assumed most people are of moderate intelligence. This assumption has severe practical implications, for tests are designed and modified in the light of it. Yet there is no clear reason to suppose that it is so. Should one suppose that moral virtue or humour are necessarily so distributed? Then why should one suppose that intelligence is, especially when we bear in mind that it is far from clear that there is anything that lies behind the word 'intelligence' to be distributed?

It is arguable that intelligence tests have their uses and that the most severe problems in connection with them come from misuse of them. In particular, individuals are **stereotyped** as being intelligent or unintelligent in the light of such tests, and then sorted and treated accordingly.

One of the main claims of intelligence testing is that good performance correlates highly with academic success as measured by other tests, and to a lesser extent with job success. But it is difficult to see in this a very strong case for intelligence tests. In the first place intelligence tests are themselves a form of academic success, partly because they test what is to some extent learned, partly because they test some things that are a necessary part of academic success, partly because they usually take place in an academic context. Secondly, knowledge of the IQ of an individual will in many cases alter the teacher's attitude to him, and his own to himself. In the third place, no doubt the kind of homes that nurture the one nurture the other. A moderate correlation between IQ and job success is likewise to be expected: those who do badly on basic tests of vocabulary, numeracy, and observation of the everyday world are not likely to prosper at school and subsequently in the professions. (Furthermore, while IQ tests may be reasonable predictors of overall achievement they are relatively poor predictors of achievement in specific subjects, which is of more practical concern to educators. Finally, it should be noted that some quite large changes in IQ have been recorded, e.g. in conjunction with the Headstart program, which suggests that part of what is being measured is achievement.)

The question remains why anyone should relate good performance on such tests to being intelligent, which one presumes should be taken to mean having a disposition to behave intelligently, and why they should make administrative decisions on the basis of them. When all is said and done we have not advanced beyond the days of Binet–Simon, except that the claims have become more grandiose in proportion to the statistical engineering (*education, generic fallacy, nature, normative, quantitative/qualitative research).

REFERENCES

Boring (1957), *Environment, Heredity and Intelligence* (1960), Fontana (1981), Gage and Berliner (1979), Kleinig (1982), Simon (1971).

Interaction analysis

In the last thirty years a great deal of energy has been spent trying to find out what goes on in classrooms. Researchers have been primarily interested in finding causal connections between the behaviour of teachers and the **learning** achievement of students. They have adopted a variety of principles and procedures that are illustrative not only of alternative types of methodology, but also, to some extent, of different national traditions in educational investigations.

Conducting research in classrooms, and indeed in almost all educational settings, is extraordinarily complex (and many of the steps taken to simplify the task are frequently misleading). Note the conditions: two dozen (or more) people in a classroom, possessing different personalities and backgrounds; no clear or accepted agreement on the nature or purpose of the meeting; a great variety of activities and exchanges (and understandings of what they mean); and, in an experimental setting, the intervention of the observer, whose welcome may be at best half-hearted, and whose presence almost certainly changes the nature of the situation. Furthermore, the classroom experience of teachers and students is a cumulative matter that extends over several hundred hours. How is a researcher to make sense of such complex events on his brief intrusions?

One solution in the United States, especially in the period up to the mid-1970s, was to pay particular attention to capturing and measuring the interaction of teacher and students, that is, the 'verbal behaviour' of teachers and students as they talked to one another. Given the prevailing social scientific and **quantitative** research methodology, researchers devised specific **behavioural** categories or activities capable of being checked off with a high degree of accuracy by trained observers. So intense was this effort that the phrase 'classroom observation' became almost interchangeable with 'interaction analysis'. A well-known example of this attempt to analyse teacher and student talk is the Flanders Interaction Analysis Categories system (FIAC), which has been used in a great variety of experimental settings for almost three decades. In that system, the details of which have varied over the years, an observer is given ten categories of verbal behaviour (seven for the teacher, e.g. 'asks questions', or 'lecturing', two for the student, e.g. 'student talk – response', and one for 'silence or confusion'), and required to note at three-second intervals the type of talk that is occurring. The tallies derived from observing a particular class enable the observer to analyse the interaction between teachers and students, that is, calculate the percentage of teacher or student talk, and the extent to which a teacher is indulging in 'direct' or dominating behaviour as opposed to 'indirect' or integrative and democratic behaviour. FIAC was used so frequently, and adapted to such a wide variety of other category systems, that it may serve as an icon of the entire type of research.

Many benefits have been claimed for FIAC. Comparatively easy to learn and apply with a high degree of accuracy, FIAC encouraged teachers, particularly those in pre-service training, to reflect upon certain alternative styles of **teaching**. The notion of direct and indirect teaching styles (or equivalent terms) has stimulated discussion about how teaching ought to take place in the classroom. But as a piece of social scientific research, FIAC has been found wanting, even by those whose commitment to this type of research is unequivocal. It is not clear, for example, how exclusive the categories are, or how useful the teaching **skills** that are encouraged by repeated use of the system. Very few **empirical** claims have been securely established by researchers using FIAC, and in certain important respects (for example, the relationship between teaching styles and student learning – one of the principal focal points of the scheme), it appears clear that no positive conclusions can be drawn.

In more general terms, the criticism of FIAC, and the research principles on which it is based, is more biting. Pre-specifying a limited number of categories (especially in a frugal way) inevitably caricatures what actually happens in the classroom. The assumption that teachers (or students) are always involved in only one behaviour at any given time, let alone the particular behaviour cited by FIAC, is logically and demonstrably false. The Flanders system is insensitive to the quality and content of classroom discussion (indeed it 'works' with nonsensical talk), and unresponsive to the different demands of different types of subject matter. In short, the use of FIAC in the classroom does not tell us very much, and what it does tell us is unimportant.

Critics in Britain (where psychological methods in education have not been so dominant among researchers) have noted that the principles on which FIAC is designed run true to the behaviourist assumptions of social scientific psychology in the United States: the system is typically based on pre-specified categories that are both atomistic and reductionist. In addition, the system contains a built-in **ideological** bias, despite its cool, social scientific appearance, in that it encourages, or requires, teachers to adopt those 'indirect' methods presumed to correspond to the American way. FIAC necessarily ignores the real life of students in the classroom, and disregards the particular meanings that students and teachers bring to any meeting. The example of FIAC offers a cautionary tale about the problems inherent in educational **research** over the last thirty years.

REFERENCES

Amidon and Hough (1967), Amidon and Hunter (1966), Barrow (1984), Delamont (1976, 1983), Delamont and Hamilton (1976), Dunkin and Biddle (1974), Flanders (1970), Freiberg (1981), Furst (n.d.), Jackson (1968), Rosenshine and Furst (1973), Simon and Boyer (1968), Walker and Adelman (1975).

Interdisciplinary study *see* Integrated studies

Interests

The claim that education should be based upon children's interests is ambiguous. It may mean: (a) that education should be based on what is in their interests; or (b) that it should be based on what interests them. In either case there is further equivocation in a phrase such as 'based upon'. One's agreement or dissent from the view might be very much affected by whether one takes 'based upon' to mean something like 'take note of' or something like 'essentially governed by'. The latter would usually be a more challenging claim, but by the same token a more debatable one.

First, that education should be in the interests of children seems almost a truism. **Education** is by definition something of value; we provide it because we believe it to be in the individual's interests to have it. Certainly, nobody would commit himself to the claim that education should be contrary to students' interests. However, the fact that education should be in the interests of children does not preclude the possibility that it should also take other interests (such as those of the state, parents, and teachers) into account, does not preclude the possibility that while being to some extent based on children's interests it should also be affected by other facts (such as considerations of educational worth, **cultural** claims, and the structure of **knowledge**), and, most importantly, does not in itself tell us what is in the interests of children. In short, while it is probably true that education should be based on children's interests, it is a most unhelpful remark. To make it meaningful one would have to offer a detailed account of what is in children's interests, and to what extent education should be based upon them. Such elaboration, besides taking us a long way from the simplistic slogan with which we started, would also render the claim considerably more open to debate.

Secondly, that education should, without qualification, be concerned only with what interests children at any given moment is not a position that anybody has actually ever defended. John Dewey and Jean-Jacques

Rousseau, who are often associated with an emphasis on children's interests, did not propose anything so dramatic. None the less, great stress may be laid upon what interests children as a criterion for selecting content, sequencing material, or motivational strategies.

The notion that curriculum content should be selected by reference to children's interests is hard to sustain. The **curriculum** is, after all, a school curriculum, and as such should meet the particular purposes that **schooling** is concerned with. Curriculum content must, therefore, at the very least, be selected by reference to the demands of such things as education and **socialization**, and not simply left to evolve in line with current interests of children, which may conceivably be trivial, antisocial, or non-educational. It might, perhaps, be suggested that as a matter of fact children are invariably (or generally) interested in educationally **worthwhile** things, or that the measure of educational worth is the interest of the student. But neither claim seems plausible: the evidence suggests that children are very often interested in pursuits that have no obvious value, educational or otherwise, and the notion that anything down to and including breaking other children's toys or painting the living room carpet have educational worth, provided that the individual is interested in the activity, is counter-intuitive.

It would be different and rather more plausible to suggest that interests should play a part in determining how to sequence material or when to encourage particular activities. Granted that some things may be valuable or trivial, regardless of student interest, it surely makes sense none the less to take advantage of those situations and occasions on which student interest is active. However, interests should not be taken as **necessary** or sufficient conditions of introducing material. It may be a good idea to override a present interest, there may be better reason to do something else, and sometimes it may be reasonable to refuse to await the spontaneous expression of interest. Many would argue that one of the prime responsibilities of the teacher is to create and evoke interest in matters regarded as being independently worthwhile, rather than to wait upon the expression of interest from students. (There is in addition the problem of how one estimates somebody else's interest in something. The teacher who is trying either to respond to or to cultivate interests would be ill advised to equate interest with, for example, expressed interest.)

The most obvious point at which interests should be stressed is that of motivation. Although there are other kinds of motivation (e.g. praise, reward, criticism, punishment, peer group pressure, success, competition), it is clearly advantageous to motivate, when one can, by taking advantage of students' present interests or by seeking to cultivate new interests. Indeed, some might say that **teaching** should by definition involve evoking not only understanding of, but also interest in, what is learned (*child-centred education).

REFERENCES

Dearden (1968), Wilson (1971).

Intrinsic value *see* Value judgements, Worthwhile

IQ *see* Education, Intelligence, Validity

K

Knowledge

It is common to distinguish propositional knowledge (knowing that . . .), skill knowledge (knowing how to . . .) and knowledge by acquaintance (knowing Smith or Paris). The logical relationship between these types of knowing (for example, the connection between knowing how to X and knowing that Z) has been much debated.

'To know' in the propositional sense is generally taken to mean: (a) having a belief; (b) that is true; and (c) that one has adequate evidence for. It is thus to be distinguished from simply having a belief (which might be false), from having a belief which though true is not established as true by reference to adequate evidence, and from being aware of something that is in fact true and shown to be so by the evidence, but which one does not believe. It should be remembered that the three criteria indicate what is *meant* by knowing; it is not suggested that every actual claim to knowledge meets the criteria. Indeed, because it is sometimes debatable what evidence would count as adequate to establish the truth of a belief, it is sometimes unclear whether we may properly claim to know something or not. We may talk of knowing that metal expands when heated, because there is no dispute about the adequacy of the evidence that supports the statement. Equally clearly, it is improper to talk of knowing that God exists, since there is considerable dispute as to what kind of evidence should count for or against such a claim. (Note that this is not to say that it is untrue to claim that God exists. It may be true or false; but we do not know whether it is, however strong our conviction.) But when we consider a claim such as 'kindness is good' there is dispute as to whether we have or have not established criteria for adequate evidence. At a deep level, one might say that all claims to knowledge (except analytic truths) are in fact conjectural, since what we take to be adequate evidence may turn out not to have been. At an everyday level, it seems rather pointless to deny that there are many things we may legitimately claim to know: for example, truths about the historical past, scientific truths, truths about our everyday existence, mathematical truths, and even truths about values. How is it, then, that throughout history some have sought to argue that there is no such thing as knowledge? What meaning are we to give to claims such as 'man is the measure of all things' and 'everything is as you see it' (***facts**)?

It is necessary to distinguish between epistemological theses and sociological theses. The former, strictly speaking, are concerned with questions about what knowledge is, its nature, while the latter are concerned with questions about social forces and their effects on knowledge claims. Social forces cannot have effects on knowledge itself, in the sense of the nature of knowledge, any more than they can on God himself or God's existence; they can have a bearing only on mankind's view of, or grasp of, knowledge or God. However, this important distinction has sometimes been confused by sociologists of knowledge.

There are certain philosophical theses that look superficially like attempts to assert the position that everything is a matter of opinion: for example, Descartes' questioning of his right to be certain about the existence of anything, saved at the last moment, according to him, by the conclusion that at any rate I know I exist (*cogito ergo sum*: 'I think therefore I am'), and Berkeley's theory that to be is to be perceived (*esse est percipi*). But neither were actually sceptical about there being **objective** truth and our having knowledge of it. Berkeley was seeking to give an account of the nature of such truth (in his view the unchanging reality of the world is guaranteed by God's perpetual sight of it), and Descartes was searching for a basis that nobody could logically deny, on which to build the edifice of knowledge.

Such views are to be sharply distinguished from sociological theses to the effect that what we claim to know, what knowledge we value, and what we choose to advance knowledge of, may be or are in various ways affected by social or cultural factors. Though the extreme view that what we think is entirely the product of the manner of social organization has little to recommend it, the weaker thesis that what we choose to regard as **worthwhile** knowledge (particularly in the context of **schooling**), what we are capable of **understanding**, and what we can regard as adequate or relevant evidence in various matters, are to some extent affected by time and place, is eminently reasonable. But such an admission does not have any bearing on the question of whether some claims are true, as opposed to merely a matter of perspective or viewpoint, and whether we either might or do have knowledge concerning some of them. Shifting opinions on the matter do not change the shape of the world, and few will take seriously the claim that we do not know that it is spherical. But, at any rate, it is clear that we should wish to distinguish between the belief that God exists, which is not supported by what is accepted as adequate evidence, and belief that the world is spherical, which is. Given the meaning of the terms, to say as much is to recognize a distinction between belief and knowledge, and that we know certain things.

Besides such **empirical** knowledge claims, it should be noted that there are various truths of logic and definition that are quite beyond cultural variation. Though the terminology might vary and though bachelors might not exist in certain societies, it remains an abiding truth that all bachelors are unmarried. At a more sophisticated level, a number of mathematical truths and philosophical principles are similarly inviolable. Since a lot of knowledge claims are built up out of logical entailment from undisputed premises, we can rapidly arrive at a considerable number of illuminating and important claims that we may properly be said to know. It has been argued against such a view that, for example, even '2 × 2 = 4' is not always true, but only if one is working in what is termed base 10, while there have been social groups that do not recognize such basic principles as the law of non-contradiction. But these objections do not succeed in establishing that everything is relative to **culture**. '2 × 2 = 4' is always true, provided that one is working in base 10, and it would remain true in the context of a society that could not count, let alone understand what is meant by base 10. Cultures that allegedly do not recognize the law of non-contradiction turn out to be societies that do not object to contradiction as a form of social interchange, which is quite different. That is to say, certainly there have been societies in which self-contradiction or contradiction of others is not regarded as being of any consequence. But if, which we believe is not the case, there has ever been a society that thought that argument could legitimately advance by self-contradictory steps, then such a society would plainly be in error.

A question of particular interest to educationalists is what the pattern of knowledge may be. Granted that there is a substantial body of knowledge (i.e. beliefs shown to be true by reference to adequate evidence) are they all of the same type? A related question is whether distinctions between various subjects are just a matter of different subject matter or have some logical rationale.

The term '**discipline**' is commonly used to characterize those subjects that involve a distinctive type of procedure, which may or may not be brought to bear exclusively on a limited range of subject matter. Thus physics, history, sociology, and philosophy are all disciplines, while education, studying French, and philately are not. The former involve not merely their particular subject matter but a particular kind of activity in relation to it, while the latter are subject matters that may invite treatment by a number of disciplines. Thus, historians study the past in certain characteristic ways, whereas educationalists may study education from a psychological perspective, a philosophical perspective, or indeed a historical perspective. Studying French does not necessarily involve one in one particular kind of procedure, nor does philately. But the sociologist, the physicist, and the philosopher do proceed in limited and identifiable ways.

So at least the assumption goes, though it may be argued that the distinction between a discipline and a subject is both artificial and fluid. There are, after all, many different kinds of sociology, many quite distinct activities or procedures that may be brought to bear on sociological subject matter; in what way does that differ from the many different activities or procedures that may come into play in reference to education? Perhaps it would be safest to say that at any given time in any given culture inquiry into certain subject matters will be seen to have taken on a recognizable and relatively single-minded form, and that it is then regarded as a discipline.

A number of educationalists have tried to produce slightly more clear and specific accounts of the nature of knowledge, prominent among these being Hirst, Phenix, and Barrow. Hirst argues that by reference to three criteria (**concepts** peculiar to the subject, a logical structure unique to the subject, and the manner in which claims are assessed for truth or falsity in the subject) seven forms of knowledge may be discerned. (These forms are: mathematics, physical science, religion, philosophy, literature and the fine arts, moral and interpersonal.) Thus the natural sciences and mathematics each have their distinctive central concepts and their own logic, such that how one determines whether or not it is true that a combination of two chemicals will have a certain effect is quite different from how one determines whether the square of the hypotenuse is equal to the sum of the squares of the opposite sides of a triangle. By contrast, stamp collecting or geography do not give rise to propositions that have to be answered in a unique philatelic or geographical way. They are, rather, fields of knowledge in which more than one form may be deployed.

Criticism of Hirst has been made on the grounds that in many of the forms (e.g. morality, literature and the fine arts) it is not at all clear in what way claims are to be examined, let alone that they are unique in kind. For example, while it is reasonably clear how one sets about assessing the truth of a claim such as that metals expand when heated, there is considerably less agreement about how one sets about determining the truth or falsity of a moral claim such as that happiness is good, and even less about what would be involved in assessing the truth value of a work of art (*aesthetic value, art education, ethics, moral education).

Phenix believes that the appropriate schema involves recognizing six realms of meaning (symbolics, empirics, aesthetics, synnoetics, ethics, and synoptics). Barrow refers to two forms of knowledge (empirical and logical), two types of interpretative attitude (religious and scientific), and four kinds of awareness (moral, aesthetic, religious, and scientific), preserving Hirst's essential distinctions, but seeing them as being to some extent different in kind. However, while the classifications of Phenix and Barrow may avoid some of the logical problems facing Hirst's, they are also of less practical significance, since the curricular implications of the latter's view are considerably more telling. Whereas it would be odd to question the educational importance of initiating people into the forms of knowledge, if they truly exist (since **education** is concerned with the development of cognitive understanding), it would require further argument to establish the educational value of introducing people to all of Phenix's realms or Barrow's kinds of awareness (*religious education**).

Note should also be taken of J. P. White's rather different view that the main distinction of interest is between those activities which, as he sees it, cannot be understood without actually engaging in them (**communicating**, appreciating art, the natural sciences, philosophy, and higher mathematics) and those that can (everything else). His thesis is that, in the interests of increasing scope for choice, which he favours because he is committed to the view that what a person would on reflection choose to do for its own sake is *ipso facto* **worthwhile**, the compulsory element in the curriculum should concentrate on the first group of activities mentioned.

Despite arguments about the precise logical structure of knowledge, it seems widely accepted that **education** should involve bringing individuals to recognize logically distinct kinds of question and issue for what they are: the educated person does not confuse a moral question with a religious one, or treat either as if it were open to examination in the manner of the empirical sciences. Consequently, opposition to concern with the nature of knowledge for curriculum purposes has generally taken the shape of objecting to the emphasis on knowledge (as opposed to, for example, **emotions**), or to the way in which concern with knowledge is operationalized, in **curriculum** terms. (The emphasis on propositional as opposed to **skill** knowledge has also been criticized.) But it may be felt that such criticism has usually been misplaced. The concern of epistemologists has invariably been primarily to establish what the nature of knowledge is – what ways of knowing or types of knowledge we are able to recognize. They have seldom wished to draw any specific conclusions about the relative weight the school curriculum should attach to such propositional knowledge, still less about how best to teach in order to develop it. It is, for example, a mistake to see Hirst as arguing either that the seven forms ought necessarily to be taught as separate subjects, or that knowing how and various affective and creative responses are unimportant in the curriculum. The issue, so far as knowledge goes, is simply: what is it like? (*integrated studies, reconceptualists, value judgements**)

REFERENCES

Barrow (1976a), Berkeley (1948), Chisholm (1966), Degenhardt (1982), Descartes (1931), Hamlyn (1971), Hirst (1974c), Hospers (1967), Phenix (1964), Pring (1976), White (1973), Young (1971).

L

Language

The development of the individual's command of language is widely agreed to be one of the central concerns of **schooling**. Language, besides being the medium through which teachers and students primarily communicate in any subject, is also a major element within most subjects. Indeed, some talk of, e.g., science education as initiation into the language of science, mathematics education as initiation into the language of mathematics, and **art education** as initiation into the language of art. It is also increasingly common to find educationalists referring to various different types of language, such as body language, computer language, the language of music. (Note the different implications of, for example, 'the language of art', meaning the words and phrases associated with knowledgeable talk about art, and 'the language of music', meaning the features of musical composition considered as a distinctive language.) Our concern here is with verbal language, whether written or spoken, which is immeasurably richer and more important than any other type of language as a means of human **communciation** and of **understanding** our world. (To avoid confusion, perhaps one should refer to 'the specialized language' of science or art, in order to indicate that particular 'languages' in this sense are merely parts of the whole, and not alternatives. A full command of language, whether in the English, French, or Japanese tongue, would include the ability to understand the vocabulary of, e.g. mathematics and art.)

Areas and questions of interest in relation to language, in this sense, include the following:

1. How is our ability to learn language initially to be explained? Is it peculiar to humans?
2. How may we most effectively facilitate the continued **learning** of language in children?
3. Do we devote enough attention to language in the schools?
4. What is the relationship between social **class** and language?
5. Are there different, not to say competing, languages of different value to choose from?
6. How is command of language related to capacity to think?

1. The first two questions have received a great deal of scholarly

171

attention. But it may be suggested that they are of less immediate educational significance than is often supposed, and that they are in any case currently unanswerable questions, notwithstanding various conflicting and entrenched views in relation to them. For example, the view associated with Chomsky, to the effect that the human brain is programmed to develop linguistic understanding, would seem to resemble the more general **nature/nurture** issue in being ultimately unprovable. More to the point, what does it matter from an educationalist's point of view? We know that, whatever the ultimate explanation, children in a social setting do acquire the rudiments of language; and we know that, once the rudiments are there, we can help the individual develop a sophisticated command of language by means of communicating through it, building, naturally enough, on the rudimentary foundations.

2. But how may we most effectively develop command of language once a basic grasp has been acquired? Here, there may be answers to the question of what techniques and strategies we should or should not employ, and we may be able to establish them (indeed we may already have some); and we should certainly welcome them if we could get them. Nor is there any shortage of proposed answers. The question is whether the means of **research** that have been employed are appropriate to the inquiry in hand and may be relied upon to give us true answers. It is debatable whether research into matters relating to the development of command of language (for example, into the teaching of reading) can be said to have clearly established many helpful, positive rules about how one ought to proceed. Various techniques and strategies, particular reading schemes for example, may have been shown to be usable to good effect, and some approaches may have been shown to be, at least whenever tried, undesirable or ineffective in some way or another. But it remains doubtful whether it would be legitimate to provide a list of prescriptions for teachers seeking to develop command of language, unless it were confined to more or less self-evident or tautological suggestions, such as 'time spent on reading . . . is associated with growth in [the] area, whereas time spent in other areas appears to detract from growth in reading' (Rosenshine, 1976), make sure that children understand the material you use, reinforce new vocabulary by some form of repetition, and do not take particular steps before children are **ready** for them.

As with the conclusions of research into **teacher effectiveness** generally, the conclusions of research into the **teaching** of reading include too many that are true by definition (e.g. 'the good reader is expert in word recognition techniques'), or unclear as phrased (e.g. 'all reading should be meaningful'), or impossible to act upon unless the general rule can be interpreted in a particular case, (e.g. 'reading instruction should be attractive to the child') or straightforwardly contentious, (e.g. 'every activity must be related to the whole scheme').

In the above comments reference has been made to the teaching of reading by way of example. Obviously, developing command of language will involve most other aspects of schooling such as the study of **literature**, the writing of **history**, and, as was noted in the first paragraph, mastery of various subjects. A coherent account of a way or ways in which to foster command of language therefore comes close to being a coherent account of successful teaching, and that is something that it is easier to note instances of than to offer a definitive explanation of.

3. The question of whether we devote enough attention to language in the schools does not admit of any simple definitive answer, inasmuch as any reasonable answer would require the detailed knowledge about effective means to ends that we lack, and a full account, and justification, of some ideal in respect of language proficiency. It is also appropriate here to draw attention to the fact that there are various aspects of language, some of which may be of more concern to us than others. For example, language may be used primarily as a vehicle for describing, explaining, or arguing something; it may be used primarily to express emotion or to elicit a response in others; it may be used with emphasis on style rather than substance.

It is far from easy to establish how much time is spent on language work in our schools, because of difficulties both in the way of acquiring reliable data and in providing an account of language work that is both clear and monitorable. (A recent survey in England by Her Majesty's Inspectors estimated that about a third of the school day is spent on language, but it is not very clear what it meant by 'time spent on language'.) What does seem to be clear is that many people leave school with a very imperfect grasp of the language, particularly for purposes of acquiring, storing, and communicating **discriminating** understanding of our world and of engaging in complex and sophisticated reasoning. It is also noticeable that much educational writing about language does not emphasize these functions so much as various expressive and affective functions. It does not, of course, follow that the same emphasis is to be found in the schools, nor that, if it were, there is any causal relationship between that emphasis and the shortcomings in command of language amongst school-leavers referred to. None the less it remains the case that our achievement in respect of developing command of language in the rational mode falls a long way short of ideal.

4. If one categorizes styles of language use according to certain features, a **correlation** may be observed between particular styles and social

classes. For example, Bernstein claims that working-class families tend to talk in terms of particulars and concrete instances, while middle-class families use more abstract and general terms. (Bernstein labelled the former type of language use, fully characterized, 'a restricted code', and the fully characterized version of the latter 'an elaborated code'.) Such information is useful to the teacher, since different styles of language use may inhibit communication between teacher and student, yet talk in many areas of the school curriculum is necessarily conducted in something like an elaborated code. Certain criticism of Bernstein's research, especially that made by followers of Labov, appears largely to have missed the point. Labov made a limited number of case studies (including verbatim transcripts) of individual children using various dissimilar codes or modes of speech; he then argued for the quality and value of the more restricted codes, while scorning some features of more elaborated codes such as their hesitant and qualified long-windedness ('hemming and hawing, backing and filling', as Labov puts it). But the issue here is not whether one code or type of language use is superior to another without qualification. It is whether particular codes or styles are more suited to particular purposes. Labov hints that Bernstein's elaborated code may be 'simply an elaborated *style*, rather than a superior code or system'. But it is absolutely clear that, notwithstanding the various defects of the elaborated code for some purposes and various virtues of the restricted code for some purposes, the former is essential for understanding and communication in, for example, the disciplines of science and history. For the elaborated code is defined in terms of features that are necessary features of a developed **discipline**. (For example, it is universalistic, context-free, and rational; **metaphorical** and other types of illustrative discourse are not.) This is not to endorse out of hand the school's tendency to smooth out distinctive styles of language, whether working-class, upper-class, or outer Hebridean, rather as it tends to smooth out differences of dialect and accent. There are qualities in, and uses for, most styles of language too obvious to need listing, and there are dangers in trying to eradicate distinctive styles, such as undermining the confidence of individuals, that are equally apparent. For example, an individual with a restricted code may express himself most vividly, refreshingly, directly, and perhaps more spontaneously than another who naturally employs an elaborated code. None the less, if the school's business is to continue to include educating, then it is bound to initiate all children to some extent into use of a common language code (whatever it may be called), the features of which will be determined by the nature of the disciplined inquiry presupposed.

5. General arguments about the competing value of different

languages are largely as misconceived as more specific arguments about the competing value of the mode of language use associated with different classes. The question of educational importance is not whether, for example, non-standard black English is as good as white middle-class English (whatever such an unqualified question may be supposed to mean), but whether one can effectively pursue the patterns of thought and argument demanded by education without going beyond the features and conventions of non-standard black English, and whether one can engage with the existing heritage of thought, especially in the written form, without at one and the same time engaging in what is classified as white middle-class English. The answer in either case seems fairly obviously to be that one cannot.

6. How is command of language related to the capacity to think? Since we know that some people who cannot speak at all, or who cannot speak well in the sense of expressing themselves unhesitatingly and audibly in public, or who cannot write at all, can none the less think, and sometimes think well, it is clear that being able to speak well or write well is not necessarily coterminous with being able to think well. However, such has been the preoccupation with noting and arguing the respective merits of various styles, functions and species of language (see above), that there is a danger that some may regard facility with language, especially if facility is judged in terms of the school's preponderantly middle-class tone, as being something quite distinct from being able to think. At its most extreme such a view may give rise to utterances of the type 'It is true that he cannot express himself well, but he has a very good mind.' Such a remark is very odd, to say the least, and such a disassociation of language and thought is to be strongly resisted.

The definition of language ('any means of expressing or communicating, as gestures, signs, animal sounds, etc.') is such as to make it a necessary truth that one thinks in a language (for thinking is a species of expressing). The language that a person thinks in might conceivably be picked up from others or devised by himself, understood by others or incomprehensible to them, articulated silently, publicly, in oral form or written form, and couched in virtually as many systems of gestures, signs, or sounds as one cares to imagine. However, it is safe to assert that the majority of humans do most of their best thinking in their native language as a matter of **contingent fact**. More importantly, if somebody were in fact to think in a language private to themselves, while not being familiar with any other public language, so that mere translation from the one language to the other was not possible, in order to think well he would have to arrive at all the insights, deductions and flights of reasoning by himself, and acquire all the experiences that contribute to

knowledge and understanding for himself, that we normally gain access to vicariously, by listening to, hearing from, and reading about others. The world's heritage of thought is couched in language, and to gain command of a sophisticated language is to gain command of a way of understanding the world. (From this, incidentally, we may conclude that some languages may clearly be regarded as superior to others, inasmuch as they allow of more sophisticated thinking.)

In seeking to develop such things as vocabulary, understanding of subtle differences between ways of expressing matters, basic grammatical categories and construction, concern for precise wording, and other aspects of command of language, the school is at one and the same time making a positive contribution to developing powers of thought. To learn in a science lesson what 'atom' means is to be introduced to the concept of an atom, notwithstanding the fact that words and **concepts**, language and thought, are not to be identified with one another. To be taught to distinguish between 'imply' and 'infer' is to learn of two distinct possibilities. To be required to **discriminate** between **indoctrination, socialization**, and influence is to be brought to recognize a broad category or genus (influence) that may take many distinct particular forms (e.g. indoctrination or socialization), and it is thereby to be led a step away from the kind of sloppy thinking that indiscriminately lumps together similar but importantly distinguishable activities or phenomena. The person who knows the difference between 'e.g.' and 'i.e.', trivial as the example may seem, thereby acquires a necessary facility for proper understanding of an argument in which the symbols are used, no less than the person who knows the difference between two chemical formulae is in that respect better equipped to be a chemist than one who does not. After all, good thinking involves such things as the ability to distinguish between an example of something (e.g.) and a complete account of something newly stated (i.e.).

It is not being claimed that the individual who lacks a particular word, or is unfamiliar with a particular way of expressing something, cannot think of whatever the word refers to or entertain the thought the expression conveys. But one may ask how one could expect to be sure that persons understand things that they are unable to give an articulate account of. Why should I believe that you have a sophisticated grasp of the history of the war in Vietnam if, for whatever reason, you are unable to give expression to that view in the public langue that we presume is the most developed communication system you have? More generally, why should I assume that someone 'has a very good mind, even though he cannot express himself well'? In the absence of thoughts clearly articulated in the language in question, where would the evidence come from? (It need not be disputed that many basic matters may be shown to be understood by means other than language, such as demonstration, action, miming, or achievement. But, whereas a person may without words demonstrate that he is a good carpenter, a fine painter, or a great composer, he surely cannot show that he is a great thinker without articulating thoughts in a language that others can understand.)

Schools have generally thought that command of language, both in general and in certain important specialist areas, was important. It may, however, be felt that the extreme importance of a very precise use of language has very often been forgotten, both in **theory**, when such things as **creativity** and expressiveness are stressed at its expense, and in practice, when teachers show reluctance to correct or interfere with the chosen form of expression of the student. We shall not here go into the detailed questions of what aspects of reading, writing, and speaking a language are crucial to quality of thought expressed, which to style (itself to some extent a factor in quality of thought), and which merely to conventional appearance. (How important is accurate spelling of strangely spelled words, for example? It might be argued that the mere insistence on precision here as everywhere else has value, or that the etymological facts that often lie behind seemingly strange spellings are important; on the other hand, it may be countered that spelling 'sleigh' 'slay' doesn't get in the way of having or communicating a clear conception of sleigh. Was the Roman orator Quintilian on to something when he tried to link neat handwriting with clear thinking?) But we shall conclude by suggesting that contemporary schooling might well make more exacting demands on students' use of language (***bilingualism, core curriculum, critical thinking, feminism, ideology**).

REFERENCES

Barrow (1982b), Bernstein (1971–3), Chomsky (1968), Cooper (1978), Holly (1974), Labov (1966, 1969), Lawton (1968), Rosenshine (1976).

Lateral thinking

'Lateral' means sideways. The phrase 'lateral thinking' is closely associated with Edward de Bono and is more or less synonymous with 'divergent thinking'. Both are to be contrasted with 'convergent thinking', which refers to thinking carried out within accepted or traditional lines. Lateral and divergent thinking refer to those moments when we make the unexpected move or connection. 'Lateral thinking' does not mean anything specific, although it is commonly referred to as if it were a particular type or way of thinking. De Bono suggests that the ability to answer a number of open-ended puzzles and problems (note that there are 'correct answers' determined by de Bono), and/or practise with them, constitutes/leads to greater **skill** at so doing on future occasions. There is no clear evidence presented to support this suggestion, and it seems most unlikely that skill at such problem solving in the abstract would **correlate** with skill at solving real-life problems in an off-beat but intelligent manner, since the latter would require understanding of the nature of the real-life problems and the limits of real life. To illustrate: the student might be required to explain what lies behind the following scenario. 'In a locked room Antony lies dead in a pool of water and broken glass, while Cleopatra lies asleep in the sun.' The answer might be that Antony is a goldfish, and Cleopatra a cat who has knocked the fish bowl over and broken it. The conventional, convergent thinker, is by implication criticized for trying to puzzle out an account that will fit with the historical figures Antony and Cleopatra; yet it might be argued that that would be the sensible thing to assume, if given no information to the contrary. Why the 'given' answer should be regarded as in any way distinguishable from any number of other possible explanations of this fairly open scene (once the only 'clue' has been revealed to be deliberately misleading) is not clear. Why one should regard it as in any way a **worthwhile** achievement to provide the given answer, or any other to fit the few facts presented, is not clear. What connection the ability to do this has with the ability to come up with a good and unexpected solution when one faces a real-life problem, such as running across an intruder in the house, finding the class one teaches in revolt, or wondering how to cure one's depression, is not clear (*critical thinking, creativity, dilemma).

REFERENCES

De Bono (1970), McPeck (1981).

Learning

Learning is clearly central to the enterprise of **schooling**. And (though this is disputed by some) there do not appear to be any major **conceptual** problems here. That is to say, we know what 'to learn' means, we know what learning is, even if we do not know various things about it such as how to help Johnny learn X or what lies behind man's drive to learn. 'To learn' is 'to acquire understanding of something that one did not have before.' One may learn propositions (that such and such), skills (how to do things), or to recognize things. What is involved in learning certain particular things (e.g. moral theory) may indeed lead to conceptual problems; but there is no real conceptual puzzle about what is embodied in the idea of, for example, acquiring understanding of a proposition.

There may, however, be problems in determining whether the criteria for learning have been met. For example, learning X obviously implies a complete **understanding** of X. If I have learned to write Latin, then I must have a thorough grasp of Latin; if in fact I have only learnt to decline the first three declensions of nouns, it would be more accurate to say that. This draws attention to the problem of determining what counts as a thorough grasp of Latin. However, that is not a conceptual problem about learning, but a conceptual problem about learning Latin.

There is no need, therefore, to argue that we should promote learning with understanding, as some have done. Learning without understanding is not learning. If you do not understand what is meant by 'the angles of a right-angled triangle add up to 180 degrees' then you have not learned that proposition; you have merely learned to recite those words. The main questions to be asked about learning are under what conditions do various people learn various things most effectively and what things do we want children to learn at various stages of schooling (e.g. to recite dates or to have historical understanding?).

Educationalists often talk of learning processes or the learning process. This is in line with a general tendency to **reify** everything (cf., e.g. **skills, critical thinking, creativity**). Rather than accept that 'learning' is a generic label covering a number of distinguishable species or types (as 'living' is a broad term that covers thousands of disparate life styles and cannot reasonably be seen as the name of a specific activity), it is presumed that we can focus on the business (the **process**, the **phenomenon**, the faculty) of learning in itself (or the processes). At its most extreme this manner of thinking may lead to the view that one can learn how to learn, again in the abstract, without any reference to what one might learn how to learn, as if learning how to learn were a skill as specific as the skill of standing on one's hands. Such thinking is dangerously confused.

There is not one process of learning. That is to say, there is not an activity or a set of steps which, when engaged in on any occasion in respect of any subject matter, will result in the matter in hand being learned. There may be some very general elements common to all acts of learning – indeed there must be some, arising out of the definition: just as all animals, while being very different, must be living organisms, because that is part of the meaning of 'animal', so all acts of learning must involve the acquisition of some new ability or understanding because that is part of the meaning of 'learning' – but what is involved in any particular act of learning must be partly dependent on what is being learned. To learn to ride a bicycle is to acquire a skill (or set of skills), and it can clearly only come about through trial and error or practice. To learn German involves at least acquiring the ability to use it correctly. Learning philosophy and sociology require coming to understand various concepts and procedures. Learning in each of these cases is a quite distinct business. The notion of the process of learning only makes sense in the way that the notion of the skill of critical thinking does (as a reference to a generic category) and as such it is redundant: 'the process of learning' means no more than 'learning' (*generic fallacy).

It may seem that we may more reasonably talk of the processes of learning. If that is taken to mean that we can classify different instances of learning as in the previous paragraph (the process of learning to ride a bike, the process of learning German, etc.), then evidently we can, though we should beware of assuming that the process whereby you learn German is necessarily the process whereby I learn it. But, in any case, reference to processes of learning in this sense would lead to a list of processes as long as the list of possible objects of human learning. The idea of studying the processes of learning, in this sense, would be absurd. If, however, the phrase 'processes of learning' is taken to refer to a limited number of types of learning, then it remains questionable whether this is a sensible approach. Once again it is far from clear that large numbers of acts of learning can be classified together, by reference to what they have in common, in any useful way. Learning to ride a bicycle, learning to tie one's shoe laces, and learning to hold a knife and fork are all instances of acquiring physical skills, but it is not clear that there is much to be gained by focusing on the features they have in common at a general level. Whether or not they could be classified together by some criteria, they remain very distinct instances of learning, such that one's ability to learn one tells us very little about one's ability to learn the others. Learning to tie one's shoelaces requires a conception of what one is trying to do combined with a certain degree of manual dexterity, while learning to ride a bicycle requires a different conception of what one is about and a sense of balance. At a more complex level, learning ancient history, for example, is quite distinct from learning physics, and very likely either one might reasonably be approached in different ways by different people (and possibly by the same person). In short, what is common to all instances of learning ancient **history** and physics, is, without a doubt, the very least of it.

But may we not, none the less, seek to identify some steps that are common to any instance of learning, some stages into which the business of passing from ignorance to understanding may be divided, whether one is learning to count or learning to compose music, and is this not what learning **theory** has in fact done? The phrase 'learning theory' is ambiguous: it may refer either to attempts to plot stages in learning or to accounts of conditions that may impair or facilitate learning. To take it in the former sense: of course learning, in whatever context, involves some sequence of very general phases such as 'environment triggers reaction in receptors', 'sensory register makes initial perception', 'information enters short-term memory', 'information either processed through response generator which activates behaviour or proceeds to long-term **memory** whence it may later be recalled'. And certainly one may choose to classify and label these phrases in this sort of way, as learning theorists such as Gagné have done. But it is difficult to see what is gained by constructing learning theories in this sense. They do not purport to be physiological accounts. They appear to involve no more than labelling, in somewhat pretentious and perhaps misleadingly mechanistic terms, very broad divisions that are conceptually required rather than **empirically** discovered (if there is any warrant for locating them at all). This labelling in no way helps to explain what is going on when people learn, or to bring us to a greater understanding of how to enhance learning. What, after all, is involved in saying that 'information, derived from the sensory register which has been activated by the environment, enters the short-term memory' beyond 'he remembered something he came across, for a short time'?

Learning theory in the sense of theory about the conditions that facilitate effective learning is potentially more interesting. 'Effective learning' may be taken to suggest learning that takes place economically and/ or has staying power. (There is no need for it to imply thorough understanding, since that is part of the meaning of 'learning', but perhaps we should add that effective learning involves hitting the right target, that is, learning that which it was intended one should learn.) It should, however, be said that research into effective learning (sometimes coupled with effective teaching, the former being used as a measure of the latter, albeit neither a **necessary** nor a sufficient condition of it), often fails to specify what it means by effective learning, and in practice appears to mean no more than learning that does indeed take place.

It has been claimed that learning may be inhibited by various forms of low self-esteem (in turn caused by a variety of personal and social factors), by anxiety and other psychological states, by perceptions of teachers and other aspects of schooling, and by distraction, failure to understand, and lack of motivation, while it may be enhanced by minimizing those hindrances and creating an encouraging climate, in which what is to be learned is expounded clearly, interestingly, and at appropriate times. It is necessary, however, to draw attention here to weaknesses and difficulties to be found in **research** into such issues. Different studies often produce inconsistent data; individual studies can often be severely criticized on methodological grounds; some of the conclusions arrived at appear to be more or less tautologous; others are of little practical value because they yield general injunctions of the type 'be interesting', without being able to provide any guidance as to what will prove interesting in particular cases. Furthermore the conditions that make such research difficult (in brief, the complexity of classroom life) make particular judgements about specific situations difficult, even if we accept the research claims. As the research itself shows, the factors that might be contributing towards a particular child's achievement as a learner are so many and various as to make it impossible to be confident of any specific view. The most sensible thing the individual teacher can do is confine himself to abstracting from the research a working-list of factors that might conceivably be relevant to the learning successes and difficulties of the particular children he encounters.

Some educationalists have advocated particular approaches to learning. One approach quite often commended is learning by discovery. Here there is an immediate problem, for the phrase might mean a number of things. Are we to understand by 'learning by discovery': (a) a case where the child is placed or left on his own to discover whatever he may about anything; (b) a case where the child is provided with materials carefully designed to limit the range of what he is to find out for himself; (c) a case where the child is provided with careful guidance, albeit with the object that he shall come to see some conclusion for himself (as in the celebrated example of Socrates teaching an untutored slave some geometry in the *Meno*); or (d) a case in which, though the teacher may explain, the child none the less comes to see the point of something for himself?

The last type of teaching, whether it is appropriate to call it learning by discovery or not, presumably has something to be said for it, since awareness of the point of something is logically tied up with what we mean by 'learning'. But 'learning by discovery' in this sense would be quite compatible with teacher-instruction, with which it is usually contrasted, and it would not appear to have any very distinctive meaning so far as manner of teaching went. The problem with the first sense is that there is no reason to suppose that the individual put in this position will see or find out anything of importance. The second sense cuts down the danger of the child failing to see or gain anything of educational **worth**, but is open to the objection that learning in this way takes up a relatively large amount of time, while the third sense, besides also being time-consuming, comes close to instruction. (None the less, for some, the third example, whether to be called 'learning by discovery' or not, comes close to a picture of ideal teaching inasmuch as the teacher knows clearly what the student is to learn, but takes positive steps to enable him to see the various steps of the argument for himself, on the grounds that this approach guarantees that he does see them, and may lead to a more vital grasp of them.)

Learning by discovery (in whatever particular sense) is usually advocated on the grounds that it is more enjoyable, more likely to prove memorable, and/or more economic in that (time-consuming or not) it leads to a more thorough grasp of a matter than might result from a number of attempts at explanation or instruction by the teacher. However, there is no firm evidence to support any of these assumptions. There is a widespread belief that what is learned by discovery will be retained better, but this surely rests on a confusion. It is what we truly understand that we most naturally retain in our mind. The connection is that what we see for ourselves we evidently understand, and what we discover for ourselves we evidently see for ourselves. In other words it is not that learning by discovery necessarily leads to better retention or clearer understanding than instruction (for clearly instruction can be well enough done to lead to good understanding and excellent retention); it is rather that we can be more certain that the individual has learned something by discovery (since it involves him articulating what he has discovered) than we can that the individual has learned what we tried to instruct him in (he may, for instance, simply parrot back at us what we have said). On balance, it does not seem at all clear that either learning by discovery or instruction is to be preferred in general on any count. It would seem reasonable to conclude that there is room for a wide range of both types of approach in any teacher's repertoire.

Finally, we return to the issue of learning how to learn. It seems to follow from what has been said about the idea of a process of learning that it is mistaken to think that there can be a skill of learning how to learn, which, once acquired, can be readily put to use in learning about anything from stamp collecting to deep-sea diving. There may be some techniques or strategies that are likely to prove equally useful whatever one may be about to start learning. But these will tend to be peripheral to the major problems involved in learning particular things. Thus one might acquire the ability to speed read, or pick up some useful little tricks to enable one to concentrate for long periods, but these, though helpful on occasion, are not in fact necessary for learning anything, and are certainly not sufficient for learning, for example, atomic theory, how to build a house, or how to get on with people. Learning always has an object: you learn this or that, one thing or another; you are learning something, and not simply learning. Learning that something can only take place when you understand that something, and to understand it is to have learned it. Students of learning would be well advised to concentrate on seeking to understand the nature of those things that are to be learned (*behavioural objectives, child-centred education, class, knowledge, operant conditioning, programmed learning).

REFERENCES

Bruner (1966), Clayton (1965), Dearden (1967, 1976), Fontana (1981), Gagné (1970, 1974), Hamlyn (1967, 1978), Handley (1973), Hilgard (1956), Kleinig (1982), McFarland (1960), Peters (1967), Plato (1961), Ryle (1949).

Learning by discovery see Learning

Learning how to learn see Learning

Learning theory see Learning

Liberal arts see Art education, Core curriculum, Culture, Emotions, History, Utilitarian

Liberal education

Charles Bailey's title *Beyond the Present and the Particular* (1984) encapsulates the essence of the argument for a liberal education. It is a conception of education as a means whereby the individual may be liberated from a pattern of thinking that is dominated by the actual here and now. Those who understand their trade, have the developed skills of their kind, and can calculate means to their immediate ends, are well qualified to survive, at any rate in a stable world. But such training and skill development will not enable them to evaluate, question, challenge, or change their world in any significant degree. They will be of little use in changed circumstances, and they do not help the individual to live a fully human life.

The argument between advocates of liberal education and those who favour more utilitarian conceptions goes back a long way. Plato did not need to use the phrase 'liberal education', since for him true education just is liberal. But notwithstanding a widespread sentiment in Greece to the effect that education was both liberating and only for free men, Plato's near contemporary Isocrates argued for a far more professional, skill-based kind of upbringing; and indeed some of the fifth-century BC sophists turn the dichotomy on its head by claiming to engage in, e.g. metaphysical or moral inquiry only in order to teach people how to function effectively in the world.

Through the intervening centuries the argument has implicitly continued, but so long as education has been confined to the few – those whose customs, habits, and professions are themselves rather general and unaffected by the passing of time – it has not been an issue of great importance. With universal education situated in strongly materialist **cultures** that are heavily dependent on the continued success of a particular kind of economy, the matter is one of considerable importance.

There are few, if any, outright attacks on liberal education. Rather, there are suggestions that so-called liberal education is in fact no such thing, attempts to discredit particular aspects of liberal education, specific appeals for more attention to various practically important skills and **subject** matters, and the odd argument in favour of vocational education. On the other hand, the system itself, and much of the theoretical work devoted to education, takes place in the light of **concepts** and assumptions that, if they do not overtly challenge the ideal of liberal education, none the less militate against it.

Successive inquiries and reports earlier in this century took the idea of liberal education for granted, pausing only to suggest that the scope of such study should be enlarged to do justice to, for example, science, or to nod in the direction of a contemporary need for, say, more qualified mathematicians. But today, ironically, although the dominant conception and the one that has been most fully articulated is one that almost defines education as liberal education (Peters, 1966), the idea is clearly threatened.

Testimony for that conclusion is to be found in a variety of **facts** and events: for example, the contemporary concern with **objective** modes of **assessment** at the expense, if necessary, of educational considerations; the **behaviouristic** tendency of much **research** and **theory**; the view that mental concepts are adequately characterized in terms of skills; the new curriculum proposals being brought forward in the United Kingdom, which, whatever the intentions behind them, suggest a more pragmatic and economy-orientated view than before; the proposal for a new integrated English curriculum in British Columbia, which barely concerns itself with, e.g. literature, such is its preoccupation with functional **literacy**, albeit broadly conceived, and with other 'socially useful' skills and information; the nature of the criticism put forward in the United States by authors as diverse as Adler, Bloom, and Hirsch. In each case, and similarly in many other incidents and proposals, we find evidence that the **aim** of producing cultured and literate individuals is being replaced by the goal of producing skilled manpower, albeit of a high order of complexity and quality.

One argument for liberal education has always been the claim that it is good in itself. This is what it is to be a free and developed human. But increasingly advocates are arguing that in the long run a liberal education is to be valued also on utilitarian grounds. (Thus, the view of the sophists comes round again.) Industry and business now tend to the view that broadly educated graduates are more use to them than specifically skill-trained personnel. Rapid shifts in technology in any case make skill-training a hazardous approach, particularly given that our ability to predict future **needs** is notoriously bad. And even hard-headed business-men now acknowledge that social problems and moral issues have to be taken into account, and that therefore they need something more than a band of technocrats, however sophisticated and able (*****ethics**).

REFERENCES

Adler (1982), Bailey (1984), Bloom (1987), Hirsch (1987), Hirst (1974c), Peters (1966), Phenix (1964), Proctor (1988), Wall (1968), White (1973, 1982).

Life history

Those scholars interested in 'life history' methods argue that the tradi-tional social scientific approach to the study of **education** misrepresents essential features of what happens in **schools**. In its emphasis on gener-alizable characteristics of **teaching** and **learning**, such an approach tends to render teachers and students 'voiceless' by ignoring those experiences which may be classified as particular or unique. To recapture the per-sonal experiences of an individual, life historians suggest that a particu-lar instance should be studied in very broad context: in terms of his previous career and life outside school on the one hand, and in terms of contemporary social, political and economic conditions on the other. Such a two-pronged personal or 'life history' approach, it is argued, will not only encourage a participant to express his own views on his educa-tional experiences, but also provide scholars with access to additional data and sources of explanation that have previously been ignored. Given such arguments, scholars in the last ten years have studied per-sonal histories of administrators, teachers, and students (with particular emphasis on teachers' work and careers).

Such methods make use of varied historical and philosophic sources. Their indebtedness to autobiographic and biographic forms is obvious (although not always acknowledged). Some researchers draw support from nineteenth-century interpretative theories, or from approaches derived from **phenomenology** and hermeneutics. Others (perhaps the larger part) draw inspiration from sociological approaches to the study of personal lives developed at the University of Chicago in the inter-war years. In so doing, they benefit from the examples offered by other scholars in their work on institutional life and on personal studies on particular individuals in society (especially those that have been ignored in main-line historical studies). In recent years, researchers interested in life histories have also used interpretative techniques derived from such diverse sources as **critical** and **feminist theories**, notions of **professional** practice, and principles of personal therapy.

Nevertheless, the task that life historians have set themselves is difficult, and the results of their efforts remain controversial. Three major problems may be identified: the question of the subject of study, difficulties in the methods used, and the nature of final accounts.

Examining the lives of living persons is a very difficult undertaking, and the injunction to relate those lives to the broader **history** of their own times makes the task even more problematical. Many persons (in education or other occupations) do not retain significant personal documents (or, if they have them, do not make them readily available). Legal considerations (real or perceived) on the treatment of living subjects may restrict the range of a historian's comment. The **ethical** problems raised in situations in which instructors encourage students to use their personal biographies as a form of critical self-awareness or therapy are particularly thorny. In addition, the task of interpreting contemporary affairs is acknowledged as one of the most difficult that a historian can face, even without the additional requirement that a personal biography be related to that wider setting.

Life historians in education tend to use such traditional methods of **research** as interviews, participant observations, and the analysis of personal writings, diaries, journals and other documents, although a few have experimented with other media. Some researchers have been accused of being somewhat uncritical in their use of such sources. Over-reliance on interviews, for example, may lead to a one-sided picture of the subject under study. Although personal recollections (even of comparatively recent events) are notoriously unreliable, some researchers appear to accept them without checking their veracity. The dangers inherent in diaries and journals (especially those created at the request of a researcher) also appear to be underestimated. In general terms, the nature of personal evidence presents formidable problems to both subject and researcher.

The problems in interpreting the evidence are also tenacious. Given the range of sources upon which life historians draw, it is not surprising that their final accounts differ markedly. Some life historians seem to cast their reports in the categorical language familiar to main-line social scientists, or to place their interpretations in **ideological** frames. Others prefer subjective approaches derived from the humanities. Whatever the variety of interpretative structure, no consensus appears to have developed on the question of how representative or how typical the final story may be. Thus a reader may be placed in the position of deciding for himself whether a particular life history may be interpreted as indicative of general conditions of the period, or as a (possibly very interesting) aberration.

REFERENCES

Ball and Goodson (1985), Bertaux (1981), Butt (1989), Butt and Raymond (n.d.), Clifford (1983), Connelly and Clandinin (1988), Dollard (1935), Goodson (1983b), Hodysh and McIntosh (1989), Milburn (1989), Pinar (1980), Plummer (1983).

Linguistic errors

Despite attempts to argue that all **languages** are equal, there is clearly such a thing as linguistic error. 'I deaded her' may be comprehensible, and may even evolve into a culturally acceptable way of saying 'I killed her'; it is none the less, currently, incorrect. (If it is not, the conclusion is not that there are no incorrect usages, but that there is no such thing as incorrectness. That is a conclusion that no normal person, who makes daily judgements about the wrong fuel for the car, incorrect change, a badly fitting suit, mistaken identity, incorrect reference, etc., could accept.) (*relativity, subjectivity)

At a given time, certain changes in linguistic practice may have become sufficiently common for it to be a matter of contention whether they are acceptable or not. For example, despite the **etymological** origins that dictate that 'datum' is the singular of 'data', and hence that the former should take a singular verb and the latter a plural one, one might argue that the word in its anglicized form is 'data', singular and plural.

But certain linguistic uses are objectionable because they break down important distinctions, because they weaken our **discriminatory** powers, and/or because they cause confusion amongst an audience some of whom are aware of correct usage. Examples of such unacceptable usages which are none the less commonly to be found in the writing of professors of education include the following:

1. Confusing 'infer' and 'imply', or treating them as interchangeable.

(The listener infers, i.e. draws a meaning from the speaker. The speaker implies, i.e. conveys a meaning by what he says.)

2. Confusing 'refute' with 'reject', 'rebuff', etc. The latter terms imply only that one is in disagreement with, distances oneself from, objects to, etc., the point at issue. To refute something is to establish that it is incorrect. One does not refute an argument by mere dissent; one has to show where and how it is wrong. Hence the wittiness of Dr Johnson's response to Bishop Berkeley's theory of the non-existence of matter. Boswell observed that though they were satisfied it was not true, they were unable to refute it. Johnson kicked a large stone, evidently feeling the force of the blow, and said: 'I refute it thus'.

3. Perhaps the confusing of 'fewer' and 'less', like the technical misuse of 'hopefully' to mean 'I hope' when actually it means 'full of hope', is something we will have to learn to live with. But, for the record, 'fewer' is used of countables, and 'less' for collective quantity. Thus, fewer chocolate bars and less sugar. And, possibly, to object to 'forward planning' (done any backward planning lately?), 'at this point in time', and other such redundant phraseology, is veering into questions of taste and style.

4. The use of 'to rationalize' to mean simply 'to provide reasons' can be very misleading. 'Rationalization' is a pejorative term meaning 'the provision of false reasoning to account for an action'. It may be done consciously or unconsciously.

Literacy

There is little agreement among educators on the meaning of 'literacy'. It is accepted that being literate involves being able to read and write, but few are agreed on the level of competence required, or on the nature of the tests that should be used to demonstrate competence. Some jurisdictions define a person as being literate if he has attended school for a given number of years (and thus ignore the question of the quality of that experience). Others reduce the notion to a set of identifiable **skills** required to survive in the contemporary world (e.g. an ability to complete a job application, read the telephone book, and understand instructions on medical prescriptions). Some educators interpret the term more broadly as a capacity to appreciate through **language** a broad range of achievements in civilized society.

Nor is discussion of the term made easier by its use in other contexts. Almost every subject in the **curriculum** claims its version of literacy; 'computer literacy', 'technological literacy', **visual literacy**, 'musical literacy', 'mathematical literacy', 'legal literacy', and 'scientific literacy' are a few of the related terms in common use in contemporary educational discourse, again without any widely accepted agreement on what they mean.

Tests used to **assess** literacy rates among school-aged or adult populations are blunt instruments. Often based on questionable criteria, or conducted in far from perfect conditions, these tests may produce results that are subject to many interpretations.

Many governments have attempted to improve literacy rates among adult populations as a step towards ameliorating social conditions within their jurisdictions. Despite some successful campaigns in many countries, such efforts have often been diminished by soaring birth-rates. Although adult illiteracy remains more widespread in the less-developed world (particularly in rural areas and among women), rates in developed countries such as Canada have been calculated by some as 1 in 8 or even higher. Adult illiteracy is therefore far from being exclusively a third-world problem.

In the United Kingdom and North America, attention in recent years has focused on the failure of school-age students to demonstrate desired levels of achievement in reading, writing, and the so-called **basics**. There is evidence that some high-school graduates have been unable to follow simple directions on labels or in manuals. University professors have also bemoaned the standard of written work by first-year students. While many reasons have been offered for these inadequacies, ranging from the results of permissive forms of curriculum, to the decline of authority within school systems, no consensus has been reached.

An important segment of literacy research is related to questions about how very young children learn to read and write. An important distinction has been made by linguists between language competence and language performance: language competence has been defined as naturally developed tacit knowledge of linguistic functions which all children acquire in the years before they attend school, while language performance refers to the actual uses of that knowledge in specific classroom contexts. Performance calls for the appropriate display of a known linguistic **concept**, and it is such displays that can be encouraged, reinforced, and evaluated – not the mere knowing of a word, grammatical structure, or register. Debates on language competence and performance have affected such related issues as the role of dialects, the nature of **readiness**, the value of formal grammar instruction, and alternative methods for teaching reading and writing.

REFERENCES

Bailey and Fosheim (1983), Britton (1970), Cooper (1981), Copperman (1978),

De Castell, Luke and MacLennan (1981), Freire (1973a), Harste and Mikulecky (1984), Hirsch (1987), Holdaway (1979, 1984), Kozol (1980), Raymond (1982).

Literature

For many the word 'literature' is most familiar in its recent sense of 'all the writings dealing with a particular subject' (as in the literature review beloved of **academic** thesis writers). Here we are concerned with literature in its older sense of 'writing in prose or verse of an **imaginative** or **critical** character, having quality of form and deemed of permanent value'. Literature in this sense was once considered a necessary part of the subject English. Many took the view that literature was itself the teacher, in a way that, e.g. economics could not be (Engell and Perkins, 1988).

Recently, however, literature has played a smaller and smaller part in conceptions of the study of English, which tends instead to be dominated by concern for such things as **creative** expression, functional **literacy**, and linguistics (Knight and Robinson, 1989). The change no doubt has many causes, but amongst them we must surely count the rapid growth of the subject of linguistics itself, and a widespread fear of making judgements of absolute **worth**. The notion of there being a corpus of timeless classics of literature, worth studying in their own right, is frequently dismissed as **élitist**, while **child-centred** approaches to **education** have led to an increased emphasis on the child's own products and **interests**. In addition, and from a quite different direction, the scientific nature of much educational **research** has led to approaches to reading that emphasize it as a set of **skills** to be exercised, reinforced, and developed piecemeal, rather than as a matter of immersion in literature. The so-called '**whole language**' approach would seem to have originated in rejection of this tendency, but perhaps too readily become a catchphrase and a bandwagon itself, rather than a clearly articulated **theory** of **language** acquisition.

Is there a case for studying literature in schools? If so, in what way? P. H. Hirst (1974) argued that literature and the fine arts constituted a (single) form of **knowledge**. While there was perhaps more debate and uncertainty over what he meant by this than any other aspect of his general theory, it seems that he was maintaining that a work of art in itself constitutes a unique kind of proposition. Thus, for example, Leonardo da Vinci's painting the Mona Lisa would itself be a statement parallel to, but distinct from, the moral statement 'kindness is good', just as the latter is parallel to, but distinct from, the mathematical statement 'the angles of a triangle add up to 180 degrees'. More recent statements by Hirst (1989) suggest a less controversial view. This sees the work of art not as a unique kind of proposition, but as a product that has **aesthetic** quality and hence gives rise to aesthetic judgements that are unique in kind. The claim is, then, that the study of literature, music, painting, sculpture, etc., has educational value because it involves students in, introduces them to, a particular type of expression, namely aesthetic judgement.

Some have objected to this kind of justification for teaching literature (or any other **art** form) on the grounds that it presupposes the transcendent or universal **value** of certain works. But it need not do so. In the first place, it may be maintained that, while, say, Bach's *B Minor Mass* is a great work of art in itself, and that this is a **fact** rather than a personal predilection, it is none the less an instance of art that belongs to a particular culture; as such it is not likely to be understood or appreciated by those from a radically different culture. Thus, one need not claim that Bach's *B Minor Mass* is superior to Inuit throat music, merely that the former is an undoubted of work of art, while some instance of the latter may be too. If that is still too strong a claim for some, for the purpose of this argument it may even be conceded that Bach's *B Minor Mass* is not objectively superior to, e.g., Andrew Lloyd Webber's *Requiem*. All that the present argument demands is that the material studied be a work of art, as opposed to something with no such pretentions. Good or bad, Lloyd Webber's *Requiem* is clearly a work of art, and as such invites aesthetic response and judgement in a way that a *Times* obituary does not (normally) do. (Whether it *is* fallacious to believe in the transcendent value of a work is another question.)

There is, however, a problem with this view. It may be conceded that a work of literature is a work of art and, consequently, that in studying literature one is coming face to face with a species of art. But by arguing for the study of literature in this way one paradoxically provides an argument against the necessity of studying it: for if one is to study literature because it is a species of art, one might just as reasonably study painting or music instead, which, by the argument, are also species of art. Studying literature may be a way, but it is by no means the only way, to begin to understand the nature of art. To be compelling, the argument would require additional reasons for studying this form of art rather than another.

This is not to dispute that literature is a form of art and that one aspect of **teaching** it is to provide **understanding** and appreciation of its artistic quality. But in order to justify taking up limited **curriculum** time with the study of literature (or anything else), it is necessary to provide reasons for concluding that it is the only or the best way to provide something of relatively great educational worth.

A very different view is that students should study literature primarily for the sake of its content. Before considering the argument for and objections to this view, certain qualifications should be noted. First, such a view might degenerate into the inculcation of various **moral** and political beliefs by means of carefully selected reading material, or lead to **censorship** of literature. However, it is not necessary that it should lead to either **indoctrination** or censorship. Secondly, the word 'primarily' should be emphasized. Few would deny that the nature of literature is such that the artifice that the author employs is an integral part of the work, and, indeed, that the manner of the telling affects the form of the tale. Awareness of the art involved in a work of literature, rejected above as a sufficient reason for study, is not therefore to be ignored as a feature of such study, and an important one at that.

The argument is that literature, by definition, explores the nature of human beings and their responses to each other and to circumstance. As such it provides an invaluable source of data relating to such matters as friendship, love, disappointment, courage, and despair. To those who are already avid students of literature such a claim tends to seem self-evident (and the fact that in countries such as the United States and Canada fewer than half the population read a book from one year's end to another, seems correspondingly frightening in its implications). Certain objections should therefore be considered.

First, it may be said that it is bizarre to seek to promote understanding of, for instance, friendship vicariously through literature rather than directly through experience. (A stronger version of this argument would have it that those who are heavily influenced by literature may have erroneous views of real life.) But this argument, though popular and superficially seductive, seems very weak on close examination. Experience, for most people, will be a relatively restricted business; that is to say, one's direct experience of friendship (its variety, its possibilities, its subtleties) is likely to be considerably more limited than the dimensions and types of friendship explored in literature. Furthermore the simplistic polarization here implied between reality and fiction is highly suspect. What we experience, what we see in daily life, is heavily informed by the conceptual schemes (the beliefs, ideas, and assumptions) by which we organize our experience, and reading clearly develops those conceptual schemes. In addition, the individual learning about friendship solely through personal experience is faced with the twin disadvantages of being directly involved and having no (necessary) further external guidance or counsel. By contrast the student of literature studies friendship with the detachment possible to an outsider and with the benefit of the insight of the author. While there is, no doubt, no substitute for experience, literature surely adds a great deal to our study and understanding of such concepts as friendship.

It may, secondly, be observed that there is no evidence to support the claim that the student of literature is more perceptive about such things as love and jealousy. But is that true? There is certainly no evidence that it necessarily has beneficial consequences, and there are certainly instances of students of literature who seem unaffected by the material they have studied. But the claim is not that students who study literature will thereby become paragons of human understanding. It is rather that it is an obviously sensible procedure, if we wish to enhance people's understanding of such **concepts**, to encourage them to immerse themselves in refined and sophisticated studies of them – which is what literature provides. Thirdly, this approach to the study of literature implies that a large part of **moral education** and development of the **emotions**, and, possibly, **critical thinking** would be well conducted in this way. It may be objected that it is preferable or more efficient to deal with these matters directly. However, that view would seem to involve the **generic fallacy**.

By and large, well-read people are notable for the breadth and depth of their understanding of the human condition. And while that says nothing necessarily for their behaviour, since there are such things as weakness of will, greed, and hate, to get in the way, it must be preferable that such understanding should exist than that it should not. A world in which people have not read, and cannot with ease read, such authors as Jane Austen, Shakespeare, Ernest Hemingway, Robertson Davies, Scott Fitzgerald, and Margaret Atwood, is by definition a world that lacks the combined insight and understanding of such authors. It is, perhaps, as simple and deadly as that.

There is at least a tangential relationship between the view put forward here and the aspirations of three recent and influential books (very different from each other though they are in particulars): Adler's *The Paideia Proposal*, Bloom's *The Closing of the American Mind*, and Hirsch's *Cultural Literacy*. What these three have in common is a conviction that education is no longer rooted in a sustained cultural tradition. The centre of that tradition lies in its literature. Ideally 'literature' here pertains to all subjects: thus, the study of maths and medicine, no less than physics and philosophy, should include an understanding of the **historical** development of these subjects and of the classic contributions to the field over the centuries. But here we are referring to literature in the sense of fiction, drama, poetry, biography, *belles–lettres* (etc.). (Most of what has been said applies most obviously and directly to fictional literature perhaps, but the other genres have similar claims to make while adding further distinctive contributions.)

The educational or curricular question, in essence, is: what can we reasonably hope that our students will gain from a guided and sustained engagement with literature, that otherwise they would gain only by chance? The answer appears to be: they would become directly involved with perceptive and well-wrought attempts to describe, express, and analyse complex human relationships, emotional states, and motivations. A large part of the stuff of life. How is this so? Because George Eliot, Shakespeare, Thomas Mann, or whoever, are classified as great literary figures because they are judged to be not only great artists (i.e. masters of form and manner), but also great students of human nature: they see and express better than most teachers can, and certainly than most students can, those aspects of the human condition that they choose to illuminate. The nature of that contribution is in addition something quite distinct from that of the social sciences, and cannot be replaced by, e.g. the study of psychology and sociology.

The emphasis placed on content as the educational justification for insisting on the importance of literature in the **curriculum** does not mean that content is all. The aesthetic dimension (what some would regard as the 'literary' aspect of the fiction, story, or content) is important for two reasons: first, aesthetic understanding is important in its own right, and it has not been denied that literature is a species of art. Secondly, as has also been observed, the art of the story-teller affects the precise nature of the content. It is because the way that Shakespeare tells the story of *Antony and Cleopatra* makes it somewhat different from the story as told by Plutarch, or in a comic-strip version, that we value his play: his manner of telling makes the tale richer, deeper, and more significant. And that is why we study his play – thanks to the quality of the art the content is more telling.

(For consideration of the question of whether literature necessarily or **contingently** does or does not provide something that cannot be equally well or better provided by, e.g. film, see **mass media**.) (*evaluation, **nationalism, religious education**)

REFERENCES

Adler (1982), Bantock (1981), Bloom (1987), Engell and Perkins (1988), Hirsch (1987), Hirst (1974c, 1989), Knight and Robinson (1988), Steiner (1961).

Logic *see* Critical thinking, Knowledge, Logical order, Transference

Logical *see* Logical order

Logical necessity *see* Contingent, Necessary condition

Logical order

The word 'logical' has two distinct senses that are often run together or confused in educational discourse. On the one hand, we have truths that are matters of logic in the strong sense of **necessary**. It is a logical truth that all bachelors are unmarried, that the angles of a triangle add up to 180°, or that 'brighter people can learn things that less bright ones cannot'. These things had to be, given the meaning of the terms involved. No **contingent** change in the world could conceivably make them untrue. Similarly there may be 'logical' implications in a statement or argument, in the sense of points that arise inescapably out of what has been said. But, on the other hand, the word 'logical' is often used to mean no more than reasonable, as when one says, 'It is logical to suppose that teaching children mathematics will be of use to them in later life.'

This distinction may have some bearing on the question of the logical order for presenting material, or the logical order of a subject. It is sometimes stated that subjects should be taught in logical sequence, but it is not always clear what is meant by this, or whether it makes much sense in the strong sense of logical. In the weak sense 'organize your physics or history programme in a logical (i.e. reasonable) way', makes sense, and is good advice. But it is not very helpful, since there may be many ways of organizing the material logically in the sense of reasonably, and whether a programme is logically organized in this sense will depend upon numerous factors, such as what you hope to achieve, what the students know, what they are **interested** in, what their particular strengths, weaknesses, problems and states of mind are, what resources are available, and what the teacher's strengths and weaknesses are. So great is the number of variables that what is a logically organized curriculum in one set of circumstances may not be in another, and many different ways of organizing a programme may be equally logical.

It would be of more practical significance to determine the logical order to sequence material in the strong sense. But is there a necessary order for sequencing material in a subject? Some might argue that the logical order in which to study **history**, for example, is chronological sequence: one should start with prehistory, move on to the earliest civilizations that arose in the Near East, advance to the emergence of Mediterranean cultures, and so on to the present day. Not only does this have a certain intuitive plausibility about it ('we should look first at what came first'), but arguments can be advanced to support the approach, most notably that to truly **understand** historical events one has to know what has led up to them. However, although a case can be made for the chronological approach, it is not correct to claim this is the logical way to proceed in the sense of the way that is necessarily demanded by the nature of studying history. It might equally reasonably be argued that students, particularly if they are young children, will study history more effectively if they begin by focusing on something with which they are broadly familiar, such as the contemporary history of their own society. (This is the thinking behind the so-called 'expanding horizons' curriculum.) There are in fact a good number of a priori reasonable ways to sequence history, and none of them could claim to be the logical way in the strong sense. Besides a chronological and expanding horizons approach, one might propose a thematic approach, an approach based on theories of child-development, concentration on the grand sweep of world history, the sharper focus of national history, or an approach designed to illustrate patterns of historical development. Any and all of these might in principle be a reasonable way to proceed. None may claim to be the logical way, and whether one is more suitable than another must depend to some extent on particular circumstances.

Some subjects may be thought to lend themselves to a logical order more obviously than others. Could one not legitimately talk of the logical order in which to teach, say reading or mathematics? It might seem so, but is there anything about the nature of mathematics that makes it necessary (as opposed to very often sensible) that one should master addition before multiplication or numeracy before algebra? Surely not. It is true that the way in which most of us handle multiplication involves addition, but it need not do so, and in any case that would not prevent us from introducing addition as part of multiplication, rather than prior to it, if we chose to. Similarly, there is no necessary reason why algebra should not be taught to people who have no prior **training** in numeracy. The argument is not that these might be sensible approaches that we should seriously consider. It is rather that, even in such a seemingly hierarchical subject as mathemtaics, it is far from clear that anything can be unequivocally identified as the logical order of sequencing in the strong sense. Likewise, though there may be some good reasons to support one approach to the **teaching** of reading rather than another, those reasons will need to be articulated and considered in respect of particular situations: one cannot simply maintain that it is logical to proceed by teaching the letters first, the syllables first, or whole words first, or by teaching reading before writing, or vice versa.

The truth is that there are very few logical restraints on how we might sequence the school **curriculum**. Rather, there are a number of contingent restraints in the spheres of resources, teacher competence, and student competence, which place limits (that might in principle be challenged) more on how we can effectively proceed than on what material we can introduce. Despite the likely ignorance of young children about politics, there is no logical bar on introducing them to the notion of democracy, provided that one handles it in some ways rather than others. Despite warnings about children's inability to handle abstract concepts (derived from **developmental theory**), one *could* successfully introduce topics such as death or love to five-year-olds, provided that one did so in certain ways rather than others. The only truly logical restraints on what we teach arise out of our **conception** of what we want to achieve. Given a certain level of intellectual development, then, *if* one's object is to plunge straight into a Socratic dialogue about death, it does necessarily follow that one cannot achieve one's objective. (Though, even in this extreme and implausible example, it is not a necessary truth that five-year-old children should be incapable of such discourse, and it is not impossible that a teacher should lead children to some degree of competence at it.)

The sensible approach to sequencing curriculum material is therefore to ignore the notion of looking for the logical order in which to present it, and instead to determine the approach in the light of one's **aims** and one's knowledge of the particular situation one confronts.

M

Mainstreaming

In the first half of the twentieth century, many educational authorities segregated handicapped students (a category that includes the deaf, blind, physically handicapped, learning disabled, mentally retarded and maladjusted) in separate schools. Such arrangements for schooling for the handicapped have been sharply criticized in the last twenty years. Some have argued that integration of all students will encourage greater acceptance of the handicapped in later life by reducing their isolation and helping to remove stigmas and **stereotypes**. Others have suggested that the criteria on which separation had been previously based were sometimes unclear or incompetently administered and often racially biased, and in consequence may have violated the civil rights of the handicapped. As society as a whole became more understanding of the nature of specific disabilities, some reasons for excluding students from regular classrooms lost their substance. Integration of special-education and regular students was advocated as a means of providing a more stimulating environment for all students. Parents' groups, in particular, became powerful political advocates of change, and assisted in success-ful legal challenges to existing patterns of segregation. Integration of special-education students was also seen in some cases as a means to reduce costs; **ethical** arguments became irresistible when linked to eco-nomic pressures.

In the last two decades, ameliorative action to integrate handicapped students into regular schools (a set of practices often labelled 'main-streaming') has been required by law in many jurisdictions in North America and Europe, particularly after the example set in the United States by the passage of Public Law 94–142 in 1975, and the debates caused by the Warnock Report in Britain in 1978. Consequently, a variety of alternative arrangements, depending at least in part on the nature of the disabilities, has been made in regular school accommoda-tions, **curricula**, and classroom groupings, to provide educational ser-vices to handicapped students. Some authorities have attempted to integrate as many handicapped students as possible into existing class-rooms, and often provided consultants, additional teachers, or para-professionals to assist teachers with their new responsibilities. For other students, special services have been provided for part of the day in separate facilities, while some classes remained integrated. In some regular schools, a resource room has been provided to offer instruction for those students who could not benefit from integration. For the most serious handicaps, special schools have been retained.

It is not surprising that the implementation of mainstreaming was very uneven across jurisdictions. In some cases, handicapped students were integrated before guidelines were provided or curricula changes were completed. Some placements of handicapped students were somewhat indiscriminate (some handicapped students found themselves relocated from special-education classrooms in which minorities were over-represented to regular classrooms of precisely the same type). Many non-handicapped students or their teachers were not prepared in any systematic way for the social changes that successful integration required. Some teachers failed to modify their **teaching** practices to accommodate special students, or resented the additional burdens that such students placed on them (especially the number of forms that some were required to complete). Additional funds promised by some authorities failed to appear in school budgets. At best, many schools seemed to muddle through, with not very satisfactory results.

The findings offered by **empirical** research on the effectiveness of mainstreaming are not encouraging (although it is not entirely clear what part inadequacy in **research** methodology plays in these inconclusive results). Implementation of mainstreaming policies seems very uneven, and subject to significant reinterpretation by school officials and teachers in local communities. No single mainstreaming programme has been shown to be more successful than others in improving the academic achievement of special-education students. There appear to be few differences in students' self-esteem as a function of class placement. Many of the anticipated benefits of mainstreaming have failed to materialize in the findings of social scientific research.

Many educators now regard mainstreaming as an over-simple solution to a series of very complex problems related to the **education** of handicapped students. While mainstreaming may benefit some students, at some ages, in some locations, programmes designed to apply to all handicapped students appear misguided. The range of disabilities that must be accommodated, and the social issues related to the education of handicapped students, require consideration of much more sensitive solutions than mainstreaming seems to provide.

REFERENCES

Allen (1980), Bogdan (1983), Crealock and Sitko (1983), Croll and Moses (1985), Grossi (1981), Kendall (1980), O'Donnell and Bradfield (1976), Salend

(1984), Semmel, Gottlieb and Robinson (1979), Swann (1985), Tomlinson (1985), Wang and Birch (1984), Weatherley and Lipsky (1977).

Mass media

The mass media (film, television, radio, newspapers, etc.) have an important bearing on **education** in at least two respects. First, it is widely believed that on balance they may have a malign and anti-educational effect on children. Secondly, and notwithstanding the first point, they are sometimes seen as providing valuable alternative modes of **communication**, perhaps even a superior manner for educational purposes. Thus the study of film, for example, might be considered as good a way or as a better way to come to grips with the subject matter of **literature**.

The question of the effects of (most particularly) television on children has been studied to the point at which no wise man would commit himself to any extreme and categorical position. **Empirical research** into such a question is notoriously difficult, and even if that were not so and all studies were taken to be unexceptionable, the conclusions drawn have been conflicting and varied. No doubt we may take it as established that television sometimes does put ideas (good or bad) into people's heads; no doubt it may desensitize them to horrors; no doubt it often leads people to a supine acquiescence in junk. But it is equally certain that it can help people to become more **critical** (even of the ideas it implants), by providing information, argument, and example. It can also promote awareness of and evoke sensitivity to issues. And some television fare is decidedly not junk, while some viewers manage to remain **discriminating**. In short, we do not know whether on balance the mass media are having a beneficial or a deleterious effect, and it would be rash to assert any dogmatic conclusions in relation to particulars (such as, e.g., whether television leads to an increase in violent crime). It would thus seem premature and unwarranted to worry about the effects of the medium as such. Far more important is to recognize that television, radio, newspapers, etc., just as literature, may be a force for good or evil. This raises other questions such as how one determines worth and quality in the various media, how one determines moral truth, whether some media are more prone to **indoctrination** than others, and whether **censorship** can be justified. None the less, there seems no reason to regard the mass media a priori as anti-educational or malignant (***ethics**).

Indeed, as noted, they clearly can be the very opposite, as countless excellent, informative, and critical nature, political, and **cultural** programmes testify. What then of the more particular argument, sometimes advanced, that since this is the age of electronic media rather than newsprint, and since many children more readily watch film/television than read, we should study film rather than literature? After all, if Dickens' *Christmas Carol* is going to be shown every year on television, why struggle to get children to read it, especially since the style of this particular book is relatively arcane and old-fashioned? Why go through the tired motions of staging *Macbeth* or *Waiting for Godot* as a school play, when the students could be making a video of their own? Why grant institutional esteem to the artistry of Henry James and not the artistry of Alfred Hitchcock?

There seems no reason to deny either that the medium of film (video-tape, etc.) may be as **worthwhile** (intrinsically or educationally) as that of print, or that particular works may be qualitatively equal to or superior to particular works of literature. The use of other media, including the mass medium of television, thus seems educationally desirable. However, this should not be confused with the idea that schools might reasonably choose to dispense with study of the written word in general and literature in particular. There are very strong educational reasons why the study of literature should remain central to the **curriculum.**

First, notwithstanding the admission that some products of the mass media are of high cultural and intellectual quality, the quality of most television is poor by any educationally **relevant** criteria. Secondly, television does not merely treat of trivia but also trivializes important subject matter. Even *The Dating Game/Blind Date* could be argued to involve the trivialization of a serious subject rather than treatment of a trivial matter, but quiz shows and certain news and current affairs programmes clearly do. One of the particular ways in which material is trivialized constitutes a third objection to the medium: the refusal (mainly thanks to the demands of advertising) to treat anything for a sustained period of time. Fourthly, despite the burgeoning of the film and television industries, the vast bulk of quality literary work, whether in the form of essays, novels, poems, biographies, etc., is simply not available, nor ever likely to be, in any other form. (We are obviously not here referring to the mere transcription of a printed page to, for instance, a microcomputer.) Finally, one might add that the tendency to highlight star-quality is inherently inimical to serious study: if the talents of the writer/presenter/actor make the point clearer, the impact greater, that is one thing. It is quite another when the audience's conviction is the product of the charisma of the commentator or the glamour of the actor.

The above are all **contingent** points, although none the less important for that. There are, however, two considerations that arise out of the nature of thought and its connection with **language.**

While a visual medium might well do a particular job better than a verbal medium, it cannot hope to do all that the latter can do or to do large parts of it, such as analyse, describe, and explain, as well. Our verbal language is complex and sophisticated. By comparison our visual language is not. A film may portray the emotional turmoil, the anxiety, and ambiguity of a character as well as a book, but it can succeed in doing this only with an audience that already has sophisticated understanding of the **concepts** in question, and that comes about through mastery of the verbal language. If I do not have words (any words) in which to refer to the concept of jealousy, then, I do not have the concept of jealousy. If I do not have the concept of jealousy, it is inconceivable that I should see it in people's behaviour, for to 'see' jealousy is to filter some particular **phenomenon** through an understanding of the idea of jealousy.

The second point is closely allied to the first. The written word is more monitorable than the visual image; it is more educable. That is to say, teachers can more readily see whether students understand a scene, and more readily develop their understanding of it, when working in the verbal medium. To make educational use of film one has to discuss it in words. Command of those words (the language) is not, however, going to be developed other than by engagement with it. The written word is not the only means of fostering such engagement, but it is the most obvious and best way. (An oral approach would be fine if the students, teachers, peers, family and so on could maintain the degree of insight, precision, and wisdom of the best authors.)

REFERENCES

Golding (1974), Postman (1985).

Mathematics *see* Change, Core curriculum, Correlation, Critical thinking, Curriculum, Discipline, Feminism, Knowledge, Language, Logical order, Nationalism

Measurement

A more specific term than **assessment**, measurement may be defined as 'the assignment of numerals to entities according to rules' (Stufflebeam, 1968). I may assess something in any way I choose: impressionistically, holistically, by reference to particular criteria, formally, informally, making my procedure public or private, etc. But to measure is to assess by reference to a publicly agreed scale or set of rules of some sort or another. The reason that we cannot measure, e.g., beauty, quality in literature, or degrees of being educated, is not necessarily that such things are inherently unmeasurable. It is rather that nobody has yet proposed a set of criteria that are both monitorable and generally agreed to be sufficient conditions of beauty, literature, or education (*necessary condition). That might be because it cannot be done (in which case they would indeed be unmeasurable), but it might not be. Is the idea of measuring the extent to which a person is educated any more far-fetched than the idea of measuring blood-pressure? On the other hand, is measurement much to be desired in a domain such as education, given that it involves limiting our assessment to a select number of monitorable features and defining whatever we are concerned with in those limited terms? Do we, for example, want to confine our attention to what is involved in multiple-choice examinations rather than in writing essays, just because we can measure success in the former but not the latter? These are not questions that easily yield incontestable answers. Perhaps the main point to stress is that, until such time as we arrive at clear and uncontested criteria for key educational concepts that are also directly and unambiguously monitorable, to seek to subject the entire educational enterprise to measurement is to distort it unwarrantably (*quantitative/qualitative research).

REFERENCES

Shufflebeam (1968), Thorndike (1971).

Memory

Memory commonly comes into educational discourse yoked to the more prominent topic of learning. This connection is encouraged in part because of the way in which we assess and evaluate learning. Typically assessment and evaluation involve discovering what students have remembered of what they were earlier taught. However much we might be concerned with other, perhaps more profound, products of learning – such as understanding – it is very difficult to disentangle these from what may be a more superficial form of memorization. And while 'rote-memorization' has long been disparaged as an educational activity or aim, it is obvious to any student facing a typical test or examination that such memorization is crucial to successful performance. So we have a slightly odd situation in which virtually everyone in the educational systems of the Western world agrees that 'cramming' or superficial memorization of information is of little or no educational significance, yet every student and teacher knows that success at this limited activity counts for a large measure of what is assessed and evaluated throughout these systems.

Research on memory has been generally rather unspectacular. Some of the commoner distinctions established – between, say, long-term and short-term memory, or between memory for **skills** and memory for events (Gregory 1969) – have simply elaborated fairly standard intuitive distinctions. Part of the problem is lack of clarity about what establishes a memory record. There are three main theories: (a) a change in the standing pattern of brain activity; (b) a change of some specific chemical molecules; (c) a change in the pathways between neurons within the nervous system. (For a clear elaboration of these, see Young, 1978.) The more informal, practical efforts to improve or 'develop' memorization – 'Develop a miraculous memory in just ten days!' – all rely on techniques that were old, and rather more sophisticated, in the Middle Ages (Spence, 1984; Yates, 1966).

One of the most significant pieces of research on memory was that conducted by Bartlett (1932). Earlier, behaviourally orientated, research (prominently that of Ebbinghaus, 1913) had tended to focus on non-sense syllables, because there would thus be no contamination of the memorizing process by earlier experience or associations. Bartlett showed, however, that memory relied on schemata, which people built up through their whole **cultural** experience. These schemata would help to determine what would be remembered, what could not be assimilated, and what would be changed over time in the memory. Bartlett's research has led to the development of 'schema-theory' in modern educational research (Anderson, 1977) and helped to show that memorizing is a more complex socially and culturally determined activity than **behaviourist** research could indicate.

Another facet of memory in **education** is emerging from the more recent research on morality and **literacy** (Goody, 1986; Havelock, 1986; Ong, 1982). In particular the progressivist distrust of rote-memorization, and the consequent move away from having children learn material 'by heart', is being questioned and challenged. It is becoming clear that the active human memory is quite unlike a coding of information in a book or in a computer. Indeed when the memory is actively stimulated it evokes vivid images. The case has been made (Egan, 1989) that memorization and the use of the **imagination** are closely related, and that the progressivist distrust and deprecation of 'rote-memorization' threw a baby out with some bath water. This newer argument is supported by a very much older one, evident in ancient Greek psychology: Mnemosyne, the goddess of Memory, was the mother of the artistic Muses.

REFERENCES

Anderson, Spiro and Montague (1977), Bartlett (1932), Ebbinghaus (1913), Egan (1989), Goody (1986), Gregory (1969), Havelock (1986), Ong (1982), Spence (1984), Yates (1966), Young (1978).

Mental faculties/faculty psychology

Faculty psychology refers to a particular view of what the mind is, and how it works. Conceived in philosophical discussions during the eighteenth-century Enlightenment, faculty psychology regarded the mind as an integrated entity, but with distinct capacities (or 'faculties') having specified functions, most of which are intellectual, such as remembering, perceiving, judging, and reasoning. Given such a view of the mind, the task of **schooling** was thought to be to provide **training** or **discipline** for each of the faculties – a task for which the classical **curriculum** was seen to be particularly appropriate. By thorough training of the faculties (many nineteenth-century schoolmasters did not economize on repetitive exercises), a person would be able to deploy these intellectual abilities in a variety of situations.

Empirical research in the first part of the twentieth century, however, demonstrated the weakness of such reasoning, especially on the question of the **transfer** of training, and most of the claims for the mental discipline view of **learning** were found to be unwarranted. At the present time, faculty psychology persists as a primitive historical antecedent to several more complex notions of mind, such as those derived from factor analysis and computational **models**. Nevertheless, in popular parlance, the **metaphor** of separate mental faculties in a variety of subtle ways continues to affect how many people view school organization, curriculum and methodology (*creativity, critical thinking, intelligence, reification).

REFERENCES

Boring (1957), Kantor (1969), Murphy and Kovach (1972).

Metaphor

As a figure of speech, metaphor has been used in a variety of ways over the centuries. A commonly held view relegates it to a largely ornamental function in which pre-existing **concepts** are dressed up in more colourful language. Others take metaphor more seriously by regarding it as inseparable from **language** and reality. They perceive reality itself as a metaphoric interaction between specific words and the particular objects that the words denote. New interactions, it may be argued, produce new realities. Identification of metaphors in specific situations may lead, it is assumed, to important insights about the nature of educational thought and practice.

It is against the background of this second interpretation that interest in metaphors should be examined in a contemporary educational context. Many educators have begun to express dissatisfaction with prevailing **research** methodologies (for example, the taken-for-granted nature of the use of categorical behaviours on the one hand, and **objective, quantitative** reporting on the other). What is perceived as the poor record of traditional research in its self-proclaimed task of predicting and controlling educational **phenomena**, and the poverty of what passes as contemporary educational **theory**, have driven many to reassess the basic principles upon which the field of inquiry is founded. What is needed, some have said, is a shift of emphasis to enable scholars and educators to break out of scientific-technological approaches and develop new perspectives. 'What I propose', Eisner (1977), for one, has written, 'starts not with a scientific paradigm but with an artistic one.'

Some researchers are studying the nature of metaphors in **education** from a philosophic point of view. Others are interested in detecting and identifying metaphors in the talk of in-service or pre-service teachers in the hope that such investigations will tell us why those teachers behave in the ways that they do. Specific metaphors, it is argued, may exercise a powerful effect on a teacher's style of **teaching** and pattern of **curriculum** innovation. In consequence, discovery of metaphors used by teachers may lead to important insights into the educational assumptions of practising teachers.

Others are involved in searching the fine arts and humanities (especially literary criticism, journalism, music, theatre and drama) as sources for alternative metaphors for examining educational phenomena. The pattern adopted is usually this: first, the original source (e.g. a branch of **aesthetics**, or a specific **discipline**, within the humanities) is examined to identify key concepts or understandings that have a capacity to throw light on educational phenomena. For example, from journalism, such concepts as 'scene-by-scene construction', 'use of dialogue', 'third-person perspective', and the 'symbolic detail of the subject's life' are extracted for possible use in educational settings (MacDonald, 1976). Secondly, particular methods of reporting are identified. Vallance (1975) identified several features (including 'simile', 'implied technique', 'implied movement', and 'overlapping adjectives') that she claimed were not only typical of art criticism but also appropriate for descriptions of educational situations.

Significant criticisms have already appeared in response to such research. It has been argued that those searching for alternative metaphors within the humanities may have neglected the effects of the great variety of images within particular disciplines. Drama, for example, offers so many distinct forms that the selection of a particular metaphor from all those available within the discipline may require careful description and definition. Since this example is by no means unique, the prospect emerges of the existence of hundreds of metaphors within the humanities awaiting transfer to education. If a selection is to be made, some criteria for determining good or useful metaphors will be required.

Secondly, little account has been taken of the difficulties that exist in the transfer of metaphoric images from one person to another. Although there are common understandings in such metaphors as 'man is a wolf', no common understandings exist in such metaphors as 'teaching is a drama'. A small amount of **empirical** research suggests that transmission of images from the humanities may be relatively difficult. Thirdly, some of the published examples of educational reporting using humanistic metaphors have been criticized for the quality of their prose and the type of judgements they have made – 'painful to read', according to one critic (Gibson, 1981) (***analogy**).

REFERENCES

Black (1962), Brown (1977), Egan (1988a), Eisner (1977, 1979), Gibson (1981), Huebner (1984), Kelly (1975), Kliebard (1982), MacDonald (1977), Milburn (1984, 1985), Rico (1976), Schlechty and Joslin (1984), Scribner (1984), Taylor (1982), Vallance (1975), Willis (1978).

Methods of teaching *see* Teaching

Microteaching

Microteaching involves providing a setting outside the regular classroom in which teachers or student teachers may meet small groups of their peers or pupils for various types of small-scale practice teaching sessions. Just as prospective lawyers hone their skills in moot courts, and accountants simulate audits of a large company's books, so teachers meet to carry out simplified skill-development exercises in teaching. Although features vary from one location to another, a microteaching session often comprises the following stages: a specific **skill** is identified, a video-tape is shown of a teacher demonstrating that skill, a student teacher prepares a brief teaching episode (about five to ten minutes in length) which puts that same skill into practice, a video-tape of that session is reviewed with an instructor, the student attempts a second, revised lesson with a second group of students, and a second video-tape is reviewed, and so on.

Several advantages are claimed for this procedure. Short **teaching** sessions based on specific skills not only reduce the normal classroom to manageable proportions, but also permit the teacher to focus on his own development rather than the immediate **needs** of his students. In selecting such skills, priority may be given to those considered essential to good teaching, for example reinforcing, questioning, and probing. Unlike the teacher in a regular classroom, a teacher in a microteaching session may repeat short-duration tasks as frequently as he wishes, until the desired competence (or mastery) is achieved. From video-tapes of such microteaching sessions, a student teacher, perhaps with the guidance of an instructor, may reflect upon his previous performance, assess his own development, and make adjustments for future practice.

Research reports suggest a certain amount of success with microteaching experiments. If teachers practise certain selected techniques, they are likely to demonstrate improvement in successive microteaching sessions. Improvement has also been noted in the ability of teachers to **evaluate** their own performances, and to accommodate criticism constructively. In addition, beginning teachers usually rate microteaching highly as a technique for introducing them to the complexities of the classroom in a programmed and systematic way. It is worth stressing, however, that not all research results have been favourable, and that on such key issues as the effects of microteaching on pupil **learning**, the results are at best ambiguous.

Despite the favourable reputations that microteaching enjoys, several observers have raised questions about its **worth**. First, microteaching remains embedded in the traditional psychological approach to teacher improvement. Because it is based on a piece-by-piece introduction to specific teaching skills, it consistently treats the means of teaching as the ends, as do such other skill-development systems as competency-based teacher training. Secondly, those advocating the use of microteaching rarely try to justify the selection of skills included in microteaching systems. They have assumed: (a) that teaching is a **behaviour**; (b) that such behaviour consists of identifiable skills and sub-skills; and (c) that the **modelling** of such skills is at least likely to lead to success in the classroom. All three assumptions are questionable.

Thirdly, given the fact that microteaching sessions are frequently artificial in nature (after all, the micro-classroom is not the real class-room), and that teaching skills in series may become somewhat mechan-ical, the notion that teachers will successfully **transfer** their microteaching experience into the complex world of the classroom seems optimistic. What is important in the classroom, for example, is not the ability to demonstrate a wide range of skills, but the ability to know what skill is appropriate to particular situations. Fourthly, only in comparatively rare instances have microteaching training programmes been sensitive to the demands of different types of subject matter taught in school.

Some observers have also pointed to the anti-intellectualism of some aspects of microteaching. Since teaching is a profession that demands an ability to treat difficult **concepts** and ideas in a way that is clear to a variety of students, those kinds of **training** that emphasize simplified skills may not be appropriate. Given differences in personalities among teachers, the stress in some forms of microteaching on standardized approaches seem inappropriate (and dangerous). Microteaching may be yet another example of an approach to training that threatens important **educational** ideals by its very success (*simulations, teacher education).

REFERENCES

Allen and Ryan (1969), Cooper (1980), Davis (1982), Gibbs (1980), Hargie (1982), Hargie and Maidment (1979), McIntyre, MacLeod and Griffiths (1977), McKnight (1980), Spelman and St John-Brooks (1972), Stones (1984), Trott (1977), Turney, Clift, Dunkin and Traill (1973), Weil and Joyce (1978).

Mixed ability *see* Core curriculum, Giftedness, Integrated studies, Integration, Mainstreaming

Models

The term 'model' has many meanings in educational discourse, and, as such, has been a source of some confusion. It is used to indicate a scale replica or icon (as in a model of the human heart), or an exemplar (as in a model lesson) – in both cases, with little ambiguity. However, the term is also used to indicate a simplified statement of relationships (as in a model of **curriculum design**), or to denote an abstract representation system (as in a model of social behaviour). Some scholars also use the term in a technical sense to show a series of relationships between variables in the workings of a social scientific theory. It is in these more interpretative senses that difficulties arise in educational talk.

Practitioners frequently notice the term being used in educational texts in such phrases as models of curriculum development or models of **teaching**. In the former, a model is often indicated by means of a two-dimensional diagram, with arrows or circles linking several curricular **concepts**. In the latter, a model may be analysed in terms of such categories as syntax, social system, principles of reaction, and support systems. Such loosely designed interpretative schemata are obviously far removed from the structural certainty of iconic models.

But educators often fail to distinguish the differences between interpretative and iconic models. In so doing, they confer on any representation of educational **phenomena** labelled a 'model' an internal consistency and coherence that may not be warranted or justifiable. This tendency to treat a so-called model with greater reverence than it deserves is one reason why many critics argue that the term is dangerous in educational discourse. They also maintain that it may be inappropriate to attempt to reduce educational phenomena to a relatively inflexible pattern of requirements and procedures. The very act of distinguishing a series of models in the complex world of **education** – even in those instances, as in models of teaching, in which a large number have been identified – may be limiting and restrictive. In addition, so-called models are frequently presented to audiences that are not aware of the questionable assumptions on which they are based.

Models may serve a function in representing, describing, explaining, or predicting educational phenomena. But, being yet another example of the tendency to bootleg from the natural sciences those concepts that give an aura of scientific knowledge to the study of education, they also may seriously mislead.

REFERENCES

Barrow (1984), Black (1962), Brady (1985), Brodbeck (1959), Hunt (1971), Jenkins and Shipman (1976), Joyce and Weil (1980), Kaplan (1964), MacIver and Holdaway (1966), Nuthall and Snook (1973), Snow (1973).

Moral education

Moral **education** is to be distinguished from moral **training, socialization** and **indoctrination**. Since education implies promoting **understanding**, to provide moral education is to give people understanding of the moral domain – understanding of the way in which moral language works, what makes behaviour and people moral as opposed to, say, prudent, popular, or selfish. Being morally educated does not necessarily imply being educated in the full sense; and while being educated (in the full sense) does imply having moral understanding, it does not necessarily imply being moral in the sense of behaving morally. The relationship between moral behaviour and moral understanding is a complex one, that cannot be examined fully here, but it is clear that the latter can exist independently and is the obvious goal of moral education. To promote moral behaviour may well be considered an aspect of socialization, and will certainly be one aim of early moral training, by which is meant the cultivation of morally desirable habits prior to any attempt to offer reasoned justification for them; socialization and training may well be proper parts of **schooling**, but they are to be distinguished from moral education. (Moral indoctrination would consist in the deliberate attempt to instil unreflective commitment to a particular set of moral rules.) It will be seen, therefore, that moral education is in principle compatible with being an immoral or amoral person. This may lead some to argue that, particularly in the early years of schooling, it is socialization and moral training that are required rather than moral education.

Moral education is also to be distinguished from **religious education**. Historically the two have often been interrelated, it being assumed that God is the author of goodness. But to take such a view is to ignore the point that morality and religion are logically distinguishable. God may demand the good of us, but only if the good has some independent status. (If God were not thought to demand the good of us, but rather it was thought that the good is whatever God demands of us, then it would not be clear why we should wish to do the good or indeed be commended for doing it. It would seem to be more a matter of power – do this because God is powerful and commands it – than morality – do this because it is good, a fact that God in his wisdom can see.)

Moral education will no doubt benefit from an earlier period of moral training, since to seek to understand the nature of, for example, obligation, promise-keeping, and beneficence, must be difficult if not impossible for one who has not been acclimatized to a sense of any of them. But moral education itself will consist in coming to understand such features of moral utterances as their **prescriptive** nature (their logically necessary tendency to lay obligation on one or to prescribe; for example 'this is good' means, partly, 'this is an ought-to-be-done thing'), their **emotive** quality (moral terms imply commitment on the part of the speaker) and their universalizability (for instance 'hitting that person is wrong, Johnny' logically implies, in default of special explanations that may justify a difference, that nobody, including the speaker, should hit that person). In addition, various logical features of moral behaviour, such as that only an agent acting freely, as opposed to on orders, under threat, or without thought, can be credited as a truly moral agent, that the fact that something is the case cannot in itself constitute a conclusive argument for showing that it ought to be, and that morality, whatever else it is about, is essentially about impartial treatment and human welfare, will need to be understood by the morally educated man (*contingent, ethics).

Those being the kinds of issue to be explored in true moral education, two practical questions arise: do we need special lessons devoted to moral education and do programmes of values clarification and other similar exercises in discussing moral problems represent adequate ways of providing a moral education? The answer to both questions, as phrased, appears to us to be no. Although there is no overwhelming objection to the idea of lessons specifically devoted to a basic course in moral philosophy (which, to be blunt, is what moral education involves) it is clear that moral education could arise out of thought and discussion generated in other contexts, particularly in history and English where moral problems are often the overt focus of attention, but also in many other subjects, including the sciences, where moral problems may emerge (e.g. nuclear weapons, abortion or industrial espionage). If there are special 'moral education' lessons and they are given over to certain types of values clarification then a true moral education is not being provided. For, typically, values clarification programmes seek to give practice in thinking about what one would do, faced with hypothetical moral problems or dilemmas (e.g. to steal for a very good cause, when all other avenues seem closed). But (a) skill in articulating what one would do in hypothetical situations is not known to have any clear relationship to doing things in real situations; (b) being articulate about one's actions, that is, having a clear explanation to offer of what one would do and why, though possibly desirable in itself, is not the same thing as having a justification or being able to offer a moral argument for what one would do; and (c) such programmes proceed as if they are developing a skill of clarifying values, without distinction as between moral, aesthetic, or other values. This seems as unwarranted as the assumption that there is a skill, or even a set of skills, of critical thinking. Whatever else it does, a programme designed to help individuals clarify moral values must be based upon an attempt to provide specifically moral understanding. It must therefore concern itself with exploring the kinds of point made above (*caring, censorship, core curriculum, developmental theory, objectivity, subjectivity, values clarification).

REFERENCES

Hirst (1974d), McPhail, Ungoed-Thomas and Chapman (1972), Peters (1974), Sizer and Sizer (1970), Straughan (1982), Wilson (1973a), Wilson, Williams and Sugarman (1967), Wright (1971).

Motivation *see* Discipline, Interest, Research, Teacher effectiveness

Multiculturalism

'Multiculturalism' is not an easy term to define. The meaning of '**culture**', on which the notion of multicultural logically depends, is far from clear, and 'multiculturalism' is not easily distinguished from such related terms as 'multiethnic', 'multiracial', 'intercultural', 'polyethnic', and 'multicredal'. These related terms, in their turn, are subject to various interpretations.

Attitudes to multiculturalism in schools depend, in large measure, on attitudes in society in general. Some claim, for example, that value systems of all cultures should be considered of equal worth, since there are no accepted grounds for judging one set of moral values to be superior to another. Others reject that form of **relativism** by arguing that certain principles of social justice pre-empt positions based on cultural identity. Members of majority groups often have difficulty coming to terms with other cultural groups within society, and some governments have enacted repressive laws to restrict the lives of minorities. Others view members of minority groups as curiosities to be accommodated by dance festivals or grants to ethnic artists and writers – a latter-day version of bread and circuses. Even in societies sympathetic to aspirations of cultural minorities, individual citizens exacerbate difficulties by regarding minorities as 'peculiarities' within an otherwise 'normal' system, or as 'problems' requiring administrative solutions. A habit of treating citizens as objects to be controlled or regulated is unlikely to lay the groundwork for constructive relationships between majority and minority groups.

School multicultural programmes, in consequence, vary widely. Some governments have attempted to identify, and offer compensatory measures for, those cultural groups that seem to be deprived. Examples of such policies include the Headstart programme in the United States, and Indian education programmes in Canada. Others have been more interested in extending special **language** programmes to satisfy a particular demand. In some areas special attention has been paid to ensuring that all students are aware of, and understand, the cultural differences that exist within a particular society. Attempts have been made to broaden the cultural base of many subjects studied in schools (for example, in **literature**, **history**, and related social sciences) to ensure a more balanced recognition of the contribution of previously neglected cultures. Special programmes have also been initiated to combat **stereotyping** and prejudice. Other governments have introduced programmes to encourage and confirm a pluralistic society, and, on occasion, separate schools have been established to serve particular religious or ethnic groups.

These educational policies remain contentious. Some critics condemn multicultural programmes on the grounds that all attempts at providing for the needs of diverse cultural groups within a single educational system are assimilationist at heart. Others argue that the demands of contemporary society require a common and restricted range of curriculum offerings. Heated debates take place on the nature and cost of compensatory programmes designed for particular cultural groups (and on the frequent lack of success of such programmes). Some groups within the educational community resist (occasionally for good reasons) affirmative action policies or second-language programmes, especially those that threaten teachers' jobs. Extremists on both the left and right wings often view multicultural policies as grist for their **ideological** mills. There appears to be little optimism that such different points of view can be reconciled (*core curriculum, ethics, moral education, positive discrimination, religious education).

REFERENCES

Banks (1981), Crittenden (1982), Grant and Sleeter (1985), James and Jeffcoate (1981), Kehoe (1984), Little and Willey (1981), Lynch (1983), McLeod (1984), Partington (1985a, 1985b), Sarup (1986), Verma and Bagley (1979), Werner, Connors, Aoki and Dahlie (1977), Wright and Coombs (1981), Young (1979).

Multidisciplinary *see* Discipline, Integrated studies, Knowledge

Multiple choice *see* Assessment, Objectivity, Research

Music *see* Language

N

Nationalism

'Nationalism' very often has pejorative overtones. It suggests patriotism ('love and loyal support of one's country') carried to excess, or chauvinism and jingoism. But the word may also specifically refer to commitment to the doctrine that national interest is more important than international interest, or to commitment to the objective of national independence.

The issue of nationalism may be of concern to education in a number of ways. First, even patriotism, though it generally lacks the undesirable connotations of nationalism, may be criticized, and many question the propriety of any steps to cultivate patriotism, let alone nationalism, in schools by such means, direct or indirect, as saluting the flag, remembering those who fell in war, displaying portraits of heads of state, presenting one's national story from one's own point of view, or overtly claiming one's superiority. The most sweeping rejection of such practices might simply insist that they are not truly **educational**. However, it is arguable that some at least are a reasonable part of **socialization**, and therefore acceptable as part of **schooling**. It would seem essential to distinguish carefully between: (a) providing information about the nation's customs and beliefs; (b) initiation into rituals that are part of the national way of life; (c) cultivating respect for features of the way of life; (d) cultivating respect for figures in national authority; and (e) **indoctrination**. One might argue against any of these procedures, but only indoctrination is self-evidently objectionable.

Secondly, a nation concerned with establishing its independence may very often face the problem that its education system is dominated by resources (ideas, textbooks, teachers, etc.) from other **cultures**. Whether and to what extent this is acceptable presumably depends to a large extent upon the nature of the external resources. There is nothing necessarily wrong with importing educational ideas or textbooks from other countries, even when the other countries in question are distinctly different culturally. A Scandinavian mathematics textbook, for example, might, once translated, conceivably be a very desirable commodity in a school system being developed in some newly independent South American state. On the other hand, a geography or sociology textbook that takes all its examples from the United States might reasonably be thought to be a bad choice for schools in Africa, partly because it would fail to illuminate the children's world directly and partly because it would be indirectly conveying a message about the importance of America and its values. (The question of the provenance of a textbook generally becomes less important as one moves from the level of providing introductory information about the findings of a **discipline** to immersion in the nature of the discipline. University graduates whose interest is in being sociologists, for example, may more profitably study texts from foreign sources than children who are being introduced to basic claims about the way society functions.)

Sometimes a nation may have good reason, as a matter of priorities, to reject the schooling and education that outsiders offer. One may object to a state that conceives of education as, for example, military training (***analysis, education**). None the less a state, for good or bad reasons, may determine to put military **training** before education, or to do a number of other things that accord ill with education, such as forging a national self-consciousness and identity, teaching people to survive on the land, or training technicians. In short, the claims of nationalism may legitimately override the claims of education. But in so far as a nation, emergent or established, is trying to educate, then much of what goes on in schools should be supra-national, since, for example, the nature of science, sociology, and even literary study, the canons of rational discourse, and the essential features of a moral, as opposed to a non-moral, position are all supra-national matters. It is anti-educational to teach sociology as if it were Marxism, a particular theory of human motivation in the name of psychology, or a particular religious doctrine as if it were an introduction to religious study (***ethics, moral education, religious education**).

This brings us to the question of perhaps most practical interest: should a nation deliberately seek to maintain or impose its own culture on the school system? Should, for example, Canadian schools seek to provide a **curriculum** that helps to define and establish a distinctively Canadian body of art, set of attitudes and values, way of life? (The very **concept** of a nation-state may be called into question at this point, especially as we have examples of Welsh, Scottish, and even Cornish nationalism seeking to extricate themselves from a British confederation, even as we see some struggling to forge a Canadian identity out of such disparate elements as Quebec, Ontario and British Columbia. Where does a nation begin and end?) Assuming, however, a people and territory under a single, stable, government, it is surely clear that there is no simple 'yes' or 'no' answer to the question of whether it should deliberately foster its own culture (even if we ignore the problem of **multiculturalism**). Certainly a nation will socialize its young, and that involves initiating children into at least part of the national culture. But to attempt to make the school curriculum concentrate on the geography, **history**, and **literature** of the nation, just because it is 'of the nation', besides being very likely unproductive, if not counter-productive, in terms of cultural advance, is highly questionable: the educated mind cannot be defined in terms of local information, local experience, and local examples. The educated mind is concerned with supra-national principles and data culled from the entire world. Besides which, thorough understanding of one's own world is to some extent dependent on the **understanding** of other people's worlds.

REFERENCES

Hodgetts (1968), Milburn and Herbert (1974), Scruton (1982), Symons (1975), Weldon (1953).

Natural

The word 'natural' has considerable **emotive** force. Indeed there is one sense of the word that makes it synonymous with 'right', 'fitting', or 'appropriate', and thus gives us a **normative** term. For example, heterosexuality is natural in some people's view, meaning that it is the proper kind of sexual relationship, as opposed to homosexuality, which would be condemned as unnatural. However, the word has a number of other senses. Natural may be contrasted with unnatural in the sense of unusual, acquired as opposed to innate, artificial, cultivated, or contrary to certain norms. For example, 'his natural expression' suggests his usual expression; the claim that the competitive instinct is natural may imply that it is an inevitable part of man's make-up rather than an acquired disposition; 'natural food' is to be contrasted with food that is artificial in the sense of processed or tampered with by man; 'natural behaviour' may suggest spontaneous, instinctive behaviour, as opposed to learned behaviour according to some code of manners: the migratory instinct may be described as natural in certain birds, meaning that it is the norm for the birds in question to have such an instinct.

An illustration of the resulting ambiguity that use of the term often involves is provided by two lines from a song that Bing Crosby once sang: 'When a cat on a fence keeps his darling in suspense, that's because it's the natural thing to do.' This might mean that keeping one's darling in suspense is: (a) the right and proper thing to do; (b) an inevitable part of the love-making game; (c) a genetically programmed behaviour; (d) what is conventionally expected of lovers; (e) a defining characteristic of love-making, or any combination of these, and no doubt other, implications. Whatever might be meant precisely, it remains clear that in such an example referring to the behaviour as 'natural' is to commend or approve it, and yet it is not self-evident that it should be commended. It is not, for example, always the case that what is natural in the sense of conventionally expected is desirable.

More formally it may be observed that in some senses of natural it is not clear why one should believe that what is natural is good, and in other cases it is far from clear what is in fact natural. The mistake of assuming that, because something is the case (and is therefore in some sense natural), it is good or right that it should be the case, is sometimes loosely referred to as the naturalistic fallacy. To conclude that, because mankind is naturally combative (if such were the case), it is commendable that people should be combative, would involve the naturalistic fallacy. (The phrase initially comes from G. E. Moore, who referred to a more specific version of the mistake involved – namely, attempting to define 'good' in terms of some natural quality such as happiness.)

The idea that education should be natural or according to nature is particularly associated with Rousseau, although it is one that has some adherents at almost any time in history, including today. Rousseau did not manage to avoid the ambiguities and confusions in the term, but it is fair to say that two of his central tenets were that children should learn from nature in the sense that they should learn from the consequences of their actions in the world at large (as opposed to the schoolroom), and that the individual has an innate nature that will realize itself in appropriate conditions, as the acorn will develop into an oak tree rather than anything else, given the right conditions. There are many severe problems in such a view. They may perhaps be summarized in the counter-view that **education** is by its very nature not a natural business in this sense. To educate people is to introduce people to ways of thinking and **understanding** that are the product of man's attempt to gain control of and give form to nature. To school people is precisely not to leave them to respond to their environment as they will, but to initiate them into various conventions and man-made meanings. It is, in any case, very unclear that it is appropriate to see individual moral, aesthetic, social and intellectual development as comparable to the physical development of mineral and plant life (*aesthetic value, child-centred education, intelligence, knowledge, moral education**).

REFERENCES

Barrow (1978), Moore (1903), Rousseau (1972).

Nature/nurture

Belief in the power of heredity is to be distinguished from belief in the power of genetic endowment, and both are to be distinguished from belief in innate differences between groups. (It is, for example, conceivable, if not very likely, that my intelligence should be determined by my genetic make-up, and that that should be determined by environmental conditions during the period surrounding my conception and birth. It is also quite conceivable that whatever factors account for my intelligence would not produce the same result in others of my class and race.) None the less, such is the heat that surrounds this topic, that it is sometimes difficult to disassociate the belief that the environment is not the sole determinant of human development from a belief in the innate superiority of a particular race.

Research into the respective power of genetic and environmental factors is severely constrained by the fact that it is not possible to produce a single instance of a being known to be free of either one. Even experiments with identical twins, which have anyway been rare, cannot entirely eliminate environmental differences. It is not necessarily true, therefore, that 'when there are no variations in hereditary factors – as is the case for identical twins – all variations in intelligence result from variations in environmental factors'. Any observed difference could be attributed to the distinct combinations of that particular genetic inheritance and the particular environment rather than to environment alone. (Besides 'no variations in hereditary factors' is not the same thing as 'no genetic variation'.) In the event researchers in this area have hotly disputed one another's findings and interpretations of the data, as well as made contrary claims.

The basic question is to what extent human attributes such as **intelligence** are the product of environment (including **teaching**), and to what extent they are governed by the individual's genetic make-up. Researchers have generally concentrated on cognitive and emotional factors. But physical characteristics, which may or may not develop in the same kind of way, could also raise interesting and difficult questions: how different would my physical state be, if I had been placed at birth in some other family, differing in wealth, style of life, geographical location, etc.?

However, it is arguable that this question as well as being unanswerable, because of the difficulties in the way of isolating factors (*research), is less important than it at first seems. If we had reason to believe that it might well be entirely a matter of either environment or genetic make-up, then it would be of some importance to determine which. For, if environment was the sole determinant of intelligence, then there would be certain things that we could and arguably should do to increase people's intelligence. If, on the other hand, the issue were solely a matter of genes, then, short of genetic engineering, there would be nothing we could do. But as a matter of fact few people, if any, do believe that it is an either/or question. Intuitively, since the time of Plato, it has seemed plausible to regard intellectual growth as governed both by some innate endowment and by the nature of the environment. And **empirical** research, while it has not settled the issue, has thrown up too many examples of similarities between subjects in different environments, and differences between subjects from similar environments, for it to be reasonable to conclude other than that a person's intelligence (and other similar characteristics) is the product of the interplay between environment and genetic factors. It is not possible to quantify (or even, most would say, **assess**) the relative importance of either one, if only because the determining power of either one in isolation, if it could be monitored, would not necessarily be the same as its power in relation to the other. (Compare, for example, the question of the relative importance of sugar and flour in a cake.) That being so, and it being admitted by all that environmental factors, not least the **schooling** system, will make some difference to the cognitive and **emotional** development of individuals (and no doubt to other areas such as physical development), it is clear that we need to continue to inquire into questions about the effects of environment, regardless of whether to some extent genetic factors may stand in our way.

The importance of dwelling on the genetic element (leaving aside its intrinsic academic interest) is presumed to be that, in so far as we have some knowledge of genetic limitations, we would be able to assess individuals in terms of their potential, and to categorize and organize them more efficiently. But since, even if there is an important element of genetic control in intelligence, etc., we are neither able to monitor it nor distinguish its workings in the abstract from its workings in particular environmental contexts, it would seem wise to concentrate on establishing what individuals can do at a given point in time, and what we can do about environmental conditions that seem to facilitate progress from that stage, rather than to concern ourselves with attempts to make long-term predictions on the basis of a genetic theory. In other words, in the current state of our knowledge, we should confine ourselves to establishing that an individual can do particular things and draw appropriate conclusions about what he may reasonably be expected to do next. That seems more acceptable than labelling him intelligent on the basis of tests, and assuming that has predictive value to warrant placing him in the A stream.

REFERENCES

Environment, Heredity and Intelligence (1960), Fontana (1981), Jensen (1969), Kleinig (1982), Simon (1971), White (1974).

Necessary condition

The ideal **analysis** of a **concept** will set out the necessary and sufficient conditions for something being an instance of the concept in question. Thus, one might argue, an act is only truly punishment (as contrasted with revenge, the administering of pain, intimidation, etc.), if (a) some kind of penalty is imposed, (b) by some person in duly constituted authority, (c) on some person to whom it is unwelcome, (d) because he has committed some offence. If that is our view, each one of the items listed represents a necessary condition of punishment. (For example, if a judge arbitrarily imposes a fine on me when I am innocent, then he has not 'punished' me, whatever it feels like to me, since the fourth condition is not met. If I see a burglar, chase him and beat him up, I am not 'punishing' him because I am not acting as a duly constituted authority – the second condition is not met.) Taken together, the four conditions would represent sufficient conditions of punishment. That is, whenever all four conditions are met we have sufficient grounds to call it 'punishment', whatever else may be going on. It is usually easier to arrive at some necessary conditions (for example, having **understanding** is a necessary condition of being **educated**) than to gain agreement on a complete set of necessary and sufficient conditions. (For example, could we in fact accept the above as sufficient conditions of punishment? Suppose a judge sees a criminal breaking the law, chases him and beats him up, because of the wrong-doing. All the conditions suggested are met, but surely it would not count as an instance of bona fide punishment?) (***contingent, logical order**)

Necessary truth *see* Contingent, Facts, Logical order

Needs

What a person needs is not a straightforward question of **empirical fact**. One cannot simply observe what a person needs. For the **concept** of need implies some objectives – one needs penicillin to recover, one needs food to survive, one needs to read to gain certain benefits – and there is room for argument about the importance of various objectives. A 'need' may therefore be defined as 'something that may or may not be lacking, necessary to some desired objective'. (Usually we talk of 'needs' when we lack something, e.g. 'I need money; I don't have any.' But there is nothing logically odd about observing that 'I need air (to breathe)', even though I happen to have it.)

A need is not the same thing as a want. I may want something that in fact I do not need (e.g. an aeroplane. I have no discernible objective to which this is a necessary means). And I may need something that I do not want (e.g. an injection to ward off some disease. I want the objective – my survival – and therefore I have the need of the injection, but I do not want the injection). It follows that an individual is not necessarily the best judge of his own needs. Most obviously he may lack knowledge about what is necessary to attain his objectives (e.g. what drug will make him better); but conceivably he may also be unclear about what he wants (e.g. does he need to leave his wife? Well, does he really have a clear idea about the kind of life he can most readily live?) Children in particular, through ignorance of means to ends and relatively unsophisticated awareness of options open to them, not to mention a certain lack of self-knowledge, are very often going to be poor judges of their own needs. However, we must also be cautious of the idea that needs can be readily judged by outside experts. An expert such as a doctor may know the appropriate medical means to various ends, but he is not qualified *qua* doctor to determine ends. For example, whether a woman needs an abortion is not a question to be determined by medical knowledge alone. There are also many areas where so-called experts are not particularly well informed about means. For example, most doctors today know rather more about medicine than their predecessors of five centuries ago did, and they know more than contemporary soccer managers know about what their players need to do in order to attain the major objective of winning. It may well be thought that educationalists are more akin to soccer managers than to doctors.

At any rate, it is evident that any needs-based approach to **curriculum** will invite the prior question of determining ends; and, although it has been argued that what ends are truly educational is a much more circumscribed question than some would seem to appreciate, it none the less remains the case that educationalists do dispute the proper ends of their business. (It should also be noted that many educationalists implicitly commit themselves to certain ends, when they assert that children need such and such, without showing awareness of the fact that they have done so.) To agree on what children need in terms of **schooling** would be to agree on what the various functions of schooling should be, and what each one entails, as well as to agree on the most suitable and/or necessary means to achieve those **aims**. There is a very real sense therefore in which at present we are not agreed and in some respects do not know what children need.

This claim may seem to fly in the face of a number of quite well-known catalogues of human needs, particularly those devised by psychologists such as Maslow, who enumerated five basic categories of need: the need for safety, the need for self-esteem, social needs, physiological needs, and the need for self-actualization. But such lists invariably present items that are too general to offer practical guidance (e.g. social needs: what are children's social needs in specific terms?), unclear although more specific (e.g. what counts as safety?), in need of interpretation in particular cases (e.g. what will in fact enhance this particular person's self-esteem?), or simply obscure (e.g. the need for self-actualization). Nor is it clear that any needs such as these have much to do with **education**.

Some have attempted to circumvent the problem of who should determine needs by adopting various types of needs assessment programme. (For example, individuals may be interviewed or asked to fill in questionnaires concerning their own needs and/or those of others such as schoolchildren.) But, whatever the manner of collecting data in such programmes, what is being gathered is, at best, information about what people think they (or others) need. It is not necessarily information about what people do need. In order to arrive at that information, it is necessary to arrive at a clear articulation of one's objectives and some strong reasons (whether derived from reasoning, observation, or both) to see particular things as necessary means to those ends (*child-centred education).

REFERENCES
Barrow and Woods (1982), Dearden (1972b), Maslow (1970), Pratt (1980).

Needs assessment *see* Needs

Neutrality

The term 'neutrality' occurs frequently in educational discourse. Some scholars have tried to find out whether and how schools (and the school **curriculum**) can remain neutral in the political sense, and avoid inculcating by precept or example particular political philosophies, while others have been interested in the relationship of the concept to such issues as a child's moral development. The concept also surfaces in **administrative theory** in education, especially in relation to boards of inquiry and the roles of supervisory officers in educational **evaluations** or disputes. Neutrality, however, is usually identified with the work of the Humanities Curriculum Project, directed by the late Lawrence Stenhouse in England during the years 1967–72. Although not the only point of interest, the Project's advocacy of neutrality, as a distinctive strategy in **teaching** certain types of controversial subject matter in the school curriculum, prompted discussions that have relevance far beyond the original source.

The chief purpose of the Humanities Curriculum Project was to encourage teachers to extend the notion of the humanities in the curriculum to include the **understanding** of significant (and, necessarily, controversial) contemporary issues. To that end, packs of materials were developed in trial schools, and eventually published, on such topics as 'the family', 'education', 'war and society', 'relations between the sexes', and 'poverty' – all of which not only drew upon perspectives in several **disciplines** (e.g., **literature**, art, **history**, religious studies, and sociology), but also provided a rich base for the exploration of value-laden issues considered appropriate for a secondary school age-group that Stenhouse considered under-challenged in schools. Given the social and intellectual significance of the subjects of study and the stimulating variety of materials in each published pack (with over 200 printed and pictorial items in each one), it is not surprising that the Project attracted attention not only in Britain but in other countries as well.

One of the objects of special attention was a particular teaching strategy recommended by Stenhouse and the other members of the Project team. Eager to avoid an all-too-common classroom teaching style in which the authority of the teacher (either as a licensed employee or a subject-specialist) was used either to inculcate partisan opinions in value-laden matters, or to offer simplistic solutions to problematic human issues, Stenhouse suggested that the traditional classroom format be replaced by a discussion group in which the teacher served as neutral chairman. Some responsibilities of the chairman were identified in detail in the Project's publications: to encourage discussion, identify the subject of study, foster commitment to inquiry, introduce evidence, mediate critical standards, ask questions, summarize main trends, provide stimulus, introduce other points of view, and so forth. He was not, however, to offer answers to students during discussions of controversial issues; rather, he was to be 'neutral'.

In the many references to neutrality in his writings, Stenhouse was concerned lest teachers use their positions of authority and power to propagate their own views, or (even worse) promote their own opinions in a way that permitted insufficient room for thorough exploration and sympathetic consideration of other positions. Consequently, teachers were encouraged, in the name of neutrality, not to express their personal commitments on public value issues. Rather, they were to concentrate on the rational examination of evidence and the democratic discussion of opposing points of view. By means of such procedures, under the guidance of a neutral chairman, students would be encouraged to reflect upon appropriate evidence, **discriminate** among alternative opinions, and understand different points of view. What the members of the group aimed for was not merely argument for its own sake, but reflective discussion that would encourage careful consideration of value-laden issues.

Other educators were not sure that the concept of neutrality could carry the burden that Stenhouse and his colleagues placed upon it. First, given the widespread use of the term in contexts not related in any way to education, it is scarcely surprising that many teachers and other observers read into 'neutrality' meanings other than those intended by the members of the Project team. Some incorrectly concluded that the Project team was recommending that teachers should not interfere in any circumstances in classroom discussions. Secondly, some were concerned that exploration of alternative points of view for their own sake, encouraged by the neutral teacher, would lead students to treat all value-laden opinions as equally valid. Given Stenhouse's commitment to the open search for alternative points of view, it is to be expected that observers would read into that commitment a greater tolerance for **subjectivity** than may actually have been the case. Thirdly, some commentators were concerned about what they perceived as a reluctance to deal with the definitional difficulties involved in a teacher being neutral in questions related to procedures, **facts** and values. Some argued that the Project team took insufficient care to indicate that value questions were also capable of being explored and analysed on a rational basis, not merely for purposes of identification and review but also for possible solution (*value judgements).

A persuasive case was made that a neutral role left the teacher exposed to the criticism that he was not sufficiently committed to truth-seeking. However justifiable in other ways the use of carefully devised procedures for rational discussion may be, to some extent those procedures will be wanting if they do not lead to truth. Given a situation in which some views are demonstrably more reasonable than others, a truth-seeking teacher has no option but to intervene, something that a neutral teacher cannot do. In short, there are defensible grounds for greater teacher intervention in discussions than some Project statements seemed to indicate. The term that seemed appropriate, therefore, was not 'neutrality' but 'impartiality', a term that allows commitment to a given position warranted by logic or reason. As Stenhouse himself (1972) commented on this issue: 'the idea of neutrality implies that all views should be subjected to critical discussion and handled fairly. Some of us now feel that impartiality or objectivity would have been a better choice of word.'

The discussions that took place in the educational literature on the nature of the Humanities Project have relevance to other curricular and educational issues. They indicate the importance of a full and frank discussion of the meaning and implication of key **concepts** before curricular or empirical investigations are undertaken. Debates on the nature and role of neutrality also illustrate the dangers inherent in giving priority to process in education rather than the pursuit of truth. In that respect, comparisons with **learning** by discovery, **values clarification**, and curriculum development are instructive.

REFERENCES

Aston (1980), Bailey (1971, 1973, 1975), Bricker (1972), Elliott (1971, 1973, 1975), Ennis (1961), Hare, R. M. (1976), Hare, W. (1979), Hipkin (1972), Parkinson and MacDonald (1981), Snook (1972c), Stenhouse (1969a, 1969b, 1970a, 1970b, 1972, 1975a), Warnock (1975).

Norm-referenced tests *see* Assessment

Normal distribution *see* Intelligence

Normative

A normative term is one that logically implies evaluation, e.g. 'beautiful', 'clever', 'helpful'. Normative is to be distinguished from **emotive meaning** in that the latter involves evaluation only **contingently**. (For example, in a certain context the word 'critical' may carry evaluative overtones, but it does not necessarily do so. 'He is a critical man; I can't decide whether that's good or not' makes sense, whereas 'She is beautiful; I can't decide whether that's good or not' doesn't.) 'Normative' is almost always used of words that imply positive evaluation, but there seems no reason why one should not also classify words that logically imply negative evaluation as normative, e.g. 'ugly', 'sinful', 'nasty'.

It is widely held that '**education**' itself is a normative term, that is, that it would not make sense to deny any value to education (genuine education, that is to say, and whatever that may be, as opposed to what may pass for education at particular times and places). Other normative educational terms include: '**creativity**', '**culture**' (in one of its senses), '**indoctrination**', '**intelligence**' and '**understanding**'. Contrast these with terms that generally have emotive meaning, but are not normative, such as '**deschooling**', '**open education**' and '**child-centred**'. A normative word may also have emotive meaning. It may be debated into which category some words, such as '**autonomy**', should be placed.

Numeracy *see* Core curriculum, Curriculum, Intelligence, Teacher effectiveness

Nurture *see* Nature/nurture

O

Objectives *see* Aims, Behavioural objectives

Objectivity

Objectivity is particularly prized in three important areas in education: **research** techniques, **value judgements**, and the **assessment** of pupils. We would like our performance in such areas to be objective in the specific sense of based on publicly assessable criteria that are pertinent to the matter in hand, rather than on whim or personal bias (which are usually associated with **subjective** judgements). However, there is a question mark over the widespread assumptions that so-called objective techniques and measures are objective and that value judgements must be subjective.

'Objective' is not synonymous with 'sound', 'reliable', or 'apposite'. Thus, a value judgement that is not objective is not necessarily unsound or unreliable (e.g. 'I like tea'). Technically objective procedures may lead to absurd or questionable claims, since they are not necessarily any more reliable or apposite than informal, impressionistic, or other frankly subjective procedures (for example, the undoubted objectivity of a lie detector does not make it necessarily any more reliable as a detector of lies than the judgement of an experienced lawyer). A problem in the sphere of research has been a tendency to link 'objective' and 'formal' styles, and to contrast them with 'subjective' and 'informal' styles, despite the fact that a formal style of research is not necessarily more objective than an informal style. Relying on my own observation would generally be classified as an informal style of research, but for certain things it may be a more reliable style, and it is not necessarily subjective in the sense of based on whim and bias and divorced from publicly acknowledged criteria. For example, some psychoanalysts employ informal techniques that, whatever else they may be, are not simply subjective. Many parents make accurate judgements about their children on the strength of their own observation alone.

Our essential concern is to be objective in the sense of 'without bias or prejudice; detached and impersonal'. This does not of course mean, indeed cannot mean, 'without any influence from the individual perspectives of those engaged in the research, value judgements or assessing'.

For in that sense (i.e. free from individual perspective) nothing is completely objective. The multiple-choice test, for example, is no more objective than the essay, since the choice of test items is the product of somebody's decision. What is required is not the exclusion of any individual influence, but the exclusion of irrelevant criteria for judgement that emanate only out of the individual judge's predilections. It is not at all clear that all systematic or so-called objective procedures do that.

1. Since the time that Greek civilization first recognized the need to distinguish between the intuited, the reasoned, and the **empirically** validated truth, argument has continued about the objectivity of value judgements (in **ethics, aesthetics**, or generally). Two important views have been that of the **positivists**, who denied any truth value to such judgements, and that of the cultural relativists. There clearly is a problem concerning how to validate a value judgement of the type 'this is good'. Such an utterance cannot be empirically tested (such a procedure might tell us what people believed to be good, but not whether their belief is correct), nor can it be logically established by reason in any formal way (one could give one's reasons for the judgement, but it is not clear how one could establish, in general, what makes reasons compelling). Intuition may indeed be a means of discerning truth, but that would leave the problem of how to determine whether a particular intuition was reliable or not. Two points, however, should be noted: First, the impossibility of establishing that a value judgement is correct (if indeed it is impossible) does not lead directly to the conclusion that value judgements are not capable of being true or false. Here is one instance where the term 'objective' may prove dangerous. One might argue that value judgements are not objective in the sense of based on publicly assessable criteria, without it following that they are subjective in the sense of matters of taste or arbitrary whim. Secondly, more important is that it surely is not the case that value judgements are subjective in that sense. For judgements to be coherent at all they must at least be constrained by the nature of the activity in question. What makes a good footballer, for instance, though hard to determine in detail, is governed by the nature of football. This fact alone lends a considerable degree of objectivity to value judgements. It may be true that we cannot establish the correctness of ultimate value judgements, and, at the level of judgements such as 'happiness is good', that we therefore have to rely on intuition, and it may be true that, whether true or false, the claim that Trollope was the greatest writer of nineteenth-century prose could not be proven. But it is none the less an objective **fact** that Trollope was a good writer in a way that many writers were not, and this can be publicly demonstrated by pointing to features of Trollope's writing and

connecting them to the nature and purpose of writing fiction. Clearly, we need to recognize this and to preserve the distinction between remarks of the type 'I like X' and 'X is good', for we all know that we mean distinct things by the utterances (*culture, relativity, worthwhile).

2. In the assessment of pupils, the epitome of subjective judgement would involve assessment by personal whim, that is, personal estimation based on irrelevant criteria, as when I give A grades to a boy simply because I like him. An objective assessment, though inescapably bound up with my judgement, differs in that it is made by reference to publicly accepted criteria. The assumption that tests that have only right or wrong answers, as opposed to, say, the writing of essays in response to open questions, are more objective than the latter, blurs the distinction between objective and subjective. Clearly, such a test removes itself from influence by the whim of the marker. However, it does not necessarily remove itself from the whim of the person who devised the test, and the criteria for judgement implicit in the test, though made public, are not necessarily any more appropriate, or indeed appropriate at all, to the task in hand. An essay marked by teachers in accordance with particular criteria is as objective as any test. The relevant criteria for marking an essay are often difficult to judge, but that does not make the essay less objective as a form of testing. It makes that particular essay (defined and evaluated by reference to particular criteria) difficult to assess accurately. No novel technique, no so-called more objective form of test, can serve as a satisfactory substitute: what makes some things hard to assess is their sophisticated and abstract nature.

3. In research, the objectivity of schedules (i.e. itemizations of what is to be observed, when, and how) is defined in terms of **validity** and **reliability**. This may be misleading. For a test may have validity and reliability, but none the less be constructed in terms of irrelevant criteria. Similarly, research techniques that successfully iron out the chances of interference from the researcher only have objectivity in that sense: they may still be very poor techniques for getting an accurate picture of that on which they are focusing.

The essential point is that there is a sense of 'objective' in which traditional claims to being objective are entirely legitimate. That is to say that a number of standard ways of testing and observing people in education are successfully devised to exclude interference from the whims and fancies of tester or researcher. However, important as that may be, a much more important sense of objectivity would demand that objective assessment and research be conducted in the light of clearly articulated, publicly accepted criteria of relevance to the matter in hand.

It is doubtful whether many so-called objective tests or research techniques are 'objective' in this sense (*interaction analysis, systematic observation).

Open education

Open education flourished between 1960 and 1970, then became embroiled in claims, counter-claims and controversies, and finally went out of fashion. Such a history is not unusual for educational concepts (although the speed with which open education went through the cycle was remarkable). It serves as a case study in the progress of an educational fad and an example of good intentions, poor thinking, and sloganeering.

Although it has theoretical roots reaching back into the eighteenth century, open education (under a variety of names) came to prominence as changes occurred in infant and primary school education in England after the Second World War, and received an official cachet in the Plowden Report in 1967. After several prominent American educators and writers had commended the English experience, open-education practices were adopted with varying degrees of enthusiasm in many parts of the United States and Canada. Shortly thereafter, schools in a great many parts of the English-speaking world were adapted (and occasionally specially built) to accommodate open-education principles.

The notion of open education, although enthusiastically endorsed by groups of educators, was never very clearly defined. Its intentions were clear enough: it was a well-meaning attempt to rid early elementary education of many of the insensitive, routinized, and examination-riddled practices of the pre-war period. But there was not a matching clarity in its principles or theoretical justification. Its advocates drew from a very mixed bag of sources, including progressivism, the free-school movement, developmental learning theory, and humanistic education. Much of the jargon and emotive language that is characteristic of talk about open education is very similar in its lack of focus to talk about child-centredness: education is to be personalized, student choice maximized, evaluation individualized, curriculum non-graded, reinforcement positive, and the environment flexible. So diffuse were the aims and methods suggested for open education that even those sympathetic to the cause had difficulty pinning down exactly what it meant, or how it should be differentiated from such related (but different) terms as 'free day', 'integrated day', 'free school', or 'informal school'.

Nevertheless, the particular web that advocates of open education wove from progressive ideas had certain distinctive features. First, many open-education schools were encouraged to offer instructional services according to the wishes and choices of students as individuals. Selection by the student, and a desire to cater to the **interests** of particular students, were important criteria in **teaching** methods, content selection, and school design. Secondly, an attempt was made within open-education schools to integrate the curriculum by breaking down what were regarded as artificial boundaries among various types of subject matter. Since children were provided with a wide range of materials and invited to work at topics of interest to them, no set **curriculum** or schemes of work based on regularly defined subject matter were possible. Thirdly, many open-education advocates recommended a reliance upon play in learning. Play, it was argued, was essential to intellectual growth in general, and social and **language** development in particular. Fourthly, many schools adopted an open-plan design in which the traditional box-like classrooms were replaced by extremely flexible work stations catering to the individual demands of students at various tasks. In older schools, corridors and broom closets were pressed into educational service by groups of students, and in newer schools movable walls provided larger spaces for a wide variety of activities and learning centres.

Open education ran into criticism at both the practical and **theoretical** levels. Advocates seemed to underestimate the power of professional traditions and political realities. Some teachers disliked the informality of open schools and proved unwilling or unable to change previous habits to meet the demands of open-area classrooms. Some practices (for example, combining singing and reading stations in the same area) were silly, and in some schools the curricular selections made by students were unwise. Many parents (on occasion, in well-publicized disputes) were hostile to what they perceived as lack of **discipline** or failure to enforce good manners. Researchers using **empirical quantitative** techniques were unable to find significant differences in achievement between students from open-plan schools and those from other schools. As politicians, especially in the United Kingdom and the United States, began to observe what they regarded as lower standards (particularly in results of tests of language and numeracy **skills**), open education became enmeshed in the prevailing backlash against progressive ideas at all levels of education. Soon tighter budgets and cries of back to the **basics** scattered the armies of open education.

The theoretical objections to open-education arguments were particularly telling. Those advocating open-education changes were often guilty of naive optimism, excessive sloganeering, and even, in the words of one critic, 'yellow journalism'. A lack of clarity in stating educational aims (especially evident in such phrases as 'open education is a state of mind') left open-education schools vulnerable to the charge that they offered no image of the educated person. Some suggested that the emphasis upon process in the open-education curriculum meant that important considerations about the nature of **knowledge** were often ignored. Other critics suggested that open-education schools possessed a hidden political message: that the emphasis on free choice had political implications that students could not realize in later life. Some sociologists argued that open-education privileges were extended to students before teachers were equipped intellectually to make those educational decisons that the new system required (*integrated **studies, research, team teaching**).

REFERENCES

Arnstine (1975), Barth (1969), Bennett, Andreae, Hegarty and Wade (1980), Brown and Precious (1968), Egan (1975), Harrison and Glaubman (1982), Kohl (1969), Murrow and Murrow (1971), Musella, Selinger and Arikado (1975), Myers (1974), Nyberg (1975), Plowden (1967), Rogers and Church (1975), Sealey (1976), Silberman (1970), Traub, Weiss, Fisher and Musella (1972), Weber (1971).

Open plan *see* Open education

Operant conditioning

Behavioural psychologists distinguish between classical conditioning (associated with Ivan Pavlov and John B. Watson) and operant conditioning (associated with B. F. Skinner). Classical conditioning occurs when a conditional stimulus causes a reflex response, as when Pavlov's dog salivated in response to a ringing bell rather than to the sight of food. Watson later applied the same technique to condition a child to fear a rat by banging against a piece of steel when the child was about to touch the rat. Note that in classical conditioning the rewards for a response are not important; what matters is that the learning occurs.

Operant conditioning stresses the importance of rewards as reinforcements in observed responses (the 'operants'). To encourage animals to learn, Skinner and his associates used food as a reinforcer of desired behaviour (with spectacular results in some cases). From these experiments came the notion that all **learning** depends on rewards or reinforcers to be found in the environment. Operant conditioning, therefore, became a powerful tool for the prediction and control of animal behaviour.

The findings of such animal-based research were applied to human beings also. The behaviour of human beings may be more complex than that of animals, behaviourists argued, but it follows the same principles. All human learning, like all animal learning, is determined by reinforcement as humans interact with their environment. From that position it is but a small step to arguing that an ideal society can be created, not by reliance upon human aspirations or free will, but by deliberate social engineering.

There can be no doubting the importance of certain experiments in changing human behaviour using practices derived from operant conditioning. A great degree of success has been reported in the amelioration of particular medical conditions (e.g. stuttering) and certain activities deemed anti-social (e.g. fetishism and alcoholism). In **educational** applications, the record is less clear. Notions derived from operant conditioning have been used in experiments in **programmed learning** and teaching machines, both of which have had limited success.

The critical attack on operant conditioning is part of a more extensive commentary on **behaviourism**. Skinner and his associates have been criticized for assuming that a complex human behaviour is a string of simple behaviours capable of being identified and modified. Yet, to take one example, it is by no means certain what string of simple behaviours comprises the act of writing an essay. Others have pointed out that operant conditioning theories are based on a limited range of animal experiments, rather than human experiments. In such a situation, the similarity of animal behaviour to human behaviour remains an assumption. Finally, critics have argued that simplistic notions of reinforcement are unlikely to account for the extraordinarily intricate patterns of human behaviour.

REFERENCES

Cosgrove (1982), Honig and Staddon (1977), Kazepides (1976), Schwartz and Lacey (1982), Skinner (1938, 1971), Wheeler (1973).

Originality *see* Creativity

P

Painting *see* Art education, Creativity

Paradigm

The word 'paradigm' is derived from the Greek verb, *paradeiknumi*, meaning 'to exhibit beside' or 'show side by side'. It has strong implications of comparison, but it is comparison for the purpose of identification, and came in practice to mean an example or a pattern whereby to judge, as Plato called his account of the ideal state in the *Republic* a *paradeigma*, an exemplar. Although the term has been used in a variety of **disciplines**, especially linguistics and literary criticism, to mean a formal **model** or type, it entered common academic discourse only after the publication of Kuhn's *The Structure of Scientific Revolutions* (1962), in which the author used it, albeit not very clearly or consistently, to denote a comprehensive system of thinking that from time to time governs scientific research.

Kuhn argued that scientific reasoning and methodology in any age were governed by an accepted model or tradition (a 'paradigm') of **theory and practice**. Activity within the accepted paradigm of an age is the normal practice of scientists, who devote their lives to articulating the paradigm's details, extending findings, and refining the theoretical framework. Not all of these findings are consistent with the paradigm; anomalies are noted that eventually may lead to the collapse of the accepted paradigm and its replacement by another. For examples of paradigm change, Kuhn drew on the history of Copernican theory, Lavoisier's theory of oxidation, Newton's laws and Darwin's theory of evolution, among others.

Kuhn's controversial notion of a paradigm had several features that attracted researchers in other disciplines. That scientific reasoning and methodology in any age are governed by an accepted model proved a particularly bewitching notion to those in fields beyond the natural sciences. The argument that scientists tend to suppress innovative techniques or findings as they search to refine the details of a paradigm, seemed a useful line of attack for scholars eager either to locate particular power structures within established disciplines, or to work outside accepted traditions. (What was frequently ignored in **education** was the

236

scepticism with which Kuhn's work was greeted by an important part of academe, and which persuaded Kuhn himself to discard the term 'paradigm'.)

At a superficial level, it may seem plausible to adapt Kuhn to the field of education. Educational **research**, it might be argued, is derived from the natural sciences, and, as such, is characterized by a methodology that stresses categorization, observation, and quantification in the pursuit of generalization and theories. Indeed, so.ne educational theorists explicitly outlined the scientific basis of their research with reference to Kuhn: 'at least for the foreseeable future', Gage (1978) notes, 'research on teaching will proceed as "normal science" . . .; that is, investigators will follow the elaborated process-product paradigm and work on cleaning up an enormous number of details in the unfinished business of the field.' At the same superficial level, educational researchers pursuing alternative methodologies (e.g. those derived from the humanities, or those applying Marxist analysis to educational problems), may be said to belong to other paradigms, with their own sets of procedures and understandings about the nature of educational research.

Nevertheless, applying Kuhn's notion of paradigms to education appears, on more serious reflection, to be an enterprise of dubious worth. Education is in many ways very dissimilar from the natural sciences: there is much greater agreement in the latter about the **concepts** to be studied and the methodologies to be applied; their areas of inquiry are much more precise, and their boundaries much more clearly delineated. Education does not have, and cannot have, that degree of certainty that we label 'scientific'; many of its essential questions are speculative in nature, requiring forms of analysis drawn from a variety of sources. Since education manifestly lacks the cohesion and structure of a scientific discipline, the very notion of a paradigm in Kuhn's sense seems inappropriate.

'Paradigm', however, has been used indiscriminately in educational contexts. Some have used it to label specific theories: thus Pavlovian conditioning and **operant conditioning** become paradigms. Others attach it to different approaches to research on **teaching** (e.g. the machine paradigm), to different sections of the research process (methodological paradigms), or to the ideas of individuals (e.g. Smith's paradigm). It is also used to denote 'value bases' for different types of programme (e.g. futures paradigm), to distinguish various philosophies of education (e.g. classical as opposed to general education paradigm), or to indicate the sexist nature of **knowledge** (e.g. male-dominated paradigm) (***feminism**). In short, 'paradigm' in education, like 'paradigm' in science – in Suppe's (1977) words, 'bloated to the point of being a philosophical analogue to phlogiston' – means almost anything, and virtually nothing.

If not entirely removed from our educational vocabulary, it should be used only with extraordinary care.

A final note. Particularly mischievous is the habit of some **academics** of using the term as a means of protecting their flanks from awkward questions. At conferences or meetings of learned societies, researchers using a particular set of theories or methodology avoid disabling criticism by declaring their critics to be 'in another paradigm'. Whether there is truth in the assertion is not the point; such a defensive move suggests that particular educational issues are off-limits to rational examination. Thus, 'paradigm', a term that began its contemporary career playing an interesting role in the assessment of research traditions, is recast as a stooge to thwart the search for truth: a classic example of linguistic debasement in education (*critical theory).

REFERENCES

Barrow (1985a), Gage (1972, 1978), Kuhn (1962, 1977), Lakatos and Musgrave (1970), McNamara (1979), Masterman (1970), Shapere (1971), Snow (1973), Suppe (1977), Tafel (1984), Tuthill and Ashton (1983), Vanderbosch and Swoboda (1984).

Peace education see Topic-centred education

Personal practical knowledge

Arguments persist about the type of **knowledge** that **professional** educators possess or should possess. Some scholars maintain that teachers should have a command of the principal **theories** and generalizations found in main-line educational **research** so that they may apply them in specific **school** situations. Others reject such a notion as inadequate and misleading; a professional teacher, they say, deals with a multitude of possibilities in specific situations in which the types of propositional knowledge produced by social scientists are not necessarily helpful. In order to cope with classroom situations that are unique, unexpected, and uncertain, a teacher requires, and develops in practice, a special form of contextually dependent knowledge that is both personal and tacit. That knowledge, it is argued, is characterized by inquiry, deliberation, and reflective action that is both dialectic and non-logical. This practical wisdom, or personal practical knowledge, is an essential aspect of **teaching** that has been downgraded in the past.

Given these arguments, it is not surprising that many familiar procedures in **education** have been questioned, especially those related to educating teachers in pre-service and in-service programmes. Because teacher-training programmes tend to emphasize social scientific generalizations and theories, and in-service programmes tend to rely on top-down managerial **models**, essential 'practical' arts are played down or diminished. In some circumstances, the emphasis upon scientific knowledge and management may be so great that the competence of teachers may be adversely affected – in short, they may be 'de-skilled'. In consequence, some researchers have argued that **teacher-education** programmes should be redesigned to accommodate greater study of personal practical knowledge (indeed, only by so doing, may school reform be effective).

Capturing the nature of such knowledge is by no means easy. Some scholars argue that a teacher's past experience (upbringing, schooling, personal beliefs and attitudes, and social relationships) should be taken into account. Others have used ideas drawn from **phenomenology**, hermeneutics, **critical theory**, or non-positivist philosophies in an attempt to describe the everyday life of the classroom. A few scholars have identified specific categories (such as 'image', '**metaphor**', and 'rhythms') and developed a special **language** in which to capture the on-the-job techniques, arts, or practices that a professional masters in order to shape the unstable patterns of his classroom interactions. Reports of these studies are often cast in the form of personal journals, **life histories**, or narratives of experience.

Many difficulties persist in both the identification of personal, practical knowledge, and the techniques used to discover its nature in particular situations. Because each case is considered unique, it is not surprising that scholars disagree on the basic characteristics of personal, practical knowledge, or on the definitions to be attached to categories that have been devised. **Academic** studies and reports on the nature of practical wisdom depend in no small part on the disciplinary or **ideological** sources from which particular investigators draw inspiration. Some scholars argue that the search for personal practical knowledge is inherently misleading, if it ignores the determining effect on teachers and teaching practice of the prevailing social and political climate. Many of the research techniques used in the search for such knowledge – participant observation, journal writing, and life histories – are contentious. Other commentators have pointed out that investigation of the personal beliefs of teachers has sometimes been conducted without due regard for the **ethical** questions connected with privacy and student-teacher relationships.

On the broader question of the role of such wisdom in teacher education programmes, some scholars have suggested that, while the study of personal, practical knowledge is important, its place in the **curriculum** should not be ensured at the expense of **disciplinary** subject matter and formal pedagogic knowledge.

REFERENCES

Butt, Raymond, and Yamagishi (1988), Carr (1986), Clandinin (1986), Connelly and Clandinin (1988), Elbaz (1983), Munby and Russell (1989), Olson (1988a), Polanyi (1962), Reid (1978), Schon (1983, 1987), Schwab (1970), Shulman (1987).

Phenomenology

Certain scholars in **education** have been interested in research methodologies and approaches derived from non-positivist sources, particularly **critical theory** and hermeneutic phenomenology. These scholars agree on one point: the inadequacy of traditional social scientific principles and research methods in the field of education. They note the social and political effects of the underlying social scientific interest in experimental observation, generalization, control, and prediction. Given these principles, they argue, educators at all levels concentrate on the means or management of education rather than on the **values** and the relations underlying it. Some critics argue that main-line educational research carries with it a deeply ingrained **positive ideology** that dehumanizes **schooling** and reduces the capacity of teachers and students to engage in self-responsible thought and action.

Scholars in education who have attempted to apply principles from phenomenology to education face two large problems. First, the field itself is far from clearly defined. More than one critic has argued (with an element of truth) that there are as many definitions of phenomenology as there are phenomenologists. Secondly, many of the important writings in phenomenology are not easily accessible, being available only in a foreign language even when not inherently complex.

Despite differences, phenomenologists interested in education have several points in common. They are concerned first of all with concrete and particular educational **phenomena**, not with generalizations or preformed social scientific **theories**. They wish to reveal the meaning of the everyday experiences of children, youths, and teachers within particular educational settings – not by using survey methods or traditional experimental techniques, but by a form of interpretative description. Phenomenology literally means the account/study (*logos*) of appearances (*phainomena*); hermeneutics (from Hermes, the Greek messenger of the gods) means interpretation. In order to grasp the lived meanings of the phenomena, researchers attempt to examine educational phenomena without the interposition of preformed assumptions, categories, or explanations. Their search is for articulations of the structures of lived experience of human beings in educational situations and relations. The sources for their approaches may be traced to the work of such scholars as Husserl, Dilthey, Sartre, Heidegger, Merleau-Ponty, Gadamer, Levinas, and Ricoeur.

The epistemological stance of the human scientist does not pose a research 'problem' for which some 'solution' must be found; rather, the phenomenologist poses a research question which is then reflected upon. The fundamental attitude is one of wonder and attentiveness to the details of lived experience. How is such phenomenological, or human science, research conducted in educational situations? If the principles and specific techniques of main-line social science research are rejected, what alternatives are suggested? Answers to those questions tend to be elusive. Some researchers claim that their 'method' is to have no method whatever – to rely on forms of insightful interpretation. Others point either to the traditions and practices within their scholarly community or to philosophic discourses, as sources for examples and inspiration. One scholar within the field (van Manen, 1990) has offered several research activities that characterize the endeavour ('turning to a phenomenon which seriously interests us', 'investigating experience as we live it', 'describing the phenomenon through the art of writing and rewriting', etc.).

Criticism of such an approach is not difficult to make. Different phenomenologists make very different claims about the nature of their research and the means by which it is undertaken. Scholars of experimental traditions argue that the conclusions of phenomenologists remain essentially descriptive and lacking in any explanatory power, and consider the uncontrolled methodology and lack of **objective** standards in their work unacceptable. Some critical theorists claim that the interpretative work of phenomenologists in education tends to ignore the social factors that produce particular meanings – a focus upon the meanings of lived experiences of individuals tends to draw attention away from the effects of deeply ingrained social structures. Thus the effects of distortive ideologies operating within the wider society are obscured rather than revealed. Consequently, to those critics, phenomenological research in education tends to encourage passivity and conservatism among participants, rather than social action and radical politics. To practising teachers, the **academic** talk of phenomenologists often appears difficult, inaccessible, and even mystical.

None the less, phenomenology's interest in the humanistic

investigation of lived experiences in schools stands in striking contrast to prevailing assumptions in contemporary educational theory and practice. The insights that it seeks to offer into the human side of education are perhaps not available from other sources, and the concern for a thoughtful and tactful pedagogy may point the way to a reconceptualization of teachers' practical knowledge (*reconceptualists).

REFERENCES

Carr and Kemmis (1986), Gadamer (1975), Greene (1985), Merleau-Ponty (1962), Radnitzky (1970), Roche (1973), Schutz (1972), Truzzi (1974), van Manen (1986, 1990).

Phenomenon

Phenomenon (singular); phenomena (plural). Although it has a use meaning 'an extraordinary occurrence or event', 'phenomenon' seems generally to be used as a synonym for any event, happening, occurrence. However, something of its root meaning (which has to do with the appearance of things, often in contrast to the reality behind it) is retained in phenomenology: the **theory** that **knowledge** has to be limited to phenomena in the sense of what we perceive or otherwise sense, since any reality that there may be behind appearances is unknowable. In **education**, the label '**phenomenologist**' has been applied to a variety of people, ranging from those directly concerned with expounding particular phenomenological theories to those seeking a new label for species of **research** that are of the informal, case-study, participant observation type (*ethnography). Some see phenomenology as having significant implications for human (specifically student–teacher) relationships.

REFERENCES

Curtis and Mays (1978), Roche (1973).

Philosophy of education see Analysis, Research, Theory

Play see Child-centred education, Open education, Simulations

Politics *see* Critical theory, Deschooling, Class, Reconceptualists

Positive discrimination

Most jurisdictions in the Western world now have equal opportunity laws of some sort, such that advertising, hiring, and employment of persons should take place without reference to gender or race. Notwithstanding the undoubted change of practice that this involves since even very recent times, there does not seem to be anything very problematic about it. Regardless of yesterday, today we regard it as axiomatic that one's gender and race are not relevant criteria to determining one's competence for a particular job. (In fact the matter is not entirely straightforward: it is not patently absurd to argue that certain jobs, roles, or activities are better suited to males or females. For example, it might be suggested, prima facie plausibly, that at least certain nursing tasks would be better undertaken by, variously, men or women. Nor is it self-evident that if a group of females or Jews wants to form a club that excludes men, or non-Jews, they should not be allowed to.)

Far more contentious is the principle of positive (sometimes termed reverse) discrimination. The basic intent of this principle is to secure preferential treatment for a particular group on the grounds that the group in question has hitherto suffered disproportionately. For example, the argument goes, since black people have been deliberately and consciously disadvantaged in respect of, say, admission to medical school in the past, since, consequently, they are relatively underrepresented in medicine today, they should now be given advantageous or preferential treatment. Thus a better qualified white candidate may legitimately be rejected in favour of a worse qualified black candidate. It is important to distinguish positive discrimination from the practice of regularly preferring a black to a white candidate *other things being equal*, on the same grounds. Whatever the logic of this latter approach (and it is not entirely clear that it is unproblematic either – might one not say that natural justice is offended, if, in every otherwise arbitrary decision, blackness supersedes whiteness?), it does not have the same capacity to antagonize: 'after all', the rejected candidate must concede, 'I am not more deserving than the other candidate, and a decision had to be made somehow. Better perhaps to serve the good of increasing black representation than to toss a coin.'

Arguments in favour of the principle of positive discrimination range from the bold declaration that such partial treatment is morally owed by way of recompense, to the more practical reasoning that any individual from a disadvantaged group who is formally as well qualified as other non-disadvantaged individuals must have overcome greater obstacles and hence may be presumed to have greater inherent talent. But, to some, these and other reasons put forward in support of the principle remain unconvincing and smack of rationalization of what is really no more than an emotional feeling that old wrongs should be redressed. The problem with that very natural sentiment is that it has no logical stopping point: if, for the sake of example, places in medical school are to be allotted to worse qualified blacks today, then tomorrow the disadvantaged and better qualified whites may presumably cry 'foul' and demand positive discrimination as recompense. (Many think it simply unwise in the long run to declare that members of certain groups may gain admission to a profession on lesser qualifications.)

Another point that needs consideration is that what may be true of groups is not necessarily true of individuals. Thus, blacks, women, native Indians, or the working class, may historically have been taken advantage of, systematically disadvantaged, etc., but it does not follow that the individual who is currently offered compensatory advantage has had any particular difficulties to contend with.

Advocates of positive discrimination tend to shrug off rather than refute these objections, pointing out that without some such affirmative action the moral obligation to be impartial cannot in practice be observed in respect of certain groups: the odds are still stacked against blacks and women in that in general terms society is still dominated by white males. It is difficulty to deny this: positive discrimination would certainly hasten the advancement of various groups, for which progress will otherwise be at best slow and steady. On the other hand positive discrimination, despite the determined attempt to make the phrase **emotively** attractive, is quite certainly a species of **discrimination**: it involves favouring certain individuals in particular situations on criteria which are not **relevant** to that situation.

In **education** it may be thought to be particularly dangerous. For education is not, or need not be, a limited good. That is to say, one man's access to education should not in principle diminish the store available for others. And since education is concerned with mastery and **understanding**, it would seem very dangerous to advocate admission to educational institutions or courses on any grounds other than an individual's ability. (If entry to a given programme were to be decided essentially by reference to **intelligence** or other standard tests of achievement, the conclusion may very well be different, for there is plenty of evidence that such tests are culturally biased and may therefore militate against particular groups.) (*feminism)

REFERENCES

Barrow (1982a), Richards (1980), Sher (1975), Singer (1979).

Positivism

Although its origins may be traced back as far as Francis Bacon, positivism is associated primarily with the work of Auguste Comte in the nineteenth century, who believed in the power of 'positive' (i.e. scientific) **knowledge** to solve human problems. In the first half of the present century, the term reappeared in 'logical positivism', a philosophic doctrine that rejected metaphysics and attempted to construct mathematical and scientific discourse on the basis of **analysis** and **logic**. In more recent years, the term has come to be used in a very general sense to label all valid knowledge as scientific, thus excluding the belief that non-sensory experience could provide a basis for such knowledge.

The term appears frequently in discussions about whether educational studies can legitimately be considered 'scientific'. Scholars who argue that, as a social science, **education** should be concerned with observable data, **empirical** methods, and **scientific objectivity** are often labelled 'positivistic' in this general sense. Other scholars, however, maintain that adherence to such principles has had harmful effects on education. Philosophers of education have argued that interest in positivistic methods tends to distract attention from important issues concerned with the nature and purposes of education. Others point to fundamental **conceptual** flaws in much social scientific **research** in education. **Phenomenologists** have maintained that traditional scientific methods ride roughshod over the experience of the individual student, and **critical theorists** have argued that positivist concern with prediction and control of educational phenomena serves the vested interests of powerful groups within society. Indeed, the clash of opposing points of view towards positivism lies at the heart of many of the issues considered in this volume.

Practical *see* Curriculum change, Personal practical knowledge, Practical principles, Relevance, Theory and practice, Utilitarian

Practical principles

In recent years the influence of Polanyi, and particularly his idea of tacit **knowledge**, has been slowly growing in educational circles. (Tacit knowledge refers to the understanding of principles, etc., that we take in and then act on habitually, without conscious reflection, thus allowing of fluent and immediate behaviour.) A recent study to some degree affected by the idea is Furlong, Hirst, Pocklington and Myles' *Initial Teacher Training* (1988), where reference is made to the significance of what are termed 'practical principles'. Behind the terminological equivocation – for what are 'practical principles'? Principles governing practice? Practicable principles? Principles arising from practice? Is the contrast with impractical or theoretical principles? Can a practical principle be theoretical? Can a theoretical principle be practical? Can a principle be other than theoretical? – apparently lies a thesis to the effect that the traditional view that prescriptions for practice should be derived from theoretical studies is no longer tenable.

It is necessary to distinguish two claims here. The first is that the traditional approach to teacher training that was based on the idea of introducing students to the findings of the various disciplines, in the light of which they were supposed to examine and establish practice, has not proved particularly effective. That is probably true enough. The second claim would be that it is false to imagine that the principles that govern practice actually do derive from **theory**.

This second claim is implicit in Paul Hirst's argument in his introduction to *Educational Theory and its Disciplines* (1983), in which he departs significantly from the position he adopted in his contribution to a previous volume of the same type (Tibble, 1966). It has also been evident in his most recent public lectures, in which he has explicitly drawn an analogy with the baking of cakes, maintaining that the principles that can now be set down in recipe books as directions (prescriptions for practice) were not (could not conceivably have been?) set down in advance of the practice of cake making, but were derived from that practice: a process of inference and deduction being based on trial and error in experience.

But the argument is unconvincing. The analogy is highly unhelpful to consideration of what practical principles there may be for teachers, where they come from originally, and how they should be communicated now. Are cake baking and teaching truly analogous? Hirst has also used the **analogy** in connection with **moral** knowledge, where it clearly begs the question, for one of the central points of contention in the sphere of morality is whether it is indeed a notion that mankind has conceived and evolved out of experience, or whether it is, so to speak, a

God-given set of principles that would obtain whatever people did and whether they recognized them or not (*ethics). We might accept Hirst's view of the way we establish principles for baking cakes, but argue that it is not the way we arrive at (though it might be the way in which we validate) principles in physics or education. Furthermore, even if we were to concede the point that principles are initially derived from practice, once we have them, why should we necessarily refrain from presenting them to students as prescriptions for practice? (The origin of cake-baking principles in practice has not led to an end to recipe books.)

A more important consideration, however, is that nothing specific follows for the training of teachers. For, even if it is true that principles governing cake baking are derived from practice, in order to assess and formulate those principles we need to have a clear conception of what constitutes success in baking cakes. One cannot simply see from experience that adding soda is good: one establishes empirically that adding soda has an effect which one deems desirable in respect of cakes. Exactly the same is true of teaching, except that both the empirical and the conceptual work are considerably more complex. To discover from practice that a certain approach is desirable in a particular teaching situation must necessarily involve: (a) perceiving an effect; (b) doing something in the way of observation or other empirical inquiry to warrant the conclusion that there was cause and effect; and (c) producing some reasoning to support the idea that such an effect is educationally desirable.

Hirst's view appears to be that the above contention is correct and that therefore the theoretical disciplines need to be drawn in at this point. For, in step (b) one will need to consider properly conducted empirical studies, or at least conduct one's own inquiry in the light of an adequate theoretical understanding of the techniques of empirical research; in step (c) one will need to be familiar with the reasoning of philosophers relating to the concept of education, and hence the criteria for educational success, or at least to be adept in the sphere of philosophical theorizing. In this conclusion he is undoubtedly correct, but it leads to the further conclusion that any argument in favour of 'practical principles' must itself be a practical argument of the first type noted, i.e. of the form 'let's see if prospective teachers teach better as a result of thinking about their own practice than they do as a result of studying educational theory.' It cannot coherently be maintained that the truth of a claim about practice can be determined or validated by practical experience rather than by theoretical reflection. The latter is a necessary condition of any genuine confirmation of a prescription.

Thus, we may make the following points: (a) that as a matter of fact a lot of educational wisdom is enshrined in and known to experienced practitioners; (b) that during (probably more accurate and precise than 'through') practice individuals, including novices, may come to recognize a lot of truths for themselves (since of course they bring some theoretical knowledge with them, which allows them to interpret and assess experience); (c) that a lot of data is particular to particular situations and therefore only recognizable in practice as a potential variable; and (d) that there are sometimes particular (and therefore **contingent**) practical restraints on theoretical wisdom. (For example, theory says one ought to do X, but there is no funding to do X today. Sensible people quite often accept that, rather than instigate a revolution to get the funding, without making the mistake of thinking that this somehow shows the theory to be faulty.) These points all seem to be true, but they also seem to be familiar, and it is far from clear that anything logically follows for our approach to **teacher-education**. To ignore the individual's practical experience would be absurd, but so would it be to dispense with concern for theoretical understanding.

The most puzzling part of this remains what is meant by a 'practical principle'? Perhaps some connection with Aristotle's remarks on practical reasoning is intended.

REFERENCES

Aristotle (1953), Furlong, Hirst, Pocklington and Myles (1988), Hirst (1983), Polanyi (1962, 1966), Tibble (1966).

Prescriptive

Prescriptive language is language that directs, commands, or prescribes. For example, 'Shut the door', 'All those on the left will stand up'. An interesting issue is the extent to which evaluative words and phrases, most notably in the moral sphere, logically imply prescription. For example, 'You ought to do this' is plainly a prescriptive utterance, even though somewhat milder in tone that the imperative 'Do this'. But the very words 'good', 'right', 'duty' seem necessarily to prescribe: one's duty is something that ought to be done (*ethics, moral education).

REFERENCE

Hare (1964b).

Problem solving see Creativity, Critical thinking, Dilemma, Lateral thinking

Process

'Process' is used in a variety of contexts in **educational** discourse. Educators talk of 'the process of **curriculum** development', 'the process of **teaching**', 'the process of **learning**', and 'the process of inquiry', as if the chief interest in such matters was to answer the question 'how?' Such an interest is understandable: teachers are eager to ensure that the ideas they consider in the classroom are understood by their students, and researchers are eager to reflect upon the methodology that they use in their work. But attention to process often seems to take precedence over consideration of underlying educational **aims** or goals. A teacher may go so far as to say that what is important is how learning occurs, not what is learned; or a student teacher may argue that his sole concern is teaching strategies, not content. In those situations, what began as an important but secondary concern has become a sterile substitute for a primary objective (*research, teacher effectiveness).

Process/product *see* Teacher effectiveness

Professional

There is considerable confusion surrounding this word. It is a 'hurrah' word, one that teachers as a body lay claim to with an uncertain grasp, one that is used within the educational business to distinguish some forms of behaviour from others and one that is also used to demarcate some studies from others.

A profession is 'an occupation requiring special training in the liberal arts or sciences', according to the standard dictionary definition. Traditionally this has meant that the prime professions are law, theology, and medicine, although few would perhaps think of the church as a profession now. The **etymological** origin of the word is in the Latin *profiteor* meaning 'I acknowledge', 'profess'. Initially it was confined to professing one's faith, but later came to indicate a claim to **knowledge** in some specialized area (a sense that is still to the fore in 'professor'). The contrast between amateur (from Latin *amo*, 'I love') and professional presumably arises from the contrast between one who takes part for the love of it, and one who takes part having engaged in extensive preparation. Since extensive preparation takes time and money, the professional athlete becomes one whose livelihood is gained this way.

Teachers, no doubt like nurses, architects, and various other groups, wish to see their line of work as a profession. Indeed, most people probably classify them as professionals without hesitation. (Kenneth Hudson, 1983, defining a professional as 'someone who takes the job seriously, who has specialised experience and possibly formal qualifications, an expert,' and remarking that 'the true professions are those which can be practised only by those who have satisfied an examining body that they have followed an approved course of training and reached a satisfactory level of competence', inexplicably concludes that they do not include teachers, whom he classes with actors and journalists. 'Anyone,' he says, 'is free to work as a teacher.' Not so, Mr Hudson, although, maybe, as with doctors, some are **empowered** to who ought not to have been.) But the truth is that the **emotive** force of the word is now its prime force. Granted that descriptively 'profession' refers to an occupation that requires qualifications and expertise, its actual use reflects our judgement as to the relative status of jobs. Teaching is a profession now because we take it seriously and value it in a way that was not done in the past.

Much more important than whether teaching has a right to be labelled a profession, is what we think professional conduct should involve for a teacher. It goes beyond mere competence as a teacher, however that might be estimated. It incorporates **ethical** conduct in general, and conformity to the constitutive rules of **education** and **teaching**. Thus, if teachers are to be seen as professional, as contrasted with tradesmen, they have a duty to do more than control their classes and impart knowledge. A doctor and a lawyer are expected to be upstanding citizens, they are expected to act when necessary beyond the call of duty, and they are expected to be accountable for the honesty of their dealings, in a way that the plumber and the garbage collector are not.

REFERENCES

Hudson (1983), McPeck and Sanders (1974).

Profiling

'Profiling' appears in educational discourse in a variety of senses, some ordinary-language, others fairly technical. It may indicate the principal features of a case (e.g. profile of a city high school) or procedure (e.g. profile of an interview schedule). In educational **research**, a profile has specific properties: a set of different measures of an individual or group of individuals, with each measure being expressed in identical units of **measurement** (e.g. in percentiles or standard scores). Analysis of a profile based on such measures requires a high level of technical and interpretative competence.

The term has been recirculated in recent years (especially in the United Kingdom and several other European countries) to denote a particular approach to **evaluating** or **assessing** student progress. Because many students were leaving school without any form of assessment, or with only a set of scores derived from formal examinations in traditional subject matter, they were unable to supply employers, registrars, counsellors or parents with evidence of progress or achievements in any aspect of their education or training. Some school critics have argued for decades that over-reliance on formal written examinations had limited the range of educational experiences available for students, especially those in the middle or lower ranges of abilities.

A profile is a record of attainment in a wide range of **knowledge, skills,** and attitudes considered desirable in educational or **training** institutions. A vocational-preparation course profile, for example, may include assessments of social abilities, **communicative** abilities, numerical abilities and decision-making skills, evidence of a range of activities related to societal, economic and environmental **understanding**, and comments on work-experience or extension studies. These assessments are rarely in the form of marks or grades; written comments indicating that prescribed activities have been completed are preferred. Profiles also serve as guides to course content for students, and as detailed schedules of progress in the **formative** sense.

The dangers of such an approach to assessment are not difficult to identify. The task of dividing broad educational goals into specific tasks or skills is extraordinarily difficult, and those who attempt it often fall into such a trap as believing that all such goals are capable of being expressed in terms of observable **behaviours**. The kind of record-keeping and consultations (with students, parents, and employers) required in constructing profiles makes heavy demands upon teachers. The absence of national standards for profiles renders them less useful, and even suspect, in the eyes of prospective employers. Because most comments on profiles are anecdotal and subjective, invalid, untrustworthy, and even libellous documents may be circulated.

Advocates of profiles have drawn attention to the importance of such formative measures in encouraging teachers to identify student weaknesses at an early stage. Contemporary reflections on profiles underscore the importance of reconsidering the role of secondary schools in providing **education** for greater numbers of students of varying abilities. Only a cynic (and perhaps a person who had studied other measures designed to encourage educational egalitarianism) would be pessimistic of the outcome of such discussions.

REFERENCES

Broadfoot (1986), Burgess and Adams (1980), Dockrell and Broadfoot (1977), Evans (1979), Law (1984), Mansell (1982), Nunnally (1967), Stevenson (1983).

Programmed learning

'Programmed learning', a term more popular in the 1950s and 1960s than now, is derived from **theories** of behavioural psychology, especially the ideas of **operant conditioning** associated with B. F. Skinner. The label is usually applied to systems of dividing given subject matter into sequenced, step-by-step tasks for individual learners or small groups, with each task carefully related to pre-specified **behavioural objectives**. A sequence of programmed tasks usually provides for choices for learners (in a variety of patterns), and offers immediate reinforcement of correct or preferred answers. Such programmed learning systems are usually loaded on teaching machines or computers.

There are many advantages in such an approach. **Learning** from the programmes requires active participation by students; learners may proceed at their own pace; wasted time in the learning process may be significantly reduced; instant feedback provides encouragement and assistance at each stage of the task; tasks may be repeated until a very high level of competency is achieved; and those **skills** or processes considered essential may be thoroughly mastered. In addition, aspects of selected subject matter may be taught through programmed learning, for example, languages and basic skills.

But it is clear that the high hopes of those who devised the first programmed learning systems have not been realized. Theoreticians often underestimated the difficulty of designing and writing programmes that lived up to the advance billing, with the result that many such programmes provided for school use were judged of low quality. School jurisdictions were unwilling to spend the money that some programmed learning systems required. Soon teaching machines began to gather dust on classroom bookshelves. Many of the more ambitious claims for programmed learning – that it would supplant teachers, or solve the problems of mass education in developing countries – remained ill-founded fantasies.

Critics argue that these difficulties are symptomatic of the poverty-stricken nature of the **educational** principles underlying programmed learning. Given the restrictive nature of objectives expressed in behavioural terms, and the choices of interactive processes required from learners, it is not surprising that programmed learning devices had such limited applications.

REFERENCES

Hawkridge (1983), Kulik, Schwalb and Kulik (1982), Pocztar (1972), Richmond (1970), Skinner (1954, 1968), Stones (1981), Taber, Glaser and Schaefer (1965).

Psychology of education *see* Developmental theory, Learning, Research, Theory

Punishment *see* Discipline, Necessary condition

Q

Qualitative research *see* Quantitative/qualitative research

Quantitative/qualitative research

One characteristic of educational **research** is that it has no techniques and approaches that are exclusively its own; all its research methods are shared with other **disciplines**. A major source has been the social sciences (especially psychology and sociology – both of which very often depend upon research principles derived from the natural sciences), although there have always been educationalists using techniques and approaches derived from philosophy, history and other humanities. It is these two traditions in educational research – the social sciences on the one hand, and the humanities on the other – that provide the basis for the very rough (as well as misleading and inaccurate) division into 'quantitative' and 'qualitative' approaches, a topic which has been the subject of intense debate among educational researchers in recent years.

The principal tradition (some call it the 'prevailing **paradigm**') in educational research, especially in North America, is that derived from the social sciences, especially the so-called hard disciplines. Most people conducting such research view **educational phenomena** as essentially natural events, subject to **systematic observation**. Their basic task is to isolate observable variables (such as teacher characteristics, **learning** outcomes, motivation, and **class**) that may be subject to treatment in experimental settings. The relationship between those variables may be expressed in the form of educational generalizations, which in turn are capable of providing guidance (possibly even predicting and controlling) in similar settings. Researchers investigating the relationship between variables or behavioural categories usually follow the standard scientific method: hypothesis formation, **empirical** testing, and control of variance. To assist them, a large number of statistical techniques have been devised, the range of which has been extended in recent years through use of the computer. Two particular experimental concepts, **reliability** (the consistency or accuracy of a measuring instrument) and **validity** (the extent to which a **measurement** instrument measures what it is supposed to measure) are considered to be fundamental to the usefulness of social scientific experiments. The results of such empirical experiments are usually expressed in numerical terms. Those conducting such experiments particularly prize replication (i.e. similar findings from repeated application of the research) and **objectivity** (i.e. elimination of the effects of their own personalities from the conduct and reporting of experiments).

The principles underlying this type of quantitative research are widely accepted within the profession. Most graduate students in education are required to take courses in this research methodology (although there is not a great deal of evidence that many pay much attention to it later in their careers). Many funding agencies expect (or require) applications for financial support for educational research to be couched in the language and form indicated by experimental design of this type. Indeed, to some people the very word 'research' is confined exclusively to such experimental methodology, with those following other research traditions consigned to 'armchair theorizing'.

It is difficult to assess the results of seventy or eighty years of empirical research. From the long list of doctoral theses that are completed annually, and the shelf-miles of research reports and journals, it is not difficult to recognize an enormous amount of research activity. Some of the claims made in this mass of research have been very influential in affecting school **curricula** and practice, and the professional training of teachers; witness the interest in **behaviourism** at all levels, in stages of child **development**, in various forms of teacher-interaction schemata, and, in particular, in many types of standardized tests.

The quantitative tradition has never lacked critics. Philosophers and historians of education have for a long time been critical of its domination. Sociologists frequently portray main-line social scientists within education as agents of class domination in the school system, slotting students by means of **intelligence** tests into state-required employment routes, or correcting deviance to accommodate middle-class notions of law and order. The most visible products of quantitative research – standardized test instruments – are regarded by many critics as the principal components of the image of the school as a factory assembly line.

In addition, many people (including some social scientists) have questioned the effectiveness and worth of quantitative methods. Some claim that the demands of social science methodology exercise a determining effect on the type of educational questions that are investigated. Some doubt the value of what appear to them to be highly simplistic behavioural categories, and others argue that the types of generalizations characteristic of social scientific research are either ambiguous or tautologous. Some philosophers have noted the atomistic nature of much social scientific research, especially the very short experimental timespans on which generalizations or conclusions have been based. Others point out that the enormous amount of labour and cost put into social scientific research has produced very little in the way of helpful results (indeed, in some areas of social scientific research, especially in the study of **teaching**, what is perceived as a lack of progress in the last two decades has caused disappointment even to the most committed). In addition, a few observers have made powerful attacks on the social scientific tradition by arguing that examining education as though it were a series of natural phenomena is misguided.

Partly as a result of these criticisms, a relatively small number of researchers have shown interest in alternative methods that bear the rough-and-ready label of qualitative research. Despite the claims of some of the more naïve or enthusiastic adherents, the methods in question are by no means new, and by no means original to education: qualitative research bears much of the heritage of humanistic analysis, elements of so-called soft social science methods (especially those derived from anthropology and sociology), and substantial borrowings from **phenomenology**. In some ways, qualitative research in education may be described in terms that are contrary to main-line social science: it is concerned with the character of particular occurrences, not the forming of predictive generalizations; its results are written up in personal prose (in which the literary skills of the author may become a factor) rather than in numerical form; it takes its **concepts** and methods from the humanities rather than from the sciences; and its subject matter tends to be more comprehensive than the minute studies characteristic of some social science. In short, qualitative research represents, in many respects, the introduction of what has been variously labelled as an 'illuminative' or 'artistic' approach.

Its methods are various. Some stress the importance of so-called naturalistic techniques that are concerned with understanding personal insights and behaviour from the point of view of the chief actors or participants. To that end, field-study approaches, case studies, and interviewing are encouraged. Others have derived concepts and approaches from, for example, literature, fine art, drama, music, and journalism. Thus such concepts as scene-by-scene construction, dialogue, third-person perspective, and symbolic detail, derived from the so-called new journalism, may be used to throw a fresh light on selected educational phenomena. The work of researchers using qualitative approaches seems particularly prominent in detailed field studies of classrooms, and in **evaluation** reports of materials, curricula, and schools.

Qualitative approaches have been no less vigorously criticized than quantitative approaches. Some claim that the movement to qualitative research is not an alternative method, but a response to the difficulties inherent in any attempt to control human beings in experimental situations. Others find the prose of some of those using qualitative techniques so impenetrable that its meanings are incapable of being shared. More generally, it has been said that some research reports of such studies are opinionated, inconsequential, or highly damaging to the characters or livelihood of the persons under study.

The argument that there are two distinctly different research methodologies seems unconvincing in logic and practice. In discussing either quantitative or qualitative methods, there seems to be a tendency to over-simplify the issues, or caricature the traditions, of one or other approach. Given the complexity of contemporary schools, and the difficulties inherent in any type of study, a wide range of research tools and approaches is a necessity. Some of those tools will be more scientific than others; in some situations, and for some purposes, different types of approach will be needed. What is at stake is not the future of this or that research tradition, but the treatment of important educational issues. To encourage a sensitive and intelligent reflection upon those issues perhaps we should place an embargo on certain researchers in both traditions (especially those in publish-or-perish university settings): mindless number-crunchers on the one hand, and opinionated scribblers on the other. (At the very least such an embargo would dramatically reduce the costs of stocking libraries and render valuable wood-products available for more productive uses.) (*action research, phenomenology)

REFERENCES

Barrow (1984), Bliss, Monk and Ogburn (1983), Bogdan and Biklen (1982), Campbell and Stanley (1963), Cook and Reichardt (1979), Dumont and Lecomte (1984), Egan (1983), Eisner (1979), Guba and Lincoln (1982), Hamilton, Jenkins, King, MacDonald and Parlett (1977), Howe (1985), Kerlinger (1973), Maling and Keepes (1985), Nolan and Short (1985), Patton (1980), Sherman and Webb (1988), Travers (1973), Walker (1985), Webb, Campbell, Schwartz and Sechrest (1966), Willis (1978).

Quasi-experimental research *see* Ethnography, Interaction analysis, Quantitative/qualitative research, Research, Systematic observation

R

Rapport *see* Communication, Understanding

Rationalization *see* Linguistic error

Readiness

We know what the word 'readiness' means. The **concept** is not obscure. The question is how to turn such truisms as 'the child should not do anything until he is ready to' into useful prescriptions for **educational** practice, or, more generally, how to make constructive sense out of too much glib talk about readiness. It is clear that the child should indeed not do anything until he is ready to, for if he is 'not ready to do something', then, though the reason why he is not ready may not have been specified, it is a matter of definition that he is not well placed to do it. However, it does not follow that he should do something when he is ready. (There may be moral constraints or competing claims on his attention, for instance. Or, though he is ready to do X now, it may be more profitable in some way to do it later.) And, rather more importantly, in order to act on the principle of following children's readiness, we have to be able to recognize it. How do we do that?

Being ready to do something is not the same thing as expressing one's readiness. (A three-year-old may think she is ready to swim and be mistaken; an adult may express readiness that he does not even feel, let alone have, from a variety of motives.) Nor is it to be identified with being **interested** in something, wanting to do something, or starting to do something. There is no reason to suppose that readiness **correlates** with any observable feature of **behaviour**, or that children necessarily (or even generally) show particular competence at tasks that they have expressed readiness for performing, shown interest in, etc. Being ready to do something means both having some kind of favourable attitude or some impetus towards doing it and being possessed of whatever abilities, **skills, knowledge**, etc., are necessary to embarking on it. There therefore cannot be any general signs of readiness, common to all instances of being ready, and to know whether someone is ready to do something specific is one and the same thing as knowing whether the person is mentally, physically, and psychologically equipped to do it.

Thus, despite its popularity, the notion that, for example, children should not learn to read until they are ready to is somewhat vacuous (unless it is explicitly explained in terms of particular observable criteria for readiness, in which case it 'may be doubtful whether it is correct to label the state 'readiness', and in any case, the efficacy of the particular scheme will have to be **assessed**). It has not been established that one should wait until the child is judged ready by any particular criteria. Yet, if no criteria are specified, it remains unclear how we are to judge readiness (*child-centred education).

Reading *see* Language, Literacy, Logical order, Readiness, Skills

Realistic *see* Relevance

Recapitulation

Recapitulation theories have an obvious attraction for educationalists. It is possible, and deceptively easy, to characterize the history of our cultural development and of individual development in similar terms. Becoming educated is in significant part a matter of accumulating the most valuable capacities the initial creation of which is part of our cultural history. Also, it may be argued, a causal sequence is evident in our cultural history. Certain things are discovered, invented, or made possible. There is a semblance at least of logical progression from a Ptolomaic to an Einsteinian universe, from crude ethnocentric self-glorifying stories about one's ancestors to sophisticated modern historiography, and so on. These developmental sequences seem **logical** in perhaps a loose sense, but it is a sense that has repeatedly suggested some guidance to the **curriculum designer**.

One might also see in these sequences of discovery and invention the product of certain psychological predispositions: given the nature of human cognition we have of necessity had to construct human **culture** in these general sequences. It is psychologically impossible that we should begin writing **history** from anything but an egocentric view, progress to an ethnocentric view, and then, maturing historiographically, try to describe things as they were. (This kind of argument, using Piaget's theory as its basis, has been made by Hallpike, 1979.)

That is, whenever we describe our cultural history as some kind of causal sequence, which one can hardly avoid, we are asserting a logical and/or psychological underpinning to the scheme. If there is a logical sequence or psychological predispositions or both underlying the process of our cultural development, then a curriculum sequence recapitulating cultural history will be based on that logical sequence or those psychological predispositions or both. And as logic and/or psychology are attractive bases for a **curriculum**, so recapitulation schemes have an obvious attraction.

However, certain problems with this principle become quickly apparent when we try to work out detailed curricula from it. Also, despite its general plausibility, recapitulation ideas tend to be little regarded today because of the particular and, so it seems at this remove, obtuse interpretations of them that were implemented towards the end of the last century. Most commonly a marriage of Rousseauian and Darwinian ideas led to the belief that evolutional theory provided nature's guidance for the curriculum. G. S. Hall (1904) claimed that the study of evolution for **education** 'when explored and utilized to its full extent will reveal pedagogic possibilities now undreamed of'. The development of civilization was seen, **analogously** to the evolution of species, as a **natural** growth whose shape should thus, naturally, dictate the shape of the individual's **development**, and so the curriculum.

The most highly developed recapitulationist curricula were implemented in Germany. All of them made alarmingly literal translations from cultural history to curricula, producing a variety of 'culture-epoch' proposals. These curricula seem now oddly content-tied and epoch-tied (DeGarmo, 1885). In North America John Dewey was at first attracted by the ideas. He tried 'a modified system of culture epochs in his Chicago experimental school during the early 1890s. But he could not interest children in all aspects of supposedly appropriate material for their age: they loved the Roman heroes, for example, but yawned through the study of Roman laws' (Gould, 1977). But Dewey never shook off the focus on content: 'There is a sort of natural occurrence in the child mind to the typical activities of primitive people; witness the hut which the boy likes to build in the yard, playing hunt, with bows, arrows, spears and so on' (Gould, 1977).

Dewey came to deride the cruder kind of culture-epoch curricula, and their disrepute lasts even to the present. Recapitulation foundered in the early decades of this century under a two-pronged attack. The less influential came as a simple extension of the attack on recapitulation ideas in biology. It was suggested that educators 'who base their work upon [recapitulation] . . . may well ask themselves whether they are not building on shifting soil' (Bovet, 1923).

The more influential attack came from the growing present-mindedness of progressivism. Recapitulation curricula become 'absurd when tested by common sense. Although the development of the child may parallel the development of the race in certain respects, it does not follow that the curriculum should parallel the cultural development of the race. Obviously a child living in the twentieth century would pursue a twentieth-century curriculum. There is no justification for delaying the study of current events and our present community, state, and national life until the child has completed his study of the preceding periods of racial development' (Monroe, De Voss, and Reagan, 1930).

Since the early part of the century there has been no significant appeal to, or development of, recapitulation theories in education, until the recent work of Kieran Egan. In 1979 he published, in *Educational Development*, what he claimed was a 'cultural recapitulation' theory. In it he identified four stages which he calls mythic, romantic, philosophic, and ironic, and claims that these stages characterize 'kinds of **understanding**' – rather than logically more sophisticated content or psychological developments. *Educational Development* is a suggestive work, but the recapitulation dimension lacks sufficient development or **empirical** support to be taken as more than a potentially useful heuristic. More recently, however, Egan has published two books (1986, 1988b) which begin the task of articulating more clearly what he means by a 'cultural recapitulation' theory, in which what are recapitulated are 'kinds of understanding'.

REFERENCES

Bovet (1923), DeGarmo (1885), Egan (1979, 1986, 1988b), Hall (1904), Hallpike (1979), Monroe, De Voss and Reagan (1930).

Reconceptualists

It is not easy to pin down exactly who the reconceptualists are, what it is that they intend to reconceptualize, or how they intend to do it. The term became current in the 1970s among those theorists interested in extending a broad (and not always well-defined) range of alternative methods of analysis to educational issues. Despite the variety of views among those labelled as reconceptualists, there are some common elements in their positions. One of their principal targets is the current conception of educational **theory, research**, and practice in general, and

curriculum research in particular. They regard the dominant, **empirical** and technical methodology as inappropriate and inadequate, in that it fails to either uncover or appraise important issues in **schooling**. They also consider much current thinking in curriculum misleading, in that it fails to reveal important characteristics of the nature of **education** and life in schools.

Reconceptualists offer an alternative set of principles and methods for the examination of curricular and educational issues, drawing for inspiration upon at least three intellectual sources. First, they derive from Marxist thory a set of analytic **concepts** for examining and assessing the relationship between society and curriculum (and other educational **phenomena**). Secondly, they use **phenomenological** approaches to examine the experience of teachers and students in educational settings, and thirdly, they adapt notions of textual and contextual criticism from hermeneutics to curricular settings. Given such diverse sources, it is difficult to accept a claim that contemporary reconceptualists are a distinct school of thought, though they may be grouped together as adopting a 'reflexive perspective' (Eggleston, 1977). (There is always a danger in a summary of such an intellectual development of ascribing a greater degree of cohesion to members of such a group than in fact is the case; perhaps it should be emphasized here that the differences among some of those labelled reconceptualists are significant.)

A major plank in reconceptualists' arguments is the notion that schooling is essentially a political enterprise designed to maintain existing economic and **ideological** structures. They regard many of the liberal or progressive claims about the ameliorative function of schools as largely fraudulent. Schools, they argue, are used by the rich and by the privileged classes to manipulate working-class and disadvantaged students. They consider the **knowledge** generated by society, and the school curriculum derived from that knowledge, as economically determined and class-based. Given the function of the curriculum in sorting students into employment paths dictated by capitalist economies, they question the notion that schools provide equal opportunity or the chance for effective upward mobility. What is needed is a view of education, and a type of curriculum, that places schools within a much broader **cultural** and historical context. A revised curriculum, with an emphasis upon practical reasoning, would open to critical inquiry those political and economic forces that govern what type of knowledge is considered appropriate for study in schools, reveal to students the reasons for their present economic and social position, and offer opportunities for reflection upon alternative courses of action. Such a perspective would also highlight the reasons for the current pattern of social relationships among teachers and principals, and teachers and students. A general objective of reconceptualist arguments is to reveal what are viewed as distortions affecting all aspects of effective communication in schools and society.

Reconceptualists have derived from phenomenology the argument that persons involved in any aspect of schooling should examine their own place in society, not by listening to authority or by noting the results of social science research, but by suspending their belief in what had previously been taken for granted. Given the consistency with which societal institutions of all types maintain their authority from generation to generation, all aspects of life, including the world of the curriculum, must be re-examined to judge whether inherited characteristics of such institutions, or the power structures that they support, should be maintained. The nature of everyone's personal experience and **life history** needs to be examined reflectively, often in a process that subjects even seemingly trivial aspects of everyday living to critical analysis. An aim of such analysis is the identification of particular human experiences, and the examination of possible alternatives for future action. In this task, reconceptualists have borrowed from hermeneutics those techniques in textual criticism that enable them to examine the nature of such phenomena as teachers' and students' **language** on the one hand, and the context of life in classroom settings on the other. In short, the accustomed patterns of everyday living may become a form of text for critical review.

The effects of such musings have touched every branch of educational thought. Important studies have been made of life in schools using reconceptualist concepts, and the arguments of reconceptualists are regularly grist for philosophers' mills. In curriculum studies, there is greater sensitivity to the importance of cultural (and especially political and economic) settings for our understanding of curricular policy and the character of particular schools. Curricular theorists are much more aware of the importance of examining the assumptions upon which curricula are designed and implemented, and much less naïve in their attempts to introduce curricular change by means of administrative manipulation. In terms of research methods, the reconceptualists have offered arguments to support the modification (or replacement) of prevailing technical social-scientific approches to **curriculum design** and development.

That having been said, several qualifications ought to be emphasized. Reconceptualist arguments, like the sources on which they draw, are often simplistic, frequently doctrinaire, and usually based on idealistic or Utopian notions of social transformation. Their powerful givens or preconceptions sometimes lie outside the boundaries of what passes as rational discussion. In certain cases, reconceptualists' articles appear to be mystical in approach, and cloaked in a rhetoric that masks what should be considered as at least highly debatable propositions (for example, concerning the **relativity** or social origin of all knowledge). While we need to extend our understanding of the nature and forms of social control, and the effect of that control on our conceptions of knowledge and curriculum, we should also be vigilant in keeping those understandings separate from, on the one hand, questions of the validity of the knowledge we possess, and, on the other, questions of the **worth** of the curriculum that we offer or approve (**action research, class, critical theory*).

REFERENCES

Apple (1979), Eggleston (1977), Freire (1973b), Giroux (1981, 1983b), Giroux, Penna and Pinar (1981), Jackson (1980), Lawn and Barton (1981), Macdonald (1981), Macdonald and Zaret (1975), Milburn, Goodson and Clark (1989), Newmann (1985), Pinar (1974, 1975, 1983, 1988a, 1988b), Pinar and Grumet (1981), Radnitsky (1970), Roche (1973), Sharp and Green (1975), Tanner and Tanner (1979), van Manen (1984), Young (1971).

Refute *see* Linguistic error

Reification

'Reification' might be called a buzz word (cf., '**brainstorming**'). Sometimes it is used rather wildly to stigmatize a view as being too credulous or serious (for example, 'You are reifying Freud now' using the word almost as synonym for 'glorifying', 'treating as sanctified'). Given its correct and precise meaning ('to make a thing out of something that is not, i.e. to concretize an abstract idea, as one may personify God') it does label a distinct **concept**, and one that is faintly troublesome. Educationalists, for instance, are already well on the way to improperly reifying **skills, processes, critical thinking, curriculum design**, etc. Thus, for example, the ability to draw becomes talked of, and presumably in time thought of, as the operation of some physical element in the individual; the display of a critical mind in diverse situations becomes seen as the deployment of a thing – one's critical thinking skill(s). One danger in such misleading reification is that it may lead us to think that, for example, critical thinking is something to be exercised, like one's body, rather than something to be developed through **understanding**. Mention should also be made of the sociological notion of reificiation, referring to the phenomenon of making 'objects' out of, for example, institutions (**mental faculties*).

Relativity

'Everything flows', 'One cannot step in the same river twice', 'Man is the measure of all things.' These quotations from ancient Greek sources indicate that arguments about relativity of judgement are nothing new. There has always been the question of whether (and, if so, in what sense) claims of various sorts are peculiar to time and place, or **cultural** setting.

Few would dispute that customs, values, claims, and opinions are to some extent relative. That is merely to say that it is a **fact** that different peoples in different situations have had different customs and values, entertained different opinions, and made different claims. It also seems reasonable to suggest that very often these different perspectives are to some extent caused by different cultural conditions, and not merely co-extensive with them. But is it reasonable to suggest that everything is entirely relative – in other words that no proposition has any sanctity except as an expression of a particular cultural perspective? Such an extreme position is plainly not reasonable: water does freeze at a certain temperature, stones do drop when let go of, the angles of a right-angled triangle do add up to 180°, two times two does equal four, and the earth is spherical. Of course, even such familiar propositions are only true if they are understood in a particular way. That is to say, two times two equals four, provided that we are working in base ten; water freezes at 100°, provided we are working on a centigrade system and given certain specificable conditions; stones drop in places where they are affected by the pull of gravity; the earth is roughly spherical. But when such ellipses and qualifications are appreciated, which is to say no more than when these propositions are fully understood, their truth is not relative. We should not confuse the facts that things look different to different cultures or from different perspectives with the claim that they are different. Similarly, we should not be confused by the fact that claims taken to be true may come to be falsified: if, for example, it were to transpire that the earth was flat after all, this would not show that the shape of the earth is relative, but that opinions or **theories** about it can be mistaken.

What is usually intended by stress on relativity is the more moderate claim that certain types of belief are relative or, more specifically, that our perceptual categories are dominated by cultural setting. Both suggestions clearly contain some truth. We do categorize or look at the world in certain ways that might easily have been otherwise and that often do vary from time to time and place to place (for example, to use a crude example, some cultures are much affected by a particular religious outlook, others not at all). But what follows from this is not the relativity of judgements or beliefs themselves, but the relativity of human interest.

The fact that some cultures do not have any scientific understanding, but instead explain certain **phenomena** in religious terms, or, perhaps, do not seek to explain them at all, but approach them **aesthetically**, does not show that in those worlds the phenomena are not amenable to scientific explanation. Nor does one culture's commitment to a religious, scientific, or any other kind of outlook have any bearing on the truth or falsity of particular judgements. On the other hand, it should surely be conceded that the tendency of cultures to look at the world in certain sorts of way rather than others is likely to be, to a large extent, a matter of time and place (*ethics, knowledge, objectivity, subjectivity).

Relevance

'Relevance' is surely one of the most hideous words in the educationalist's vocabulary. It is frequently asserted that **schooling, curriculum**, etc., should be relevant. Nobody would seriously suggest that they should be irrelevant. The question is, to what should they be relevant? For relevance is not a straightforward property of things, as a particular shape or colour may be. It is a relational property. To establish that something has relevance, one therefore has to specify the end to which it is supposedly relevant, and show that it does indeed serve that end. In addition, if the **normative** overtones of relevance are to be justified, one will need to argue for the desirability of the end in question.

'Relevance' is often used as if it were synonymous with 'contemporary', or 'in fashion'. (Thus 'relevant' subjects include computer studies but not classics.) It is also sometimes used as a synonym for having vocational or professional advantages. (In this sense, engineering is a 'relevant' subject.) Another of the many misuses of the word equates 'relevance' with 'what seems relevant to an individual', so that a relevant curriculum becomes a curriculum that students *perceive* as being 'up to date', 'of professional value', etc.

The relevance that the school curriculum should have is relevance to some one or more of the functions of schooling and the **aims** of **education**. Whether, therefore, the study of Chinese, English **literature**, or physics has any relevance is a question of whether what is involved in studying each subject can be shown to serve as a good means to furthering some educational aim or other end of schooling. (The logic and abuse of such terms as 'useful', 'practical', 'realistic', and 'variable' is essentially the same.)

Reliability

The word 'reliability' has a particular technical meaning in **empirical research**, and it is important to distinguish that sense from the word's everyday sense, as in 'Jones is a reliable person' or 'I find this a reliable test of loyalty.' One important question is whether the reliability that researchers refer to is sufficient to warrant us in relying on their research. The answer, in brief, is that it is not, although reliability in the technical sense (which, to avoid confusion, will be referred to throughout as t-reliability) is a **necessary condition** of acceptable research instruments.

In its everyday sense, 'reliability', whether as an attribute of persons, machines, evidence, etc., refers to the trust that we may legitimately place in the person, machine, evidence, etc. A reliable person can be counted upon or trusted to do what is expected of him. By extension, a reliable machine is one that functions appropriately, and that can be counted upon to continue doing so. Reliable evidence is bona fide evidence. A reliable test will prove an accurate guide to the truth about whatever is being tested. But it is not legitimate to assume, and it is not necessarily the case, that because a test has high t-reliability (reliability in the technical sense) it is to be trusted as an accurate guide. Whether it is to be trusted will depend on other technical factors such as **validity**, but above all on the appropriateness of the test and the subtlety and sense of its devising. The key question becomes: is it sensible to test for X in this way? The answer to that question does not depend exclusively on consideration of methodological or technical matters.

T-reliability is essentially a measure of the consistency of a test under different circumstances. One cannot refer to a general t-reliability (as if to say this test is consistent under any circumstances), but must specify the respect in which a t-reliability rating is given. For example, one may refer to test-retest (sometimes called examinee) t-reliability, which is to say, the consistency of results obtained when the same test is used at different times on the same group of people. Marker (or observer) t-reliability refers to the consistency of test results regardless of which individuals do the marking (or observing). T-reliability in respect of instrument stability refers to consistency between tests (such that different tests produce the same or equivalent results with a given group).

T-reliability scores are expressed as a **correlation** between the performances at different times (with different markers, etc.) on a scale from -1.00 to $+1.00$. A perfect reliability in respect of, for example, test-retest would be expressed as $+1.00$ and would indicate a perfect correlation between the various performances of a student on this test. In fact such perfection is never attained, and reliability ratings on educational tests that are none the less regarded as adequate are often below 0.80. The fact that actual scores will thus be seen to fluctuate even on 'good' tests gives rise to the notion of the standard error of measurement. It is conceded that an individual's performance may be affected by a number of factors that do not have any bearing on the quality of the test (e.g. mood of student, motivation, luck, rapport with examiner). By calculating a margin of error around scores on a test (the manner of doing which will be found described in standard books on statistics and instructional psychology), a 'true' score can be estimated by taking the recorded score and adjusting it in the light of the error score.

It is generally believed that length of test can be helpful in improving its t-reliability (as large samples are regarded as preferable to small ones in research), that items should be neither very difficult nor very simple, and that relatively heterogeneous student groups should be used in developing a test (compare the desire for random and representative samples in research).

However, despite the common-sense wisdom of such means of seeking to improve the quality of tests, and despite the degree of qualification implied by recognition of a margin of error, there remain problems. High t-reliability scores might to a considerable extent be the product of chance or other factors (not considered in allowing for a margin of error). Furthermore, notwithstanding broad injunctions about the ideal types of question, the items on a test may be poorly chosen or poorly presented in a wide variety of ways and for a wide variety of reasons. Crudely, high reliability could be the product of puerile questioning, and – the point to stress – judging the puerility of questions is an art that has nothing to do with the skills of testing in general and such technical concepts as t-reliability in particular. Establishing whether or not various steps one has taken (e.g. lengthened the test) have in fact improved t-reliability is not simply an empirical matter, but calls for exceedingly complex judgement and estimation. (The more trivial or obvious the object of the test, the easier it is, no doubt, to make reasonable estimates: for example, a test of the child's ability to compute numbers should more readily get high marker t-reliability than an essay test. A method of marking essays that has t-reliability must be suspect, given what we know of the complexity of essay writing, the difficulty of quantifying the qualities of an essay, and legitimate differences of concern between essay markers. A system of marking essays that bypasses such differences would avoid important issues inherent in essay writing, just as an observation schedule that has high t-reliability is suspect, if it gains it with reference to situations which we know to be complex and the source of quite different kinds of perception amongst different people.)

Lack of t-reliability is certainly a defect in a test or research schedule.

But it and other technical concepts such as validity, even when taken together, fall a long way short of being a sufficient set of conditions for a good test. And t-reliability is bought at too high a price, if it is the outcome of simplistic, trivial, or in any other way inadequate conceptualization of what is at issue. Above all it should be remembered that t-reliability is not the same thing as reliability in the ordinary sense of 'to be counted on' as a gauge of truth or reality. (It is worth repeating here that tests may be t-reliabile, *and* valid and objective in technical senses, and still poor measures of the true situation.) (*analysis, assessment, concept, developmental theory, objectivity, research, teacher effectiveness, validity)

Religious education

Patterns of religious education vary from country to country. For example, there are denominational systems of schooling in Canada, often receiving state funds. In the United States private religious schools are strong. In Britain religious education is an anomaly: it is the only compulsory subject in the **curriculum**. Yet in practice the content of 're-ligious education' classes varies considerably, sometimes being more akin to general studies or discussion groups than to anything specifically religious. This presumably represents a response to changing attitudes to religion in society that have not been reflected in any change in the law. RI, or religious instruction, as it used to be known, implied the imparting of information about and even the initiation into the responses of a faith (characteristically the Anglican faith). Although such initiation is to be distinguished from **indoctrination**, to some it seemed uncomfortably like it, besides which religious faith has been thought to be fairly dramatically on the decline in general, while immigration has brought with it a number of new faiths. 'Religious **education**' has thus become the preferred phrase implying as it does that **understanding** of, rather than commitment to, religion is the aim. Seeking merely to explore and explain the nature of religious discourse and/or to describe features of particular faiths gets round the problem of the status of fundamental religious claims such as that God exists. (The problem is essentially how we are to determine what kind of evidence counts as evidence to support such claims. Nobody disputes that the Bible says X, for instance, but many do dispute that the Bible represents unimpeachable evidence; likewise, to some the appearance of design in the universe is evidence of God's existence, to others not; to some personal revelations are conclusive, to others they are mere illusion.)

Certain problems still remain, however. There is the question of which religion or religions should be examined (*multiculturalism). There is the question of whether this type of examination of religion needs to take place in lessons devoted to the purpose rather than, say, in the course of history and English lessons. There is the question of whether it should be classified as a form of knowledge as Hirst argues, or merely a subject matter inviting questions from a number of different, but not distinctively religious, disciplines. Some would question why, even in diluted form, religious education should retain its special status. To that the most immediate answer would appear to be that, like it or leave it, whether based on truth or not, religion has been and continues to be a phenomenon of enormous and unique significance to mankind, and as such deserves close attention (*moral education).

REFERENCES

Hirst (1974d), Hudson (1973), Sealey (1983).

Research

Most of the entries in this book are directly or indirectly concerned with research. Some refer to research into particular matters, whether conceptual (e.g. the nature of education, the nature of knowledge), empirical (e.g. classroom disicipline, teacher effectiveness), or both (e.g. creativity, intelligence). Some concentrate on different types of research method (e.g. ethnography, systematic observation, analysis). And some deal with specific methodological concepts (e.g. reliability, validity). Some of what is said about particular areas of research is critical. The nature of that criticism may be summarized in three parts:

1. A great deal of empirical research into education has been flawed in terms of the basic requirements of such research. (For example, samples have been too small and/or not representative; relevant variables have been ignored; interpretation of data has been questionable.)

2. A particular, widespread, failing in such research has been its conceptual inadequacy. A number of early pieces of research operated with very broad polarized categories (e.g. the research of Lewin, Lippitt and White, 1939, and Withall, 1949, centred on directive and indirective styles of teaching) or obviously inadequate conceptualization (e.g. early conceptions of intelligence and creativity). More recently, attempts to improve conceptualizations have been prone to confuse increased specificity with increased clarity, to confuse clarity of verbal definition with

clarity of conception, and to confuse clarity of analysis with empirical distinctiveness of an item. A further problem has been the reversion to operational definitions which, while they may be clear and observable, depart considerably from everyday understanding of the concepts in question (for example, definitions of 'intelligence' that enable us to monitor intelligence but bear no obvious relationship to the intelligence we ascribe to an Einstein or a Bertrand Russell) (*analysis).

3. The most serious problem may be that the nature of the educational enterprise does not lend itself to empirical research to the extent that is popularly supposed. The central concepts of the enterprise (e.g. education, **moral** development, **aesthetic** appreciation), and the things that we should be interested in observing (e.g. enthusiasm, **understanding**) do not readily lend themselves to full articulation in terms that can be observed or accurately monitored. In addition, and essentially as a result of the conceptual problems, the hope of controlling all relevant variables (in respect of, e.g. environment, individual personality, teacher behaviour, intelligence) may be vain. We may thus be on the horns of a **dilemma**. Either we confine our research to a set of monitorable concepts, in which case we impoverish reality (for in reality people may be affected by aspects of, e.g. respect for their teachers, love of learning, that we cannot adequately monitor). Or we accept the complex nature of the business and thereby accept that there is much that we cannot profitably research by observation.

The remainder of this entry will seek only to summarize points dwelt on at greater length elsewhere, to shape them into a pattern, and to indicate under what further entries to pursue particular matters.

The term 'research' is frequently used as if it were synonymous with 'empirical research'. This usage is illegitimate and misleading at best, and, at worst, could prove detrimental to education itself. It is illegitimate because, besides research that is truly based on observation, which is the hallmark of empirical inquiry, we have historical research (which some might classify as empirical,but which often is not in any plausible sense), philosophical research, and other reflective inquiries into such matters as values and aims. In so far as this point is not recognized and given due weight, the educational enterprise is in danger of being defined exclusively in monitorable means–ends terms. Thus, successful education becomes synonymous with success at readily and immediately observable tasks; a good **curriculum** becomes a curriculum of which the pay-off is easily and directly observable (*empirical, education, interaction analysis, aims, teacher effectiveness).

Given the nature of educational theory, it is important to recognize the field of educational research as one involving a number of different kinds of question (not simply different questions) and needing to call upon a number of different developed **disciplines**. Thus, besides relatively straightforward descriptive empirical questions about what is taking place in schools, we have to deal with more complex questions about cause and effect, which are only partially empirically observable, and questions about the origins and development of ideas and practices, about the coherence of theories and practices, about the nature of concepts, and about our values and ideals, that become progressively remote from empirical observation (*theory, value judgements, concept, analysis).

Traditionally, the disciplines seen as crucial to dealing with these various questions have been philosophy, history, sociology, and psychology. Recently, reliance on these four disciplines, at any rate in a form that institutionalizes them as four distinct programmes, has met with some criticism. However, while there can be no question that in some way or other the individual needs to integrate these disciplines, and while other subjects such as economics and the unfashionable comparative education are equally important for a complete and thorough programme of educational research, the vital importance of the traditional disciplines cannot coherently be denied. For what is distinctive about them, even allowing for blurring at the edges and overlap, is that, unlike subjects such as economics that are defined by reference to their subject matter rather than a specifiable methodology (or set of methodological approaches), they introduce four broad, distinguishable, types of inquiry each of which is necessary to making full sense of the educational picture. It is logically inconceivable that anyone should produce educational research of value were he to lack understanding of the concerns and techniques of philosophy, sociology, and psychology, and unlikely that he would not gain further benefit from some historical awareness. Indeed, the obvious and hideous weakness of most research to date has been that sociologists have taken little account of the possible effects of individual psychology, and vice versa, empiricists generally have shown little philosophical acumen, and philosophers have tended to analyse concepts *in vacuo*, without reference to empirical research or historical development. It borders on the shocking that the intervention of the Council for Accreditation of Teacher Education in teacher education in Britain has led directly in some instances to the abandonment of, for example, any philosophical training (*integrated studies, knowledge).

One consequence of a successful integration of disciplines in research should be that more truly educational research would take place, as opposed to research that, while it may relate to children, to **learning**, or to schools, does not obviously have anything to do with education. Thus it has been argued that research into such matters as **operant conditioning**, the effects of schooling on subsequent social achievement, and sex-role **stereotyping**, while it has its own intrinsic value, has got little or nothing to do with education or schooling. Such a view is obviously debatable, but so long as consideration of the concepts of schooling and education and our ideals and aims are pushed to the side, it cannot even be debated. In this respect, attention may be drawn to recent criticism of developmental theory that is not concerned with alleged inadequacies within such research, but with the point that as educators we should not be interested in what happens to human beings *qua* human beings, so much as in what we could and should do to enhance a non-natural educational development. The only relevance developmental theory as currently understood would have to such an enterprise would be its ability to demonstrate insurmountable restraints on our ideals. But in point of fact there is very little in, for example, Piagetian developmental theory that clearly shows we could never hope to achieve various particular goals with particular children. The essential and less controversial point remains that there cannot be coherent empirical research in education that is not grounded in an explicit and clearly articulated conception of such things as educational success, worthwhile learning, and morally acceptable teaching, none of which is in itself an empirical matter (*education, schooling, developmental theory, natural, worthwhile).

Notwithstanding the above points, it is empirical research that dominates the field, though the record is not an altogether happy one. The history of such research over the last fifty years shows a disturbing ability on the part of those engaged in the field to recognize its weaknesses surprisingly late after the event, but to remain confident that purely technical or methodological change and increased sophistication herald a more productive era. See, for example, such reviews of the research as Dunkin and Biddle (1974), Heath and Nielsen (1974), and Good, Biddle and Brophy (1975). In other words the conceptual and logical problems involved in such research are not adequately appreciated, and discussion centres rather on the relative merits of, for example, ethnographic and systematic approaches, and on the possibility of, for example, quasi-experimental research, to be distinguished both from true experiment (which is difficult to conduct with human subjects for practical and ethical reasons) and from surveys (which are easier to conduct, but harder to turn to useful account). Some current approaches to empirical research such as ATI (**aptitude treatment interactions**) are relatively sophisticated in their recognition of the complex interplay of factors that may affect what goes on in the classroom, but it remains open to debate how successful such research has so far proved in overcoming the inherent difficulties noted above (*ethnography, systematic observation, quantitative/ qualitative research, interaction analysis).

In summary, we would suggest that educational research is too much dominated by empirical research, and the latter too much preoccupied with general and abstract argument about the merits of rival styles or paradigms of research. Too little attention is paid to disentangling different kinds of question or different elements within a question, and to suiting the manner of inquiry to the nature of the particular question rather than to an a priori commitment to a paradigm of research. There is insufficient appreciation of the misrepresentation of educational success that may be involved in relying on, for example, standardized tests of achievement as indicators of progress, and the violence that may be done to notions such as intelligence and creativity by defining them in terms that can be readily monitored. There is also too great a willingness to infer cause and effect on a limited data base, even though most researchers are formally well aware that high correlations do not necessarily imply cause and effect (*paradigm, assessment, correlation).

Any improvement must depend upon integrating the skills, insights and concerns of philosophy with empirical inquiry to a far greater extent than has so far been achieved (*critical thinking, ideology, language, learning, metaphor, objectivity, open education, reconceptualists).

REFERENCES

Barrow (1984), Carr (1983), Delamont (1984), Dunkin and Biddle (1974), Egan (1983), Gage (1963), Good, Biddle, and Brophy (1975), Good and Brophy (1978), Heath and Nielsen (1974), Hempel (1966), Lewin, Lippitt and White (1939), Rudner (1966), Shulman (1979), Wilson (1972), Withall (1949).

Respect for persons

This concept was given considerable prominence in the 1960s by philosophers who argued that it was an integral part of the ideal teaching relationship. Respect for persons is not conceived of in terms of feelings of personal affection, agreement with a viewpoint or moral approval. To have respect for a person is to recognize another as a person in his or her own right as an autonomous being, and, as such, to be accorded certain rights and treated with consideration. To show lack of respect would be, for example, to use someone merely as a means to our ends. The importance of the concept lies precisely in the fact that it is in a sense depersonalized: even if one admitted that one did not like one's neighbour, thought one's father-in-law stupid, or regarded a child as obnoxious, one would none the less be called upon to recognize that as individuals they were entitled to consideration.

The phrase appears to have waned almost to the point of disappearance. The idea or **concept**, however, has not been entirely abandoned. '**Caring**', while it very often is taken to mean 'having sentiments of affection', can be used to mean essentially respect for persons. The idea should certainly not be allowed to die; of particular concern to the philosopher Kant, the concept is still thought by many to be an essential element in **ethics**.

REFERENCES

Downey and Telfer (1969), Langford (1968), Peters (1966).

Role playing *see* Simulations

S

Schooling

'Schooling' is the most general term that describes the enterprise we are primarily interested in. It is true that the word 'education' is sometimes used to refer to the educational system, and therefore becomes more or less synonymous with schooling, and that 'education' in a narrower sense is not the business of schools alone. None the less, it is convenient to mark a distinction between schooling, which has a variety of purposes and functions, and education which is one of the things with which schools are concerned.

At different times and places different views of schooling have been held. The classical Spartans, for example, for reasons to do with their own internal politics, sent boys to military boarding school at the age of seven, where the main concern was to provide military **training**, character building, and commitment to the Spartan way of life. There was very little emphasis on reading and writing, let alone the kind of intellectual development that we associate with education. Today the instilling of commitment to communism is a straightforward element in Soviet education, while in many states circumstances give rise to a military training for the young, often at the expense of the intellect, and character building remains a proud boast of many private schools throughout the world. But the **conception** of schooling prevalent in the Western world today differs from these examples. Military training seldom has any place in it, character building, when it is considered, has a much more open quality, and the overt attempt to instil **ideological** commitment is condemned as **indoctrination**. Instead the emphasis falls on **education, socialization**, physical education, **moral** and **emotional** development. (One might add vocational training, university or more generally social role selection, and child minding. Some, including **deschoolers**, have argued that schools in fact fail to achieve various desirable ends, because they are too bound up with serving various other incompatible or inherently undesirable ends.)

Although the question of what schools do and what they achieve lies behind much **empirical research**, the question of what they ought to do has seldom been considered in any depth, other than in the speculative treatises of philosophers such as Plato and Rousseau. Perhaps John Dewey was the last man to attempt, by implication at least, a comprehensive theory of schooling. Yet the question is important: for, without a clearly articulated view of what schooling ought to be trying to do, we are in no position to assess either the suitability of the **measures** of success and achievement used in empirical research or the adequacy of our schooling systems (*culture, knowledge, language, learning).

REFERENCES

Barrow (1981c), Peters (1966).

Science *see* Core curriculum, Curriculum change, Discipline, Feminism, Indoctrination, Knowledge, Language, Moral education, Paradigm, Research, Sex education

Selective-response tests *see* Assessment

Self-education *see* Education

Self-esteem *see* Communication, Creativity, Learning

Self-expression *see* Creativity

Sequencing material *see* Deschooling, Interests, Logical order, Recapitulation

Setting *see* Integration

Sex education

What role should schools play in respect of sex education? Is sex education a matter for schools at all, or should it be laid at the door of parents? How secure is our knowledge on matters to do with sex? Should we treat, for example, Freudian theories of infant sexuality as

established, probable, unlikely, or false? Have we good reason to conclude that pornographic material does or does not affect people? If so, in
what way? Is it cathartic or causative? Do we even have agreement on
what constitutes pornography?

The first issue that requires settlement is what is meant by 'sex education'. Genuine sex **education** (as opposed to, say, providing helpful advice on how to combat sexual attacks) would involve providing
understanding of the **facts** of sexual activity, the facts of sexual mores,
and the facts of argument about sexual morality. As with, for example,
moral education, it would be a matter of promoting **understanding** of the
domain, rather than fostering particular attitudes or behaviours. But
then, if that is what sex education is, is it truly sex education that we are
interested in? Much actual 'sex education', or writing about it, is far
more concerned with promoting current sexual mores as morally desirable or counselling children into acceptance of/coping with them. A
society is bound to influence children to accept current sexual mores to
some extent, both in school and out, and may legitimately do so in the
name of **socialization**. But one may question whether some so-called sex
education does not border on overt moralizing and even **indoctrination**.
And, in any case, socialization should be distinguished from sex
education.

Another question to be asked is whether sex education should constitute a distinct subject. The answer must to some extent be related to
the previous question, and may in turn give rise to the further question
of whether this is a subject that should be taught by specialists. (If so, of
what sort should they be? Counsellors, moralists, biologists, a new breed
of specialist teacher selected according to a novel set of criteria?) If, for
example, sex education is seen as a distinct subject that involves preparing children to cope with their own developing sexuality, then it well
may be that it requires teachers who are specifically trained to do this. If,
on the other hand, it is seen as the provision of an amalgam of information about physical development and sexual reproduction, it might well
be regarded as falling within the province of biology.

The fact appears to be that lack of a clear consensus on what sex
education is leads at present to some confusion over how and by whom
it may best be provided. At the risk of seeming unwarrantably **prescriptive**, we may suggest that science education for young children should
certainly include description of the biological facts concerning sexual
development and reproduction, issues of sexual morality should certainly be discussed with older children, either in the context of, for
example, literature and history, or as a subject matter in its own right,
and that care should be taken to prepare children for changes in, and for
coping with, their own sexuality, as well as for dealing with sexual

harassment and the sexual advances of others. The majority of teachers are ill equipped to deal with the last element, and specialists, perhaps drawn from those with a background in psychology and counselling, would be needed here (*stereotyping).

Sex-roles *see* Feminism, Stereotyping

Sexism *see* Feminism

Simulations

A simulation ought to be distinguished from role-playing and games, although all three share some characteristics. Role-playing occurs when someone assumes or acts out the persona or function of another (a common feature of simulations), and a game is a contest (again, a common feature of simulations) played according to certain rules (usually pre-determined) and decided by skill, strength, or good fortune. The single most important characteristic of a simulation, however, is the deliberate construction of a **model** of a particular **process**, the working of which demonstrates selected characteristics without incurring some of the costs of a real-life situation. In pilot training, for example, the device which the novice operates includes, by carefully designed replication, almost all the features of the real event (take-off, cruising and landing), except the most dangerous one: it does not fly. As a social science research tool, a simulation may be based on a model of a social or psychological process (for example, a carefully designed sequence of stresses in a family group), in which selected variables may be manipulated and inter-relationships examined, again without incurring the costs (both personal and financial) of the real-life situation. Simulations are particularly useful to cybernetic psychologists, who use the **analogy** between machines and man to provide opportunities for **conceptualizing** persons (including learners) as self-regulating feed-back systems. Although features of simulations may be traced back to hunting rituals of early man (and the board games of early Chinese civilizations), the device came into its own in modern times with the popularity of the war game, in which the major features of the battlefield may be reproduced without incurring the costs of actual warfare. Simulations are widely used in such fields as industrial training, business, computer applications, and social scientific research.

In schools, simulations are used primarily as training devices to introduce students to a working model of some abstract, symbolic or real-life process. The structure of educational simulations commonly includes the following features: (a) a scenario that sketches a background or plot; (b) a set of roles (occasionally for each individual, but usually for groups of persons representing various interests in the scenario); (c) a sequence (often repetitive) of procedures for the individuals or groups to follow; (d) a simplified model from real life enshrined in a set of data that the players are expected to operate; and, (e) an opportunity for participants to examine the consequences of their actions and reflect upon the relationship of the simulation to the real-life situation. For example, at a fairly simple level a class may be broken up into groups representing countries (each equipped with a Prime Minister, Foreign Affairs Minister, etc.) involved in examining (by means of a regular series of internal and inter-nation meetings) a series of economic and political difficulties based on the national realities of pre-1914 Europe. Decisions in each international session may be based on a set of statistics governing the economic and political well-being of each nation, which the teacher (or game director) feeds to the participants as the events of the scenario unfold and the players' decisions are made. At the end of the action, participants are provided with the opportunity to compare their own actions with those taken by national governments before the First World War.

In the last twenty years, many types of simulations (a few designed by teachers, but most produced commercially) have appeared in school classrooms, particularly in such subjects as politics, international studies, business, geography, conservation, personal and career guidance, and computer studies. Evidence of this increased interest in the technique is found in new professional societies and journals in the United States, Britain, Canada, and other countries.

Many claims have been made to justify the introduction of simulations into the classroom. Observers have pointed to the intense **interest** and involvement (the terms are never defined very precisely) stimulated by simulations. Some have argued that such involvement is particularly helpful (in both academic and personal senses) for slower-learning students. In a few cases improvement has allegedly been noticed in the ability of students to make decisions, or in the development of particular **skills**. But the major defence of such a technique is that it places students in situations in which they make some of the decisions, play out important features of the roles, and experience some of the consequences, of real-life situations that would otherwise be closed to them. A political simulation, for example, provides a first-hand opportunity for students to experience some of the pressures facing elected representatives in a way not otherwise available. On the question of the relative efficiency of simulations, as opposed to other methods, in increasing students' knowledge of a particular subject, the **research** evidence (as might be expected) is inconclusive.

The critics of educational simulations (in conception and in practice) can marshal some powerful arguments. The origin of simulations (lying as it does within **behaviourist** theory) does not inspire confidence in those concerned with **intellectual** growth of students. Some educators argue that simulations are essentially mechanistic instruments designed primarily to change student behaviour by means of relatively crude feed-back methods. The very notion of operating a model, frequently at a simplistic level, raises the question of the **academic** appropriateness of the technique, as well as the issue of the efficient use of students' time. Would it not be wiser, it is argued, to read a life of Harry Truman rather than play the role of President, especially if the simulation time consumes (as it frequently does) many hours? Such critics remain unimpressed by the interest argument, unless that interest can be linked firmly to positive findings on the achievement of desired educational goals. While simulations, it is suggested, may be useful in improving certain skills or behaviours, they are inappropriate in the humanities, and very demanding upon the skills of teachers, many of whom are ill-prepared (both professionally and personally) for the pressures of a lengthy classroom simulation.

Despite years of study, the jury is still out on the value of simulations. Some claims made by their proponents remain attractive, but the research data to support those claims seem unconvincing. Interest in educational simulations appears to have declined in the last decade, but it is not clear whether this decline is due to disenchantment with educational simulations, or simply the result of a conservative mood affecting schools throughout the Western world (*microteaching).

REFERENCES

Cruikshank (1979), Inbar and Stoll (1972), Joyce and Weil (1980), Raser (1969), Tansey and Unwin (1969), Taylor and Walford (1972), Wilson (1970).

Skills

'Skill' is an overworked word in **education**. It is applied indiscriminately to mechanical skills (e.g. grasping an object, practising sleight of hand), intellectual skills (e.g. reasoning, **analysing**), **emotional** skills (e.g. relating to people), perceptual skills (e.g. recognizing and differentiating between musical notes), and creative skills (e.g. writing poetry). It is applied to skills that appear to develop naturally (e.g. walking), those that appear to be, while not **natural** in the sense of automatic, none the less acquired through the environment (e.g. talking), and those that in most cases need to be learned, with or without the aid of teachers (e.g. writing essays). Particular skills, sometimes of very different type, may sometimes arise spontaneously and in other cases be the product of teaching (e.g. musical composition, riding a bike). Some skills are simple (e.g. holding a pen), some are very complex (e.g. the skill of the historian or soccer player). This varied use of the word 'skill' is acceptable, provided that it is recognized that it makes it a very general term meaning little more than 'ability'. It is a general term covering as many diverse species as the word 'animal'. To say that one has a certain skill is to say no more than that one is able to do something; and, just as to be told that the spider and the shark are both animals is to be told virtually nothing about how to recognize or treat either one, so to be told that grasping an object and reasoning are skills is to learn next to nothing about how to deal with or foster either one.

While being used in a wide variety of contexts, 'skill' is wrongly allowed to retain connotations deriving from its basic use to denote a simple, mechanical skill that can be best developed by continued practice. But, while such skills as those of dribbling a ball and pirouetting on one's toes *are* essentially the product of practice, such skills as those of **critical thinking** and **creative** expression are essentially the product of **understanding** and **learning**. Talking in terms of, for example, the skill(s) of critical thinking may mislead us into regarding critical thinking in terms of the exercise of skill(s) that can be trained by extensive practice without regard to particular context. Thus, rather than promoting the understanding that allows the individual to be, say, a critical historian, we may be tempted to set him to critical thinking exercises, rather as we may set him on a bike. (If it be said that this is not the implication of referring to 'the skill' of critical thinking, we must ask why in that case we continue to refer to it as 'a skill', for the word would now appear to be redundant: 'the skill of critical thinking' means no more than 'critical thinking'.)

The insidious effects of over-using the word 'skill' are apparent in certain approaches to **curriculum design**. Reading, for example, as nobody would in fact dispute if pressed specifically on the point, though often referred to as 'a skill', is no such thing. It is a complex activity involving a number of different kinds of aspect, some of which may perhaps reasonably be seen as skills (e.g. decoding), some of which may not (e.g. understanding the logic of a particular passage or appreciating the imagery). Seeing reading as a skill or set of skills (notwithstanding the point that it certainly involves some skills) has misled some into the conclusion that the best way to teach reading is to exercise the child methodically in the practice of the various skills, introducing them one at a time. While it cannot be unequivocally asserted that that is a bad thing to do, there is no compelling evidence that it is a particularly good way to proceed, it is clearly not a necessary way to proceed, and what one might hope to achieve in the name of good reading evidently involves a great deal more than the mastery of various discrete aspects of the business of reading. The whole is greater than the sum of the parts (*brainstorming, curriculum, generic fallacy, microteaching, reification, transference).

REFERENCE

Barrow (1990).

Slogan

A slogan is a distinctive phrase that serves as a rallying cry. It is a pejorative term, implying that nothing much lies behind the phrase, apart from its **emotive** force. Politicians naturally love to adopt effective slogans, for they cause a suspension of **crictal thought** in those who are struck by them. (Consider, e.g. Harold Macmillan's famous 'You never had it so good', which suggested euphoria and stability and left unasked questions such as in what respects or at what price). **Educanto** is unfortunately full of slogans: for example, 'whole language', 'child-centred', 'relevance', 'feminism', 'visual literacy' and 'cultural literacy'. It is even arguable that a phrase such as 'curriculum development' is little more than a slogan (*interest, open education, values clarification).

Social science *see* Feminism, Quantitative/qualitative research, Research

Socialization

Socialization is an important (and unavoidable) function of **schooling**, and it invites a number of questions, particularly in the area of how to do it effectively, to which we do not have very clear answers; but it is not a particularly complex **concept**. Socialization is the business of adjusting people to the way of life of the community, usually by way of initiation into its customs, beliefs, rituals, conventions, expectations, and demands, combined with instruction and the setting of examples. In socializing individuals we habituate them to our **culture** or way of life, we make them one of us. It is important to distinguish carefully between socialization and other types of influence such as **indoctrination, education** and **training** (*emotions, emotive meaning, moral education, sex education**).

REFERENCES

Barrow (1981c), Kazepides (1982).

Sociology of education *see* Research, Theory

Sociology of knowledge *see* Knowledge

Special education *see* Giftedness

Standardized achievement tests *see* Assessment

Stereotyping

A stereotype – derived from the Greek *stereos* meaning solid or firm, and *typos* meaning the mark of an impression or blow – is a set of value-laden beliefs held by one person or group concerning traits of another group, **class**, or category within the society. A stereotype may thus range from being a rather unsavoury indicator of over-simplified or exaggerated judgements of others, especially those of other ethnic groups, to being a fairly neutral term that identifies an important factor in all social relationships. But some educationalists unwarrantably seem to assume that a stereotype is by definition one extreme or the other.

Those who believe that a stereotype is necessarily always of the former type have in mind that when a person is asked to give an opinion about traits of groups to which he does not belong, his response is frequently over-simplified, erroneous, and negative. A man may hold the view that women are naturally shy and submissive, an American that Canadians are friendly, a young man that the old are feeble and slow-witted, and so forth. Such generalizations often influence how a person may regard a specific member of the group in question, whether the characteristics fit that individual or not. In consequence, grave social, political, and economic injustice has often been done to individuals within society, especially members of visible minorities, native peoples, religious groups, the aged, and women, by persons holding such stereotypical beliefs.

Some social psychologists, on the other hand, have suggested that these examples do not tell the whole story. When we face new social situations, they argue, we act on generalizations derived from similar experiences in the past. Stereotypes therefore serve a purpose in helping us to sort out the various roles that others occupy in society. Many of these roles, particularly those related to occuption or rank, are played with a high degree of consistency. In short, the argument goes, stereotyping *per se* is a neutral term denoting something that serves an essential social function; what is highly objectionable about particular stereotypes is not that they are stereotypes, but that they are untenable stereotypes for one of any number of reasons (e.g. they are false, ethnocentric in origin, or based on a misconception of the nature of generalizations).

Many features of **research** into stereotyping remain controversial. Investigations into the accuracy of cultural stereotypes are notoriously difficult to conduct, for how are we going to be able to establish clearly what are the characteristics of certain groups, such as women or the elderly (surely an important question to be answered before charges of false stereotyping may be laid)? Other questions that do not lend themselves to **empirical** research have not been adequately explored: the relationship between the stereotypes used by persons and their attitudes has not been thoroughly reviewed, despite its obvious importance (for example, do people's attitudes lead to stereotypes, or vice versa?). It is not clear to what extent preconceptions held by researchers have affected their views of the differences between groups or **cultures**. In addition, the question of the truth or falsehood of some research claims has been ignored in view of political arguments surrounding them, especially claims related to the self-fulfilling role of some victims of stereotypes.

Educational institutions have been accused of playing a part in encouraging dissemination of harmful and false stereotypes. School readers and textbooks, in particular, have been charged with confirming attitudes that are not supported by the available evidence, or offering interpretations that are based upon a selective twisting of the same evidence. In other studies, some teachers and administrators have been accused of harbouring ill-founded or erroneous attitudes towards other groups.

An enormous effort has been made in many countries to harness the resources of educational systems to the task of diminishing the force of damaging stereotypes, especially those involving ethnic or religious groups, and women. Teaching materials have been prepared that provide a more balanced picture of the role of groups which have suffered from negative and misplaced stereotyping, and school-books considered harmful have been removed from the curriculum or extensively revised. Students have been encouraged to improve their knowledge of other groups within society, either directly by personal contacts, or vicariously through an enriched **curriculum**. In many countries, there are reports of significant changes in the extent to which certain stereotypical beliefs are held by students and other members of the community, for which schools should take some credit (even though legal and social changes may have been largely responsible).

These efforts are not without their critics. Some educationalists are unhappy with the principle of **positive discrimination**. Others have argued that attempts to remove all stereotyping is singularly naïve. A government programme to avoid sex-role stereotyping in the upbringing of the young will not result in the abolition of stereotyping *per se*, but only in the abolition of a particular form of stereotyping, which will inevitably be replaced by another perhaps better, perhaps worse, form. In some cases, efforts to remove all evidence of various stereotypes from school programmes has involved some reformers riding roughshod over certain other principles, witness the removal of certain books of acknowledged literary worth from school libraries. Given the confusion over the nature and accuracy of stereotypes, such difficulties are likely to persist (**censorship*).

REFERENCES

Allport (1954), Barrow (1982a), Brigham (1971), Fishman (1956), Johnston and Ettema (1982), Lippman (1922), McDiarmid and Pratt (1971), Miller (1981), Roy (n.d.).

Subject-centred education *see* Child-centred education

Subjectivity

The suggestion that an opinion is subjective usually serves to diminish its credibility. This may be misleading. A basic meaning of 'subjective' is 'in the mind' as opposed to 'out there in the world' or 'real', hence it comes to mean 'incapable of being externally verified', and hence 'unreliable, transitory, personal' or, more generally, without any truth value. Obviously, if an opinion is subjective in the sense of being unreliable, transitory, and personal to a point at which the question of its truth or falsity cannot arise, by definition it is of little value in respect of determining truth. However, it is clear that some claims, while being subjective in the sense of 'in the mind' are none the less reliable guides to truth, e.g. 'I am in pain', 'I dislike him', 'It is cold'. Indeed, such subjective utterances may be a much more reliable guide to the truth of certain affairs than a host of **objective** measures: the psychologists' battery of tests does not establish the presence of happiness as certainly as the individual's subjective belief that he is happy. (This is essentially because the **concept** of happiness is such that an individual cannot intelligibly be said to be happy if he does not feel that he is. Conversely, if he feels that he is, though others may wonder at it in certain circumstances, he must be acknowledged to be so. See Barrow, 1980.)

Furthermore all opinions have a subjective element, inasmuch as all by definition involve belief, which is by definition a subjective state or 'in the mind'. For example, it may be the case that John F. Kennedy is dead, just as it may be the case that I am sad, but my opinion on either issue is necessarily partly subjective in the specific sense that it is located in my mind. Whether there is anything objective (in the sense of 'corresponding to reality' or 'true') about either opinion is a further question, and one that should be distinguished from the question of whether either opinion is 'capable of being externally verified'. (For an opinion may be objective in the sense of corresponding to what is in fact the case in the world, while not being open to confirmation by external verification.)

An important distinction is, therefore, between those claims and opinions which are purely subjective and those which have a degree of objectivity in the sense that they are based on some publicly accredited and assessable criteria. What these are may on occasion be difficult to determine and hotly disputed (for example, what are the publicly accredited and assessable criteria for determining God's existence?). None the less, 'two times two equals four', 'pearls dissolve in acid', 'the earth is spherical', even, it may be argued, 'the Mona Lisa is a great work of art', and 'torture is evil', are clearly objective utterances to a degree that 'roses are the most beautiful flowers' or 'coffee tastes better with sugar in it' are not.

Subjectivity should not be confused with **relativity**, although the two are often found together. Subjectivity implies (allowing for the variations and qualifications of degree noted) that the opinion arises out of the individual's personal perspective; relativity implies that the opinion arises out of some **cultural** setting. Thus a subjectivist view of moral utterances equates 'this is good' with 'I favour this', while a relativist view equates it with 'this is favoured in this time and place (i.e. by this group or community)' (*ethics, research, systematic observation, value judgements).

REFERENCE

Barrow (1980).

Subjects

The traditional secondary school curriculum subjects are: science, maths, history, English, and, more tentatively, religion, physical education, art, a foreign language, and geography. Their continued importance, at any rate in official thinking, is testified for by the content of the new curriculum proposals in the United Kingdom. While different jurisdictions give priority to different subjects and sometimes organize them differently (geography, for instance, may become part of social studies), few entirely ignore any of them.

This volume includes entries on **history, literature, religious education**, and **art education**. But it should not be inferred that these are necessarily judged to be more important than other subjects mentioned. There are entries on history and literature, because the nature of these subjects and the purpose of teaching them are currently more disputed than is, say, the nature and purpose of teaching mathematics. Furthermore, there seems a real danger that these subjects, which are crucial to the humanities and a necessary part of a **liberal education**, may become distorted, if not actually removed from the curriculum, in these **utilitarian** times. There are entries on art education, **aesthetic value**, religious education (and **moral education**), because the domains of religion, art and morality are **conceptually** complex, to an extent and in a way that, e.g. physical and science education are not. (The absence of an entry for a particular subject matter does not imply that there are no practical difficulties or questions about the best way to teach that subject. It suggests only that there are relatively few conceptual, **logical**, or evaluative difficulties.)

The issue of whether the curriculum should be subject based is considered in the entries on **topic-centred** curriculum and **knowledge** (*core curriculum, critical thinking, discipline, integrated studies, sex education, understanding).

Sufficient condition *see* Necessary condition

Summative evaluation *see* Formative/summative evaluation

Syllabus *see* Curriculum

Sympathy *see* Communication, Understanding

Systematic observation

A major distinction in **empirical research** is that between formal and informal approaches. A variety of labels and minor differences in practice are associated with either approach. For example, systematic observation and **interaction analysis** are species of the formal approach, while case study, **ethnographic** research, and participant observation are types of informal approach. A useful pair to concentrate on in an attempt to get at the underlying strengths and weaknesses of either approach, are systematic observation and ethnography.

Essential characteristics of systematic observation (a tradition pioneered by N. A. Flanders' Interaction Analysis Categories system) are that an observer should classify subject behaviour, according to a previously drawn-up schedule of behaviour categories, at regular intervals. The intervals are usually short (e.g. three seconds to three minutes) and the moment of classification theoretically instantaneous and dogmatic (i.e. the subject has to be classified according to only one of the categories). The observation schedule is usually (though it need not be) **behavioural**. The subjects will be individual students or teachers. In practice the procedure may be fairly complex in that the observer is likely to have several target subjects (e.g. the teacher and a number of individual students) and to be looking out for specific behaviours or responses relating to a variety of general categories (e.g. teacher/pupil interactions, pupil/pupil interactions, location). In addition he may need to code reactions of non-target pupils from time to time. A necessary consequence of this approach is that the time spent observing an individual is not continuous and is considerably limited relative to the overall time spent in the classroom. (For example, assuming a coding at two-minute intervals, and allowing for the fact that not all subjects can be coded at once, a particular target pupil's responses might only be coded fifteen times in a three-quarter-hour lesson.)

It will be apparent that the phrase 'systematic observation' is somewhat misleading. There is indeed system in the observation schedules referred to, but so there may be in the informal studies with which they are often contrasted. The most obvious and notable characteristic of so-called systematic observation is rather its commitment to a pre-specification of the behaviours to be looked for.

The crucial distinction in types of educational observation, notwithstanding the large number of labels and the genuine variations in approach to be found, would therefore appear to be that between those who approach the classroom with a preconceived set of categories of behaviour to look out for, and those who arrive at a set of classroom behaviours as a result of judging what appear to be salient characteristics of behaviour. Clearly there may be something to be said for both approaches: the former is useful in so far as the observation schedule is realistic, imaginative, and wide ranging, and the observers themselves otherwise limited in awareness; the latter's greater flexibility gives more scope for describing classroom life as it actually is, provided that observers have the ability to recognize and categorize different behaviours as they occur. (A further quite important distinction in the latter case is that between participant observers, who advertise their presence and become part of the observed community, interacting with others who are described as 'informants', and those who resemble systematic observers in that they observe as if from the outside, albeit informally.)

The usual argument in favour of systematic observation is that it is relatively **objective** in the limited and specific sense that others may know the basis of the claims eventually made. Because we know from the observation schedule, and accompanying explanation of the category, precisely what is meant by, for example, 'paying attention', and because we know the system whereby the judgement was arrived at (i.e. it is based on a stated number of codings at particular intervals over a given period of time), we have a proper understanding of a claim such as 'boys pay attention 50 per cent of the time'. This, it is sometimes alleged, we do not have if an informal study makes a similar claim.

However, this argument is flawed. First, in principle there is no reason why an informal approach should not make it clear on what basis it makes its judgements. There is no inherent reason why an informal study should not clarify in advance what it would recognize as 'paying attention', and certainly there is nothing to prevent it offering clear statements after the event of what it understood as instances of various types of response. Secondly, it is not necessarily the case that we know the precise basis for judgements following systematic observation, because even a clear statement of what observers were looking for does not guarantee that the judgements of observers were dependable. Thirdly, the quality and accuracy of systematic observation will depend not upon the fact of pre-specification, but on the quality of those specifications, and in point of fact, because of inherent difficulties in conceptualization, many observation schedules will necessarily be inadequate to deal with other than relatively trivial and straightforward behaviours. (Many actual observation schedules have been of very poor quality, simply because researchers have not been sufficiently aware of the requirements of adequate conceptualization.) (*concept, analysis, teacher effectiveness)

A further claim to be made for systematic observation is that it is objective in the sense that there is consistency between different observers and/or between observations made on different occasions. This, however, is not necessarily true, since different observers, though using the same categories and coding system, none the less have to make judgements, and it is conceivable that what one person sees as, for example, 'looking out of the window' and hence categorizes as 'being distracted', another will see as something different. However, it is likely to be generally the case, partly because categories of behaviour in systematic observation tend to be relatively simplistic and easy to observe, and partly because observers are usually trained beforehand to ensure that they do make similar judgements. And it is also true that informal observation, by its very nature, cannot guarantee conformity of judgement in advance: two observers in two different classrooms may encounter entirely different situations and consequently not even describe the same kinds of behaviour. But it is important to recognize what the reason for this is: if one's object is to have different observers looking for the same things in different classrooms on different occasions, then one does indeed need prior agreement on a clearly articulated set of behaviours to look for. (Even that does not necessarily imply the need for the type of observation schedule typically employed in systematic observation, though such a schedule might well make things easier.) If, on the other hand, one's object is to give a realistic description of various classrooms that may in fact present very different pictures, then it is highly misleading to insist on the description of each one being confined to a number of predetermined behaviours. (In either case what is required is not in fact a determinate pre-specified list of behaviours, so much as clearly articulated and agreed concepts.) An important question therefore is what kinds of thing we want to research. If we want to describe or build up understanding of particular classrooms, then systematic observation is not needed, and will in fact prove a hindrance inasmuch as it limits the aspects of the classroom life that are considered significant. If we want to foster understanding of classroom life in general, then systematic observation is not necessarily required; provided that informal observation is carried out by observers who **communicate** with one another and use clearly articulated concepts, their various findings can be coherently pooled together. It is only if our concern is to arrive at statistical generalizations about particular, easily recognizable, behaviours, that systematic observation would seem to have an obvious edge on informal techniques.

We now come to the main problem: granted that systematic observation has a relatively high degree of objectivity in the specific senses noted, and that it may have its value for a particular limited kind of inquiry, a price has to be paid for these advantages. The price is a distorted picture of reality, since the items on a manageable observation schedule (highly unlikely to number more than, say, one hundred): (a) add up to only a partial description of all the behaviours that actually occur; and (b) are either: (i) relatively trivial; or (ii) inadequately conceptualized; or (iii) not as straightforwardly observable and monitorable as the argument in favour of systematic observation demands they should be.

To elaborate:

(a) A description of classroom life that is confined to tabulating the relative incidence of some hundred such behaviours as 'listening to the teacher', 'talking to peers', and 'being distracted' cannot provide very sophisticated understanding of the complex interactions of classroom life.

(b) If the observers are to make accurate and uniform judgements about the categorization of behaviour in a split second, then:

    (i)   they will have to concentrate on trivial matters that would be equally unproblematic for informal observers (e.g. whether a child is in or out of the classroom; whether a teacher is addressing an individual student), or

    (ii)   they will be treating complex and subtle matters as if they were unproblematic (e.g. in order to make a snap judgement about whether children are or are not distracted, inadequately conceptualizing 'being distracted' in terms only of crude behavioural signs, such as 'looking out of the window', which are in fact neither **necessary** nor sufficient conditions of being distracted); or

    (iii)   in trying to do justice to the complexity of a concept such as 'being interested', they will face all the problems of the informal observer despite the observation schedule. (For example, if the systematic observer has a category such as 'being interested', and has been given a sophisticated understanding of this concept that cannot be couched in crude behavioural terms, then he faces the problems that anyone else faces in trying to determine whether an individual is interested at a particular moment; he will simply be unable to make a snap decision with confidence; and will have no guarantee that other observers, even if trained for the same project, would have made the same decision.)

In sum, in so far as systematic observation is seen as essentially concerned with a limited number of items of behaviour, pre-specified and defined in such a way as to allow of instantaneous unambiguous judgement, it is open to the following objections.

1. At best it gives us only a partial view of classroom life, and it determines what that partial view shall be concerned with without any reference to what may actually be the essence or dominant features of life in the particular classrooms observed.
2. There are some things that can be well quantified using this approach, such as the relative incidence of teacher talk, the location of students, or transparently disruptive behaviour. But precisely because such things are relatively easy to observe they are not very difficult to research by means of informal techniques either. In addition, one may question the relative value of this kind of information, unless it is allied to a more sophisticated understanding of classroom life.
3. Many of the concepts that are crucial to the enterprise of schooling cannot legitimately be treated in the way that systematic observation requires. Such things as **creativity**, enthusiasm, **interest, learning**, and being **educated** itself cannot be defined, without gross distortion, in ways that enable an observer to make instantaneous decisions about whether people are enthusiastic, interested, learning, etc.
4. Since systematic observational research has often not confined itself to the limited number of appropriate concepts referred to under (2), it is to that extent guilty of promulgating inadequate conceptions of, for example, distraction, interest, and attention. Indeed, it may reasonably be said that it is not systematic observation that is to be criticized so much as the grandiose claims made in its name about, for example, 'providing an objective description of classroom life', and the conceptual murder that has taken place in its cause.

None of this is to say that informal techniques are free from difficulties (the most obvious one of which is indeed the weakness that systematic observation is supposed to remedy – namely, the difficulty of knowing precisely how judgements were arrived at). But we must surely conclude that the problem in classroom research is not so much one of which method to adopt, as how to conceptualize important elements in a way that both does justice to the elements and allows us to recognize them in practice.

REFERENCES

Amidon and Hough (1967), Barrow (1984), Croll (1986), Delamont (1984), Flanders (1970), Galton (1980), Galton and Simon (1980), Galton, Simon and Croll (1980), Mcaleese and Hamilton (1978), Milburn (1985).

T

Task words *see* Achievement words

Taxonomy

'Taxonomy' (from the Greek *taxis* – plural, *taxa* – meaning 'arrange-ment', 'division'), like a number of other educational terms, ideas, and practices, is a word originally associated with biology; it refers to a system of classifying animals and plants, typically by division, class, order, family, genus and species. In education it just seems to mean any systematic organization. One of the most famous is Bloom's taxonomy of educational objectives, which catalogues large numbers of elements within the cognitive and affective domain, and seeks to relate these to specifiable and observable **learning** objectives. (Bloom acknowledges that his is not truly a taxonomy, since the **discrimination**, categorization, and arrangement of the various cognitive and affective levels is some-what arbitrary.)

More importantly, Bloom's taxonomy may be criticized on the grounds that some of his **concepts** are rather rough and ready, and consequently difficult to assess in practice. (For example, what actually counts as 'willingness to respond' or 'satisfaction in response'?) Yet, the fundamental concern is to isolate **skills** and attributes that can be **mea-sured**. That concern may itself be criticized on the grounds that all is not measurable that is of educational importance. Thirdly, throughout the taxonomy Bloom ignores questions of what is **worthwhile**. For example, in the affective domain, as an illustrative educational objective related to 'commitment' we find: 'devotion to those ideas and ideals which are the foundation of democracy'. Such an objective clearly raises crucial ques-tions such as, what are those ideas and ideals? How do you tell whether an individual has such devotion? What counts as devotion? Is it indeed right to encourage such devotion? By any means? Is such an objective appropriately **educational (*behavioural objectives)**?

REFERENCES
Bloom (1956), Krathwohl, Bloom and Masia (1964).

Teacher education

The first edition of this book contained no entry on 'teacher education'. That is to be explained in terms of the **fact** that there were a number of entries on related **concepts**, and there did not seem much to say about teacher education *per se*. After all, are not all the researchers and theorists whose work is drawn on in this volume involved with teacher education? And are not teachers and student teachers who care to read this thereby making some small contribution to their own **education**? Our thinking on this matter has not substantially changed, but the pragmatic wisdom of a specific entry has been brought home to us by recent political activity in a number of countries which suggests that teacher preparation is likely to expand over the next few years, while debates about how to conduct that preparation period will once again take centre stage. What form should teacher education take? And who is a teacher educator?

In earlier ages, teachers, like most other tradesmen and professionals, learnt their craft on the job, usually by some form of apprenticeship to an experienced individual. When people considered the qualifications of teachers it was almost always in terms of their wisdom, moral probity, or the like, rather than in terms of any strictly **professional** knowledge (e.g. of teaching techniques, child psychology). In essence, one's knowledge of some teachable subject matter was one's qualification for teaching, and one's competence as a teacher was developed through practice, with or without the guidance of a more experienced mentor. Despite isolated but, over the centuries, repeated objections to one or other of these features, the pattern remained much the same well into this century. (Comenius, for example, was appalled at the lack of a science of pedagogy and tried to develop one; Rousseau did not regard the wisdom of the book-learned as worth teaching.) A comparison of contemporary tests for qualifying teachers with those of nearly a century ago in the United States, reveals that the major change (and it is a marked one) is from testing the would-be teacher's knowledge of subject matter to testing his **knowledge** of educational **theory** (Shulman, 1986).

The perennial issue these days is therefore the relative weight to be given to theory and practice and the nature of the relationship between them in practice. (So far as logic goes, there is no room and no excuse for the divorce that some have assumed to be there. The two are necessarily connected.)

In the early days of this century the tendency was to refer to 'teacher training'. Since the 1960s 'teacher education' has been the preferred term, a natural consequence of the recognition of the distinction between educating and training that philosophers such as R. S. Peters

(1966) brought out, and a self-conscious concern that the business of teaching be seen as a profession rather than a trade. More generally, the impetus of solid and exciting work in educational theory contributed to the strong leaning towards 'teacher education' – pre-service teacher programmes, while they had their teaching practices, none the less involved considerable attention being paid to such issues as 'the concept of education', 'the sociology of knowledge', 'the forms of knowledge', '**creativity**', and '**moral education**'. Quietly, that enthusiasm and that degree of intellectual activity have subsided.

Today, many opt for the **neutral** 'teacher preparation', since it is clear that training does play a part in the business, even though one might not wish so to characterize the whole process. The emphasis now falls more on practice and theoretical reflection arising out of practice, than on the study of the constituent theoretical **disciplines**. Indeed the integrity and logical status of those disciplines have themselves been challenged from a variety of angles. In some jurisdictions the emphasis is now on wide practical experience and development of allegedly **generic skills** of **teaching**, rather than detached consideration of the **research** behind and arguments for one's practice and skills. **Subject** knowledge is accorded quite different weight according to institution and locality. Some university departments in Britain still take it for granted that subject knowledge is crucial, and devote much of the teacher-training year to consideration of, and practice at, ways of delivering specific content material. At the other extreme certain North American programmes for certifying teachers pay no direct attention to subject knowledge, and concentrate on developing generalized techniques of teaching.

Increasingly initial teacher training is being supplemented, to some extent replaced, by professional development, in-service, or continuing study. Some have argued that ideally initial preparation should be a careful, but unambitious, process of training on the job, provided that at a later date, when realistic fears about controlling a class, etc., have disappeared, teachers might have access to thorough theoretical study of education. But the recent increase in the time allotted to professional development days (North America) and Baker days (United Kingdom – so called after the Minister of Education) would bring little joy to such people. For other developments in recent years have included a strong shift towards 'practical', '**relevant**', or 'useful' in-service courses, by which is meant essentially a move away from detached intellectual study in the direction of the execution of specific currently required programmes, projects and tasks. The single professional development days that are a noticeable feature of, e.g., Canadian education, while sometimes productive as why should they not be, seem all too often to involve teachers in uncritical adulation of a self-serving bandwagon without intellectual grounding or repute.

The salient question in all of this remains: what ought a teacher to know and be able to do? (And what, if it is different, ought someone who is going to teach study or do beforehand?)

1. There are certain personal characteristics that few would deny a teacher should have. Some of these, such as integrity and kindness, are **moral**. Others, though they may not be unique to the profession, are none the less professional virtues, such as patience and sense of humour. Such characteristics cannot be cultivated or developed in a programme of teacher training. They therefore have to be used as criteria for selection (amongst others) to a programme.

2. Practical experience, with guidance, is, of course, a *sine qua non* of adequate preparation. Experts often debate the relative merits of one long practicum, or two shorter ones, how long a time should be spent in the school, how long should be spent observing, how long teaching, whether the student should be observed a lot or a little, how the observer should respond, etc. No doubt all such things make a difference. No doubt also we do not know enough to say with assurance what would prove best in any particular case. The important point is that practice is needed in order to experiment, to fail, to feel the satisfaction of success, to see how incomplete one's theory is, to perfect, and so on.

3. The single most important thing is probably the most neglected. A teacher must have a solid understanding of the subject that he teaches. You cannot teach **history**, physical education, or anything else well, if you do not know your history or your physical education. This logically inescapable point has belatedly been recognized by some empirical researchers (e.g. Shulman). Clearly, initial teacher-training programmes differ in the extent to which mastery of subject matter is their immediate concern. (A college of education offering a B.Ed. degree has a direct responsibility; a department of education offering a one-year postgraduate certificate does not.) But any teacher-training programme should pay due care and attention to the point: subject qualifications should be an important criterion of selection, and the study of teaching (however carried out) should be undertaken in reference to the teaching of specific subject matter. Thus, in order to avoid the **generic fallacy**, students need to be taught about teaching **history**, science, a diverse curriculum to seven-year-olds, etc., rather than about teaching *per se*.

4. The previous comment brings us to the main issue: what should the role of educational theory be? Should it be studied in its own right? If so

before, after, or during classroom practice? Should it arise out of practical experience? Should it be based on the study of philosophers, sociologists, and the like, or on the inquiries of practising teachers? Such questions currently exercise our minds considerably. But should they do so? Is it perhaps six of one and half a dozen of the other? Certainly, reasons that seem prima facie sensible have been advanced for a variety of approaches, but it is far from clear that reasoning or **empirical** data lead to the conclusion that any particular approach is better than another. What is undeniable is that while good teaching may and often does take place without any conscious reflection on, let alone examination of, the corpus of knowledge relating to the nature of education, any attempt to assess, improve, change, criticize, or otherwise comment on one's educational practice, if it is to be informed comment, presupposes a theoretical position. Equally, while a sound theoretical position is conceivable in one who has never formally studied education, it is unlikely in the extreme that most teachers would not benefit, so far as their powers of theorizing about education go, from a close study of the findings and arguments of scholars in the field. In short, while it is not obvious that it matters when or how it is done, there is a strong case for saying that prospective teachers ought to make a close study of educational theory. (The inescapable fact that many practitioners, and, indeed, some teacher educators, deny the importance of theory arises in our view from the diversity and in some cases poor quality of theory. There is without question more bad theory in a multidisciplinary subject such as education still struggling for academic respectability, and still threatened by those who want to see it as a **professional** study as distinct from an **academic** one, than there is in an established discipline. Bad theory is indeed, by definition, irrelevant to practice.)

If teacher education should ideally involve the four elements mentioned, who are the teacher educators? Some faculties draw a distinction between those individuals who are involved with teacher education and those who are involved with, e.g. graduate work. Such a division merely marks out initial teacher training from in-service work; all work in a faculty of education should be presumed both to involve academic respectability and to be professionally orientated. Though in principle a professor of instructional psychology might deal only with PhD students working on pure research, in fact almost all of them work with practising teachers on research that is located in schools or the like, and their ultimate objective is to enlarge the pool of wisdom available for practising teachers. It therefore seems unfortunate that such an artificial division should have arisen.

Worse is the attempt to distinguish between those who are and those who are not involved with teacher education by reference to the focal point of their scholarly interests. 'A teacher educator' to some by definition means an empirical investigator of teacher-training programmes. Why the concept should be so narrow, why a sociologist who has devoted his life to examining, say, the social milieu that produces teachers, or the philosopher who has concerned himself with examining the idea of teacher education should be excluded, is, in logic, far from clear. In practice, alas, we know that it is another symptom of the contemporary confusion over what is needed to achieve a coherent theory of education (*practical principles).

REFERENCES

Comenius (1969), Peters (1966), Rousseau (1972), Shulman (1986).

Teacher effectiveness

The unwary may turn to this entry in order to find a summary of effective teaching techniques. They will be disappointed, partly because this is not that kind of dictionary (see Introduction), and partly because, as will be argued, we are not in a position to say much with confidence on this subject, other than what should be self-evident because logically necessary and, more specifically, what follows necessarily from the nature of the **educative** task teachers are engaged in.

Over the last fifty years there has been a mass of **empirical** research into **teaching** strategies, classroom organization and management, and teacher and school effectiveness (various summaries of such research are readily available, for example, Dunkin and Biddle, 1974, and Good and Brophy, 1978). Various specific claims have been made as a result of the research, and many of these have passed into textbooks, at one time or another, as more or less reliable rules. For example, 'indirect styles of teaching are preferable to directive styles'; 'one should vary one's style of questioning (there being five particular questioning techniques that should ideally be used)'; 'in introducing material to children one should pass from the particular to the general'; 'teachers who predominantly address the whole class and ask many open-ended questions are relatively effective at teaching mathematics and language skills'; 'the optimum number of alternatives in a multiple-choice question is four'.

However, there is a danger that those who are not thoroughly immersed in the **research** itself will remain unaware of the very serious problems and pitfalls endemic to it, and as a result will be far too impressed by and trusting of these findings. (The logic of research into, for example, classroom management, teacher effectiveness, and effective schools being essentially similar, this argument should be seen as relevant to all empirical research into matters pertaining to good teaching and desirable schooling.)

For the most part, research has taken the form of surveys or field studies. That is to say, classrooms have been observed, as a result of which descriptions of student and teacher behaviour can be provided and **correlations** can be noted between various behaviours or facets of student or teacher personality or background and the progress of students, as determined by particular criteria (e.g. relating to good behaviour) and/or specific tests of achievement. The manner of observation may take various forms ranging from very formal styles (e.g. **systematic observation**) to very informal ones (e.g. **ethnographic** studies). Some approaches, such as **aptitude treatment interaction** studies, overtly recognize the complexities of classroom life and some of the problems in describing teacher–student interaction to be noted below (and by implication criticize other approaches for being too simplistic and partial), but give rise to difficulties of their own when it comes to extrapolating generalizable conclusions from their studies. True experimental situations to test hypotheses (i.e. setting a group of children in an artificially controlled situation to see whether A leads to B) have been rare, no doubt largely for practical and **ethical** reasons. It would, for example, be a heavy responsibility, even if it were permitted and individuals were willing, to take a group of children and subject them to a three-year experiment in which teachers offered no guidance, just to test the hypothesis that no progress is made where no guidance is offered. And it would in addition be extremely difficult to so construct the experiment that we could be confident that any lack of progress noted was indeed specifically the result of no teacher guidance, rather than a host of other factors.

It is evident that even at best, when we can be confident that we have accurately described what is going on and correctly discerned progress, a field study provides only weak or tentative guidance. In an uncontrolled situation, inferring cause and effect is necessarily a chancy business, and, in the absence of experimental follow-up, must remain on the level of hypothesis. Thus the fact that a teacher of a certain type is found to end the year with students who make relatively good progress at mathematics, cannot automatically be interpreted to mean that that type of teaching is relatively effective in mathematics. (And it could never be said to have been demonstrated by this form of research.) In the first place, the student progress in question could have been the result of any number of other factors, personal, social, or whatever. It may be said in response to this that it would be reasonable to attribute the progress to the teaching style, if nothing else correlates highly with progress. (That is, if all students who make good progress were taught in this particular way, but they have nothing else such as background, personality, or experience in common.) But that is not in fact self-evidently so, for when we are dealing with the multiplicity of factors that we are, and with human subjects who are affected in different ways by different factors, we cannot be sure that it is not different combinations of factors that are producing similar results in different cases. For example, simplifying, it may be that three students made progress simply because they were intelligent hard-working students who would have made progress in most situations, four made progress as a direct result of the teaching, two made progress because of home support, three more made progress because their liking for the teacher enabled them to accept his style, one made progress because he was motivated by awareness of being engaged in research, and so forth. In the second place, we cannot be sure that our understanding or description of the style of teaching in question in fact hits upon the characteristics that might be thought to be the cause of the progress. For example, we may characterize the teaching as directive, supportive, and demanding. But perhaps it was also amusing and interesting, and perhaps those are the characteristics, which might well be encountered in a teaching style that is not directive and demanding, that actually occasioned the progress.

The means of assessing student progress constitute another problem in such research. Too great a reliance on simple tests of achievement in, for example, numeracy, literacy, or particular tasks such as drawing a map of the classroom, is open to the objection that such abilities, though in themselves sometimes important, represent a very limited and narrow view of successful education, quite apart from the fact that they necessarily only take into account immediate gains and tell us nothing about the long-term impact of a programme of teaching. More ambitious tests of, for example, creativity or IQ are open to criticism on the grounds that they do not truly assess **creativity** or **intelligence**. Relatively informal approaches run into the difficulty of providing clear and convincing accounts of the criteria whereby progress has been assessed. The importance of this kind of problem should not be underestimated: without a clearly articulated and defensible account of educational progress that can also be adequately **assessed** or **measured**, no programme of research into teaching styles or techniques can presume to draw conclusions about effectiveness, since effective teaching must at least be teaching that promotes **educational** progress to a high degree.

The major difficulty with such research is that of controlling all the variables that come into play, regardless of the mode of observation employed. In the developed natural sciences it is relatively easy to arrive at a convincing statement of what is causing a particular effect. For example, we mix chemical A with chemical B and note effect C. Conceivably, the effect is not the result (or not simply the result) of mixing A and B; perhaps the temperature, the light conditions or the properties of the container in which the mix is made have something to do with it. But:

(a) the developed state of the science itself allows us to severely limit the number of possible variables to be considered (for example, we do not have to take seriously the suggestion that the day of the week or the structure of the laboratory have anything to do with it);

(b) the nature of the subject matter allows us to ignore a range of variables that only come into play with human subjects (e.g. motivation, consciousness of experimental situation);

(c) the business of **conceptualization** of potentially relevant factors is more advanced, partly perhaps because of inherent features of the factors in question, partly perhaps because of the developed state of the science. For example, if we wish to check whether temperature is a relevant factor in contributing to the observed effect, conceptualizing and recognizing temperature is considerably easier than conceptualizing and recognizing student intelligence or enthusiasm would be in a comparable piece of social science research;

(d) it is relatively easy to artificially isolate and control material variables, as compared with mental or emotional variables. For example, one can alter the temperature of a room more readily than one can alter the mood of an individual, even assuming that one could meet the previous point and correctly discern a particular mood.

In the classroom, in the current state of our knowledge, we have to allow for the possible relevance of, in practical terms, innumerable factors related to, for example, physical conditions, individual experience, individual ability, individual temperament, social and family background, in addition to the focal point of attention, i.e. teacher behaviour. There are so many possibly relevant factors that previous research cannot give us any clear guidance on, that we also have to allow for the possibility of the total count of relevant variables being multiplied tenfold as a result of different combinations. (For example, teacher praise combined with one kind of student personality may produce a different effect when the student has one kind of temperament and has experienced one sort of parental support, from that which it produces with a different combination of temperament and parental support.) In addition, there are many potentially crucial variables that have not been conceptualized in a way that is uncontentious (e.g. intelligence, creativity), and perhaps cannot satisfactorily be. Furthermore some of these variables, even if we agree on their conceptualization, cannot in fact be isolated. For example, although one might distinguish intelligence and creativity conceptually, it is not clear that one could in practice conduct research that genuinely isolated the one from the other. It is far from clear that statistical exercises that are designed to review data, holding particular variables constant, can logically meet this point. Suppose, for example, that our research reveals a significant positive correlation between a specific teaching style and student progress in mathematics. It is of course possible to check, after the event, whether certain other variables on which we have collected data (e.g. IQ of students, parental support, previous experience of students) also correlate with such progress. But we cannot deduce from low correlation in respect of such other factors that they are irrelevant to the effect noted, for it may conceivably be that the style of teaching was effective for different reasons in the case of different students, i.e. for some, because it integrated well with their previous experience, for others because it suited the nature of their intelligence, etc. This problem is more serious than may at once be apparent, since in reality we are dealing with many more possible relevant variables and the permutations they give rise to, and no actual research can conceivably monitor all the factors that might be relevant.

Behind this basic problem of controlling variables lies a very real problem of conceptualization. While some factors, such as age, sex, and previous experience can be fairly easily conceptualized and noted, others such as the interest of the student, the student's liking for the teacher, and the teacher's capacity to generate enthusiasm, cannot. Whatever cannot be clearly and adequately conceptualized in such a way that it is also reliably discernible (and we would argue that a number of possibly crucial concepts in relation to successful interaction between teacher and students inherently cannot be) obviously cannot be taken into account in research. And if our research proceeds without taking certain potentially relevant factors into account, we do not simply have gaps in our knowledge, we face the possibility of a distorted reading of the situation.

For the most part research has been more poorly constructed than it need have been: (a) samples have tended to be too small and unrepresentative; (b) conceptualization has been poor even when it need not have been; (c) less often, but still to a noteworthy degree, technical matters such as the **reliability** and **validity** of research instruments have not been up to scratch; (d) studies have in any case (and not surprisingly in the circumstances) produced a great many contradictory findings. Those four criticisms have been endorsed in many reviews of the research. In addition, we would claim that: (e) many of the claims made by empirical researchers turn out to combine an element of logically necessary truth with a particular empirical element that has not in fact been established (*contingent). For example, research claims that 'with-itness' is shown to be advantageous, but in fact the meaning of 'withit-ness' (essentially, 'making interventions at the appropriate time in respect of the appropriate target') is such that it has to be the case that a successful teacher should be with it rather than without it, while the research has not satisfactorily answered the truly empirical question of whether the specific interventions made by teachers in the research sample would always (or even generally) have the same effects in other classrooms.

All these considerations, which taken together would seem to be more serious than merely the sum of the individual parts suggest, incline us to the view that there are very few claims about effective teaching that can legitimately be said to have been demonstrated to be both true and significant for education. And indeed it is possible that the underlying premise of such research (that there is a determinate list of good teaching techniques) is mistaken: it well may be that there are hundreds or thousands of combinations of teaching techniques that in one situation or another will prove effective.

It should not be concluded either that it does not much matter what the teacher does, or that there is nothing that can be said about what constitutes good or effective teaching. Evidently there are better and worse teachers, and their ability is related to the things they do. Furthermore, many of the claims made by researchers may in fact be reasonable, at least at the level of generalization. (For example, it well may be that it is often a good idea to present various different types of question to students.) All that is being pointed out is that many such claims have not been satisfactorily demonstrated to be true, and in some cases it is difficult to see how they could be. None the less, guidance about effective teaching could be gained by a combination of better conducted research on more limited and carefully chosen issues (i.e. essentially on those matters that lend themselves to adequate conceptualization and recognition, such as whether a mathematics programme is better suited in general to six-year-olds or eight-year-olds), and a far greater reliance on thinking out the logical implications of teaching various things to various groups of students. For there is no gainsaying the point that what constitutes effective teaching is largely a matter of working out what would count as success in a particular situation (for example, that children should come to be enthusiastic about history, and meticulous and critical in handling evidence, while being given information about what pieces of evidence are relevant to a particular historical problem), and recognizing that such a conception entails some procedures rather than others (*language, learning, research).

REFERENCES

Barrow (1984), Bennett (1976), Biddle and Ellena (1964), Delamont (1983), Dunkin and Biddle (1974), Gage (1972), Good, Biddle and Brophy (1975), Good and Brophy (1978), Heath and Nielsen (1974), Kounin (1970), Sanders (1978, 1981).

Teaching

At first blush, it may seem curious in a dictionary of educational concepts to have only a short entry under teaching. It is, after all, generally supposed to be central to the enterprise, and there is a mass of research extending over many decades into what constitutes effective teaching. The two reasons for none the less keeping this entry brief are: (a) that teaching is not a particularly obscure **concept**; and (b) that the question of what we know about how best to teach is examined under a number of other entries.

1. 'Teaching' is a broad, general term. It is sometimes referred to as a polymorphous ('many-shaped') word, since it may encompass a wide variety of more specific activities such as lecturing, instructing, drilling, eliciting responses, asking questions, testing, providing information, encouraging, and conducting seminars. There is no mystery about what the word means, as there may be with, e.g. '**creativity**', and no conceptual complexity as there is with, e.g. **intelligence**. There is, however, a practical limit to the value of talking about teaching in general, rather than particular aspects or types of teaching, since what is true of teaching in one form may not be true of teaching in another form (*achievement/ task words).

2. For a long time researchers have tried to determine what kinds of teaching are most effective. Under various other headings we discuss a number of approaches to teaching and research into them. In general, it is our view that research in this area has been poorly conducted and cannot claim to have established very much of significance. In particular, we argue: (a) that it is in the nature of things very difficult to conceptualize and observe particular types of teaching in isolation. It is difficult, for example, to conduct research that focuses on instruction while controlling all other aspects of a teaching situation, even supposing that we could produce a coherent conception of instruction that was readily

distinguishable from, for example, **interesting** students, informing them, and eliciting responses; (b) that too often research has failed to take into consideration the question of the relationship between a given teaching style and different contexts and subject matter. Research into, for example, a questioning style of teaching used in sixth-form chemistry classes is surely more plausible than research into questioning techniques in general; (c) that much research has proceeded without any attempt to produce an adequate conception of what would constitute success, effectiveness, quality, etc., in a specifically educational context. A very effective way to teach history might well be to hypnotize students, if effective were to be construed merely as imparting information. But would that count as good history teaching? (***research, teacher effectiveness, aptitude treatment interactions, ethnography, interaction analysis, quantitative/qualitative research, systematic observation**)

It has been suggested (e.g. Coleman, 1966; Schlechty, 1976) that in fact teaching makes very little difference to student achievement, as compared with factors such as home background (***class**). We regard that claim as counter-intuitive, given common-sense observations and experience, and would claim that the research allegedly supporting it is open to the same kinds of criticism as have been made against research into teacher effectiveness generally. It may also be suggested that the unstated premise behind all such research (that a limited number of teaching procedures or external factors are generally causative of student achievement) is highly questionable. Why should it not be the case that a vast number of factors to do with teaching, individual psychology, and wider social context all have a bearing on successful **schooling**, and that many, perhaps all, individual cases are the product of unique combinations of these myriad variables? The more one is inclined to such a view, the more difficult must the task of empirically researching good teaching seem. A more hopeful approach to this issue would involve giving more thought to what would constitute good or successful teaching of X to particular groups of students, and confining **empirical** study to distinguishing between approaches that, while true to the conception of success, conspicuously do and do not succeed in particular cases (***indoctrination, integrated studies, language, learning, microteaching, readiness, team teaching, education, worthwhile**).

REFERENCES

Coleman (1966), Hirst (1974a), Schlechty (1976).

Team teaching

Team teaching became popular in the expansionary years of the 1960s and early 1970s when school systems in Britain, Canada and the United States were bent on providing a wider range of choice in the **curriculum**. It involves several teachers being responsible as a team, not as individuals, for a given number of students. That vague definition masks enormous variation in the size of teams, number of students, range of offerings, and duration of team-taught enterprises. Team teaching was used at all levels of **education**, although it tended to be more informal in elementary schools, and at that level more difficult to distinguish from open-plan schooling. In secondary schools, colleges, and universities, team-teaching patterns usually provided for large-group instruction (in the form of lecture, demonstrations, or guest-speakers), small-group discussions or seminars, individual counselling, and opportunities for student research, field work, or work experience. So popular did team teaching become in some jurisdictions that large-scale alterations were made to existing school buildings, or new schools built entirely on team-teaching principles (with major investments in movable interior walls). As often happens in education, what was greeted enthusiastically in one period was out of favour a decade later. Many of the movable walls introduced with such enthusiasm have not budged for ten or more years.

Many of the arguments supporting team teaching were persuasive in the 1960s, and remain attractive now. Working as a team encourages the allocation of teaching duties according to the academic or pedagogic strength of particular team members. Planned differences in sizes of students' groups (from hundreds in a lecture or demonstration to two or three in a remedial session) accommodate with ease different types of **learning** styles. Team-teaching timetables appear flexible enough to provide for an attractive assortment of field-trips or site-visits, often considered disruptive to conventional schedules. In curricular terms, scheduling of teachers for cross-disciplinary or **integrated** approaches is easier in team-teaching schools than in others. Teachers may benefit from each other's expertise, keep abreast of new developments in subject matter, use visual aids or other equipment more efficiently, and have more time for preparations and consultations, while students may benefit from a wider range of learning experiences and opportunities for individual research and one-to-one discussions with teachers. Team-teaching schedules may also be designed to provide for students with special characteritics, from the **gifted** to the learning disabled. Given such bounties, why did enthusiasm for team teaching wither away?

To some extent, enthusiasts for team teaching underestimated human factors. In some instances, team-teaching schemes were introduced hastily, without enough time for **research**, planning, and preparation. Commitments to those schemes varied among particular team members, the quality of leadership within teams was very uneven, and personalities tended to clash. Some aspects of team teaching (especially large-group instruction) made demands upon both teachers and students that some would not, or could not, satisfy. It was soon discovered that teaching in teams did not produce higher student scores on standardized tests. In addition, some school administrators seemed to view the introduction of team teaching as a means of economizing on the number of teachers required for particular schools.

But more serious flaws in team-teaching patterns (rather like those in open-plan schools) surfaced in the course of their operation. In particular, flexible scheduling and adequate provision of teaching resources perished on the rock of timetabling. Institutional requirements for system and order tended to militate against the essential flexibility demanded by team teaching. Especially at the secondary-school level, those advocating team-teaching approaches failed at times to provide for the specific needs of teachers of different types of subject matter; scheduling requirements for team teaching in French, for example, are not the same as those for physical education.

As these problems multiplied, enthusiasm for team teaching began to decline. What survived the 1970s were many types of local variant, largely small-scale ventures, built upon the notion that special groups of teachers should co-operate to meet particular curricular circumstances – and in many schools they survive to this day, long outliving the educational fad that fathered them (***open education**).

REFERENCES

Bair and Woodward (1964), Barnett (1982), Close (1974), Frankle and Hiley (1980), Geen (1985), Richmond (1967), Rutherford (1979), Seyfarth and Canady (1973), Shaplin and Olds (1964), Tallboy (1973), Warwick (1971).

Technology *see* Deschooling, Programmed learning

Tests *see* Accountability, Assessment, Behavioural objectives, Creativity, Critical thinking, Education, Intelligence, Reliability, Research, Validity

Theory

The word 'theory' derives from the Greek *theoria*, meaning 'speculative thought'. Theory, in this basic sense, thus marks the distinction between the observation of particulars on the one hand, and the attempt to formulate general observations and hence, ultimately, to construct explanatory systems on the other. Straightaway it may be noted that theory cannot be divorced entirely from practical observation: every particular observation is theory laden, if only in that one chooses to classify in one way rather than another. It may also be observed that theory may be productive even when partially mistaken, as was, for example, the case with early Egyptian astronomy, which, despite its errors and deficiencies, served several practical purposes.

Educational theory is very old, having been better developed than a number of other branches of theory by the time of Plato. The question is whether it has advanced very much since that time. (Another view has it that educational theory is relatively young, but that view presupposes that educational theory is, or should be, essentially scientific, and therefore ignores much of the highly sophisticated educational theorizing prior to the end of the nineteenth century.) It is arguable that in broad terms development in educational theory has been similar in kind to, and kept pace with, development in, for example, moral theory and political theory over the centuries. (That is to say particular **concepts** have been more fully explicated, arguments have been tested and stood their ground or found wanting, new circumstances or new insights have given rise to new forms of problem, and a fuller and wider body of understanding has accumulated. It is not to say that we necessarily have established more certainly what we ought to do morally, politically or educationally.) (*ethics)

One major issue within educational theory during the last hundred years has been the extent to which it should be seeking to adopt the form, aspirations, and manners of the natural sciences. Is it appropriate and plausible to seek a body of educational theory parallel to scientific theory? The answer appears to be no. The most obvious characteristics of developed scientific theory are: (a) that it operates with very clearly articulated, unambiguous, central concepts (e.g. physicists do not in the normal run of events have vague or conflicting conceptions of such things as force and atom); (b) that it operates with a generally accredited system of verification (e.g. physicists do not generally dispute the appropriateness of observation and controlled experiment to establish some things, axiomatic reasoning to establish others, etc.); and (c) that there are relatively few problems about ends (e.g. there is not often dispute about what constitutes 'working', 'success', or 'truth', in relation to specific problems in physics). Medical theory may be cited as an instance of a less secure but none the less plausibly scientific theory: there is room for dispute about ends (e.g. what counts as a healthy state, especially mental health?), there is argument about whether particular pieces of research have truly established what they claim and, in particular, about the appropriateness of certain styles of research to particular problems (e.g. has it been established that butter is bad for us, or hasn't it? is the research behind psychoanalytic theory well grounded?), and some crucial concepts are complex and contentious (e.g. depression). None the less, despite these grey areas, we may be inclined to say that anyone who would be a doctor would be well advised to study and master the body of medical theory, and that practice should be directed by that theory.

But educational theory has severe shortcomings on all three counts:

1. Its ends are far from clearly articulated, and to a certain extent hotly and legitimately debated. For example, it is not clear what is involved in the '**education**', '**creativity**' 'individual growth' 'critical thinking' '**socialization**', etc., that various educators call for at one time or another, and, when it is clear, it is often the case that while one person thinks education is important, another thinks that it is not, that one person values the development of **autonomy** over socialization, another vice versa, etc.

2. It has no specific methodology, since it involves a combination of various different types of claim, each requiring examination in a different kind of way (e.g. there are evaluative questions, conceptual questions, questions of observable fact, empirical questions the answers to which are not readily observable, etc.); in some crucial cases the appropriateness of types of verification may be called into question (*__teacher effectiveness, critical thinking__).

3. Its central concepts are not clearly articulated (and, indeed, as we have noted, there is not even agreement on what they should be in name): education might be agreed by some to be essentially about developing **understanding**, good teachers, effective schools, and **worthwhile learning** – but what such things actually are, let alone how one can recognize or aim at them, are matters on which educators have not come to any clear agreement. For these reasons the idea of an educational expert, comparable even to a medical expert, let alone an expert in physics, is suspect.

It seems to us a simple, but exceedingly damaging, mistake to think that the problems in educational theory can be solved by making it a species of scientific theory (and, correspondingly, to attribute all confusion, ignorance, and absurdity to the youthful state of educational theory as a science). In our view, educational theory has not been treated as a branch of scientific theory during most of its history, for the very good reason that it should not be. Educational questions and issues cannot yet (if ever) be reduced to means–end questions that are amenable to **empirical research**. There are questions of value and conceptual coherence to be examined (broadly, philosophical questions); there are questions that lie in the domains of psychology and sociology, both of which are themselves far from clearly articulated disciplines, to be examined; there are ideas and insights to be gained from the historical and comparative study of education. An educational theorist needs ideally to be adept in at least those four subject areas (***facts**).

REFERENCES
Barrow (1981a), Dearden (1984), Hirst (1973), Tibble (1971).

Theory and practice

Given what **theory** is (essentially, understanding of the principles governing practice), it is necessarily the case that theory and practice are interrelated, and those who claim to see themselves as practitioners who have no need of theory are missing the point. (No doubt they have been misled by such colloquialisms as 'it's all right in theory, but not in practice'; but, in so far as theory does not match up to reality in practice, it is poor theory.) Certainly, it is possible to be a good theoretician but a bad practitioner, and vice versa, whether in medicine, law, or teaching, no less than in engineering or sailing. The fact remains that good medical practice, legal practice, teaching, bridge-building, and sailing are so inasmuch as they exemplify the theory behind them. The theory articulates the principles and criteria whereby success is judged, and therefore it is necessary to any understanding, **evaluation**, or attempt to improve practice.

It is probably fair to say that large portions of educational theorizing are for one reason or another very poor; that helps to foster the falsehood that theory is irrelevant to practice, since many sensible practising teachers would indeed be better off without the poor theory offered to them. None the less it remains an inescapable truth that in so far as we want to explain, criticize, evaluate and improve educational practice, we have to sift through the theoretical work, hoping that in time we may produce a coherent body of educational theory that ranks at least with medical or legal theory in terms of certitude (***autonomy, communication, practical principles**).

Thinking *see* Accountability, Critical thinking, Language, Lateral thinking, Transference, Understanding

Topic-centred education

This rather cumbersome phrase is not particularly widely used. The idea of organizing the **curriculum** around topics, however, as distinct from **subjects, disciplines,** or forms of **knowledge** does have long-standing and strong appeal. Many elementary curricula are conceived in terms of problems, issues, and topics to be explored, rather than distinct subjects to be mastered (and **aims**/objectives are often couched in terms of developing **generic skills** rather than in terms of competence in particular discrete branches of study). While the secondary school curriculum in most jurisdictions continues to be based upon subject divisions (notwithstanding the movement towards **integrated studies** in the late 1960s and early 1970s), certain topics of a multidisciplinary nature have become increasingly popular, and are regularly championed as equally deserving of curriculum time as well-tried subjects such as **history**, science, and English. Prominent amongst them are: peace education, women's studies, ecological education, and global education.

Particular topics may be worth introducing to the curriculum for a wide variety of reasons (such as their relative educational value, the resources of the school, and the extent to which they would otherwise be examined by students). But the first question to be raised about the idea of introducing a topic-based approach to curriculum is what kind of argument is being introduced? Is the claim an **empirical** one, to the effect that students will be better able to think intelligently about ecological matters or the role and status of women, if they study these topics directly, than they would if they considered such matters in the light of an **understanding** of history, **literature**, science, etc? Is there, by contrast, an implied epistemological claim, to the effect that conventional subject divisions are arbitrary or, worse, incorrectly drawn – perhaps even that knowledge is a 'seamless whole'? Or is the argument primarily one of administrative convenience or organizational rationalization? Granted that we want students to become reasonable and informed in their consideration of matters to do with peace, women, ecology, and international relations (which presumbly none would deny), why is it concluded that the proper response is to include such topics as subjects in their own right in the curriculum?

Most of the traditional curriculum subjects, notwithstanding important differences between them, are based upon a distinctive mode of inquiry of one sort or another: science is defined largely in terms of the manner of scientific inquiry; history, less tidily but none the less truly, is defined largely in terms of exploring the past by a limited set of recognized procedures; mathematics is the study of a unique type of procedure; English is largely based upon coming to grips with a certain kind of medium (in general terms, the written **language**, more specifically with species of the genre such as poetry and fiction). There is, in other words, a clear commitment to the notion that **education** does not primarily seek to study and solve particular problems (e.g. how are we to cure cancer, is free trade a good thing, is *Wuthering Heights* a good novel?), so much as to provide a broad range of information and to develop a sustained grip on certain key types of inquiry; drawing on this, individuals will be able to cope rationally and intelligently with particular issues as and when they arise. On what grounds is it proposed that we should now depart from this practice and select certain particular issues for close study?

Part of the answer is that these and similar topics are perceived as being of great and urgent social importance. Children ought to study peace and views on the role and status of women because these things matter and all is far from well and secure in respect of them. But the more one considers this prima facie common-sense argument, the more peculiar and unconvincing it seems.

In the first place, the claim that these (or any other) topics are of considerable importance is far from self-evident and is in fact directly disputed by many. For example, some would question the educational importance of women's studies or global education.

Secondly, there is too little clarity about what precisely might be being proposed in any given instance to make it possible to give a reasoned response to the claim that a certain topic ought to be studied. What, for example, are we being asked to decide upon, when women's studies are proposed as a curriculum subject? Similarly, what precisely is meant by peace education or global education? Does the plea for ecological education refer to providing scientific information relating to ecology, and philosophical insights into our obligations to each other and to future generations, in a dispassionate manner, or are we referring to the presentation of a particular point of view concerning ecology? If the latter, we obviously need to be very careful that we do not drift into **indoctrination**. Beyond these general concerns about the nature of what is being proposed, lie more complex, more difficult, and no less important conceptual problems: what, for example, is peace?

Thirdly, even if we knew precisely what we were talking about in a given case and agreed on the social importance of the issues, it would not follow that the topic should necessarily be studied in the school curriculum. For social importance is not identical with educational importance. It is of great social importance that individuals should drive carefully and that they should respect democratic procedures. But it does not follow that educating people has anything to do with teaching them to drive, or that the school should instil and enforce respect for democracy. On the contrary, the former would constitute skill-training that a school might provide, but which is none the less non-educational, and the latter would be positively anti-educational. Conversely, there are things that schools necessarily should do in the **interests** of education, that have no immediate direct social importance. For example, schools should teach students history, because without such understanding they will be imperfectly educated; but, none the less, my neighbour will not necessarily be a worse citizen for being ignorant of history.

If we were convinced that a particular topic needed to be studied in schools, we would still be left with the question of the best way to proceed. Granted that issues of war and peace need to be considered, is this best done by introducing peace studies into the curriculum, or by teaching certain existing subjects in ways that include clear reference to the topic? To some extent, the answer to this question may depend upon one's particular aims: what heightens awareness, for example, does not necessarily sharpen perception, and vice versa. If our aim is primarily to get students into the frame of mind that leads them to join Greenpeace or the women at Greenham Common, we should probably insist on teaching ecology and peace (and women's) studies as such. But this consideration in turn raises the question of whether some objectives are not inappropriate in an educational context. It is not legitimate to seek to advance particular **ideological** stances in the name of education. It might be argued that while it would be wrong to indoctrinate, it is none the less reasonable to intend that students should come to be moved to appropriate action in the light of barely disputed truths. Thus, it may be said, there are certain facts about what we are doing to the environment that in themselves ought to lead right-minded persons to seek to change the nature of what we are doing. But, it may be concluded, the only way to get people to take the issue seriously is to treat the topic as a subject in its own right. Perhaps there is some truth in this empirical claim that would warrant investigation. (It cannot be entirely true as it stands, since the obviously deeply concerned advocates of this view are witness against it, being invariably the products of an educational system that did not teach the topic as a subject in its own right.)

Whichever way one approaches such topics, it is surely clear that at the end of the day informed opinion upon matters to do with peace, women, ecology, etc., is dependent upon a broad base of information and the capacity both to sift and analyse individual pieces of information and to organize and evaluate the whole. Putting it more graphically, if you do not have a great deal of historical understanding (about women, about peace and war, about man's relationship with the environment), if you do not have a good grasp of contemporary science, if you do not have access to the cumulative wisdom on these topics enshrined in literature, then it does not matter how closely you have concentrated on some contemporary issue, you will not be able to do it justice. Superficially therefore the problem disappears as six of one and half a dozen of the other: either we teach the traditional subjects (drawing attention to the topics in question as appropriate), and thereby enable the student to arrive at an informed position on the topic; or we teach the topic and in doing so introduce the historical background, the scientific understanding, the literary contribution. But while in the abstract this makes sense, it is difficult not to conclude that on balance the former way is preferable. The danger of the topic-centred approach (even when it is not indoctrinatory or partial) is that the student does not develop historical, scientific, literary understanding as such – elements which are essential both to education and to developing rational understanding. The corresponding danger of the traditional subject-centred approach is that students may leave school capable in principle of a rational response to, e.g. ecological issues, but without a strong body of information on the subject and without a heightened awareness relating to it. But perhaps one may conclude by observing again that this is less of an educational problem than a social one. If society wants to turn our attention to, e.g. ecological problems, it can (and does), e.g. by means of the **mass media**. The school's role is primarily to educate people, so that they can respond intelligently to different social problems as and when they arise.

Training

To train a person is to provide them with know-how or the ability to perform certain actions. Training may take place in respect of intellectual matters (e.g. one may train a person to conduct **research** in a particular way) as well as physical matters, but it is probably more common to talk of it in the latter context (e.g. trained mechanic, trained chef, trained clerk). We may distinguish between training somebody to do something specific, training them in a **skill** (e.g. training them to strip automobile engines) and training them as something such as a clerk, mechanic, or researcher. In every case the key characteristic of the trained individual is that he has the ability to carry out some operation, but he lacks the **theoretical** understanding that lies behind it. Once such understanding is added we move from the merely trained state towards that of being educated. These are both **degree** words: few people, if any, are simply trained mechanics or trained nurses, and few are fully educated. In practice, we should distinguish between the automatic performance of operations (the mark of the trained person), and the understanding of operations, with or without skill in performance (a sign of the educated person). The distinction should not be taken to imply either lack of connection between the two or lack of value in training. Training may be of great value in its own right in some contexts, and a necessary preliminary to **education** in others. Children have to be trained to read and write, for example, before any education worth noting is likely to take place in our **culture** (**moral education, sex education*).

REFERENCE

Peters (1966).

Transference

What is usually referred to as 'transference' is misleadingly so termed. It would be more accurate to talk of certain things being 'common to' various different activities or operations than to talk of them being transferred. Concern for truth, for example, and the ability to count to ten are not well thought of as capacities (or **skills**) that we possess and transfer from one sphere of operations to another; rather, they are capacities we have, that have relevance to a wide variety of settings. If one can count, one can count, and there is no obvious sense in wondering whether one will be able to 'transfer' the ability to count displayed in the supermarket yesterday, to the question of pocket-money before us today. Of course one can 'transfer' the ability, since it is an ability one has that happens to be common to both operations. (Whether one recognizes that, whether one is disposed to counting in a new setting, etc., are quite different questions, though it seems likely that some 'transference' talk has arisen out of a failure to distinguish the ability to do something from such things as the desire to do it and recognition of the need to do it.)

Talk of 'transference' also tends to lead to **reification**. For, if one talks of transferring the skill of, e.g. analysing from one context to another, one suggests that there is some discernible operation that may be set in motion in a variety of contexts, as a chain-saw may be used to cut the dining-room table or the garage. But **analysing**, and many so-called skills, are not identifiable entities that can be meaningfully referred to in the abstract and set going wherever required: one may be skilled at historical analysis and nothing else, for example. The ability to analyse must always be context bound (i.e. one can analyse historical data, country and western songs, chemical data, or indeed everything, so long as there is something specified); and if it is broken down into various elements (such as concerns for pattern and coherence, and the ability to understand that if A is B and all Bs are C, then A is C) those elements do not have to be 'transferred': for, if one has the disposition and the understanding, one has them, and they may in principle be displayed in any appropriate context.

What may inhibit a display of, for example, logical understanding, is an unfamiliarity with a new context. Thus, anybody who appreciates that if A is B and all Bs are C, then A is C, should appreciate that the argument that George Jones is a 'possum', on the grounds that all persons who fail to show up are nicknamed 'possum' and George Jones frequently fails to show up, is sound. But if one has never heard of George Jones, knows nothing about country and western music, and is unfamiliar with the word 'possum', one is unlikely to see the logic. It will be noted that even in this very simple example (compare switching from nuclear physics to the finer points of morality), it is not a question of whether the ability to understand a point of logic can be transferred, but whether a new context is sufficiently well understood to allow the point of logic to be recognized. The point of logic itself is simply common to many examples.

The above suggests that some of the assumptions behind **empirical research** into transfer of training have been seriously confused. It is clear, for example, that looking to see whether a mind trained to think logically in the study of biology can transfer that logical ability to the sphere of **literature** is absurd. It cannot be expected to proceed logically in the latter context, until it has studied the subject sufficiently to be adept in recognizing the distinctive form that the formal points of logic take there. On the other hand, it must be the case that skills (e.g. using a library index, reading, typewriting), understanding points of logic, and dispositional features (e.g. love of precision), that are common to a variety of pursuits, can be made use of in different contexts, provided that the context is understood. Therefore, whether, e.g. courses in logic improve **critical thinking** would seem to be a question that cannot meaningfully be researched empirically by concentrating on critical thinking courses alone. Practice on logical exercises may or may not make one better able to perform such exercises, but it cannot in itself enable one to be logical in various specific contexts. Conversely, the increased capacity to proceed logically in historical or scientific reasoning incorporates points of formal logic along with contextual understanding. To establish that critical thinking courses do (or do not) make a material difference, it would be necessary to monitor a large number of, e.g. critical historians, some of whom take part in critical thinking courses and some of whom do not, and to examine whether there is any **correlation** between doing the course and being a better historian (*****generic fallacy, learning**).

U

Understanding

Understanding is one of the crucial **concepts** in education – one of the select band of organizing concepts that help to define the enterprise, comparable in this respect to concepts such as God, prayer and sin in religion, or beauty, harmony and form in aesthetics. For **education** is essentially about the achievement of understanding; whether we think of formal or informal education, self-education, education through experience or through deliberate teaching, education as purveyed in schools or through life, etc., the idea that someone might be educated to the extent that he lacks understanding is scarcely tenable. Yet, curiously, the concept of understanding has not received much direct attention from philosophers, nor often been the chosen focus of study for psychologists.

Knowledge and **learning**, rather than understanding, have attracted the attention. This may be a matter of some concern. In the first place the connotations of 'knowledge' and 'understanding' are rather different. The former may suggest the acquisition or possession of information in an inert form. While the latter necessarily implies that the information in question is imbibed in such a way that it cannot lie inert. Secondly, by concentrating on knowledge and learning we have to some extent kept the two distinct: while philosophers consider the nature of knowledge in the abstract, psychologists study the mechanics of learning, without paying much attention to what is being learned. But what is of prime interest to us as educators is precisely the experience or act of understanding that encompasses both the agent and the subject matter. Our minimal aim is to promote understanding, i.e. to ensure that students fully comprehend, grasp, or perceive the nature, character or function of the subject matter. (What it is that is to be fully comprehended may change with different students. For example, historical understanding in nine-year-olds may be conceived of in terms of the acquisition of information about dates and events, while in the case of older students it would include the ability to put pattern on, and to see the significance of, events.)

One may understand another person in the sense of comprehending what they are saying or doing. One may understand that person in the sense of feeling rapport or being in sympathy with him. One may understand how to do something, either in the sense of having understanding of the principles that lie behind appropriate actions, or in the restricted sense of knowing what to do to achieve something. But the understanding that education is primarily concerned with is 'understanding that such and such', or propositional understanding, for it is propositions that enshrine our explanations, perceptions, and interpretations of the world.

The question therefore arises as to what we want children to understand, since they clearly cannot be expected to understand everything. Does it perhaps not matter what they come to understand, provided that they continue to enlarge their understanding? Such a view, though it has been put forward seriously from time to time in one guise or another, seems plainly untenable. Understanding may be of trivial or even vicious matters. An individual who acquires a more and more sophisticated understanding of ways in which to humiliate and hurt people, or an increasingly complex understanding of the finer points of matchbox collecting, is scarcely to be considered well educated. (More to the point, whatever he is called, he would not be representative of what we hope to achieve in **schools**.) But then how are we to determine what subject matter should ideally be understood?

Since we do not think that education should become a trivial or immoral business, we need first to differentiate amongst various potential subjects on those grounds. Secondly, in so far as it is education we are concerned with, we should distinguish between those subject matters understanding of which contributes to developing breadth of mind, and those where that is not so. (Schools have other purposes besides providing education, and those other purposes may also guide us towards selection of particular subject matter.) But, finally, the decision as to whether children should study, e.g., soccer, politics, nineteenth-century poetry, mathematics, or frogs, has to be made by reference to economy and logic. Expending energy on teaching certain things would be more unnecessary, and hence more wasteful, than expending energy on others; and certain types of subject matter have considerably greater illuminative power than others.

For example, to understand the game of soccer is not very difficult for most people, given that they already have some understanding of **competitive** team ball games, and that new concepts (e.g. offside, indirect free-kick, sweeper), though they may have unusual names, can be explained fairly easily in language that is already familiar. The principle is no different with, for example, physics; but explaining such concepts as atom, force, and pressure, is likely to take longer and to require more patient and subtle elaboration. When we add that coming to understand certain subject matters, such as physics, moral philosophy, **history** or mathematics gives one powerful means to increase one's understanding of the world, because they not only incorporate a method for acquiring further understanding but also focus on important subject matters, it seems reasonable to conclude that such subjects should have a priority in the school **curriculum**. It is not that there is anything inherently unworthy or unrespectable about understanding all there is to know about soccer; but it is less mind-broadening than understanding physics (***aesthetic value, art education, ethics, language, moral education, normative**).

REFERENCES

Barrow and Woods (1982), Cooper (1983), Hamlyn (1978).

Universalizability *see* Ethics, Moral education

Useful *see* Relevance, Utilitarian

Utilitarian

It is important to distinguish two senses of this word: (a) of utility, i.e. being of practical use; (b) pertaining to, conforming to, or in line with utilitarianism, conceived of as the doctrine that the rightness of any action lies in its propensity to maximize happiness.

The first sense is (unfortunately) the one usually intended by journalists and politicians when they call for **schooling** to be more utilitarian, or for the **curriculum** to have more utility. Furthermore, it is common for people to interpret usefulness by reference to economic considerations. 'A utilitarian curriculum' in this sense would usually be a curriculum that caters to the industrial and economic demands of society.

What a utilitarian curriculum in the second sense would be is not very clear. Nor, despite the fact that happiness was cited as a prime educational goal by a large number of teachers in a survey in Britain (Ashton, Kneen, Davies and Holley, 1975), is it immediately obvious that utilitarianism has got a great deal to do specifically with **education**. None the less, it has been argued that an essentially **liberal** arts curriculum is justified on the grounds that it is reasonable to suppose that it would contribute more than alternatives to leading people to care for the happiness of others, and to enabling them to some extent to be masters of their own happiness and to contribute to that of society as a whole. It should be added that this thesis is specifically argued within the context of a democratic state, and that it leans heavily on a conception of happiness as having 'a sense of enmeshment with one's world' (Barrow, 1980) (*aesthetic value, ethics).

REFERENCES

Ashton, Kneen, Davies and Holley (1975), Barrow (1976a, 1980).

V

Validity

'Validity', when used as a technical term in reference to tests or research schedules, is closely associated with '**reliability**' and '**objectivity**' in their technical senses. Like 'reliability', 'validity' is a word that may confuse, because it has a broad everyday sense as well as the narrower technical sense. In everyday terms an argument is valid, if it is correct (logically sound, coherent, etc.). In keeping with this usage, reference to the over-all validity of a test or set of tests may be a judgement of the degree to which evidence and theory support the adequacy and appropriateness of inferences based on test information. As such it is an issue to be reasoned about rather than demonstrated empirically or statistically. But more common in research are references to various sources of evidence that may bear on the validity of our inferences, such as construct and content. Thus we have measures of content validity, where the concern is to check the extent to which the testing procedure covers or matches the field or domain in question. (For example, a test for a social studies course would have high content validity, in so far as it matched the range of the course content.) Criterion validity (also known as predictive validity) is the phrase used to refer to **correlation** between prognostic test scores and subsequent measures of success. (For example, a test designed to select students for admission to a philosophy programme has high criterion validity, in so far as high scores on the test correlate with high scores on some subsequent test of philosophical competence.) Construct validity, perhaps one of the most important considerations, refers to the quality of a test so far as actually testing what it claims to test goes. (For example, a test of IQ has high construct validity in so far as it does indeed test IQ. Note that in practice this usually means in so far as it correlates with accepted IQ tests. There is thus a danger of circularity in establishing construct validity.)

Concern for validity is, then, essentially concern for whether tests are suited to their task. It is important that a test should have high validity ratings as well as high reliability ratings, since it could have high reliability (i.e. produce consistent results under various different conditions), but none the less be invalid, because it is not in fact testing what it is supposed to test. For example, one can imagine a multiple-choice exam in a philosophy course that would have high reliability, but poor construct validity and poor content validity, since the manner of testing bears little relation to the nature of a philosophy course and one's assumptions about what it is to be a competent philosopher. Again, if one wanted to test students' response to a complete programme, it would presumably be wiser to adopt some form of examination rather than a single extended essay question, since the latter would be likely to have relatively low content validity.

It is evident that we must desire tests to have high validity. What is not so clear is whether in fact many educational tests have it, and, more particularly, whether the ways in which validity is measured are reliable (in the everyday sense) or adequate. We have already seen, for example, that the fact that a new IQ test has high construct validity only means that its results correlate well with the results of accepted tests such as, e.g. Stanford-Binet. But where is the critical probing and questioning of whether Stanford-Binet should be treated so reverentially? Where is the evidence that it is a good test and a desirable model? The answer to that, of course, lies in prior claims to the effect that the Stanford-Binet IQ test has high construct validity. But one may reasonably raise the question: are we satisfied that the way in which accepted IQ tests have been given high validity ratings truly establishes that they are good tests of what they seek to test? (As with 'reliability', in using 'validity' in its technical sense, we must dispense with connotations that derive from the ordinary-language use of the word: in normal discourse validity is a matter of logical coherence, and a valid argument is in itself a good one. But a technically valid test is not necessarily a good one. Quite apart from the fact that it may be marred by a lack of reliability, or by having validity only in a limited number of respects, even a test that does test what it intends to test, tests it fully, does so regardless of who is marking it, or when, etc., may be objected to, on the grounds that what it is testing is not worth testing or not what it claims to be testing. For example, a creativity test may have high construct validity on its own terms, but none the less not test true creativity.)

The majority of educational tests claim indirect validity rather than direct validity. They do not directly test what they wish to know about, as a driving test or an eyesight test does. Rather they test various performances or achievements which are believed to be indicative of that which is of real interest. For example, one does not directly test the creative act, one tests the ability to think of uses for a brick or to devise suitable titles for short stories, in the belief that such abilities betoken creativity. Sometimes connection between performance on the items of a test and whatever the test is indirectly concerned with may be severely questioned. Many have argued that performance on IQ tests cannot be regarded as having indirect validity as a measure of **intelligence**, since nobody has convincingly established a relationship between the **concept** of intelligence and performing on the test items. Hence some are content to say only that IQ tests test what they test.

The main problems with measuring validity is that, for all the statistical devices for computing scores, the rules of procedure, and the specialist vocabulary, estimating validity is at rock bottom a matter of judgement, and not a matter of observation and **measurement**. Some tests that do have high validity in various respects according to their authors, do not deserve those scores, since the conceptualization of the authors has been poor. For example, the question of whether an IQ test has indirect validity depends for its answer both on evidence of correlation between test performance and intelligence, and on an adequate conceptualization of intelligence. Similarly, claims about the predictive validity of tests cannot be based simply on observation; they depend crucially on somebody's view of what counts as achievement. (One should also note that so many and various are the factors that may affect individual performance that it is extremely difficult to be satisfied that a test really has been shown to have predictive validity: a test that is a very good test for predicting future counsellors might seem to fail to make sound predictions for countless reasons, and, similarly, a test that is in fact poor might seem to be quite good, thanks to a variety of chance and irrelevant circumstances, not least that it lends impetus to its own predictions by the fact of making them.)

Tests are typically only checked for ratings in respect of certain particular reliability and validity measures, and only on a small scale at that, while the conceptual work and the element of judgement involved are poorly executed. The serious practical problem that this leads to is that we have a great many tests which are said to have high reliability and high validity, and in some sense may in fact have so (at any rate they have been honestly calculated to have so), but which may none the less be thoroughly bad, silly, or useless tests. And short of a thorough examination of each test, the research behind it and the main concepts in question, there is no way that we can form a reasonable view as to which are to be trusted and which not. We certainly cannot take a high validity score as any kind of indication of the worth of a test (*creativity, developmental theory, research**).

Value judgements

It is an axiom of moral philosophy that one cannot derive ought from is. The mere fact that something is the case cannot establish that it should be. Although, therefore, empirical **facts** may have considerable bearing on whether something is right, valuable or **worthwhile** (e.g. in assessing the moral rightness of an act it may be relevant to know that it led to a great deal of misery), establishing whether it is, is ultimately not an **empirical** issue. Whether a particular **curriculum** is worthwhile, for example, cannot finally be decided by any process of observation.

This has led some to take the view that value judgements are **subjective, relative**, or simply a matter of opinion, arbitrary belief, or preference. Whatever truth there may be in such claims, it is clear that value judgements in any sphere can to some extent be reasoned about, and that there are limits to what may sensibly be claimed. These limits are set by the nature of the activity in question. Thus, however much opinion may differ amongst mountaineers on the finer distinctions between first-rate mountaineers, it is clear that certain clear criteria have to be met for it to make sense to suggest that an individual is a good mountaineer. If it were to be suggested that I, who suffer from vertigo, have never climbed a mountain, have weak ankles, and would not recognize a crampon if offered one, am a good mountaineer, this should not be described as subjectively true or a matter of opinion. It would be objectively false. It is true that many activities are more complex and less well understood than mountaineering. But even though the nature of, for example, morality and art are less clear cut than the nature of mountaineering, the fact remains that value judgements in these areas have to conform to some rules (again, derived from understanding the nature of the enterprise), and it is not the case that an individual is entitled to any opinion.

Value judgements in the sphere of **education**, or any other part of **schooling**, therefore have to be constrained by the limits of what education, **socialization**, etc., actually are. A teacher who manages to get children to learn something false, to learn something trivial by rote, or to learn something of value by threat and intimidation, may be said to be a poor teacher; for each of these, in different ways, is at variance with the nature of education. In a nutshell, a clear understanding of the various proper functions of schooling is necessary for making clear and reasonable judgements in that area, and sufficient to establish that many such judgements are clearly true or false.

This fundamental observation has repercussions for a number of other issues. It suggests that **values clarification** exercises, in so far as they tend to examine problems detached from any clear domain, may ignore the crucial elements of value judgements. It explains why such things as **needs** assessment, or research into **teacher effectiveness**, have a problem when they proceed without clear delineation of the nature of the enterprise. It also has a direct bearing on **aesthetic** and **moral education** (*culture, essentially contested concepts, ethics, language, objectivity**).

REFERENCES

Barrow (1975), Sloan (1980).

Values clarification

During the 1960s and 1970s, when anti-traditionalist and anti-authoritarian feelings were common, teachers were provided with new curricular materials to assist them in discussing values and morals in their courses. Several projects were undertaken, including those led by Lawrence Kohlberg and Donald Oliver in the United States, Peter McPhail and John Wilson in England, and Clive Beck in Canada, each of which purported to explore a variety of theories and approaches to moral development. Important discussions took place among these scholars about the nature of values and **moral education**, and about the characteristics of materials designed to help children make or justify moral judgements. Given the sensitive nature of the subject matter and the vested interests that others in the community had in the same endeavour, it is hardly surprising that the publications of these **research** efforts, provoked wide interest and a certain amount of controversy.

Few projects, however, aroused more bitterness and personal invective than values clarification. This term achieved prominence following the publication of *Values and Teaching*, by Louis Raths, Merrill Harmin and Sidney Simon (1966), and became very popular among teachers and administrators when a succession of practical classroom guides (of which Sidney Simon was the principal author) appeared almost annually in the educational market-place. The arguments that arose about the nature and worth of values clarification procedures were of classic (and instructive) proportions: on the one side were arrayed well-meaning and dedicated theorists who developed very practical methodologies, and on the other side, philosophers and curricular theorists who demanded more than a visible result in the classroom as a criterion for assessing the **worth** of an **educational** idea.

Simon and his colleagues were worried by the failure of school systems to provide the assistance students needed in considering and resolving personal difficulties that they were experiencing at critical periods in their development. Young people, the authors argued, are frequently so puzzled, uncertain, flighty, or apathetic, while they are undergoing rapid physical, emotional, and intellectual change, that they are unable to make choices or decisions with any degree of certainty or wisdom. Such traditional means of rendering assistance as providing rules, dogma, and heroic examples had not been very successful; what was required was a fresh approach that would show students how to identify values, consider alternatives, make personal choices, and act upon those choices. An emphasis on choosing and acting became an important tenet in values clarification **theory and practice**.

The central ideas and methodology of values clarification are simple – often deceptively so. The process of valuing is defined in terms of seven steps that include choosing, prizing, and acting; it is the teacher's function to encourage students to follow these steps in clarifying their own positions on a wide range of value questions (e.g. is reading a book preferable to going to the movies?) and moral questions (e.g. is stealing right or wrong?). To encourage students to consider alternative positions on important value and moral questions, a wide range of exercises, or strategies, was offered for teacher use, including rank ordering (e.g. personal choices about kinds of entertainment), public interview (e.g. about family experiences), either/or forced choices (e.g. about personal charcteristics), or role-playing exercises (e.g. considering which characters should be thrown over the side of a life-raft to save others), most of which may be adapted to a variety of age-levels and **disciplines**. By means of these exercises, students were expected to examine alternative positions on issues considered important and **relevant**, make their personal decisions on those issues, and then act on those decisions.

The success of such strategies, it was claimed, required a particular style of **teaching**. The teacher was to avoid making any statements that might be read as **indoctrinatory**, preaching, or even suggestive of a particular position. Given the purpose of the undertaking (to encourage students to consider choices, and act upon those choices), Simon and his colleagues argued that teachers should not intervene in the process of selecting choices, but should provide a discussion climate in which students might come to their own decisions. This notion that it is the teacher's job to focus upon the process of valuing, but remain **neutral** as to alternative values or moral positions, became a major point of disagreement between Simon and his associates, and their critics.

The fact that values clarification ideas and techniques were widely adopted is a factor to be considered in the debates that took place on their worth. There can be no doubting the popularity of values clarification exercises among teachers; carefully designed to be easily adapted to classroom use at almost every grade level, copies of Simon's 'handbooks' have sold in their hundreds of thousands. Values clarification techniques were given official cachet by principals and superintendents in many schools, and recommended in the curriculum guidelines of a great many provincial and state ministries or departments of education in such countries as the United States, Australia, and Canada.

Why, then, object to values clarification? The subject matter of the exercises appears important, relevant to student concerns, and open to expression of diverse opinions; students seem willing to participate in the exercises and to enjoy their experiences; teachers find that the strategies are a refreshing change from traditional classroom practices, and appear to work very well with many types of students. Why criticize such an approach?

Firm answers to that question are not difficult to find. Empirical psychologists, philosophers, curriculum specialists, and members of the public have found the suggestions put forward by Simon and his associates to be wanting in a number of important respects, ranging from some of the effects observed in classrooms, to profound issues concerning the nature of value judgements in various fields. First, several observers (especially teachers) have found that values clarification exercises fail to sustain **interest**. In some classrooms in which the technique was greeted with enthusiasm at first, the level of interest dropped rapidly when it became clear that discussions did not lead to any form of conclusion or resolution. For how long, it was argued, will students rest content with simply clarifying their own values? Secondly, many observers (especially, in this case, those outside education) pointed to the frequency with which values clarification exercises led to invasion of students' privacy. Despite the protective devices offered in the exercises (in particular, an invitation to refuse to participate), many students found themselves placed in a position in which they were required to reveal very personal (and highly charged) **emotions**, to examine publicly intimate details of their family life, or to discuss their relationships with their peers of both sexes. Some observers have expressed alarm about the introduction of what appears to be a disguised form of client-centred therapeutic methodology. Thirdly, it has been argued that some of the exercises are so inappropriate for certain groups of students that they are likely to cause severe embarrassment, or even psychological damage, to the participants. The life-raft exercise, for example, in which students, role-playing a wide range of persons trapped on an overloaded raft, are required to decide those who will survive and those who will be tossed overboard, may affect dramatically the feelings of self-worth of sensitive youngsters. Other exercises call for expressing views on personal sexual habits that students may not be mature enough even to consider. In general, then, there is room for concern about values clarification exercises even if the theory behind them is accepted.

But such acceptance cannot be taken for granted. The major charge against values clarification is that its basic principles are wanting. In the first place, Simon and his associates have been accused of confusing, or failing to distinguish between, values in general and morals in particular: deciding whether to have ice-cream or jelly for dessert is not just less significant, it is of a different logical order from deciding whether or not one ought to steal. Secondly, critics of values clarification approaches argue that too great an emphasis appears to be placed on expressing views on issues, as opposed to investigating them in a rigorous manner. How can a student be justified in taking a stand on euthanasia, for example, without some grasp of the **facts** and arguments that lie behind such an issue? Merely selecting, clarifying, and perhaps acting on value or moral positions cannot be construed as a means of making sound judgements. The relative merit of competing moral claims in particular circumstances must be considered; yet that is a task to which the values clarification technique, almost by definition, does not address itself. In short, by stressing (and over-stressing) the importance of coming to a personal decision about values, and by denying the opportunity for critical intervention by the teacher, Simon and associates appear to condone some of the worst forms of **subjectivism** and **ethical relativism**. As a consequence, students will be left with the notion that moral judgements are simply expressions of personal points of view. Teachers, meanwhile, are placed in the awkward position of being expected to accept all points of view, and to refrain from encouraging critical consideration of those situations in which values conflict. To this important charge, Simon and associates have not offered a convincing rebuttal.

The standard of debate surrounding values clarification exercises has unfortunately declined on occasion into personal invective. Some opponents of values clarification hide their own dogmatic or indoctrinatory intentions in a cloud of critical – and sanctimonious – platitudes. But the adverse criticism has struck home: the licence to introduce values clarification exercises, so freely available only a few years ago, has now been trimmed (or revoked) in many educational jurisdictions.

REFERENCES

Beck (1971), Fraenkel (1977), Gow (1980), Harmin, Kirschenbaum and Simon (1973), Kazepides (1977), Kirschenbaum (1977), Kohlberg (1966), Lockwood (1975, 1977a, 1977b), McPhail, Ungoed-Thomas and Chapman (1972), Oliver and Shaver (1966), Partington (1984), Purpel and Ryan (1976), Raths, Harmin and Simon (1966), Simon (1974), Simon and Clark (1975), Simon and deSherbinin (1975), Simon, Howe and Kirschenbaum (1972), Stewart (1975), Suttle (1982), Wagner (1981), Wilson (1973b).

Viable

As applied to ideas (its other point of application is living organisms; e.g. a viable foetus is one that will survive outside the uterus) 'viable' means 'workable' or 'feasible'. For example, a viable plan is a possible plan. (It is not necessarily a particularly good one, except in the sense that it will work.) A viable project is a project that can be carried out. There is a depressing tendency for some to describe curriculum subjects, etc., as viable, when they mean something like 'in vogue', 'all the rage', or 'popular'. For example, business studies may be described as more viable than Russian. (Presumably the reasoning behind this would be: business studies, being more popular, fashionable, etc., than Russian, is likely to prove a more successful course; it is therefore particularly feasible.) (*relevance)

Visual literacy

Another extension of the use of the word 'literacy', which properly refers to being able to read and write words. (Its etymological origin is the Latin word *litera*, 'a letter of the alphabet'.) (cf. computer literacy) 'Visual literacy', meaning the ability to interpret and create visual messages consisting of symbols other than words, is becoming something of a catch-phrase. Fairly representative is this quotation from the preface to a popular reading programme: 'The dominance of electronic mass media such as television and films, the increased popularity of photographic communication, and the widespread use of symbols in environmental print have heightened the importance of visual literacy.' Visual literacy is thought to be important both in order to appreciate various visual media and art forms and to be forearmed against the seductive powers of, e.g. advertising.

There is a danger of schools committing the generic fallacy in presuming to teach alleged general skills of visual representation and interpretation, as opposed to recognizing the need to develop such abilities in specific contexts. One needs to teach students to understand cinematic techniques, the nature of cubist art, or principles of architecture, rather than to understand visual messages *per se*. Furthermore, it is often argued that a full understanding of specific visual symbols of any depth or complexity is dependent on verbal understanding. For example, even a relatively simple message, such as a picture of the actor Dustin Hoffman looking like a stereotypical stage Jew, would not be comprehensible as a reference to his appearance in the role of Shylock in *The Merchant of Venice* to anyone ignorant of Shakespeare's plays and current news stories relating to Hoffman. Such considerations suggest the conclusion that to develop visual literacy, we need to develop literacy itself, and understanding of various particular bodies of knowledge, art forms, and modes of communication (*language).

W

Wants *see* Interests, Needs, Open education, Readiness

Weasel words

The weasel, as Theodore Roosevelt noted in a speech in 1916, is able to suck out the contents of an egg without apparently damaging the shell. Hence 'to weasel' comes to mean 'to surreptitiously but deliberately destroy or upset the apple cart' or, simply, 'to equivocate or avoid commitment', since these are two familiar ways for pragmatists to ride with the tide. Hence 'weasel words' come to be words that sound significant but actually imply little of substance. For example, an advertising slogan of the form 'There's nothing like X' is strictly speaking probably true, and sounds like a strong recommendation, but actually could be quite immaterial. The rhetoric of **education** has its fair share of weasel words: e.g. **'empower'**, **'brainstorm'**, **'creative'**.

Whole language

The writing on the topic of whole language is extensive and very varied. It would be difficult and little to the purpose to attempt to summarize its many distinct, sometimes incompatible, and often vague claims and themes. The label 'whole language' seems to have emerged to describe a view that arose in opposition to the North American practice of seeing the teaching of reading as a matter of developing a number of discrete **skills** in and of themselves. Thus supporters of 'whole language' tend to object to, e.g. basal readers, the disassociation of reading and writing, the separation of reading from studying some specific subject matter, the distinction between learning to read letters and learning to read words. As a **slogan** it had some purpose, and some of the particular criticisms implied or stated had force (in particular the suggestions that current practice too often divorces the skills of reading/writing from **understanding** of subject matter, and that skill-based approaches to **language** tend to commit the **generic fallacy**). On the other hand, viewed as a positive thesis, the idea of whole language becomes vague and opaque. That is to say, despite the widespread use of the phrase, there is not much more to be said about the idea of whole language than that it involves a rejection of too compartmentalized, broken-down, and mechanistic a view of the various elements that go to make up the ability to read and write (*literature).

Women's studies *see* Topic-centred education

Words *see* Concept, Language

Worthwhile

Education is characteristically associated with the worthwhile, as opposed to the trivial or pernicious. A distinction may be drawn between intrinsic worth or value and extrinsic worth or value. The latter implies that something has value as a means to something else. (For example, learning to recognize letters has extrinsic value, as a means to enabling one to read.) Intrinsic value implies that something is good or worthwhile in itself, as, it may be claimed, being healthy or being able to read are.

There are problems about the notion of valuable in itself. Are we sure that those things we regard as valuable in themselves are not in fact being valued for further extrinsic reasons? (For example, do I really value reading for its own sake, or for the pleasure, profit or wisdom it may give me? Do I value being healthy for its own sake, or for what it allows me to do?) When we say that something is valuable in itself, are we attributing some quality to it? If so, is it a quality that can be discerned, as when we say this is a **creative** painting? Or is it rather a disguised way of saying 'I just value it'? There are, in addition, a number of competing **theories** of value, ranging from the extreme view that an activity has worth if, and only if, someone wants to do it for its own sake, through to the view that some activities are invested with innate value, regardless of whatever various people may think of them.

However, examination of particular areas, such as **morality**, science, football, or **aesthetics** inevitably leads to the discovery of some criteria for making value judgements. It may be that there is no agreed way of establishing the relative inherent worth of, say, a moral consideration versus an aesthetic one, but clearly there is the possibility of making **objective value judgements** within a field.

Schools, it should be noted, are concerned with judgements about educational worth, and quality in respect of other functions of **schooling**;

thus, even if judgements about the good life are not amenable to rational settlement, arguments about what is good for schools may be. At the very least, it is desirable that schools should take steps to facilitate intelligent choices on the part of the adult individual, and very probably greater agreement on what is educationally worthwhile could be arrived at by closer consideration of the various goals of schooling (*culture, interests, knowledge).

REFERENCES

Bantock (1965), Barrow (1981c), Peters (1966), White (1973).

Bibliography

Acton, H. B. (ed.) (1969), *The Philosophy of Punishment: A collection of papers*, London: Macmillan.

Adams, H. (ed.) (1971), *Critical Theory since Plato*, New York: Harcourt Brace Jovanovich.

Adelman, C. (ed.) (1984), *The Politics and Ethics of Evaluation*, London: Croom Helm.

Adler, M. J. (1982), *The Paideia Proposal: An educational manifesto*, New York: Macmillan.

Alberty, H. (1953), 'Designing programs to meet the common needs of youth', in N. B. Henry (ed.), *Adapting the Secondary-School Program to the Needs of Youth* (pp. 118–40), National Society for the Study of Education, 52nd Yearbook, Pt 1, Chicago: University of Chicago Press.

Aldrich, V. C. (1963), *Philosophy of Art*, Englewood Cliffs, NJ: Prentice Hall.

Alexander, S. (1968), *Beauty and Other Forms of Value*, New York: Crowell.

Allen, D. and Ryan, K. (1969), *Microteaching*. Reading, Mass.: Addison-Wesley.

Allen, K. E. (1980), 'Mainstreaming: what have we learned?', *Young Children*, **35**(5), 54–63.

Allport, G. W. (1954), *The Nature of Prejudice*, Reading, Mass.: Addison-Wesley.

Alston, W. P. (1964), *Philosophy of Language*, Englewood Cliffs, NJ: Prentice Hall.

American Association of School Administrators (1982), *Guidelines for the Preparation of School Administrators* (2nd edn), Arlington, Va.: the author.

Amidon, E. J. and Hough, J. B. (1967), *Interaction Analysis: Theory, research and application*, Reading, Mass.: Addison-Wesley.

Amidon, E. and Hunter, E. (1966), *Improving Teaching: The analysis of classroom verbal interaction*, New York: Holt, Rinehart & Winston.

Anderson, R. C., Spiro, R. J. and Montague, W. E. (1977), *Schooling and the Acquisition of Knowledge*, Hillsdale, NJ: Erlbaum.

Anderson, R. M. and Tomkins, G. (eds.) (1981), *Understanding Materials: The role of materials in curriculum development*, Vancouver: Centre for the Study of Curriculum and Instruction, Faculty of Education, University of British Columbia.

Annis, D. B. (1974), *Techniques of Critical Reasoning*, Columbus, Ohio: Merrill.

Anyon, J. (1981), 'Social class and school knowledge', *Curriculum Inquiry*, **11**, 3–42.

Apple, M. (1979), *Ideology and Curriculum*, London: Routledge & Kegan Paul.

Apple, M. (1987), 'Teaching and technology: the hidden effects of computers on teachers and students', *Educational Policy*, **1**(1), 135–57.

Aristotle (1953), *The Nicomachean Ethics*, Harmondsworth, Middx.: Penguin.

Arnold, M. (1932), *Culture and Anarchy*, Cambridge: Cambridge University Press.

Arnstine, D. (1975), 'Open education: an aspirin for the plague', in D. Nyberg (ed.), *The Philosophy of Open Education* (pp. 160–73), London: Routledge & Kegan Paul.

Ashton, P., Kneen, P., Davies, F. and Holley, B. J. (1975), *The Aims of Primary Education: A study of teachers' opinions*, London: Macmillan.

Aston, A. (1980), 'The Humanities Curriculum Project', in L. Stenhouse (ed.), *Curriculum Research and Development in Action* (pp. 139–46), London: Heinemann.

Austin, J. L. (1962), *Sense and Sensibilia*, New York: Oxford University Press.

Azrin, N. H. and Holz, W. C. (1966), 'Punishment', in W. K. Honig (ed.), *Operant Behavior: Areas of research and application* (pp. 380–447), New York: Appleton-Century-Crofts.

Bacchus, M. K. (1986), *The Myth and Reality of Curriculum Planning*, London: Institute of Education, University of London.

Bailey, C. (1971), 'Rationality, democracy and the neutral teacher', *Cambridge Journal of Education*, **2**, 68–76.

Bailey, C. (1973), 'Teaching by discussion and the neutral teacher', *Proceedings of the Philosophy of Education Society of Great Britain*, **7**, 26–38.

Bailey, C. (1975), 'Neutrality and rationality in teaching', in D. Bridges and P. Scrimshaw (eds.), *Values and Authority in Schools* (pp. 124–34), London: Hodder & Stoughton.

Bailey, C. (1984), *Beyond the Present and the Particular*, London: Routledge & Kegan Paul.

Bailey, R. W. and Fosheim, R. M. (eds.) (1983), *Literacy for Life: The demand for reading and writing*, New York: Modern Language Association of America.

Bailin, S. (1988), *Achieving Extraordinary Ends: An essay on creativity*, Boston: Kluwer.

Bair, M. and Woodward, R. G. (1964), *Team Teaching in Action*, Boston: Houghton Mifflin.

Baldwin, A. L. (1967), *Theories of Child Development*, New York: John Wiley.

Ball, S. J. (1987), *The Micro-Politics of the School: Towards a theory of school organization*, London: Methuen.

Ball, S. J. and Goodson, I. F. (eds.) (1985), *Teachers' Lives and Careers*, London: Falmer Press.

Banks, J. A. (1981), *Multiethnic Education: Theory and practice*, Boston, Allyn & Bacon.

Bantock, G. H. (1965), *Education and Values: Essays in the theory of education*, London: Faber & Faber.

Bantock, G. H. (1968), *Culture, Industrialisation and Education*, London: Routledge & Kegan Paul.

Bantock, G. H. (1981), *The Parochialism of the Present*, London: Routledge & Kegan Paul.

Barbe, W. B. and Renzulli, J. S. (eds.) (1981), *Psychology and Education of the Gifted* (3rd edn), New York: Irvington.

Barbee, D. E. and Bouck, A. J. (1974), *Accountability in Education*, New York: Petrocelli Books.

Barnes, D. (1982), *Practical Curriculum Study*, London: Routledge & Kegan Paul.

Barnett, C. W. (1982), *Team Teaching in the Elementary School*, Palo Alto, Calif.: R. & E. Research Associates.

Barnett, G. (ed.) (1966), *Philosophy and Educational Development*, Boston: Houghton Mifflin.

Barrow, R. (1975), *Moral Philosophy for Education*, London: Allen & Unwin.

Barrow, R. (1976a), *Common Sense and the Curriculum*, London: Allen & Unwin.

Barrow, R. (1976b), *Plato and Education*, London: Routledge & Kegan Paul.

Barrow, R. (1978), *Radical Education: A critique of free schooling and deschooling*, Oxford: Martin Robertson.

Barrow, R. (1979), 'Back to basics', in G. Bernbaum (ed.), *Schooling in Decline* (pp. 182–203), London: Macmillan.

Barrow, R. (1980), *Happiness*, Oxford: Martin Robertson.

Barrow, R. (1981a), *Educational and Curriculum Theory*, The Occasional Papers Series, Vancouver: Centre for the Study of Curriculum and Instruction, Faculty of Education, University of British Columbia.

Barrow, R. (1981b), 'Philosophy: its nature and point', in *The Philosophy of Schooling* (pp. 1–21), Brighton, Sussex: Wheatsheaf.

Barrow, R. (1981c), *The Philosophy of Schooling*, Brighton, Sussex: Wheatsheaf.

Barrow, R. (1982a), *Injustice, Inequality and Ethics: A philosophical introduction to moral problems*, Brighton, Sussex: Wheatsheaf.

Barrow, R. (1982b), *Language and Thought: Re-thinking language across the curriculum*, London, Ont.: Althouse Press.

Barrow, R. (1983), 'Does the question "what is education?" make sense?' *Educational Theory*, **33**, 191–5.

Barrow, R. (1984), *Giving Teaching back to Teachers: A critical introduction to curriculum theory*, Brighton, Sussex: Wheatsheaf.

Barrow, R. (1985a), 'The paradigm to end paradigms: reorientating curriculum research for the secondary school', in G. Milburn and R. Enns (eds.), *Curriculum Canada VI: Alternative research perspectives: The secondary school curriculum* (pp. 21–38), Vancouver: Centre for the Study of Curriculum and Instruction, Faculty of Education, University of British Columbia.

Barrow, R. (1985b), 'Misdescribing a cow: the question of conceptual correctness', *Educational Theory*, **35**, 205–7.

Barrow, R. (1986), 'The concept of curriculum design', *Journal of Philosophy of Education*, **20**, 73–80.

Barrow, R. (1990), *Understanding Skills: Thinking, feeling, and caring*, London, Ont.: Althouse Press.

Barrow, R. St C. and Woods, R. G. (1982), *An Introduction to Philosophy of Education* (3rd edn), London: Routledge & Kegan Paul.

Barth, R. S. (1969), 'Open education – assumptions about learning', *Educational Philosophy and Theory*, **1**(2), 29–39.

Bartlett, F. C. (1932), *Remembering*, Cambridge: Cambridge University Press.

Batcher, E., Brackstone, D., Winter, A. and Wright, V. (1975), *. . . And Then There Were None*, Toronto: The Status of Women Committee, Federation of Women Teachers' Associations of Ontario.

Beardsley, M. C. (1981), *Aesthetics: Problems in the philosophy of criticism* (2nd edn), Indianapolis, Ind.: Hackett.

Beattie, C. (1984), 'Human knowledge and computer knowledge: what can and should computers be used to teach', in G. Milburn and R. Enns (eds.), *Curriculum Canada VI: Alternative research perspectives: The secondary school curriculum* (pp. 121–41), Vancouver: Centre for the Study of Curriculum and Instruction, Faculty of Education, University of British Columbia.

Beauchamp, G. A. (1968), *Curriculum Theory* (2nd edn), Wilmette, Ill.: Kagg Press.

Becher, T. and Maclure, S. (1978a), *The Politics of Curriculum Change*, London: Hutchinson.

Becher, T. and Maclure, S. (eds.) (1978b), *Accountability in Education*, Windsor, Berks.: NFER.

Becher, T., Eraut, M. and Knight, J. (1981), *Policies for Educational Accountability*, London: Heinemann.

Beck, C. (1971), *Moral Education in the Schools: Some practical suggestions*, Profiles in Practical Education, no. 3, Toronto: Ontario Institute for Studies in Education.

Becker, H. J. (1984), 'Computers in schools today: some basic considerations', *American Journal of Education*, **93**, 22–39.

Bedford, E. (1964), 'Emotions', in D. F. Gustafson (ed.), *Essays in Philosophical Psychology* (pp. 77–98), New York: Anchor.

Bell, C. (1914), *Art*, London: Chatto & Windus.

Benn, C. (1981a), 'The myth of giftedness', *Forum for the Discussion of New Trends in Education*, **24**, 50–2.

Benn, C. (1981b), 'The myth of giftedness (Part II)', *Forum for the Discussion of New Trends in Education*, **24**, 78–84.

Bennett, N. (1976), *Teaching Styles and Pupil Progress*, London: Open Books.

Bennett, N., Andreae, J., Hegarty, P. and Wade, B. (1980), *Open Plan Schools*, Windsor, Berks.: NFER Publishing.

Berkeley, G. (1948), *Works*, London: Nelson.

Bernbaum, G. (1977), *Knowledge and Ideology in the Sociology of Education*, London: Macmillan.

Bernstein, B. B. (1971–3), *Class, Codes and Control*, 3 vols, London: Routledge & Kegan Paul.

Bertaux, D. (1981), *Biography and Society: The life history approach in the social sciences*, Beverly Hills, Calif.: Sage.

Biddle, B. J. and Ellena, W. J. (eds.) (1964), *Contemporary Research on Teacher Effectiveness*, New York: Holt, Rinehart & Winston.

Black, M. (1962), *Models and Metaphors: Studies in language and philosophy*, Ithaca, New York: Cornell University Press.

Bliss, J., Monk, M. and Ogburn, J. (1983), *Qualitative Data Analysis for Educational Research*, London: Croom Helm.

Block, P. (1987), *The Empowered Manager*, San Francisco: Jossey-Bass.

Bloom, A. (1987), *The Closing of the American Mind*, New York: Simon and Schuster.

Bloom, B. S. (ed.) (1956), *Taxonomy of Educational Objectives: The classification of educational goals: Handbook 1: Cognitive domain*, New York: David McKay.

Bloom, B. S., Hastings, J. T. and Madaus, G. T. (1971), *Handbook on Formative and Summative Evaluation of Student Learning*, New York: McGraw-Hill.

Bogdan, R. (1983), 'A closer look at mainstreaming', *Educational Forum*, **47**, 425–34.

Bogdan, R. C. and Biklen, S. K. (1982), *Qualitative Research for Education: An introduction to theory and methods*, Boston: Allyn & Bacon.

Bolam, D. (ed.) (1972), *Exploration Man: An introduction to integrated studies*, Schools Council Integrated Studies, Oxford: Oxford University Press.

Bolam, D. (1973), 'History and integrated studies', in R. B. Jones (ed.), *Practical Approaches to the New History: Suggestions for the improvement of classroom method* (pp. 256–85), London: Hutchinson.

Bolam, R. (1975), 'The management of educational change: towards a conceptual framework', in A. Harris, M. Lawn & W. Prescott (eds.), *Curriculum Innovation* (pp. 273–90), London: Croom Helm.

Boring, E. G. (1957), *History of Experimental Psychology* (2nd edn), New York: Appleton-Century-Crofts.

Bottomore, T. (1984), *The Frankfurt School*, London: Tavistock.

Bovet, P. (1923), *The Fighting Instinct*, London: Allen and Unwin.

Bowles, S. and Gintis, H. (1976), *Schooling in Capitalist America: Educational reform and the contradictions of economic life*, New York: Basic Books.

Boyd, W. L. (1978), 'The changing politics of curriculum policy-making for American schools', *Review of Educational Research*, **48**, 577–628.

Brady, L. (1985), *Models and Methods of Teaching*, Sydney, NSW: Prentice Hall.

Brent, A. (1978), *Philosophical Foundations for the Curriculum*, London: Allen & Unwin.

Bricker, D. C. (1972), 'Moral education and teacher neutrality', *School Review*, **80**, 619–27.

Brigham, J. (1971), 'Ethnic stereotypes', *Psychological Bulletin*, **76**, 15–38.

Britton, J. (1970), *Language and Learning*, London: Penguin.

Broadfoot, P. (1979), *Assessment, Schools and Society*, London: Methuen.

Broadfoot, P. (1986), 'Profiling and the affective curriculum', *Journal of Curriculum Studies*, **19**, 25–34.

Brodbeck, M. (1959), 'Models, meaning, and theories', in L. Gross (ed.), *Symposium on Sociological Theory* (pp. 373–403), Evanston, Ill.: Row, Peterson.

Brown, L. B. (1973), *Ideology*, Harmondsworth, Middx.: Penguin.

Brown, M. and Precious, N. (1968), *The Integrated Day in the Primary School*, London: Ward Lock.

Brown, R. H. (1977), *A Poetic for Sociology: Toward a logic of discovery for the human sciences*, Cambridge: Cambridge University Press.

Bruner, J. (1960), *The Process of Education*, Cambridge, Mass.: Harvard University Press.

Bruner, J. (1966), *Toward a Theory of Instruction*, Cambridge, Mass.: Harvard University Press.

Burgess, R. G. (ed.) (1982), *Field Research: A sourcebook and field manual*, London: Allen & Unwin.

Burgess, R. G. (ed.) (1984), *The Research Process in Educational Settings: Ten case studies*, London: Falmer Press.

Burgess, T. and Adams, E. (eds.) (1980), *Outcomes of Education*, London: Macmillan.

Burt, C. (1923), *Handbook of Tests for Use in Schools*, London: King.

Burt, C. (1975), *The Gifted Child*, London: Hodder & Stoughton.

Butt, R. L. (1989). 'An integrative function for teachers' biographies', in G. Milburn, I. F. Goodson and R. J. Clark (eds.), *Re-interpreting Curriculum Research: Images and arguments* (pp. 146–59), London, Ont.: Althouse Press.

Butt, R. L. and Raymond, D. (n.d.), 'Arguments for using qualitative approaches in understanding teacher thinking: the case for biography', *Journal of Curriculum Theorizing*, **7**(1), 62–93.

Butt, R., Raymond, D. and Yamagishi, L. (1988), 'Autobiographic praxis: study-ing the formation of teachers' knowledge (nn. 1, 2)', *Journal of Curriculum Theorizing*, **7**(4), 87–164.

Callaghan, R. E. (1964), *Education and the Cult of Efficiency*, Chicago: University of Chicago Press.

Calvert, P. (1982), *The Concept of Class: An historical introduction*, London: Hutchinson.

Campbell, D. T. and Stanley, J. C. (1963), 'Experimental and quasi-experimental designs for research on teaching', in N. L. Gage (ed.), *Handbook of Research on Teaching* (pp. 171–246), Chicago: Rand McNally.

Carr, E. H. (1961), *What is History?*, London: Macmillan.

Carr, W. (1983), 'Can educational research be scientific?', *Journal of Philosophy of Education*, **17**, 35–43.

Carr, W. (1986), 'Theories of theory and practice', *Journal of Philosophy of Education*, **20**, 177–86.

Carr, W. (1989), 'Action research: ten years on', *Journal of Curriculum Studies*, **21**, 85–90.

Carr, W. and Kemmis, S. (1986), *Becoming Critical: Education, knowledge and action research*, London: Falmer.

Carson, A. S. (1983), 'Education and the concept of ideology', *New Education*, **5**(2), 15–23.

Cassivi, D. (1988), *The Right Road*, Sydney, NS: Angeline.

Chisholm, R. M. (1966), *Theory of Knowledge*, Englewood Cliffs, NJ: Prentice Hall.

Chomsky, N. (1968), *Language and Mind*, New York: Harcourt Brace.

Clandinin, D. J. (1986), *Classroom practice: Teacher images in action*, London: Falmer.

Clanfield, D. (ed.) (1989), *Building a People's Curriculum: The experience of a Quebec teachers' collective*, Toronto: Our Schools/Our Selves.

Clayton, T. E. (1965), *Teaching and Learning: A psychological perspective*, Englewood Cliffs, NJ: Prentice Hall.

Clifford, G. J. (1983), 'The life story: biographic study', in J. H. Best (ed.), *Historical Inquiry in Education: A research agenda* (pp. 56–74), Washington, DC: American Educational Research Association.

Close, J. J. (ed.) (1974), *Team Teaching Experiments*, Windsor, Berks.: NFER.

Cohen, B. (1982), *Means and Ends in Education*, London: Allen & Unwin.

Coleman, J. S. (1966), *Equality of Educational Opportunity*, Washington, DC: US Department of Health, Education and Welfare.

Comenius (1969) (ed. John E. Sadler), *Comenius: On education*, London: Collier Macmillan.

Connelly, F. M. (1972), 'The functions of curriculum development', *Interchange*, **3**, 161–77.

Connelly, F. M. and Clandinin, D. J. (1988), *Teachers as Curriculum Planners: Narratives of experience*, New York: Teachers College Press.

Connelly, F. M., Dukacz, A. S. and Quinlan, F. (eds.) (1980), *Curriculum Planning for the Classroom*, Toronto: OISE Press.

Cook, T. D. and Reichardt, C. S. (eds.) (1979), *Qualitative and Quantitative Methods in Evaluation Research*, Beverly Hills, Calif.: Sage.

Cooper, C. R. (ed.) (1981), *The Nature and Measurement of Competency in English*, Urbana, Ill.: National Council of Teachers of English.

Cooper, D. E. (1978), 'Linguistics and "cultural deprivation"', *Journal of Philosophy of Education*, **17**, 113–20.

Cooper, D. E. (1983), 'Understanding as philosophy', *Journal of Philosophy of Education*, **17**, 145–33.

Cooper, J. M. (1980), 'Microteaching: forerunner to competency-based teacher education', *British Journal of Teacher Education*, **67**, 139–46.

Copperman, P. (1978), *The Literary Hoax: The decline of reading, writing, and learning in the public schools and what we can do about it*, New York: Morrow.

Corey, S. M. (1953), *Action Research to Improve School Practice*, New York: Teachers College, Columbia University.

Cosgrove, M. P. (1982), *B. F. Skinner's Behaviorism: An analysis*, Grand Rapids, Mich.: Zondervan.

Cox, C. B. and Dyson, A. E. (1969), *Fight for Education: A black paper*, London: Critical Quarterly Society.

Cox, C. B. and Dyson, A. E. (eds.) (1971), *The Black Papers on Education*, London: Davis-Poynter.

Craft, M. (ed.) (1984), *Education and Cultural Pluralism*, London: Falmer Press.

Crealock, C. M. and Sitko, M. C. (1983). 'Special education in the secondary school: selected issues', in R. J. Clark, R. Gidney and G. Milburn (eds.), *Issues in Secondary Schooling* (pp. 37–44), London, Ont.: Althouse Press.

Crittenden, B. (1982), *Cultural Pluralism and the Common Curriculum*, Carlton, Vic.: Melbourne University Press.

Croll, P. (1986), *Systematic Classroom Observation*, London: Falmer Press.

Croll, P. and Moses, D. (1985), *One in Five: The assessment and incidence of special educational needs*, London: Routledge & Kegan Paul.

Cronbach, L. J. (1963), 'Evaluation for course improvement', *Teachers College Record*, **64**, 231–48.

Cronbach, L. J. and Snow, R. E. (1977), *Aptitudes and Instructional Methods: A handbook for research on interactions*, New York: Irvington.

Cruikshank, D. R. (1979), *Simulations and Games: An ERIC bibliography*, Washington, DC: Eric Clearinghouse on Teacher Education.

Culley, M. and Portuges, C. (eds.) (1985), *Gendered Subjects: The dynamics of feminist teaching*, London: Routledge & Kegan Paul.

Cummins, J. (1983a), 'Language proficiency, biliteracy and French immersion', *Canadian Journal of Education*, **8**, 117–38.

Cummins, J. (1983b), *Heritage Language Education: A literature review*, Toronto: Ontario Ministry of Education.

Cummins, J. and Swain, M. (1986), *Bilingualism in Education: Aspects of theory, research and practice*, London: Longman.

Curtis, B. and Mays, W. (eds.) (1978), *Phenomenology and Education*, London: Methuen.

D'Angelo, E. (1971), *The Teaching of Critical Thinking*, Amsterdam: B. R. Gruner.

Davis, B. K. (1982), *Microteaching: From infant death to immortality?*, unpublished paper (ERIC Document Reproduction Service No. ED 224446).

Davis, J. E. (ed.) (1979), *Dealing With Censorship*, Urbana, Ill.: National Council of Teachers.

Day, E. M. and Shapson, S. (1988), 'A comparison study of early and late French immersion programs in British Columbia', *Canadian Journal of Education*, **13**, 290–305.

De Beauvoir, S. (1953), *The Second Sex* (H. M. Parshley, trans. and ed.), New York: Knopf.

De Bono, E. (1970), *Lateral Thinking: Creativity step by step*, New York: Harper & Row.

De Castell, S., Luke, A. and MacLennan, D. (1981), 'On defining literacy', *Canadian Journal of Education*, 6(3), 7–18.

De Tocqueville, A. (1863), *Democracy in America*, Cambridge, Mass.: Bowen.

Dearden, R. F. (1967), 'Instruction and learning by discovery', in R. S. Peters (ed.), *The Concept of Education* (pp. 135–55), London: Routledge & Kegan Paul.

Dearden, R. F. (1968), *The Philosophy of Primary Education*, London: Routledge & Kegan Paul.

Dearden, R. F. (1972a), 'Autonomy and education', in R. F. Dearden, P. H. Hirst and R. S. Peters (eds.), *Education and the Development of Reason* (pp. 448–65), London: Routledge & Kegan Paul.

Dearden, R. F. (1972b), ' "Needs" in education', in R. F. Dearden, P. H. Hirst and R. S. Peters (eds.), *Education and the Development of Reason* (pp. 50–64), London: Routledge & Kegan Paul.

Dearden, R. F. (1976), *Problems in Primary Education*, London: Routledge & Kegan Paul.

Dearden, R. F. (1984), *Theory and Practice in Education*, London: Routledge & Kegan Paul.

Defaveri, I. (1983), 'Ideology and education', *New Education*, 5(2), 5–13.

DeGarmo, C. (1885), *Herbart and the Herbartians*, New York: Scribner.

Degenhardt, M. A. B. (1982), *Education and the Value of Knowledge*, London: Allen & Unwin.

Delamont, S. (1976), 'Beyond Flanders' fields: the relationship of subject matter and individuality to classroom style', in M. Stubbs and S. Delamont (eds.), *Exploration in Classroom Observation* (pp. 101–32), London: John Wiley.

Delamont, S. (1983), *Interaction in the Classroom* (2nd edn), London: Methuen.

Delamont, S. (ed.) (1984) *Readings on Interaction in the Classroom*, London: Methuen.

Delamont, S. and Hamilton, D. (1976), 'Classroom research: a critique and a new approach', in M. Stubbs and S. Delamont (eds.), *Explorations in Classroom Observation* (pp. 3–20), London: John Wiley.

Descartes, R. (1931), *Philosophical Works*, Cambridge: Cambridge University Press.

Diller, K. C. (1978), *The Language Teaching Controversy*, Rowley, Mass.: Newbury House.

Dockrell, W. B. and Broadfoot, P. M. (1977), *Pupils in Profile: Making the most of teachers' knowledge of pupils*, London: Hodder & Stoughton.

Dollard, J. (1935), *Criteria for the Life History*, New Haven, Conn.: Yale University Press.

Dowdall, C. B. and Colangelo, N. (1982), 'Underachieving gifted students: review and implications', *Gifted Child Quarterly*, 26, 179–84.

Downey, R. S. and Telfer, E. (1969), *Respect for Persons*, London: Allen & Unwin.

Doyle, J. F. (ed.) (1973), *Educational Judgements: Papers in the philosophy of education*, London: Routledge & Kegan Paul.

Dreyfus, H. L. and Dreyfus, S. E. (1984), 'Putting computers in their proper place: analysis versus intuition in the classroom', *Teachers College Record*, **85**, 578–601.

Dumont, F. and Lecomte, C. (1984), 'Distortions in educational research: a lattice of constraints in the 1980s', *McGill Journal of Education*, **19**, 215–27.

Dunkin, M. J. and Biddle, B. J. (1974), *The Study of Teaching*, New York: Holt, Rinehart & Winston.

Dunlop, F. (1984), *The Education of Feeling and Emotion*, London: Allen & Unwin.

Ebbinghaus, H. (1913), *Memory*, New York: Teachers College Press.

Ebbutt, D. (1985), 'Educational action research: some general concerns and specific quibbles', in R. Burgess (ed.), *Issues in Educational Research: Qualitative methods* (pp. 152–74), London: Falmer.

Ebel, R. L. (1972), *Essentials of Educational Measurement* (2nd edn), Englewood Cliffs, NJ: Prentice Hall.

Egan, K. (1975), 'Open education: open to what?' in D. Nyberg (ed.), *The Philosophy of Open Education* (pp. 24–34), London: Routledge & Kegan Paul.

Egan, K. (1979), *Educational Development*, New York: Oxford University Press.

Egan, K. (1983), *Education and Psychology: Plato, Piaget and scientific psychology*, New York: Teachers College Press.

Egan, K. (1986), *Teaching as Storytelling*, London, Ont.: Althouse Press.

Egan, K. (1988a), 'Metaphors in collision: objectives, assembly lines, and stories', *Curriculum Inquiry*, **18**, 63–86.

Egan, K. (1988b), *Primary Understanding*, London: Routledge & Kegan Paul.

Egan, K. (1989), 'Memory, imagination, and learning', *Phi Delta Kappan*, **70** (6), 455–9.

Egan, K. and Nadaner, D. (eds.) (1988), *Imagination and Education*, New York: Teachers College Press.

Eggleston, J. (1977), *The Sociology of the School Curriculum*, London: Routledge & Kegan Paul.

Eisele, J. E. (1980), 'A case for universal computer literacy', *Journal of Research and Development in Education*, **14**(1), 84–9.

Eisner, E. W. (1977), 'On the uses of educational connoisseurship and criticism for evaluating classroom life', *Teachers College Record*, **78**, 345–58.

Eisner, E. W. (1979), *The Educational Imagination: On the design and evaluation of school programs*, New York: Macmillan.

Eisner, E. W. (1982), *Cognition and Curriculum: A basis for deciding what to teach*, New York: Longman.

Elbaz, F. (1983), *Teacher Thinking: A study of practical knowledge*, London: Croom Helm.

Eliot, T. S. (1948), *Notes Towards the Definition of Culture*, London: Faber & Faber.

Elliot, R. K. (1971), 'Versions of creativity', *Proceedings of the Philosophy of Education Society of Great Britain*, **5**, 139–52.

Elliott, J. (1971), 'The concept of the neutral teacher', *Cambridge Journal of Education*, no. 2, 60–7.

Elliott, J. (1973), 'Neutrality, rationality and the role of the teacher', *Proceedings of the Philosophy of Education Society of Great Britain*, **7**, 39–65.

Elliott, J. (1975), 'The values of the neutral teacher', in D. Bridges and P. Scrimshaw (eds.), *Values and Authority in Schools* (pp. 107–20), London: Hodder & Stoughton.

Elliott, J. (1978), 'What is action research in schools?' *Journal of Curriculum Studies*, **10**, 355–7.

Elton, G. R. (1967), *The Practice of History*, New York: Crowell.

Engell, J. and Perkins, D. (eds.) (1988), *Teaching Literature*, Cambridge, Mass.: Harvard University Press.

Ennis, R. H. (1961), 'Is it impossible for schools to be neutral?', in B. O. Smith and R. H. Ennis (eds.), *Language and Concepts in Education* (pp. 102–11) Chicago: Rand McNally.

Entwistle, H. (1970), *Child-centred Education*, London: Methuen.

Entwistle, H. (1978), *Class, Culture and Education*, London: Methuen.

Entwistle, H. (1979), *Antonio Gramsci: Conservative schooling for radical politics*, London: Routledge & Kegan Paul.

Entwistle, H. (1982), 'Class in the classroom', *Canadian Dimension*, **16**(3), 18–22.

Environment, Heredity and Intelligence (1960), Reprint Series no. 2, Cambridge, Mass.: Harvard Educational Review.

Eraut, M. (1981), 'Accountability and evaluation', in B. Simon and W. Taylor (eds.), *Education in the Eighties: The central issues* (pp. 146–62), London: Batsford.

Erikson, E. (1963), *Childhood and Society* (2nd edn), New York: Norton.

Esposito, D. (1973), 'Homogeneous and heterogeneous ability grouping', *Review of Educational Research*, **43** (2), 163–79.

Evans, K. (1979), 'Pupil profiles: a rationale', *Secondary Education Journal*, **9**(3), 21–3.

Federation of Women Teachers' Associations of Ontario (1978), *What is Basic?: A task force report July, 1978*, Toronto: the author.

Fennema, E. (1982), 'Girls and mathematics: the crucial middle grades', in L. Silvey and J. R. Smart (eds.), *Mathematics for the Middle Grades (5–9)* (pp. 9–19), Reston, Va.: National Council of Teachers of Mathematics.

Fetterman, D. M. (ed.), (1984), *Ethnography in Educational Evaluation*, Beverly Hills, Calif.: Sage.

Finley, M. I. (1975), *The Use and Abuse of History*, London: Chatto & Windus.

Firestone, S. (1972), *The Dialectic of Sex: The case for feminist revolution*, New York: Bantam.

Fishman, J. A. (1956), 'An examination of the process and function of social stereotyping', *Journal of Social Psychology*, **43**, 27–64.

Flanders, N. A. (1970), *Analyzing Teaching Behavior*, New York: Addison-Wesley.

Flew, A. G. N. (1966a), *God and Philosophy*, London: Hutchinson.

Flew, A. G. N. (1966b), 'What is indoctrination?' *Studies in Philosophy and Education*, **4**, 281–306.

Fontana, D. (1981), *Psychology for Teachers*, London: Macmillan.

Fowlkes, D. L. and McClure, C. S. (eds.) (1984), *Feminist Visions: Toward a transformation of the liberal arts of curriculum*, Birmingham, Ala.: University of Alabama Press.

Fox, R. and Tiger, L. (1971), *The Imperial Animal*, New York: Holt, Rinehart & Winston.

Fraenkel, J. R. (1977), *How to Teach About Values: An analytic approach*, Englewood Cliffs, NJ: Prentice Hall.

Frankena, W. K. (1973), 'The concept of education today', in J. F. Doyle, (ed.), *Educational Judgements: Papers in the philosophy of education* (pp. 19–32) London: Routledge & Kegan Paul.

Frankle, R. J. and Hiley, D. R. (1980), 'Course-pairs: team-teaching without tears', *Liberal Education*, **66**, 340–6.

Frazier, N. and Sadker, M. (1973), *Sexism in School and Society*, New York: Harper & Row.

Freiberg, H. J. (1981), 'Three decades of the Flanders Interaction Analysis System', *Journal of Classroom Interaction*, **16**(2), 1–7.

Freire, P. (1973a), *Education for Critical Consciousness*, New York: Seabury.

Freire, P. (1973b), *Pedagogy of the Oppressed* (M. B. Ramos, trans.), New York: Seabury.

Friedan, B. (1963), *The Feminine Mystique*, New York: Norton.

Friedan, B. (1982), *The Second Stage*, New York: Summit.

Friedenberg, E. (1982), 'Core curriculum, nostalgia, and anomie', *McGill Journal of Education*, **17**, 99–108.

Fullan, M. (1982), *The Meaning of Educational Change*, Toronto; OISE Press.

Fullan, M. G. (1988), *What's Worth Fighting For In The Principalship?: Strategies for taking charge in the elementary school principalship*, Toronto: Ontario Public School Teachers Federation.

Furbank, P. N. (1985), *Unholy Pleasure: The idea of social class* Oxford: Oxford University Press.

Furlong, V. J., Hirst, P. H., Pocklington, K. and Myles, S. (1988), *Initial Teacher Training*, Milton Keynes: Open University.

Furst, E. J. (1981), 'Bloom's taxonomy of educational objectives for the cognitive domain: philosophical and educational issues', *Review of Educational Research*, **51**, 441–53.

Furst, N. (n.d.), 'Interaction analysis in teacher education: a review of studies', in *Interaction Analysis: Selected papers* (pp. 1–11), ATE Research Bulletin 10, Washington, DC: Association of Teacher Educators.

Gadamer, H-G. (1975), *Truth and Method*, New York: Seabury.

Gage, N. L. (ed.) (1963), *Handbook of Research on Teaching*, Chicago: Rand McNally.

Gage, N. L. (1972), *Teacher Effectiveness and Teacher Education: The search for a scientific basis*, Palo Alto, Calif.: Pacific Books.

Gage, N. L. (1978), *The Scientific Basis of the Art of Teaching*, New York: Teachers College Press.

Gage, N. L. and Berliner, D. C. (1979), *Educational Psychology* (2nd edn), Chicago: Rand McNally.

Gagné, R. M. (1970), *The Conditions of Learning*, New York: Holt, Rinehart & Winston.

Gagné, R. M. (1974), *Essentials of Learning for Instruction*, Hinsdale, Ill.: Dryden Press.

Gallie, W. B. (1955), 'Essentially contested concepts', in *Proceedings of the Aristotelian Society 1955–6*, 167–98.

Gallie, W. B. (1964), *Philosophy and Historical Understanding*, London: Chatto & Windus.

Galton, M. (ed.) (1980), *Curriculum Change: The lessons of a decade*, Leicester: Leicester University Press.

Galton, M. & Simon, B. (eds.) (1980), *Progress and Performance in the Primary Classroom*, London: Routledge & Kegan Paul.

Galton, M., Simon, B. and Croll, P. (1980), *Inside the Primary Classroom*, London: Routledge & Kegan Paul.

Gardiner, J. (ed.) (1988), *What is History Today?*, Atlantic Highlands, New Jersey: Humanities Press.

Geen, A. G. (1985), 'Team teaching in the secondary schools of England and Wales', *Educational Review*, **37**, 29–38.

Genesee, F. (1983), 'Bilingual education of majority-language children: the immersion experiments in review', *Applied Psycholinguistics*, **4**, 1–46.

Getzels, J. W. and Dillon, J. T. (1973), 'The nature of giftedness and the education of the gifted', in R. M. Travers (ed.), *Second Handbook of Research on Teaching* (pp. 689–731), Chicago: Rand McNally.

Gibbons, J. A. (1979), 'Curriculum integration', *Curriculum Inquiry*, **9**, 321–32.

Gibbs, I. (1980), 'Initial caution among students towards microteaching', *Research in Education*, **24**, 45–56.

Gibson, R. (1981), 'Curriculum criticism: misconceived theory, ill-advised practice', *Cambridge Journal of Education*, **11**, 190–210.

Gibson, R. (1985), 'Critical times for action research', *Cambridge Journal of Education*, **15**, 59–64.

Gibson, R. (1986), *Critical Theory and Education*, London: Hodder & Stoughton.

Gilbert, R. (1984), *The Impotent Image: Reflections of ideology in the secondary school curriculum*, London: Falmer Press.

Giroux, H. A. (1979), 'Toward a new sociology of curriculum', *Educational Leadership*, **37**, 248–53.

Giroux, H. A. (1981), *Ideology, Culture and the Process of Schooling*, Philadelphia: Temple University Press.

Giroux, H. A. (1983a), 'Ideology and agency in the process of schooling', *Journal of Education*, **165**, 12–34.

Giroux, H. A. (1983b), *Theory and Resistance in Education: A pedagogy for the opposition*, South Hadley, Mass.: Bergin & Garvey.

Giroux, H. A. (1988), *Teachers as Intellectuals: Toward a critical pedagogy of learning*, Granby, Mass.: Bergin & Garvey.

Giroux, H. A., Penna, A. N. and Pinar, W. F. (eds.) (1981), *Curriculum and Instruction: Alternatives in education*, Berkeley, Calif.: McCutchan.

Godfrey, R. (1984), 'John White and the imposition of autonomy', *Journal of Philosophy of Education*, **18**, 115–17.

Goldberg, S. (1973), *The Inevitability of Patriarchy*, New York: Morrow.

Golding, P. (1974), *The Mass Media*, London: Longman.

Good, T. L., Biddle, B. J. and Brophy, J. E. (1975), *Teachers Make a Difference*, New York: Holt, Rinehart & Winston.

Good, T. L. and Brophy, J. E. (1978), *Looking in Classrooms* (2nd edn), New York: Harper & Row.

Goodson, I. F. (1983a), *School Subjects and Curriculum Change*, London: Croom Helm.

Goodson, I. F. (1983b), 'The use of life histories in the study of teaching', in M. Hammersley (ed.), *The Ethnography of Schooling* (pp. 129–54), Driffield, N. Humberside: Nafferton Books.

Goodson, I. (1987), 'Understanding curriculum: the alienation of curriculum theory', *Curriculum Perspectives*, **7**(2), 41–7.

Goodson, I. F. and Ball, S. J. (eds.) (1984), *Defining the Curriculum: Histories and ethnographies*, London: Falmer.

Goody, J. (1986), *The Logic of Writing and the Organisation of Society*, Cambridge: Cambridge University Press.

Gould, S. J. (1977), *Ontogeny and Philogeny*, Cambridge, Mass.: Harvard University Press.

Gow, K. M. (1980), *Yes Virginia, There is a Right and Wrong*, Toronto: John Wiley.

Graham, K. (1977), *J. L. Austin: A critique of ordinary language philosophy*, Hassocks, Sussex: Harvester.

Grant, C. A. and Sleeter, C. E. (1985), 'The literature on multicultural education: review and analysis', *Educational Review*, **37**, 97–118.

Greene, M. (1985), 'Consciousness and the public space: discovering a pedagogy', *Phenomenology + Pedagogy*, **3**, 69–83.

Greenfield, T. B. (1979), 'Organization theory as ideology', *Curriculum Inquiry*, **9**, 97–112.

Greer, G. (1970), *The Female Eunuch*, London: MacGibbon & Kee.

Greer, G. (1984), *Sex and Destiny: The politics of human fertility*, New York: Harper & Row.

Gregory, R. L. (1969), in Waddington, C. H., *Towards a Theoretical Biology*, Edinburgh: Edinburgh University Press.

Gribble, J. (1983), *Literary Education: a revaluation*, Cambridge: Cambridge University Press.

Gronlund, N. E. (1974), *Improving Marking and Reporting in Classroom Instruction*, New York: Macmillan.

Gronlund, N. E. (1977), *Constructing Achievement Tests* (2nd edn), Englewood Cliffs, NJ: Prentice Hall.

Grossi, D. L. (1981), 'A review of literature on the effectiveness of mainstreaming', *Illinois School Research and Development*, **17**(3), 33–8.

Grumet, M. (1988), *Bitter Milk: Women and teaching*, Amhurst, Mass.: University of Massachusetts Press.

Grundy, S. (1987), *Curriculum: Product or praxis?*, London: Falmer.

Guba, E. G. and Lincoln, Y. S. (1982), *Effective Evaluation: Improving the usefulness of evaluation results through responsive and naturalistic approaches*, San Francisco: Jossey-Bass.

Guilford, J. P. (1967), *The Nature of Human Intelligence*, New York: McGraw-Hill.

Habermas, J. (1974), *Theory and Practice*, London: Heinemann.

Hall, G. S. (1904), *Adolescence*, New York: Appleton.

Hallpike, C. R. (1979), *The Foundations of Primitive Thought*, Oxford: Clarendon Press.

Hamilton, D. (1976), *Curriculum Evaluation*, London: Open Books.

Hamilton, D., Jenkins, K., King, C., MacDonald B., and Parlett, M. (eds.) (1977), *Beyond the Numbers Game: A reader in educational evaluation*, London: Macmillan.

Hamlyn, D. W. (1967), 'The logical and psychological aspects of learning', in R. S. Peters (ed.), *The Concept of Education* (pp. 24–43), London: Routledge & Kegan Paul.

Hamlyn, D. W. (1971), *The Theory of Knowledge*, London: Macmillan.

Hamlyn, D. W. (1978), *Experience and the Growth of Understanding*, London: Routledge & Kegan Paul.

Hammersley, M. and Atkinson, P. (1983), *Ethnography: Principles in practice*, London: Tavistock.

Handley, G. D. (1973), *Personality, Learning and Teaching*, London: Routledge & Kegan Paul.

Handlin, O. (1979), *Truth in History*, Cambridge Mass.: Harvard University Press.

Hare, R. M. (1964a), 'Adolescents into adults', in T. H. B. Hollins (ed.), *Aims in Education: The philosophic approach* (pp. 47–70), Manchester: Manchester University Press.

Hare, R. M. (1964b), *The Language of Morals*, Oxford: Oxford University Press.

Hare, R. M. (1976), 'Value education in a pluralistic society: a philosophical glance at the Humanities Curriculum Project', *Proceedings of the Philosophy of Education Society of Great Britain*, **10**, 7–23.

Hare, R. M. (1981), *Moral Thinking: Its levels, method and point*, Oxford: Clarendon Press.

Hare, W. (1979), *Open-mindedness and Education*, Montreal: McGill-Queen's University Press.

Hargie, O. D. W. (1982), 'Research paradigms and theoretical perspectives in microteaching', *British Journal of Educational Technology*, **13**, 76–82.

Hargie, O. and Maidment, P. (1979), *Microteaching in Perspective*, Dundonald, Northern Ireland: Blackstaff Press.

Harmin, M., Kirschenbaum, H. and Simon, S. B. (1973), *Clarifying Values through Subject Matter: Applications for the classroom*, Minneapolis, Minn.: Winston Press.

Harris, A. (1977), 'The impossibility of a core curriculum', *Oxford Review of Education*, **3**, 171–80.

Harris, K. (1979), *Education and Knowledge*, London: Routledge & Kegan Paul.

Harrison, J. A. and Glaubman, R. (1982), 'Open education in three societies', *Comparative Education Review*, **26**, 252–73.

Harste, J. C. and Mikulecky, L. J. (1984), 'The context of literacy in our society', in A. C. Purves and O. Niles (eds.), *Becoming Readers in a Complex Society* (pp. 47–78), 83rd Yearbook of the National Society for the Study of Education, Pt. I, Chicago; Chicago University Press.

Havelock, E. (1986), *The Muse Learns to Write*, New Haven: Yale University Press.

Hawkridge, D. (1983), *New Information Technology in Education*, Baltimore: Johns Hopkins University Press.

Heath, R. W. and Nielsen, M. A. (1974), 'The research bias for performance-based teacher education', *Review of Educational Research*, **44**, 463–84.

Hempel, C. G. (1966), *Philosophy of Natural Science*, Englewood Cliffs, NJ: Prentice Hall.

Hepburn, R. W. (1972), 'The arts and the education of feeling and emotion', in R. F. Dearden, R. H. Hirst and R. S. Peters (eds.), *Education and the Development of Reason*, (pp. 484–500), London: Routledge & Kegan Paul.

Hilgard, E. R. (1956), *Theories of Learning* (3rd edn), New York: Appleton-Century-Crofts.

Hilgard, E. R. and Bower, G. H. (1966), *Theories of Learning* (2nd edn), New York: Appleton-Century-Crofts.

Hipkin, J. (1972), 'Neutrality as a form of commitment', *Trends in Education*, no. 26, 9–13.

Hirsch, E. D., Jr. (1987), *Cultural Literacy: What every American needs to know*, Boston: Houghton Mifflin.

Hirst, P. H. (1973), 'The nature and scope of educational theory (2)', in G. Langford and D. J. O'Connor (eds.), *New Essays in the Philosophy of Education* (pp. 66–75), London: Routledge & Kegan Paul.

Hirst, P. H. (1974a), 'What is teaching?' in *Knowledge and the Curriculum: A collection of philosophical papers* (pp. 101–15), London: Routledge & Kegan Paul.

Hirst, P. H. (1974b), 'Curriculum integration', in *Knowledge and the Curriculum: A collection of philosophical papers* (pp. 132–51), London: Routledge & Kegan Paul.

Hirst, P. H. (1974c), *Knowledge and the Curriculum: A collection of philosophical papers*, London: Routledge & Kegan Paul.

Hirst, P. H. (1974d), *Moral Education in a Secular Society*, London: University of London Press.

Hirst, P. H. (1975), 'The curriculum and its objectives – a defence of piecemeal rational planning', in *The Curriculum* (pp. 9–21), Studies in Education (New Series) 2, The Doris Lee Lectures, London: University of London Institute of Education.

Hirst, P. H. (ed.) (1983), *Educational Theory and its Disciplines*, London: Routledge & Kegan Paul.

Hirst, P. H. (1989), Unpublished paper delivered at Simon Fraser University, British Columbia.

Hitchcock, D. (1983), *Critical Thinking: A guide to evaluating information*, Toronto: Methuen.

Hodgetts, A. B. (1968), *What Culture? What Heritage?*, Toronto: Ontario Institute for Studies in Education.

Hodgetts, A. B. and Gallagher, P. (1978), *Teaching Canada for the '80s*, Toronto: Ontario Institute for Studies in Education.

Hodgkinson, C. (1983), *The Philosophy of Leadership*, Oxford: Blackwell.

Hodysh, H. W. and McIntosh, R. G. (1989), 'Problems of objectivity in oral history', *Historical Studies in Education*, **1**(1), 137–47.

Holdaway, D. (1979), *The Foundations of Literacy*, Sydney, NSW: Ashton Scholastic.

Holdaway, D. (1984), *Stability and Change in Literacy Learning*, London, Ontario: Althouse Press.

Hollins, T. H. B. (ed.) (1964), *Aims in Education: The philosophic approach*, Manchester: Manchester University Press.

Holly, D. (ed.) (1974), *Education or Domination?: A critical look at educational problems*, London: Arrow.

Holmes, M. (1984), 'Progressivism versus traditionalism', in H. Oliver, M. Holmes and I. Winchester (eds.), *The House That Ryerson Built: Essays in education to mark Ontario's bicentennial* (pp. 31–45), Toronto: OISE Press.

Holt, M. (1978), *The Common Curriculum: Its structure and style in the comprehensive school*, London: Routledge & Kegan Paul.

Honig, W. K. and Staddon, J. E. R. (eds.) (1977), *Handbook of Operant Behavior*, Englewood Cliffs, NJ: Prentice Hall.

Hornby, P. A. (1977), *Bilingualism: Psychological, social, and educational implications*, New York: Academic Press.

Hospers, J. (1961), *Human Conduct: An introduction to the problems of ethics*, New York: Harcourt, Brace & World.

Hospers, J. (1967), *An Introduction to Philosophical Analysis* (2nd edn), Englewood Cliffs, NJ: Prentice Hall.

House, E. R. (1979), 'Technology versus craft: a ten-year perspective on innovation', *Journal of Curriculum Studies,* **11**(1), 1–15.

House, E. R. (1980), *Evaluating with Validity,* Beverley Hills, Calif.: Sage.

Howard, P. (1988), *Winged Words,* London: Hamish Hamilton.

Howe, K. R. (1985), 'Two dogmas of educational research', *Educational Researcher,* **14**(8), 10–18.

Hoy, W. K. and Miskel, C. G. (1987), *Educational Administration: Theory, research, and practice* (3rd edn), New York: Random House.

Hoyle, E. (1970), 'Planned organizational change in education', *Research in Education,* **3**, 1–22.

Hoyle, E. (1986), *The Politics of School Management,* London: Hodder & Stoughton.

Hudson, K. (1983), *The Dictionary of Even More Diseased English,* London: Macmillan.

Hudson, L. (1966), *Contrary Imaginations,* London: Methuen.

Hudson, W. D. (1970), *Modern Moral Philosophy,* London: Macmillan.

Hudson, W. D. (1973), 'Is religious education possible?', in G. Langford and D. J. O'Connor (eds.), *New Essays in the Philosophy of Education* (pp. 167–96), London: Routledge & Kegan Paul.

Huebner, D. (1984), 'The search for religious metaphors in the language of education', *Phenomenology + Pedagogy,* **2**, 112–23.

Hughes, G. (1988), *Words in Time,* Oxford, Blackwell.

Hult, R. E. (1979), 'On pedagogical caring', *Educational Theory,* **29**, 237–43.

Hunt, D. E. (1971), *Matching Models in Education: The coordination of teaching methods with student characteristics,* Monograph Series no. 10, Toronto: Ontario Institute for Studies in Education.

Hurn, C. J. (1978), *The Limits and Possibilities of Schooling: An introduction to the sociology of education,* Boston: Allyn & Bacon.

Hurst, B. C. (1984), 'Means, ends, content and objectives in curriculum planning: a critique of Sockett and Hirst', *Journal of Philosophy of Education,* **18**, 17–29.

Hustler, D., Cassidy, A. and Cuff, E. C. (eds.) (1986), *Action Research in Classrooms and Schools,* London: Allen & Unwin.

Illich, I. (1971), *Deschooling Society,* London: Calder & Boyars.

Inbar, M. and Stoll, C. S. (eds.) (1972), *Simulation and Gaming in Social Science,* New York: Free Press.

Isaacs, S. (1966), *Intellectual Growth in Young Children,* London: Routledge & Kegan Paul.

Jackson, M. (1979), 'How many basics?' *ACT 3,* pp. 15–17.

Jackson, P. (1968), *Life in Classrooms,* New York: Holt, Rinehart & Winston.

Jackson, P. (1970), 'Is there a best way of teaching Harold Bateman?' *Midway,* **10**, 15–28.

Jackson, P. W. (1980),'Curriculum and its discontents', *Curriculum Inquiry,* **10**, 159–72.

James, A. and Jeffcoate, R. (ed.) (1981), *The School in the Multicultural Society: A reader,* London: Harper & Row.

James, C. (1968), *Young Lives at Stake: A reappraisal of secondary schools,* London: Collins.

Jencks,C. (1972), *Inequality: A reassessment of the effect of family and schooling in America,* New York: Harper & Row.

Jenkins, D., Kemmis, S., MacDonald, B. and Verma, G. K. (1979), 'Racism and educational evaluation', In G. K. Verma and C. Bagley, (eds.), *Race, Education and Identity* (pp. 107–32), London: Macmillan.

Jenkins, D. and Shipman, M. D. (1976), *Curriculum: An introduction*, London: Open Books.

Jensen, A. R. (1969), 'How much can we boost IQ and scholastic achievement?', *Harvard Educational Review*, **39**, 1–123.

Johnson, N. A. and Johnson-Lee, B. A. (1988), 'Ethnographic research in education: strategies for reappraisal', *McGill Journal of Education*, **23**, 231–41.

Johnston, J. and Ettema, J. S. (1982), *Positive Images: Breaking stereotypes with children's television*, Beverly Hills, Calif.: Sage.

Jones, P. (1975), *Philosophy and the Novel*, Oxford: Clarendon Press.

Joyce, B. and Weil, M. (1980), *Models of Teaching* (2nd edn), Englewood Cliffs, NJ: Prentice Hall.

Kantor, J. R. (1969), *The Scientific Evolution of Psychology*, 2 vols, Chicago: Principia Press.

Kaplan, A. (1964), *The Conduct of Inquiry*, San Francisco: Chandler.

Karabel, J. and Halsey, A. H. (1977), *Power and Ideology in Education*, New York: Oxford University Press.

Kazepides, A. C. (1976), 'Operant conditioning in education', *Canadian Journal of Education*, **1**(4), 53–68.

Kazepides, A. C. (1977), 'The logic of values clarification', *The Journal of Educational Thought*, **11**, 99–111.

Kazepides, A. C. (1982), 'Education, socialising and indoctrinating', *Journal of Philosophy of Education*, **16**, 155–65.

Kehoe, J. (1984), *A Handbook for Enhancing the Multicultural Climate of the School*, Vancouver: West Education Development Group, Faculty of Education, University of British Columbia.

Kelly, A. V. (1977), *The Curriculum: Theory and practice*, London: Harper & Row.

Kelly, A. (1985), 'Action research: what is it and what can it do?', in R. G. Burgess (ed.), *Issues in Educational Research: Qualitative methods* (pp. 129–51), London: Falmer.

Kelly, A. V. (1986), *Knowledge and Curriculum Planning*, London: Harper & Row.

Kelly, E. F. (1975), 'Curriculum evaluation and literary criticism', *Curriculum Inquiry*, **5**, 87–106.

Kelman, P. (1984), 'Computer literacy: a critical re-examination', *Computers in the School*, **1**(2), 3–18.

Kemmis, S. (1984), *The Action Research Reader*, Geelong, Vic.: Deakin University Press.

Kendall, D. (1980), 'Developmental processes and educational programmes for exceptional children', in G. M. Kysela (ed.), *The Exceptional Child in Canadian Education* (pp. 13–45), Seventh Yearbook of the Canadian Society for the Study of Education, Vancouver: Canadian Society for the Study of Education, University of British Columbia.

Kerlinger, F. N. (1973), *Foundations of Behavioral Research* (2nd edn), New York: Holt, Rinehart & Winston.

Kirk, G. (1986), *The Core Curriculum*, London: Hodder & Stoughton.

Kirschenbaum, H. (1977), 'In support of values clarification', *Social Education*, **41**, 398, 401–2.

Kirst, M. W. and Walker, D. F. (1971), 'An analysis of curriculum policy-making', *Review of Educational Research*, **41**, 479–509.

Kleinig, J. (1982), *Philosophical Issues in Education*, New York: St Martin's Press.

Kliebard, H. M. (1982), 'Curriculum theory as metaphor', *Theory into Practice*, **21**, 11–17.

Knight, R. and Robinson, I. (1988), *My Native English*, Doncaster: Brynmill.

Koerner, J. D. (1963), *The Miseducation of American Teachers*, Boston: Houghton Mifflin.

Kogan, M. (1978), *The Politics of Educational Change*, London: Collins.

Kohl, H. R. (1969), *The Open Classroom: A practical guide to a new way of teaching*, New York: New York Review.

Kohl, H. R. (1982), *Basic Skills: A plan for your child, a program for all children*, New York: Little, Brown.

Kohlberg, L. (1966), 'Moral education in the schools: a developmental view', *School Review*, **74**, 1–30.

Kohlberg, L. (1969), 'Stage and sequence: the cognitive developmental approach to socialization', in Goslin, D. (1969), *Handbook of Socialisation Theory and Research* (pp. 347–480), Chicago: Rand McNally.

Kohlberg, L. (1970), 'Education for justice: a modern statement of the Platonic view', in N. F. Sizer and T. R. Sizer (eds.), *Moral Education: Five lectures* (pp. 56–83), Cambridge, Mass.: Harvard University Press.

Kooi, B. Y. and Schutz, R. E. (1965), 'A factor analysis of classroom-disturbance intercorrelations', *American Educational Research Journal*, **2**, 37–40.

Koran, M. L. and Koran Jr, J. J. (1984), 'Aptitude-treatment interaction research in science education', *Journal of Research in Science Teaching*, **21**, 793–808.

Kounin, J. S. (1970), *Discipline and Group Management in Classrooms*, New York: Holt, Rinehart & Winston.

Kozol, J. (1980), *Prisoners of Silence: Breaking the bonds of adult literacy in the United States*, New York: Continuum.

Krathwohl, D. R., Bloom, B. S. and Masia, B. B. (1964), *Taxonomy of Educational Objectives: The classification of educational goals: Handbook II: Affective domain*, New York: David McKay.

Kuhn, T. S. (1962), *The Structure of Scientific Revolutions*, Chicago: University of Chicago Press.

Kuhn, T. S. (1977), 'Second thoughts on paradigms', in F. Suppe (ed.), *The Structure of Scientific Theories* (2nd edn, pp. 459–82), Urbana, Ill.: University of Illinois Press.

Kulik, C.-L. C., Schwalb, B. J. and Kulik, J. A. (1982), 'Programmed instruction in secondary education: a meta-analysis of evaluation findings', *Journal of Educational Research*, **75**, 133–8.

Labov, W. (1966), *The Social Stratification of English in New York City*, Washington, DC: Center for Applied Linguistics.

Labov, W. (1969), *The Study of Nonstandard English*, Champaign, Ill.: NCTE.

Lacey, C. and Lawton, D. (1981), *Issues in Evaluation and Accountability*, London: Methuen.

Lakatos, I. and Musgrave, A. (eds.) (1970), *Criticism and the Growth of Knowledge*, Cambridge: Cambridge University Press.

Langer, S. K. (1958), *Reflections on Art: A source book of writings by artists, critics and philosophers*, Baltimore: Johns Hopkins Press.

Langford, G. (1968), *Philosophy and Education*, London: Macmillan.

Law, B. (1984), *Uses and Abuses of Profiling: A handbook on reviewing and recording student experience and achievement*, London: Harper & Row.

Lawn, M. and Barton, L. (eds.) (1981), *Rethinking Curriculum Studies: A radical approach*, London: Croom Helm.

Lawton, D. (1968), *Social Class, Language and Education*, London: Routledge & Kegan Paul.

Lawton, D. (1973), *Social Change, Educational Theory and Curriculum Planning*, London: Hodder & Stoughton.

Lawton, D. (1975), *Class, Culture and the Curriculum*, London: Routledge & Kegan Paul.

Lawton, D. (1980), *The Politics of the School Curriculum*, London: Routledge & Kegan Paul.

Lawton, D. (1983), *Curriculum Studies and Educational Planning*, London: Hodder & Stoughton.

Lazerson, M., McLaughlin, J. B., McPherson, B. and Bailey, S. K. (1985), *An Education of Value: The purposes and practices of schools*, Cambridge: Cambridge University Press.

LeCompte, M. D. and Goetz, J. P. (1982), 'Problems of reliability and validity in ethnographic research', *Review of Educational Research,* **52**, 31–60.

Leithwood, K. A., Holmes, M. and Montgomery, D. J. (1979), *Helping Schools Change: Strategies derived from field experience*, Toronto: Ontario Institute for Studies in Education.

Lello, J. (ed.) (1979), *Accountability in Education*, London: Ward Lock.

Lewin, K., Lippitt, R. and White, R. K. (1939), 'Patterns of aggressive behavior in experimentally created "social climates" ', *Journal of Social Psychology,* **10**, 271–99.

Lewis, E. G. (1981), *Bilingualism and Bilingual Education*, Oxford, Pergamon.

Lewis, J. Jr. (1974), *School Management by Objectives*. West Nyack, NY: Parker.

Lewis, M. and Simon, R. I. (1986), 'A discourse not intended for her: learning and teaching within patriarchy', *Harvard Educational Review,* **56**, 457–72.

Lippman, W. (1922), *Public Opinion*, New York: Macmillan.

Lister, I. (1971), *Deschooling: A reader*, London: Cambridge University Press.

Little, A. and Willey, R. (1981), *Multi-ethnic Education: The way forward*, Schools Council Pamphlet 18, London: Schools Council.

Lloyd, D. I. (ed.) (1976), *Philosophy and the Teacher*, London: Routledge & Kegan Paul.

Lockwood, A. L. (1975), 'A critical view of values clarification', *Teachers College Record,* **77**, 35–50.

Lockwood, A. L. (1977a), 'Values education and the right to privacy', *Journal of Moral Education,* **7**, 9–26.

Lockwood, A. L. (1977b), 'What's wrong with values clarification', *Social Education,* **41**, 399–401.

Lowenfeld, V. and Brittain, W. L. (1982), *Creative and Mental Growth,* (7th edn), New York: Macmillan.

Lunn, J. C. B. (1970), *Streaming in the Primary School*, Slough: NFER.

Lynch, J. (1983), *The Multicultural Curriculum*, London: Batsford.

Lytton, H. (1971),*Creativity and Education*, London: Routledge & Kegan Paul.

Mcaleese, R. and Hamilton, D. (eds.) (1978), *Understanding Classroom Life*, Windsor, Berks.: NFER.

McClellan, J. E. (1976), *Philosophy of Education*, Englewood Cliffs, NJ: Prentice Hall.

McDiarmid, G. and Pratt, D. (1971), *Teaching Prejudice: A content analysis of social studies textbooks authorized for use in Ontario,* Toronto: Ontario Institute for Studies in Education.

MacDonald, B. (1977), 'The portrayal of persons as evaluation data', in N. Norris (ed.), *Safari: Theory in practice: Papers two* (pp. 50–67), Occasional Publications No. 4, Norwich: Centre for Applied Research in Education, University of East Anglia.

MacDonald, B. (1978), 'Accountability, standards, and the process of schooling: a British view', in M. van Manen and L. Stewart (eds.), *Curriculum Policy Making in Alberta Education* (pp. 241–74), Edmonton, Alta.: Faculty of Education, University of Alberta.

MacDonald, B. (1979), 'Hard times: education accountability in England', *Educational Analysis,* **1**(1), 23–43.

MacDonald, B. and Walker, R. (1975), 'Case-study and the social philosophy of educational research', *Cambridge Journal of Education,* **5**, 2–11.

MacDonald, B. and Walker, R. (1976), *Changing the Curriculum,* London: Open Books.

Macdonald, J. (1981), 'Curriculum, consciousness, and social change', *Journal of Curriculum Theorizing,* **3**(1), 143–53.

Macdonald, J. and Zaret, E. (eds.) (1975), *Schools in Search of Meaning,* Washington, DC: Association for Supervision and Curriculum Development.

Macdonald-Ross, M. (1975), 'Behavioural objectives: a critical review', in M. Golby, J. Greenwald and R. West (eds.), *Curriculum Design* (pp. 355–86), London: Croom Helm.

McFarland, H. S. N. (1960), *Human Learning: A developmental analysis,* London: Routledge & Kegan Paul.

MacIntyre, A. (1981), *After Virtue,* London: Duckworth.

McIntyre, D., MacLeod, G. and Griffiths, R. (eds.) (1977), *Investigations of Microteaching,* London: Croom Helm.

MacIver, D. A. and Holdaway, E. A. (1966), 'An analysis of the use of models in education', *Alberta Journal of Educational Research,* **12**, 163–88.

McKernan, J. (1988), 'The countenance of curriculum action research: traditional, collaborative, and emancipatory-critical conceptions', *Journal of Curriculum and Supervision,* **3**, 173–200.

McKnight, P. C. (1980), 'Microteaching: development from 1968 to 1978', *British Journal of Teacher Education,* **6**, 214–27.

McLaren, P. (1986), *Schooling as a Ritual Performance: Towards a political economy of educational symbols and gestures,* London: Routledge & Kegan Paul.

McLeod, K. A. (ed.) (1984), *Multicultural Early Childhood Education,* Toronto: Guidance Centre, Faculty of Education, University of Toronto.

McNamara, D. R. (1979), 'Paradigm lost: Thomas Kuhn and educational research', *British Educational Research Journal,* **5**, 167–73.

McNiff, J. (1988), *Action Research: Principles and practice,* London: Macmillan.

McPeck, J. E. (1981), *Critical Thinking and Education,* Oxford: Martin Robertson.

McPeck, J. E. and Sanders, J. (1974), 'Some reflections on education as a profession', *Journal of Educational Thought,* **8**(2), 55–66.

McPhail, P., Ungoed-Thomas, J. R. and Chapman, H. (1972), *Moral Education in the Secondary School,* Schools Council Project in Moral Education, London: Longman.

Mager, R. F. (1975), *Preparing Instructional Objectives* (2nd edn), Belmont, Calif.: Pitman Management and Training.

Maling, J. and Keepes, B. (1985), 'Educational research and evaluation', in E. Eisner (ed.), *Learning and Teaching the Ways of Knowing* (pp. 265–85), 84th Yearbook of the National Society for the Study of Education, Pt II, Chicago: Chicago University Press.

Mansell, J. (ed.), (1982), *Profiles: A review of issues and practice in the use and development of student profiles,* London: Further Education Curriculum Review and Development Unit, Department of Education and Science.

Marland, M. (1977), *Language Across the Curriculum,* London: Heinemann.

Marshall, J. D. (1984), 'John Wilson on the necessity of punishment', *Journal of Philosophy of Education,* **18,** 97–104.

Martin, J. R. (1985), *Reclaiming a Conversation: The ideal of the educated woman,* New Haven, Conn.: Yale University Press.

Marwick, A. (1970), *The Nature of History,* London: Macmillan.

Maslow, A. H. (1970), *Motivation and Personality* (2nd edn), New York: Harper & Row.

Masterman, M. (1970), 'The nature of a paradigm', in I. Lakatos and A. Musgrave (eds.), *Criticism and the Growth of Knowledge* (pp. 59–89), Cambridge: Cambridge University Press.

Mayeroff, M. (1971), *On Caring,* New York: Harper & Row.

Merleau-Ponty, M. (1962), *Phenomenology of Perception,* London: Routledge & Kegan Paul.

Michels, R. (1949), *Political Parties,* Illinois: Free Press.

Milburn, G. (1984), 'On discipline stripping: difficulties in the application of humanistic metaphors to educational phenomena', *Canadian Journal of Education,* **9,** 361–75.

Milburn, G. (1985), 'Deciphering a code or unraveling a riddle: a case study in the application of a humanistic metaphor to the reporting of social studies teaching', *Theory and Research in Social Education,* **13**(3), 21–44.

Milburn, G. (1989), 'How much life is there in life history?', in G. Milburn, I. F. Goodson and R. J. Clark (eds.), *Re-interpreting Curriculum Research: Images and arguments* (pp. 160–8), London, Ont.: Althouse Press.

Milburn, G. and Enns, R. (eds.) (1985), *Curriculum Canada VI: Alternative research perspectives: The secondary school curriculum,* Vancouver: Centre for the Study of Curriculum and Instruction, Faculty of Education, University of British Columbia.

Milburn, G., Goodson, I. F., and Clark, R. J. (eds.) (1989), *Re-interpreting Curriculum Research: Images and arguments,* London, Ont.: Althouse Press.

Milburn, G. and Herbert, J. (eds.) (1974), *National Consciousness and the Curriculum: The Canadian case,* Toronto: Ontario Institute for Studies in Education.

Miliband, R. (1977), *Marxism and Politics,* Oxford: Oxford University Press.

Mill, J. S. (ed. M. Warnock) (1962), *Utilitarianism,* London: Fontana.

Miller, A. G. (ed.) (1981), *In the Eye of the Beholder: Contemporary issues in stereotyping,* New York: Prager.

Miller, J. P. (1988), *The Holistic Curriculum,* Toronto, OISE Press.

Millett, K. (1970), *Sexual Politics,* New York: Doubleday.

Montgomery, R. (1978), *A New Examination of Examinations,* London: Routledge & Kegan Paul.

Moore, G. E. (1903), *Principia Ethica,* Cambridge: Cambridge University Press.

Monroe, W. S., De Voss, J. C. and Reagan, G. W. (1930), *Educational Psychology*, New York: Doubleday, Doran.

Morgan, M. T. and Robinson, N. (1976), 'The "back-to-the-basics" movement in education', *Canadian Journal of Education,* **1**(2), 1–11.

Morrison, A. and McIntyre, D. (1971), *Schools and Socialization,* Harmondsworth, Middx.: Penguin.

Mosca, G. (1939), *The Ruling Class,* New York: McGraw-Hill.

Munby, H. and Russell, T. (1989), 'Educating the reflective teacher: an essay review of two books by Donald Schon', *Journal of Curriculum Studies,* **21**, 71–80.

Murphy, G. and Kovach, J. K. (1972), *Historical Introduction to Modern Psychology* (3rd edn), New York: Harcourt Brace Jovanovich.

Murrow, C. and Murrow, L. (1971), *Children Come First: The inspired work of English primary schools,* New York: American Heritage.

Musella, D., Selinger, A. and Arikado, M. (1975), *Open-Concept Programs in Open-Area Schools,* Toronto: Ministry of Education.

Myers, D. A. (1974), 'Why open education died', *Journal of Research and Development in Education,* **8**(1), 60–7.

Newman, E. (1975), *A Civil Tongue,* Indianapolis, Ind.: Bobbs-Merrill.

Newmann, F. M. (1985), 'The radical perspective on social studies: a synthesis and critique', *Theory and Research in Social Education,* **13**, 1–18.

Newsome, G. L. (1974), 'Instructional behaviorism: a critique', in M. J. Parsons (ed.), *Philosophy of Education 1974: Proceedings of the Thirtieth Annual Meeting of the Philosophy of Education Society* (pp. 336–50), Edwardsville, Ill.: Studies in Philosophy of Education, Southern Illinois University.

Nicholls, A. and Nicholls, S. (1972), *Developing a Curriculum: A practical guide,* London: Allen & Unwin.

Nilsen, A. P., Bosmajian H., Gershuny, H. L., and Stanley, J. P. (eds.) (1977), *Sexism and Language,* Urbana, Ill.: National Council of Teachers of English.

Nixon, J. (ed.) (1981), *A Teacher's Guide to Action Research,* London: Grant McIntyre.

Nixon, J. (1987), 'The teacher as researcher: contradictions and continuities', *Peabody Journal of Education,* **64**(2), 20–32.

Noble, D. (1984), 'Computer literacy and ideology', *Teachers College Record,* **85**, 602–14.

Noddings, N. (1984), *Caring,* Berkeley: University of California Press.

Nolan, J. F. and Short, E. C. (1985), 'Combining qualitative and quantitative modes of inquiry to inform curriculum deliberation: a proposed framework', *Curriculum Perspectives,* **5**(1), 15–23.

Norris, N. (ed.) (1977), *Safari: Theory in practice: Papers two,* Occasional Publications No. 4, Norwich: Centre for Applied Research in Education, University of East Anglia.

Nunnally, J. (1967), *Psychometric Theory,* New York: McGraw-Hill.

Nuthall, G. and Snook, I. (1973), 'Contemporary models of teaching', in R. M. W. Travers (ed.), *Second Handbook of Research on Teaching* (pp. 47–76), Chicago: Rand McNally.

Nyberg, D. (ed.) (1975), *The Philosophy of Open Education,* London: Routledge & Kegan Paul.

O'Donnell, P. A. and Bradfield, R. H. (eds.) (1976), *Mainstreaming: Controversy and consensus,* San Rafael, Calif.: Academic Therapy Publications.

Ogilvie, E. (1973), *Gifted Children in Primary Schools*, Schools Council Research Studies, London: Macmillan.

O'Hear, A. (1981), *Education, Society and Human Nature*, London: Routledge & Kegan Paul.

Ohmann, D. (1976), 'The doublespeak of basics', unpublished paper (ERIC Document Reproduction Service No. ED 120 818).

O'Keefe, D. (ed.) (1986), *The Wayward Curriculum: A cause for parents' concern?*, London: Social Affairs Unit.

O'Leary, K. D. and O'Leary, S. G. (eds.) (1977), *Classroom Management: The successful use of behavior modification*, New York: Pergamon.

Oliva, P. F. (1988), *Developing the Curriculum* (2nd edn), Glenview, Ill.: Scott, Foresman.

Oliver, D. W. and Shaver, J. P. (1966), *Teaching Public Issues in High School*, Boston: Houghton Mifflin.

Olsen, T. (1974), 'Censorship and selection', *Journal of Reading*, **17**, 502–3.

Olson, C. P., and Sullivan, E. V. (1987), 'Beyond the mania: critical approaches to computers in education', in L. L. Stewin and S. J. H. McCann (eds.), *Contemporary Educational Issues: The Canadian mosaic* (pp. 95–107), Toronto: Copp Clark.

Olson, J. K. (1985), 'Changing our ideas about change', *Canadian Journal of Education*, **10**, 294–308.

Olson, J. (1988a), 'Making sense of teaching: cognition vs. culture', *Journal of Curriculum Studies*, **20**, 167–9.

Olson, J. (1988b), *Schoolworlds/Microworlds: Computers and the Culture of the Classroom*, Oxford: Pergamon Press.

Ong, W. J. (1982), *Orality and Literacy*, London: Methuen.

Osborne, H. (1984), 'The cultivation of sensibility in art education', *The Journal of Philosophy of Education*, **18**, 31–40.

Papert, S. (1980), *Mindstorms: Children, computers and powerful ideas*, New York: Basic Books.

Parkinson, J. P. and MacDonald, B. (1981), 'Teaching race neutrally' in A. James and R. Jeffcoate (eds.), *The School in the Multicultural Society: A reader* (pp. 206–16), New York: Harper & Row.

Partington, G. (1984), '(Im)moral education in South Australia', *The Journal of Moral Education*, **13**, 90–100.

Partington, G. (1985a), 'Multiculturalism and the common curriculum debate', *British Journal of Educational Studies*, **33**, 35–56.

Partington, G. (1985b), 'The same or different? curricular implications of feminism and multiculturalism', *Journal of Curriculum Studies*, **17**, 275–92.

Passmore, J. (1980), *The Philosophy of Teaching*, London: Duckworth.

Patton, M. Q. (1980), *Qualitative Evaluation Methods*, Beverly Hills, Calif.: Sage.

Peters, R. S. (1966), *Ethics and Education*, London: Allen & Unwin.

Peters, R. S. (ed.) (1967), *The Concept of Education*, London: Routledge & Kegan Paul.

Peters, R. S. (1974), *Psychology and Ethical Development: A collection of articles on psychological theories, ethical development and human understanding*, London: Allen & Unwin.

Peters, R. S. (ed.) (1976) *The Role of the Head*, London: Routledge & Kegan Paul.

Peters, R. S. and White, J. P. (1969), 'The philosopher's contribution to educational research', *Educational Philosophy and Theory*, **1**(2), 1–15.

Peters, R. S., Woods, J. and Dray, W. H. (1973), 'Aims of education – a conceptual inquiry', in R. S. Peters (ed.), *The philosophy of Education* (pp. 11–57), Oxford: Oxford University Press.

Peters, T. J. and Waterman, R. H. (1984), *In Search of Excellence: Lessons from America's best-run companies*, New York: Warner.

Phenix, P. (1964), *Realms of Meaning: A philosophy of the curriculum for general education*, New York: McGraw-Hill.

Phillips, D. C. (1985), 'The tendency to tendermindedness in educational research, or, the new anti-formalism', in E. E. Robertson (ed.), *Philosophy of Education 1984: Proceedings of the fortieth annual meeting of the Philosophy of Education Society* (pp. 283–93), Normal, Ill.: Philosophy of Education Society,, Illinois State University.

Piaget, J. (1930), *The Child's Conception of Physical Causality*, London: Routledge & Kegan Paul.

Piaget, J. (1947), *The Psychology of Intelligence*, London: Routledge & Kegan Paul.

Piaget, J. (1959), *The Language and Thought of the Child* (3rd edn), London: Routledge & Kegan Paul.

Pinar, W. F. (ed.) (1974), *Heightened Consciousness, Cultural Revolution, and Curriculum Theory: The proceedings of the Rochester conference*, Berkeley, Calif.: McCutchan.

Pinar, W. F. (ed.) (1975), *Curriculum Theorizing: The reconceptualists*, Berkeley, Calif.: McCutchan.

Pinar, W. F. (1983), 'Curriculum as gender text: notes on reproduction, resistance, and male-male relations', *Journal of Curriculum Theorizing*, **5**, 26–52.

Pinar, W. (1980), 'Life history and educational experience', *Journal of Curriculum Theorizing*, **2**(2), 159–212, and **3**(1), 259–86.

Pinar, W. F. (1988a), 'The reconceptualization of curriculum studies', *Journal of Curriculum and Supervision*, **3**, 157–67.

Pinar, W. F. (ed.) (1988b), *Contemporary Curriculum Discourses*, Scottsdale, Ariz.: Gorsuch Scarisbrick.

Pinar, W. F. and Grumet, M. (1981), 'Theory and practice and the reconceptualisation of curriculum studies', in M. Lawn and L. Barton (eds.), *Rethinking Curriculum Studies* (pp. 20–42), London: Croom Helm.

Plamenatz, J. (1970), *Ideology,* New York: Praeger.

Plaskow, M. (ed.) (1985), *Life and Death of the Schools Council*, Lewes, Sussex: Falmer.

Plato (1961), *Meno*, Cambridge: Cambridge University Press.

Plato (1974), *The Republic*, Indianapolis, Ind.: Hackett.

Plowden, Lady (Chairman) (1967), *Children and their Primary Schools*, 2 vols, A Report of the Central Advisory Council for Education, London: HMSO.

Plummer, K. (1983) *Documents of Life: An introduction to the problems and literature of a humanistic method*, London: Allen & Unwin.

Pocztar, J. (1972), *The Theory and Practice of Programmed Instruction: A guide for teachers,* Paris: UNESCO.

Polanyi, M. (1962), *Personal Knowledge: Towards a post-critical philosophy*, Chicago: University of Chicago Press.

Polanyi, M. (1966), *The Tacit Dimension*, London: Routledge & Kegan Paul.

Pope, D. (1983), *The Objectives Model of Curriculum Planning and Evaluation*, London: Council for Educational Technology.

Pope, M. (1979), *Sex and the Undecided Librarian*, Metuchen, NJ: Scarecrow Press.

Popham, W. (1969), 'Objectives and instruction', in W. J. Popham, E. W. Eisner, H. J. Sullivan and L. L. Tyler, *Instructional Objectives* (pp. 32–52), AERA Monograph Series on Curriculum Evaluation no. 3, Chicago: Rand McNally.

Popham, W. J. (1978), *Criterion-Referenced Measurement*, Englewood Cliffs, NJ: Prentice Hall.

Postman, N. (1985), *Amusing Ourselves to Death*, Harmondsworth, Middx., Penguin.

Power, E. J. (1982), *Philosophy of Education: Studies in philosophy, schooling, and educational policies*, Englewood Cliffs, NJ: Prentice Hall.

Pratt, D. (1980), *Curriculum Design and Development*, New York: Harcourt Brace Jovanovich.

Pring, R. (1971a), 'Bloom's Taxonomy: a philosophical critique', *Cambridge Journal of Education*, **2**, 83–91.

Pring, R. (1971b), 'Curriculum integration', in R. S. Peters, P. H. Hirst and H. T. Sockett (eds.), *Proceedings of the Philosophy of Education Society of Great Britain*, **V**(1), 171–200.

Pring, R. (1973), 'Curriculum integration: the need for clarification', *New Era*, **54**(3), 59–64.

Pring, R. (1976), *Knowledge and Schooling*, London: Open Books.

Pring, R. (1981), 'Monitoring performance: reflections on the Assessment of Performance Unit', in C. Lacey and D. Lawton (eds.), *Issues in Evaluation and Accountability* (pp. 156–71), London: Methuen.

Proctor, R. E. (1988), *Education's Great Amnesia*, Bloomington: Indiana University Press.

Purpel, D. and Ryan, K. (eds.) (1976), *Moral Education: . . . It comes with the territory*, Berkeley, Calif.: McCutchan.

Quinn, V. (1984), 'To develop autonomy: a critique of R. F. Dearden and two proposals', *Journal of Philosophy of Education*, **18**, 265–70.

Rachlin, H. (1970), *Introduction to Modern Behaviorism*, San Francisco: Freeman.

Radnitsky, G. (1970), *Contemporary Schools of Metascience*, Chicago: Henry Regnery.

Radwanski, G. (1987), *Ontario Study of the Relevance of Education and the Issue of Dropouts*, Toronto: Ministry of Education.

Ragsdale, R. G. (1983a), 'Misapplication of microcomputers in education', *Orbit 65*, **14**(1), 23–5.

Ragsdale, R. G. (1983b), 'Educating teachers for the information age', *McGill Journal of Education*, **20**, 5–18.

Rapoport, R. N. (1970), 'Three dilemmas in action research', *Human Relations*, **23**, 499–513.

Raser, J. R. (1969), *Simulations and Society: An exploration of scientific gaming*, Boston: Allyn & Bacon.

Raths, L. E., Harmin, M. and Simon, S. B. (1966), *Values and Teaching: Working with values in the classroom*, Columbus, Ohio: Merrill.

Ravitch, D. and Finn, C. E. (1987), *What do our 17-year-olds know?*, New York: Harper & Row.

Raymond, J. C. (ed.) (1982), *Literacy as a Human Problem*, University, Alabama.: University of Alabama Press.

Reid, M. I. (1979), 'The common core curriculum: reflections on the current debate', *Educational Research*, **21**(2), 97–102.

Reid, W. A. (1978), *Thinking about the Curriculum: The nature and treatment of curriculum problems*, London: Routledge & Kegan Paul.

Reid, W. A. (1981), 'Core curriculum: precept or process?', *Curriculum Perspectives*, **1**(2), 25–9.

Reimer, E. (1971), *School is Dead: Alternatives in education*, New York: Doubleday.

Renzulli, J. S. (1978), 'What makes giftedness?: a definition', *Phi Delta Kappan*, **60**, 180–4, 261.

Renzulli, J. S. and Delisle, J. R. (1982), 'Gifted persons', in H. E. Mitzel (ed.), *Encyclopedia of Educational Research* (5th edn, vol. 2, pp. 723–30), New York: Free Press.

Resnick, D. P. and Resnick, L. B. (1985), 'Standards, curriculum, and performance: a historical and comparative perspective', *Educational Researcher*, **14**(4), 5–18.

Reynolds, J. and Skilbeck, M. (1976), *Culture and the Classroom*, London: Open Books.

Richards, J. R. (1980), *The Sceptical Feminist*, London: Routledge & Kegan Paul.

Richmond, W. K. (1967), *The Teaching Revolution*, London: Methuen.

Richmond, W. K. (ed.) (1970), *The Concept of Educational Technology: A dialogue with yourself*, London: Weidenfeld & Nicolson.

Rico, G. (1976), 'Metaphor and knowing: analysis, synthesis, rationale', unpublished doctoral dissertation, Stanford University.

Robinson, F. G., Ross, J. A. and White, F. (1985), *Curriculum Development for Effective Instruction*, Toronto: OISE Press.

Roche, M. (1973), *Phenomenology, Language and the Social Sciences*, London: Routledge & Kegan Paul.

Rogers, V. R. (ed.) (1970), *Teaching in the British Primary School*, New York: Macmillan.

Rogers, V. R. and Church, B. (eds.) (1975), *Open Education: Critique and assessment*, Washington, DC: Association for Supervision and Curriculum Development.

Rosenshine, B. (1976), 'Classroom instruction', in N. L. Gage (ed.), *The Psychology of Teaching Methods* (pp. 335–71), 75th Yearbook of the National Society for the Study of Education, Pt. I, Chicago: Chicago University Press.

Rosenshine, B. and Furst, N. (1973), 'The use of direct observation to study teaching', in R. M. W. Travers (ed.), *Second Handbook of Research on Teaching* (pp. 122–83), Chicago: Rand McNally.

Ross, M. (1984), *The Aesthetic Impulse*, Oxford: Pergamon.

Rousseau, J.-J. (1972), *Emile*, London: Dent.

Rowntree, D. (1981), *Statistics Without Tears: A Primer for Non-mathematicians*, Harmondsworth, Middx.: Penguin.

Roy, S. (ed.) (n.d.), *Sex-role Stereotyping and Women's Studies: A resource guide for teachers, including suggestions, units of study, and resource lists*, Toronto: Ontario Ministry of Education.

Rudner, R. S. (1966), *Philosophy of Social Science*, Englewood Cliffs, NJ: Prentice Hall.

Rutherford, W. L. (1979), 'Questions teachers ask about team teaching', *Journal of Teacher Education*, **30**(4), 29–30.

Ryle, G. (1949), *The Concept of Mind*, London: Hutchinson.

Safty, A. (1988), 'French immersion and the making of a bilingual society: a critical review and discussion', *Canadian Journal of Education*, **13**, 243–62.

Salend, S. J. (1984), 'Factors contributing to the development of successful mainstreaming programs', *Exceptional Children*, **50**, 409–16.

Sanders, J. T. (1978), 'Teacher effectiveness: accepting the null hypothesis', *Journal of Educational Thought*, **12**, 184–9.

Sanders, J. T. (1981), 'Teacher effectiveness and the limits of psychological explanation', *McGill Journal of Education*, **16**, 67–75.

Sanders, J. and Cunningham, D. (1973), 'A structure for formative evaluation in product development', *Review of Educational Research*, **43**, 217–36.

Sarup,, M. (1986), *The Politics of Multiracial Education*, London: Routledge & Kegan Paul.

Sarason, S. (1982), *The Culture of the School and the Problem of Change* (2nd edn), Boston: Allyn & Bacon.

Sarason, S. (1983), *Schooling in America: Scapegoat and salvation*, New York: Free Press.

Sarason, S. B. and Doris, J. (1979), *Educational Policy, Public Policy, and Social History*, New York: Free Press.

Scheffler, I. (1973), *Reason and Teaching*, London: Routledge & Kegan Paul.

Schlechty, P. C. (1976), *Teaching and Social Behavior: Toward an organizational theory of instruction*, Boston: Allyn & Bacon.

Schlechty, P. C. and Joslin, A. W. (1984), 'Images of schools', *Teachers College Record*, **86**, 156–69.

Schnell, R. L. (1979), 'Childhood as ideology: a reinterpretation of the common school', *British Journal of Educational Studies*, **27**, 7–28.

Schon, D. A. (1983), *The Reflective Practitioner: How professionals think in action*, New York: Basic Books.

Schon, D. A. (1987), *Educating the Reflective Practitioner: Toward a new design for teaching and learning in the professions*. San Francisco: Jossey-Bass.

Schrag, F. (1988), *Thinking in School and Society*, New York: Routledge & Kegan Paul.

Schubert, W. H. (1986), *Curriculum: Perspective, paradigm and possibility*, New York: Macmillan.

Schutz, A. (1972), *The Phenomenology of the Social World*, London: Heinemann.

Schwab, J. J. (1970), *The Practical: A language for curriculum*, Washington, DC: National Educational Association.

Schwartz, B. and Lacey, H. (1982), *Behaviorism, Science and Human Nature*, New York: W. W. Norton.

Schwartz, S. (ed.) (1970), *Teaching the Humanities: Selected readings*, New York: Macmillan.

Scribner, S. (1984), 'Literacy in three metaphors', *American Journal of Education*, **93**, 6–21.

Scriven, M. (1967), 'The methodology of evaluation', in R. W. Tyler, R. M. Gagné and M. Scriven, *Perspectives of Curriculum Evaluation* (pp. 39–83), American Educational Research Association Monograph Series on Curriculum Evaluation No. 1, Chicago: Rand McNally.

Scriven, M. (1986), 'Computers as energy: rethinking their role in schools', *Peabody Journal of Education*, **64**(1), 27–51.

Scruton, R. (1982), *A Dictionary of Political Thought*, London: Macmillan.

Sealey, J. A. (1983), 'Religious education: a component of moral education?' *Journal of Philosophy of Education*, **17**, 251–4.

Sealey, L. (1976), 'Open education: fact or fiction?', *Teachers College Record,*, **77**, 616–30.

Sears, R. R., Maccoby, E. E. and Levin, H. (1957), *Patterns of Child Rearing*, Evanston, Ill.: Row, Peterson.

Seidel, R. S., Anderson, R. E. and Hunter, B. (eds.) (1982), *Computer Literacy: Issues and directions for 1985*, New York: Academic Press.

Semmel, M. I., Gottlieb, J. and Robinson, N.M. (1979), 'Mainstreaming: perspectives on educating handicapped children in the public school', *Review of Research in Education*, **7**, 223–79.

Seyfarth, J. T. and Canady, R. L. (1973), 'Team teaching: indicators of expectations and sources of satisfaction', *Clearing House*, **47**, 420–2.

Shakeshaft, C. (1987), *Women in Educational Administration*, Berkeley, Calif.: Sage.

Shapere, D. (1971), 'The paradigm concept', *Science*, **172**, 706–9.

Shapiro, H. S. (1982), 'Shaping the educational imagination: class, culture and the contradictions of the dominant ideology', *Journal of Curriculum Theorizing*, **4**(2), 153–65.

Shaplin, J. T. and Olds, H. F. (eds.) (1964), *Team Teaching*, New York: Harper & Row.

Shapson, S. M., D'Oyley, V. and Lloyd, A. (eds.) (1982), *Bilingualism and Multiculturalism in Canadian Education*, Vancouver: Centre for the Study of Curriculum and Instruction, Faculty of Education, University of British Columbia.

Sharp, R. (1980), *Knowledge, Ideology and the Politics of Schooling: Towards a Marxist analysis of education*, London: Routledge & Kegan Paul.

Sharp, R. and Green, A. (1975), *Education and Social Control: A study in progressive primary education*, London: Routledge & Kegan Paul.

Sher, G. (1975), 'Justifying reverse discrimination in employment', *Philosophy and Public Affairs*, **4** (2).

Sherman, R. R. and Webb, R. B. (1988), *Qualitative Research in Education: Focus and methods* (pp. 162–74), London: Falmer.

Shipman, M. D. (1974), *Inside a Curriculum Project: A case study in the process of curriculum change*, London: Methuen.

Shulman, L. (ed.) (1979), *Review of Research in Education*, Itasca, Ill.: Peacock.

Shulman, L. S. (1986), 'Those who understand', *Educational Researcher*, **15** (2), 4–14.

Shulman, L. S. (1987), 'Knowledge and teaching: foundations of the new reform', *Harvard Educational Review*, **57**, 1–22.

Silberman, C. E. (1970), *Crisis in the Classroom: The remaking of American education*, New York: Random House.

Simon, A. and Boyer, G. E. (eds.) (1968), *Mirrors for Behavior,* Philadelphia: Research for Better Schools.

Simon, B. (1971), *Intelligence, Psychology and Education: A Marxist critique* (rev. edn), London: Lawrence & Wishart.

Simon, H. A. (1965), *Administrative Behavior*, New York: Free Press.

Simon, S. B. (1974), *Meeting Yourself Halfway: Thirty-one values clarification strategies for daily living*, Niles, Ill.: Argus Communications.

Simon, S. B. and Clark, J. (1975), *More Values Clarification: A guidebook for the use of values clarification in the classroom*, San Diego, Calif.: Pennant Press.

Simon, S. B. and deSherbinin, P. (1975), 'Values clarification: it can start gently and grow deep', *Phi Delta Kappan*, **56**, 679–83.

Simon, S. B., Howe, L. W. and Kirschenbaum, H. (1972), *Values Clarification: A handbook of practical strategies for teachers and students*, New York: Hart.

Simons, H. (ed.) (1980), *Towards a Science of the Singular,* Occasional Publications No. 10, Norwich: Centre for Applied Research in Education, University of East Anglia.

Singer, P. (1979), *Practical Ethics*, Cambridge: Cambridge University Press.

Sizer, N. F. and Sizer, T. R. (eds.) (1970), *Moral Education: Five lectures*, Cambridge, Mass.: Harvard University Press.

Skilbeck, M. (1983), 'Core curriculum revisited', *Forum for the Discussion of New Trends in Education*, **26**(1), 11–14.

Skilbeck, M. (1984), *School-Based Curriculum Development*, London: Harper & Row.

Skilbeck, M. (1989), 'Revitalizing the core curriculum', *Journal of Curriculum and Supervision*, **4**, 197–210.

Skinner, B. F. (1938), *The Behavior of Organisms: An experimental analysis*, New York: Appleton-Century-Crofts.

Skinner, B. F. (1954), 'The science of learning and the art of teaching', *Harvard Educational Review*, **24**, 86–97.

Skinner, B. F. (1968), *The Technology of Teaching*, New York: Appleton-Century-Crofts.

Skinner, B. F. (1971), *Beyond Freedom and Dignity*, New York: Knopf.

Sloan, D. (ed.) (1980), *Education and Values*, New York: Teachers College Press.

Smith, B., Stanley, W. and Shores, J. (eds.) (1957), *Fundamentals of Curriculum Development*, New York: Harcourt, Brace & World.

Smith, N. L. (1988), 'Mining metaphors for methods of practice', in D. M. Fetterman (ed.), *Qualitative Approaches to Evaluation in Education: The silent scientific revolution* (pp. 153–77), New York: Praeger.

Smyth, J. (1989a), 'An alternative vision and an "educative" agenda for supervision as a field of study', *Journal of Curriculum and Supervision*, **4**, 162–77.

Smyth, J. (ed.) (1989b), *Critical Perspectives in Educational Leadership*, London: Falmer.

Snook, I. A. (1972a), *Indoctrination and Education*, London: Routledge & Kegan Paul.

Snook, I. A. (ed.) (1972b), *Concepts of Indoctrination: Philosophical essays*, London: Routledge & Kegan Paul.

Snook, I. A. (1972c), 'Neutrality and the schools', *Educational Theory*, **22**, 278–85.

Snow, R. E. (1973), 'Theory construction for research on teaching', in R. M. W. Travers (ed.), *Second Handbook of Research on Teaching* (pp. 77–112), Chicago: Rand McNally.

Sockett, H. (1976), *Designing the Curriculum*, London: Open Books.

Sockett, H. (ed.) (1980), *Accountability in the English Educational System*, London: Hodder & Stoughton.

Sparshott, F. (1982), *The Theory of the Arts*, Princeton, NJ: Princeton University Press.

Spelman, B. J. and St John-Brooks, C. (1972), 'Microteaching and teacher education: a critical reappraisal', *Irish Journal of Education*, **6**(2), 73–93.

Spence, J. (1984), *The Memory Palace of Mattea Ricci*, New York: Viking Penguin.

Spender, D. (1982), *Invisible Women: The schooling scandal*, London: Writers and Readers Publishing Cooperative Society.

Spolsky, B. and Cooper, R. L. (1977), *Frontiers of Bilingual Education*, Rowley, Mass.: Newbury House.

Stacey, J., Bereaud, S. and Daniels, J. (eds.) (1974), *And Jill Came Tumbling After: Sexism in American education*, New York: Dell.

Stake, R. E. (1967), 'The countenance of educational evaluation', *Teachers College Record*, **68**, 523–40.

Stake, R. E. (1985), 'Case study', in J. Nisbet, J. Megarry and S. Nisbet (eds.), *World Yearbook of Education 1985: Research policy and practice* (pp. 277–85), London: Kogan Page.

Stanford, M. (1986), *The Nature of Historical Knowledge*, Oxford: Blackwell.

Stanworth, M. (1983), *Gender and Schooling: A study of sexual divisions in the classroom*, London: Hutchinson.

Steinberg, I. S. (1980), *Behaviorism and Schooling*, Oxford: Martin Robertson.

Steiner, G. (1961), *The Death of Tragedy*, London: Faber & Faber.

Stenhouse, L. (1969a), 'Handling controversial issues in the classroom', *Education Canada*, **9**(4), 12–21.

Stenhouse, L. (1969b, July 24), 'Open-minded teaching', *New Society*, pp. 126–8.

Stenhouse, L. (1970a), 'Controversial value issues in the classroom', in W. G. Carr (ed.), *Values and the Curriculum: A report of the fourth international curriculum conference* (pp. 103–15), Washington, DC: National Education Association.

Stenhouse, L. (ed.) (1970b), *The Humanities Project: An introduction*, London: Heinemann.

Stenhouse, L. (1972, Feb. 4), 'The idea of neutrality', *Times Educational Supplement*, no. 2959, p. 2.

Stenhouse, L. (1975a), 'Neutrality as a criterion in teaching: the work of the Humanities Curriculum Project', in M. J. Taylor (ed.), *Progress and Problems in Moral Education* (pp. 123–33), London: NFER.

Stenhouse, L. (1975b), *An Introduction to Curriculum Research and Development*, London: Heinemann.

Stenhouse, L. (ed.) (1980), *Curriculum Research and Development in Action*, London: Heinemann.

Stevenson, M. (1983), 'Pupil profiles – an alternative to conventional examinations?', *British Journal of Educational Studies*, **31**, 102–16.

Stewart, J. S. (1975), 'Clarifying values clarification: a critique', *Phi Delta Kappan*, **56**, 684–8.

Stockard, J. and Wood, J. W. (1984), 'The myth of female underachievement: a reexamination of sex differences in academic underachievement', *American Educational Research Journal*, **21**, 825–38.

Stones, E. (1981), 'Programmed learning revisited: a case study', *Programmed Learning & Educational Technology*, **18**, 7–10.

Stones, E. (1984), *Supervision in Teacher Education: A counselling and pedagogical approach*, London: Methuen.

Straughan, R. (1982), *Can We Teach Children to be Good?* London: Allen & Unwin.

Strayer, J. R. (ed.) (1943), *The Interpretation of History*, Princeton: Princeton University Press.

Stufflebeam, D. L. (1968), 'Towards a science of educational evaluation', *Educational Technology*, **8**(14), 5–12.

Sublette, J. R. (1982), 'Back to basics in literature: where and why?' *English Journal*, **71**(6), 32–5.

Suppe, F. (1977), *The Structure of Scientific Theories*, Urbana, Ill.: University of Illinois Press.

Suttle, B. B. (1982), 'Moral education versus values clarification', *Journal of Educational Thought*, **16**, 35–41.

Swain, M. (ed.) (1976), *Bilingualism in Canadian Education: Issues and research*, Yearbook of the Canadian Society for the Study of Education, vol. 3, Edmonton, Alta.: Canadian Society for the Study of Education.

Swain, M. and Lapkin, S. (n.d.), *Evaluating Bilingual Education: A Canadian case study*, Clevedon, Avon: Multilingual Matters.

Swann, W. (1985), 'Is the integration of children with special needs happening?', *Oxford Review of Education*, **11**, 3–18.

Symons, T. H. B. (1975), *To Know Ourselves: The report of the commission on Canadian studies: Volumes I and II*, Ottawa: Association of Universities and Colleges of Canada.

Taba, H. (1962), *Curriculum Development: Theory and practice*, New York: Harcourt, Brace & World.

Taber, J. I., Glaser, R. and Schaefer, H. H. (1965), *Learning and Programmed Instruction*, Reading, Mass.: Addison-Wesley.

Tafel, L. S. (1984), 'A future paradigm for teacher education', *Action in Teacher Education*, **6**(1–2), 1–6.

Tallboy, F. (ed.) (1973), *Open Education: Review of the literature and selected annotated bibliography*, Reports in Education no. 4, Montreal: Faculty of Education, McGill University.

Tanner, D. and Tanner, L. (1979), 'Emancipation from research: the reconceptualist prescription', *Educational Researcher*, **8**(6), 8–12.

Tanner, L. N. (ed.) (1988), *Critical Issues in Curriculum*, 87th Yearbook of the National Society for the Study of Education, Pt. I, Chicago: Chicago University Press.

Tansey, P. J. and Unwin, D. (1969), *Simulation and Gaming in Education*, London: Methuen.

Tawney, D. (ed.) (1976), *Curriculum Evaluation Today: Trends and implications*, Schools Council Research Studies, London: Macmillan.

Taylor, J. L. and Walford, R. (1972), *Simulation in the Classroom*, Harmondsworth, Middx.: Penguin.

Taylor, P. (1982), 'Metaphor and meaning in curriculum: on opening windows on the not yet seen', *Journal of Curriculum Theorizing*, **4**(1), 209–16.

Taylor, P. H. (1970), *How Teachers Plan their Courses: Studies in curriculum planning*, London: National Foundation for Educational Research in England and Wales.

Taylor, P. H. and Richards, C. (1979), *An Introduction to Curriculum Studies*, London: NFER.

Thorndike, R. L. (ed.) (1971), *Educational Measurement* (2nd edn), Washington, DC: American Council on Education.

Tibble, J. (ed.) (1966), *The Study of Education*, London: Routledge & Kegan Paul.

Tibble, J. (ed.) (1971), *An Introduction to the Study of Education: An outline for the student*, London: Routledge & Kegan Paul.

Tobias, S. (1981), 'Adapting instruction to individual differences among students', *Educational Psychologist*, **16**, 111–20.

Tobias, S. (1982), 'When do instructional methods make a difference?', *Educational Researcher*, **11**(4), 4–9.

Tolstoy, L. (1898), *What is Art? and Essays on Art*, London: Oxford University Press.

Tom, A. R. (1980), 'The reform of teacher education through research: a futile quest', *Teachers College Record*, **82**, 15–29.

Tom, A. R. (1984), *Teaching as a Moral Craft*, New York: Longman.

Tomkins, G. S. (1986), *A Common Countenance: Stability and change in the Canadian curriculum*, Toronto: Prentice Hall.

Tomlinson, S. (1985), 'The expansion of special education', *Oxford Review of Education*, **11**, 157–65.

Toohey, K. (1985), 'English as a second language for native Canadians', *Canadian Journal of Education*, **10**, 275–93.

Toomey, R. (1980), 'Dreams and realities about values and core curriculum in secondary school', *Australian Journal of Education*, **24**, 13–25.

Tosh, J. (1984), *The Pursuit of History*, Harlow: Longman.

Tosi, A. (1984), *Immigration and Bilingual Education: A case study of movement of population, language change and education within the EEC*, Oxford: Pergamon.

Traub, R. E., Weiss, J., Fisher, C. W. and Musella, D. (1972), 'Closure on openness: describing and quantifying open education', *Interchange*, **3**(2–3), 69–84.

Travers, R. M. W. (1973), *Second Handbook of Research on Teaching*, Chicago: Rand McNally.

Tripp, D. H. and Watt, A. J. (1984), 'Core curriculum: what it is and why we don't need one', *Journal of Curriculum Studies*, **16**, 131–41.

Trott, A. J. (ed.) (1977), *Selected Microteaching Papers*, APLET Occasional Publication No. 4, London: Kogan Page.

Truzzi, M. (ed.) (1974), *Verstehen: Subjective understanding in the social sciences*, Reading, Mass.: Addison-Wesley.

Turner, M. B. (1965), *Philosophy and the Science of Behavior*, New York: Appleton-Century-Crofts.

Turney, C., Clift, J. C., Dunkin, M. J. and Traill, R. D. (1973), *Microteaching: Research, theory and practice*, Sydney, NSW: Sydney University Press.

Tuthill, D. and Ashton, P. (1983), 'Improving educational research through the development of educational paradigms', *Educational Researcher*, **12**(10), 6–14.

Tyler, R. W., (1949), *Basic Principles of Curriculum and Instruction*, Chicago: University of Chicago Press.

Tyler, R. W., Gagné, R. M. and Scriven, M. (1967), *Perspectives of Curriculum Evaluation*, American Educational Research Association Monograph Series on Curriculum Evaluation No. 1, Chicago: Rand McNally.

Underhill, I. and Telford, P. (1979), 'An integrated Canadian studies course', *History and Social Science Teacher*, **15**, 119–24.

Vallance, E. (1975), 'Aesthetic criticism and curriculum description', unpublished doctoral dissertation, Stanford University.

Valverde, L. A. (ed.) (1978), *Bilingual Education for Latinos*, Washington, DC: Association for Supervision and Curriculum Development.

van Manen, M. (1984), 'Practicing phenomenological writing', *Phenomenology + Pedagogy*, **2**, 36–69.

van Manen, M. (1986), *The Tone of Teaching*, Richmond Hill, Ont.: Scholastic-TAB.

van Manen, M. (in press), *Researching Lived Experience: Human science for an action sensitive pedagogy*, London, Ont.: Althouse Press.

Vanderbosch, J. and Swoboda, M. (1984), 'Anomalies and paradigms; feminist criticism and general education', *Liberal Education*, **70**, 223–7.

Verma, G. K. and Bagley, C. (eds.) (1979), *Race, Education and Identity*, London: Macmillan.

Vickery, T. R. and Smith, C. G. (1979), 'The back to basics curriculum as a social control mechanism', unpublished paper, Syracuse University (Eric Document Reproduction Service No. ED 173 259).

Volkart, E. H. (1986), *The Angel's Dictionary*, New York: Franklin Watts.

Wagner, P. A. (1981), 'Simon, indoctrination and ethical relativism', *The Journal of Educational Thought*, **15**, 187–94.

Waldo, D. (1968), *The Novelist on Organization & Administration: An inquiry into the relationship between two worlds*, Berkeley, Calif.: Institute of Governmental Studies, University of California.

Walker, R. (1985), *Doing Research: A handbook for teachers*, London: Methuen.

Walker, R. and Adelman, C. (1975), 'Interaction analysis in informal classrooms: a critical comment on the Flanders' system', *British Journal of Educational Psychology*, **45**, 73–6.

Wall, G. I. (1968), 'The concept of vocational education', *Journal of Philosophy of Education*, **2**.

Wallace, D. G. (ed.) (1982), *Developing Basic Skills Programs in Secondary Schools*, Alexandria, Va.: Association for Supervision and Curriculum Development.

Wallin, E. (1985), 'To change a school: experiences from local development work', *Journal of Curriculum Studies*, **17**, 321–50.

Wang, M. C. and Birch, J. W. (1984), 'Comparison of a full-time mainstreaming program and a resource room approach', *Exceptional Children*, **51**, 33–40.

Warnock, G. J. (1967), *Contemporary Moral Philosophy*, London: Macmillan.

Warnock, M. (1966), *Ethics Since 1900* (2nd edn), London: Oxford University Press.

Warnock, M. (1975), 'The neutral teacher', in M. J. Taylor (ed.), *Progress and Problems in Moral Education* (pp. 103–12), London: NFER.

Warnock, M. (1976), *Imagination*, London: Faber & Faber.

Warren, M. A. (1980), *The Nature of Women: An encyclopedia and guide to the literature*, Inverness, Calif.: Edgepress.

Warwick, D. (1971), *Team Teaching*, London: University of London Press.

Warwick, D. (ed.) (1973), *Integrated Studies in the Secondary School*, London: University of London Press.

Weatherley, R. and Lipsky, M. (1977), 'Street-level bureaucrats and institutional innovation: implementing special-education reform', *Harvard Educational Review*, **47**, 171–97.

Webb, E. J., Campbell, D. T., Schwartz, R. and Sechrest, L. (1966), *Unobtrusive Measures: Nonreactive research in the social sciences*, Chicago: Rand McNally.

Weber, L. (1971), *The English Infant School and Informal Education*, Englewood Cliffs, NJ: Prentice Hall.

Weil, M. and Joyce, B. (1978), *Information Processing Models of Teaching: Expanding your teaching repertoire*, Englewood Cliffs, NJ: Prentice Hall.

Weldon, T. D. (1953), *The Vocabulary of Politics*, London: Penguin.

Werner, W., Connors, B., Aoki, T. and Dahlie, J. (1977), *Whose Culture? Whose Heritage?: Ethnicity within Canadian social studies curriculum*, Vancouver: Centre for the Study of Curriculum and Instruction, Faculty of Education, University of British Columbia.

Werner, W., and Rothe, P. (n.d.), *Doing School Ethnography*, Curriculum Praxis Monograph Series No. 2. Edmonton, Alta.: Faculty of Education, University of Alberta.

Wheeler, H. (ed.) (1973), *Beyond the Punitive Society: Operant Conditioning: Social and Political Aspects*, San Francisco: W. H. Freeman.

White, J. P. (1967), 'Indoctrination', in R. S. Peters (ed.), *The Concept of Education* (pp. 177–91), London: Routledge & Kegan Paul.

White, J. P. (1972), 'Creativity and education: a philosophical analysis', in R. F. Dearden, P. H. Hirst and R. S. Peters (eds.), *Education and the Development of Reason* (pp. 132–48), London: Routledge & Kegan Paul.

White, J. P. (1973), *Towards a Compulsory Curriculum*, London: Routledge & Kegan Paul.

White, J. P. (1974), 'Intelligence and the logic of the nature-nurture issue', *Journal of Philosophy of Education*, **8**, 30–51.

White, J. P. (1982), *The Aims of Education Restated*, London: Routledge & Kegan Paul.

Whitehead, A. N. (1929), *The Aims of Education and Other Essays*, New York: Macmillan.

Williams, R. (1961), *The Long Revolution*, London: Chatto & Windus.

Willis, G. (ed.) (1978), *Qualitative Evaluation: Concepts and cases in curriculum criticism*, Berkeley, Calif.: McCutchan.

Willis, P. E. (1977), *Learning to Labour: How working class kids get working class jobs*, Westmead, Hants: Gower.

Wilson, A. (1970), *War Gaming*, Harmondsworth, Middx.; Penguin.

Wilson, J. (1964), 'Education and indoctrination', in T. H. B. Hollins (ed.), *Aims in Education: The philosophic approach* (pp. 24–46), Manchester: Manchester University Press.

Wilson, J. (1972), *Philosophy and Educational Research*, Windsor, Berks.: NFER.

Wilson, J. (1973a), *The Assessment of Morality*, Windsor, Berks.: NFER.

Wilson, J. (1973b), *A Teacher's Guide to Moral Education*, London: Geoffrey Chapman.

Wilson, J. (1979), *Preface to the Philosophy of Education*, London: Routledge & Kegan Paul.

Wilson, J., Williams, N. and Sugarman, B. (1967), *Introduction to Moral Education*, Harmondsworth, Middx.: Penguin.

Wilson, P. S. (1971), *Interest and Discipline in Education*, London: Routledge & Kegan Paul.

Winter, R. (1987), *Action-Research and the Nature of Social Inquiry: Professional innovation and education work*, Aldershot, Hants.: Avebury/Gower.

Withall, J. (1949), 'The development of a technique for the measurement of socio-emotional climate in classrooms', *Journal of Experimental Education*, **17**, 347–61.

Wittgenstein, L. (1958), *Philosophical Investigations*, Oxford: Blackwell & Mott.

Woods, P. (1977), *The Ethnography of the School*, Units 7–8; E202 Schooling and Society, Milton Keynes, Bucks.: Open University.

Woods, P. (1985), 'Sociology, ethnography and teacher practice', *Teaching and Teacher Education,* **1,** 51–62.

Woods, P. (1986), *Inside Schools: Ethnography in educational research,* London: Routledge & Kegan Paul.

Wright, D. (1971), *The Psychology of Moral Behaviour,* Harmondsworth, Middx.: Penguin.

Wright, I. and Coombs, J. (1981), *The Cogency of Multicultural Education,* Vancouver: Centre for the Study of Curriculum and Instruction, Faculty of Education, University of British Columbia.

Wright, N. (1977), *Progress in Education,* London: Croom Helm.

Yates, F. (1966), *The Art of Memory,* Chicago: University of Chicago Press.

Young, J. C. (1979), 'Education in a multicultural society: what sort of education? what sort of society?, *Canadian Journal of Education,* **4,** 5–21.

Young, J. Z. (1978), *Programs of the Brain,* Oxford: Oxford University Press.

Young, M. F. D. (ed.) (1971), *Knowledge and Control,* London: Collier Macmillan.

Zais, R. S. (1976), *Curriculum Principles and Foundations,* New York: Crowell.

Zigrami, D. and Zigrami, P. (1980), 'A personal view of the stresses of being an ethnographer', *Journal of Classroom Interaction,* **16**(1), 19–24.